WHOSE MASTER'S VOICE?

WHOSE MASTER'S VOICE?

The Development of Popular Music in Thirteen Cultures

Edited by
**Alison J. Ewbank
and Fouli T. Papageorgiou**

**Contributions to the Study of Music and Dance,
Number 41**

GREENWOOD PRESS
Westport, Connecticut • London

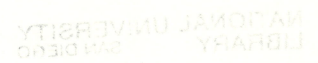

Library of Congress Cataloging-in-Publication Data

Whose master's voice? : the development of popular music in thirteen
cultures / edited by Alison J. Ewbank and Fouli T. Papageorgiou.
     p.   cm. — (Contributions to the study of music and dance,
ISSN 0193–9041 ; no. 41)
  Includes bibliographical references and index.
  ISBN 0–313–27772–9 (alk. paper)
   1. Popular music—History and criticism. 2. Music and society.
I. Ewbank, Alison J. II. Papageorgiou, Fouli T. III. Series.
ML3470.W56   1997
781.63′09—dc20   95–46060

British Library Cataloguing in Publication Data is available.

Library of Congress Catalog Card Number: 95–46060
ISBN: 0–313–27772–9
ISSN: 0193–9041

First published in 1997

Greenwood Press, 88 Post Road West, Westport, CT 06881
An imprint of Greenwood Publishing Group, Inc.

Printed in the United States of America

The paper used in this book complies with the
Permanent Paper Standard issued by the National
Information Standards Organization (Z39.48–1984).

10 9 8 7 6 5 4 3 2 1

This book is dedicated
to young musicians
and the dreams
they try so
hard to
fulfill.

CONTENTS

TABLES

PREFACE

This collection of research findings and interpretation has been produced by members of the International Communications and Youth Cultures Consortium (ICYC) which is an informal group of researchers who have conducted their own national studies, within the framework of a negotiated international project. The professional training and scholarly approaches of the group cover a range of the social services and humanities, including sociology, psychology, political science, economics, philosophy, communication, journalism, broadcasting and musicology. The scholars are employed in universities, research institutes, broadcasting organizations and the music industry. The research team represents a diversity of theoretical, methodological and philosophical approaches to the study of youth and culture. But, although this team was selected for its diversity, all members are eminent scholars within their fields who are committed to understanding the economic and social factors that influence cultures and youth.

They were brought together by their mutual interest in investigating repercussions from the development of international communication systems. In particular, they chose to look at the possibility of an international youth culture based on common global tastes and values. The question was addressed initially by focusing on popular music, its production development and application. This comprised the first stage of the ICYC study, and it is these findings that make up the content of this book.

The study set out to examine both the structure of the global culture industry and the repercussions of that global industry on national cultures at various levels of functioning. The reports concentrate on the production of popular music. Each country's musicians themselves are described. The findings are placed within a context of the historical development and the political, economic and social conditions of each country. A number of previous studies had established the existence of a largely unidirectional flow of popular music around the world from Anglo-American sources. Concern has been expressed about the possibility of a global cultural homogenization in the future.

The connection with young people was their heavy consumption of popular music and the socializing effects of this consumption. It was predicted that music could carry with it identification with lifestyles and values of other societies. The ICYC members decided to look at the local music environments to measure the effects on local production and consumption of the presence of international music and, at a later date, to look at the relationship and behavioral effects between musical tastes and the cultural mores of the young.

The research was conducted by nationals of each country. In this way the researchers were studying their own cultures. Each brought to the work a national's understanding of the complexities and idiosyncracies of their particular cultural studies: such an understanding would have been impossible for a visiting academic to acquire. It must be explained that representation was not dictated by any sampling technique, random or otherwise. The parameters of the study were not fixed in the initial stages of the project. Since we were exploring new ground we took an open stance. From the start we could make no claims about the global representativeness of our sample. However, certain guidelines of choice in broad groupings were adhered to. It was insured that there would be representatives of developed and underdeveloped countries; old countries with strong national traditions and relatively new countries with weak or no traditions, large; medium sized and small countries; economically strong and weak ones; democracies and other forms of government; old imperialists and new ones; countries where the majority of young people are allowed an adolescence and countries where adult responsibility comes in childhood. We did not consciously look for countries with important popular music industries; we were as interested in countries with weak domestic industries. We wanted to focus on the generation of and support given to weakly based domestic industries as well as on the strength and impact of exporting countries. We hoped to include representatives of countries with differing musical roots and countries with differing cultural histories. The sample eventually arrived at satisfying these criteria. The chapters present a wide variety of concerns. They succeed in illustrating the complexity and variety of contexts in which popular music is produced. The study itself had no overall financial backing and had to rely on dispersed intermittent outside sources, which were mainly directed toward funding meetings or access to meetings rather than toward research expenses. Individuals had to rely on their own resources. Each piece of work represents a degree of personal sacrifice in time and funds on the part of the contributor. This book was launched on enthusiasm, goodwill and friendship alone and this cannot be extracted from people by dictate.

Being a collection of reports from individual countries, this book is innovative in that the perspective is that of the recipient as opposed to that of the provider. The view is from inside the country. Account is only taken of the outside foci that actually are seen to impinge on the domestic musical environment. This is different from the usual accounts of the interaction of national and transactional forces, which almost invariably take as their subject the transactional aspect, describing how it affects and is accommodated to varying situations. Here external influences are not subjects of study in themselves but are viewed as part of a complex scene along with other variables operating in various national situations. Each researcher worked on an identical agenda generated by the group as a whole. This included providing descriptive information about relevant demographic, social, economic and political conditions historically and currently. The historical development of music was to be traced and the current state of the music industry in each country was to be researched in order that factual statistical details could be presented. Interviews were to be carried out with both persons working in the music and communication industries and practicing musicians. This was done in order to present a detailed, rounded picture of the musical environment in the researcher's country.

These requirements were adhered to by the majority. However, not all the agenda's components could be covered by everyone. There were variations in access to statistical information and in the comprehensiveness of information available. The resources and conditions of work of the different researchers were also very unequal. As a result, there are differing areas of emphasis, dictated not only by information availability but also by differing national concerns. The editors judge that this diversity has added to the value of the collection a dimension unobtainable by outside researchers. The book provides a platform for each author's personal perspectives and values. Information from one area that a particular author has dealt with at length can enhance the understanding of that concern in another country, where the author has chosen to emphasize another area. If connections are made by the reader, information given in one chapter may be applied to another as long as account is taken of differences in circumstances and time. The diversity of the reports also reflects the writers' differing educational and research traditions. This is shown in the concerns aired and the methods employed. Additionally the language and style of the chapters are variegated, reflecting the different cultural and linguistic backgrounds of the authors. Editorial policy has been not to impose our value judgments or West European perspectives on our colleagues. Selected parts of the material presented here have been used as source evidence in the earlier ICYC book *Music at the Margins* (Sage, 1991) by Deanna Robinson, Elizabeth Buck, Marlene Cuthbert et al. This was a comparative interpretation of the ICYC members' work. This particular volume is published to present the researchers' materials as a whole on a national basis. It is targeted neither to duplicate nor to contradict the comparative book, rather to complement and to broaden the subject's knowledge base. It is hoped that the evidence presented here will provide some answers to policy and rhetorical questions which increasingly are being raised by people with an interest in their national cultures.

ACKNOWLEDGMENTS

These contributors have indicated a wish to acknowledge the help which has been given to them during the preparation of their chapters.

Hanna Adoni offers very special thanks to the following Israeli musicians who were interested in her research and kind enough to give long and thorough personal interviews: Corina Alal, Shlomo Artzy, Shula Chen, Ricki Gal, Nurith Galron, Sassi Keshet, Oshik Levy, Yael Levy, Danny Litany, Chani Livne, Alon Oleartchik, Avi Toledano and Yehudit Ravitz. She is greatly indebted to Meir Paz of ACUM who was genuinely helpful in supplying the important statistics on the production and consumption of popular music in Israel. She would also like thank the journalists and music critics Yuval Nir, Ronen Tal and Itzik Yosha, who through their interviews helped her understanding of the Israeli musical scene. Her thanks are also given to Gilad Ben-Schach, the former Director of Music Programming and his colleagues at the Israeli Broadcasting Authority (IBA) and to the recording companies which supplied the relevant data.

Thanks are also due to students, Tali Swissa and Amit Kama from the Communications Institute, the Hebrew University of Jerusalem, for their efforts in interviewing the musicians, the IBA personnel and the music critics who supplied them with most valuable data on popular music in Israel. It should be noted that part of the data presented in this chapter was collected during a cross-cultural research project which was carried on in about 20 countries and was directed by Deanna Robinson from the University of Oregon and coauthor of Chapter 12.

Nelly de Camargo wishes to thank colleagues in the Institute of Arts, Brazil, for their comments. She directs special thanks to Antonio Marcos A. Queiroz for his help in her research work.

Alison J. Ewbank wishes to acknowledge the help given to her by Mallory Wober, who read and commented on her manuscript and provided additional data from his own work. She also thanks Ray Brown for his collaboration in writing about the local music environment.

Georgette Wang thanks Lin Chwen-hwa for her indispensable assistance in data collection, and Professor Fong Jien-sang for reading the chapter prior to publication.

INTRODUCTION

The spread of Anglo-American music around the world is often seen as threatening the extinction of indigenous musics. Over the past two decades, a rich bibliography has been produced on this theme, including a significant number of transcultural studies (see Bibliography at the end of this chapter). The argument put forward by many scholars implies a model of cultural domination or cultural "imperialism" imposed from core to peripheral countries via the international music industry, through the medium of popular music of, basically, Anglo-American nature. Thus, Frith (1989, 2) argues that "no country in the world is unaffected by the way in which the twentieth century mass media (the electronic means of musical production, reproduction and transmission) have created a universal pop aesthetic." Similarly, Hamelink (1983) regrets the "one-way traffic" which characterizes the patterns of cultural interaction in the second half of the twentieth century, based on the "synchronization" of a multiplicity of indigenous cultures with one particular cultural pattern of global dimensions. Furthermore, he thinks that the infiltration of the indigenous cultures by the dominant one has been subtle and consequently even more dangerous and destructive, leading to an immediate threat to global cultural diversity.

However, as Robinson et al. (1991) point out, "one of the major issues of the so-called information age is whether technological developments are leading to cultural enrichment and pluralism versus cultural homogenization and domination" (p. 18). Wallis and Malm (1984), in their report on the music industry in small countries, model the interaction between cultures on the basis of three patterns of change: cultural exchange, cultural dominance and cultural imperialism. But, they note that these three patterns have been joined by a forth pattern from around 1970: transculturation. This pattern of change "is the result of the worldwide establishment of the transnational corporations in the field of culture, the corresponding spread of technology and the development of worldwide marketing networks for what can be termed transnationalized culture or transculture" (p. 300). They conclude that although in its early days transculturation has had positive effects in the production of music in small countries, they could not foresee a projection of this trend into the future.

Many other factors are at play in determining cultural change and transcultural influence which cannot be easily predicted. Manuel (1988), for example, poses the question whether changing local tastes (of popular music) are due to socioeconomic developments within the culture itself or they

derive from Western influence. Fejes (1981) also notes that the media imperialism approach tends to obscure the complex relationships and dynamics
that exist among the external and internal factors and forces that shape the
cultural production of peripheral countries.

This collection of papers aims to amplify exactly these "complex relationships and dynamics" which shape the interaction between indigenous
musics and "internationalized" Anglo-American popular music. The approach shared by all the authors in this book centers on providing a historical review of the development of indigenous music in each country, in order
to highlight the endogenous as well as the exogenous influences in the for-
mulation of the mainstream and peripheral musical genres at national and
local levels.

The conceptual framework we propose for interpreting popular music
production at national and local levels is based on two main issues. The first
issue concerns the extent to which international (Anglo-American) music is
accessible to national or local populations through the mass media. The
second issue refers to the social, economic and political circumstances which
have encouraged the introduction of foreign music in a country, providing
the context for exogenous influences of varying degrees on local musical
production.

The reports included in this book take a look at popular music production in each country "from the inside" rather than attempting to prove a
model or provide a global synthesis "from the outside." This approach provides the opportunity to elaborate the concept of interaction between indigenous and foreign music or between spontaneous and imposed music on
the basis of the sociopolitical context of such interaction; it also provides
the ground to rethink the various forms "cultural exchange" may take.

The main point brought forward by this book is that popular music ab-
sorbs exogenous influences and accommodates them stylistically in new
forms that reflect the socioeconomic and political environment of the historical period it belongs to. Thus, to understand phenomena of enforcement
and domination of foreign musics on indigenous ones, we need to study the
societal factors which mediated and allowed such a pattern to develop at the
receiving end. As it is clearly shown by the chapters, popular music in each
country expresses and reflects the social and political forces which are at
play in a particular period of time and determine the dynamics of the development of each country internally, as well as its position and role in the international scene.

Some countries are endowed with a rich tradition of indigenous national
music which inspires their contemporary production of popular music; others are lacking a tradition of their own but strive to produce a contemporary
musical identity by building on elements of the international pop and rock
or regional mainstream musics (e.g., Latin America). Most countries are in
between these two models and utilize both traditions and the regional and
international contemporary musical influences as sources of inspiration for
modern popular music production. Thus, the analysis of contemporary musical production is based in most chapters on a dual problematic: it concerns
the interaction between indigenous and "external" (regional, international)
music and/or the relationship between local (peripheral) production of
popular music and the "core" production of the transnational industries.

This dual analytical model points to a simple categorization of the expected results of the interaction between the indigenous/local musics and the "external" (regional or international) popular music. Thus, three basic "situations" can be distinguished:

1. *Integration.* Foreign music or "core production" music has lent stylistic, instrumental, vocal and other elements to the local/indigenous production of music, which still retains traditional melodic or other elements but has creatively integrated the two types of music into a new type. Integrated music is invariably found in all the 13 countries presented in the book, although its appeal and share of the local market varies substantially between countries.
2. *Importation.* Foreign music is imported to the country and consumed exactly as it has been produced--that is via imported records or produced--that is reproductions of these records in local plants under license.
3. *Cloning.* Imitation of foreign music hits by local groups which either perform these hits in their own way or produce their own music, often with lyrics in the local language, to sound exactly like the foreign music they imitate.

All these situations are present in most countries, although at differing degrees, and in many cases they are complemented by the consumption and--sometimes--production of traditional or "purely" local music. The "juxtaposition" of these situations and the relative prominence each of them achieves during specific periods in the history of each country is clearly demonstrated by the reports. The patterns of such juxtaposition have aroused the interest of many scholars, and various theories and models have been produced for their interpretation (see, for example, Hamelink, 1983; Wallis and Malm, 1984; Nettl, 1985). On the evidence of the reports presented in this book, it is shown that any theory or model which tries to interpret the interaction between the peripheral and the "core" production of popular music mainly on the basis of the production and market forces may arrive at misleading results. The interplay between production/market forces and the dynamics of the national context within which these forces operate determine the model of juxtaposition of the elements defined above. However, if we accept this in principle, it is nearly impossible to model the interaction between indigenous/local and "core" musical genres. It is more meaningful to analyze in somewhat greater depth the concept of "global" musical taste, which may be created through the interaction of different musics. Undoubtedly, the phenomenal expansion of mass communication facilities is leading toward a higher degree of interaction or interinfluence between musics, and in particular between the so-far-dominant (in market terms) Anglo-American pop and the indigenous (traditional and modern) musical genres.

This trend toward "globalization" of contemporary popular music is admitted by Robinson, Banks and Breaux in their report of U.S. popular music presented in this book (chapter 12), but is also treated with a large degree of skepticism: "Globalization is offset by an equally strong trend toward indigenization, the realization that one's own local traditions are worth keeping, related to a growing need to establish a self-identity based on the immediate environment." This statement is characteristic of the change in the thinking of scholars in the late 1980s, although it may be somewhat overoptimistic, given the present composition of the international music market and the structure of the music industry. Inevitably globalization comes to be a much more powerful trend compared with indigenization, since the former is supported by a powerful transnational phonographic industry (or mass media industry more generally) while the latter represents minority interests and minority markets in global terms.

The production of what has been called "globalized" music (e.g., see Wallis and Malm, 1984) implies a two-way process, which allows the incorporation of ethnic and folk elements into the contemporary pop genres produced by the "core" international music industry monopolies, in order to diversify their product, make it more interesting and increase its market potential. A crucial question here concerns the nature of the "core": as the economic power of Japan increases, we may also expect that globalized popular music will exploit the so-far-unexploited sources of the Far East musical traditions, sounds and styles in order to produce a new generation of international pop.

The question of indigenization also has been raised by the studies presented in this book, concerning the role of popular music in defining, to a certain extent, and reinforcing, at times of crisis, the national or local identity of a population. This question has been connected with the relative significance of indigenous versus "external" or "core" musics in the contemporary popular music production in each country. In countries with a strong national tradition of music (like Greece, Spain, Japan, India) we can observe a coexistence of different music tastes, traditional and modern, connected to different age groups, socioeconomic profiles or local culture (e.g., urban-rural). In countries with a regionally defined musical tradition (e.g., the Latin American countries) the building of a national identity on the basis of the regional tradition is a strong factor in the definition of contemporary popular music, although the common denominator of regional tradition is not as strong as that of a national tradition. In younger nations (e.g., Australia, Israel) without a unique or distinct musical tradition, the building of contemporary popular music style is based more solidly on international pop and forms in itself part of the national identity building.

However, in most of these nations, an equilibrium of the traditional and the modern, of the indigenous and the foreign, determines the definition of the contemporary musical scene and forms part of the national identity. This equilbrium is sensitive to social, economic and political changes, as the recent history of most of these nations has shown. In times of economic hardship or political instability, traditional and imported musics may be played against each other in order to introduce or force upon people a new identity which complies with the economic and political circumstances of the country. As discussed earlier in this introduction, musical "integration" has been achieved in the countries presented in this book by incorporating pop/rock elements in the creation of contemporary indigenous music. Thus indigenous musics from many countries, although different acoustically and melodically, have a significant common denominator: they share a pop/rock beat, instrumentation and style. The fusion of cultures has enriched popular music and at the same time has given it an international character.

This character implies an international identity model, which may threaten the national identity (as the chapter on Taiwan shows) or reinforce it (as the chapter on Uruguay implies). Thus, one should not take it for granted that the traditional forms of music will survive and develop through an awakening of self-identity at a national or regional level. The historical context of the development of popular music in the 13 countries shows that such an awakening has come about when self-identity is threatened. Under ordinary circumstances, especially when stability and relative affluence are established, the market forces tend to operate against all minority tastes, reinforcing majority tastes through the expansion of mass communication media.

We cannot but share the skepticism of many of the contributors of the book as to whether contemporary musical production in peripheral countries or regions, as a symbol and expressive channel of an alternative culture, will continue to survive if the mainstream cultures of all these nations become "globalized," accompanied by a sense of international identity. The question "whose master's voice?" that popular music echoes is eventually a question of identity conflict and identity fusion around the world.

BIBLIOGRAPHY

Adorno, T.W. (1976). *Introduction to the Sociology of Music.* New York: Seabury.

Alexander, J.C. & Seidman, S. (Eds.) (1990). *Culture and Society: Contemporary Debates.* Cambridge: Cambridge University Press.

Bigsky, C.W.E. (Ed.) (1976). *Approaches to Popular Culture.* London: Edward Arnold.

Blankopt, K. (Ed.) (1982). *The Phonogram in Cultural Communication: Report on a Research Project Undertaken by Mediacult.* Vienna: Springer-Verlag.

Bourdieu, Pierre (1979). *Distinction: A Social Critique of the Judgement of Taste,* Trans. Richard Nice. London: Routledge & Kegan Paul.

Dexter, L.A. & White, D.M. (Eds.) (1964). *People, Society and Mass Communications.* New York: Free Press.

Fejes, Fred (1981). "Media Imperialism: An Assessment." *Media Culture and Society,* 3, 281-289.

Frith, S. (1988). *Music for Pleasure: Essays in the Sociology of Pop.* Oxford: Polity Press.

Frith, Simon (Ed.) (1989). *World Music, Politics and Social Change.* Manchester: Manchester University Press.

Hamelink, Cees (1983). *Cultural Autonomy in Global Communications: Planning National Information Policy.* New York: Longman.

Hobsbawn, E. (1983). "Introduction: Inventing Traditions." In Hobsbawn E. & Ranger, T. (Eds.). *The Invention of Tradition.* Cambridge: Cambridge University Press.

Lewis, G.H. (1980). "Taste Cultures and Their Composition: Towards a New Theoretical Perspective." In Katz, E. & Szecko, T. (Eds.). *Mass Media and Social Change.* Beverly Hills, CA: Sage.

Manuel, Peter (1988). *Popular Music in the Non-Western World: An Introductory Survey,* New York: Oxford University Press.

McCormack, T.W. (1969). "Folk Culture and the Mass Media." *Archive Europeenes de Sociologie,* 10 (2).

Mendelsohn, H. (1964). "Listening to Radio." In Dexter, L.A. & White, D.M. (Eds). *People, Society and Mass Communication.* New York: Free Press.

Nettl, Bruno (1985). *The Western Impact on World Music: Change, Adaptation and Survival.* New York: Schirmer.

Riesman, D. (1950). "Listening to Popular Music." *American Quarterly.* 2 (4).

Robinson, D.C. (1986). "Youth and Popular Music: A Theoretical Rationale for an International Study." *Gazette,* 37, 30-50.

Robinson, Deanna Campbell; Buck, Elizabeth, B.; Cuthbert, Marlene, et al.; and the International Communication and Youth Culture Consortium (1991). *Music at the Margins: Popular Music and Global Cultural Diversity.* Newbury Park, CA: Sage.

Roe, K. & Carlsson, U. (Eds.) (1990). *Popular Music Research: An Anthology from Nordicom-Sweden.* Goteborg: Nordicom.

Shudson, M. (1987). "The New Validation of Popular Culture: Sense and Sentimentality in Academia." *Critical Studies in Mass Communication."* 4(1), 51-68.

Spottswood, Richard (1990). *Ethnic Music on Records.* 7 volumes. Urbana: University of Illinois Press.

Swingewood, Alan (1977). *The Myth of Mass Culture.* London: Macmillan.

Wallis, Roger and Malm, Krister. (1984). *Big Sounds from Small People: The Music Industry in Small Countries.* London: Constable.

Weber, M. (1969). *The Rational and Social Foundation of Music.* Trans. D. Martindale et al. New York: Carbondale.

Williams, Raymond (1981). *Culture.* Glasgow: Fontana.

CHAPTER 1

THE AUSTRALIAN ROCK MUSIC SCENE

Susanna Agardy
& Lawrence Zion

INTRODUCTION

Since white settlement began in Australia two centuries ago, the development of local culture has almost always occurred in competition with its better established imported counterparts. With much older Aboriginal cultures at best ignored, culture in Australia has evolved within the context of a "new society": with few exceptions, there has been little of the prolonged isolation here that has commonly shaped the evolution of "traditional" cultures. Thus, rather than warranting an exploration of the effects of the internationalization on a well-established indigenous music scene, the Australian scene needs to be examined in terms of the developments and prospects of a pop scene that has evolved in full competition with overseas products. This competition has applied also to other cultural products. Our examination will include a historical overview which will be followed by an outline of the structure of the rock music industry in Australia.

Australia has a population of 16 million people, over one-fifth of whom were born overseas. Although the country occupies a large land mass, most of the population is concentrated near the coast, especially the Southeast coast. Most Australians live in large cities; Sydney and Melbourne alone accommodate around 6 million people. Despite the more recent trend toward higher density living around the city areas, the ideal of a "house and garden" survives for the majority of Australians. The life cycles of Australians are similar to those of other Western nations: the minimum school-leaving age is 15 years, while marriage generally occurs after the age of 20.

Culturally, Sydney and Melbourne dominate the rest of the country to an extent that has sometimes caused resentment in the smaller cities and rural areas. While many immigrants continue to speak their mother tongues, most Australians speak only English, a factor that has ensured the country's cultural integration with both Britain and North America. From the outset, for many years Aboriginal languages and cultures, like Aborigines themselves, were treated with disdain. It was only in 1966, for instance, tha Aborigines were allowed to vote in Australia. Within this environment, Aboriginal musical instruments such as the didgeridoo have been viewed as cultural exotica, and only in isolated instances over the past few years have white Australian musicians shown any interest in attempting to integrate Aboriginal music within Western musical culture.

Australia was initially established mainly as a penal colony, the earliest white immigrants being from England, Ireland and Scotland. Although the British parliamentary system was adopted, the hierarchical class structure of British society did not take root in Australia in the same form, and there is a tendency to regard Australia as an egalitarian society, although this may be a simplistic representation. New settlers in many ways tried to live out their remembered cultural heritage by proxy. Their music includes folk songs from their homelands, songs often modified to suit the new conditions.

BROADCASTING

Radio in Australia officially began in 1923. In 1985 there were 330 stations, currently organized in four sectors. Virtually all of the population is reached by radio, the only exception being the residents of some outback areas.

The largest concentrations of radio stations are in Sydney and Melbourne, with some 45 stations located in these two cities. Some regional centers may have only one or two local stations and outback areas have patchy reception of perhaps one. The broadcasting system in Australia is modeled partly on the British system, exemplified by the network of national government-funded stations, and partly on the American system, exemplified by the style of the commercial stations. The majority of the radio stations are on the AM band. FM radio was introduced during the middle 1970s, and most of the FM licenses have been issued to public stations. In 1985 there were seven FM commercial radio licenses in existence, and these stations have been so successful and profitable that AM stations are now also clamoring for access to FM bands.

The Australian Broadcasting Corporation (ABC) began transmission in 1932. The ABC runs both radio and television stations and has an overseas service, Radio Australia, to parts of Asia. The ABC is supported completely by government funding and may not undertake commercial advertising. The ABC's stated aims include the provision of a diverse nationwide service, Australian in character, with special regard for rural areas not served by other radio stations. It provides a combination of network and local programming. The ABC is often perceived by sections of the community--for example, by the commercial sector--as the organization which should serve audience segments whose tastes are not catered for by other radio stations. The ABC also maintains the local symphony orchestras located in the states and is a concert entrepreneur. In 1985 there were 133 national radio stations.

Commercial radio stations are the most numerous and reach the largest audiences, being concentrated most heavily in metropolitan cities. They are privately owned and operated and rely on advertising for revenue. Commercial stations often sponsor community activities and those oriented to rock formats sponsor rock concerts. Commercial stations have their licenses granted by the Australian Broadcasting Tribunal (ABT or the Tribunal) and these licenses are renewable every three years. A license fee based on revenue is payable annually.

The industry association of the radio stations, the Federation of Australian Radio Broadcasters (FARB) represents the interests of commercial stations. Part of its policy is "to sustain an environment for discussion and negotiation with a view to inhibiting unwarranted government intrusion into the broadcasting process" (FARB 1982, 9). FARB also carries out self-regulatory activities concerning program and advertising content. In 1985 there were 137 commercial radio stations in Australia.

Public radio stations are operated by community groups, educational institutions and specialized groups such as music broadcasting societies and religious and ethnic groups. The purpose of establishing these stations has been to provide community access and an alternative medium for the expression of diverse tastes and opinions not represented in the mainstream national and commercial broadcasting stations.

Public radio stations are nonprofit stations which are barred from advertising and are frequently underresourced and small in scale. They rely on varying combinations of income sources such as member organizations, government grants and listener subscriptions. Some community stations transmit only within a radius of several kilometers. They are largely staffed by volunteers and usually have small, if loyal, audiences. In 1985 there were 53 public radio stations in Australia.

The Special Broadcasting Service (SBS) was set up with the purpose of giving expression to the government policy of multiculturalism, which acknowledges the high proportion of immigrants in the population, and for the perceived need to give public exposure to the cultures of these peoples. The SBS provides both television and radio services in over 50 languages. There is one ethnic radio station each in Melbourne and Sydney, but ethnic television has extended to all major population centers. The service is funded fully by the government. It is expected to be amalgamated into ABC in 1987, but it is intended that its special character will be preserved.

The formats of the commercial radio stations dominate the airwaves. The bulk of audiences show a preference for commercial stations. A survey in 1979 (Meyer et al. 1983) showed that 76% of people would turn to commercial radio for "pleasant music" and this finding is borne out by the regular audience surveys of radio stations. A strong American influence is reflected in the programming practices of stations, with increasingly tighter music formats aimed at attracting the largest possible market share, which is considered to be an economic necessity. The major formats of commercial stations are described as "talk," "adult contemporary," "contemporary" (including rock), "good music" or "country" (this is mainly played by rural stations which also maintain a greater mix of formats). The music played varies within these limits--that is, varieties of rock, Top 40, light popular music and beautiful music. Virtually no classical music or jazz is heard on commercial stations. A greater diversity of music is played by the national and other noncommercial stations. The national stations play classical music and jazz, as well as some "contemporary" music, with one radio station being targeted at youth and playing some less commercially oriented rock. The SBS radio stations play ethnic music, while public stations play the greatest diversity of music. They have set out, as a matter of policy, to provide both talk and music, which is often not otherwise available. They are willing to experiment and give airtime to little-known local and overseas artists, and in some cases have provided a springboard to local artists, who were later accepted by commercial stations and achieved international success. The public stations set out to please "some of the audience some of the time," providing for a great variety of tastes at different times.

PUBLIC POLICY AND GOVERNMENT REGULATION OF RADIO

Public policy, through regulation of the electronic media, has played and continues to play an important part in the encouragement of an Australian cultural identity (which now includes multiculturism) in programming[1]. The government has encouraged the fostering and development of national identity, and this has been reflected in legislation and in some of the activities of the relevant regulatory agency, the Australian Broadcasting Tribunal. The ABT is an independent quasi-judicial body. Its major functions are:

1. To grant, renew, suspend and revoke licenses.
2. To grant approvals and authorize transactions in relation to the ownership and control of licenses.
3. To determine and enforce standards and conditions in relation to programs and advertisements.
4. To assemble and disseminate information relating to radio and television in Australia.
5. To inquire into and report on matters relating to radio and television that are referred by the minister.

The ABT's activities extend only to commercial television and radio stations and public radio stations. The ABC and the SBS are self-regulating. The provisions governing the functions of the ABT and the obligations of the relevant stations are contained in the Broadcasting and Television Act 1942 (amended), (the act). The Department of Communications is concerned with overall matters of policy, planning and development of services and technical matters.

In the past, television and radio have been subject to stringent limitations of ownership, but in 1986 the government introduced a policy of greatly expanding these limits. This policy has already set in motion large-scale trading in television and radio stations. Ownership by foreign citizens is still limited for both, and the Tribunal must approve transfers of shareholdings. The previous ownership limitations have still allowed the radio (and television) stations to join together for the purpose of joint advertising selling arrangements and radio stations are generally part of news networks.

The Broadcasting and Television Act requires that the Tribunal determine programming standards for radio and television and that the stations comply with these standards, which describe what is suitable or unsuitable material for transmission. Early governmental concerns with the development of Australian culture have continued, and thus in order to reinforce government policy of providing an "Australian sound" on the electronic media, both the Broadcasting and Television Act and the ABT's Program Standards contain detailed requirements. The act now prescribes a minimum amount of Australian-originated music on radio: a minimum of 5% of the time that music is played on radio must consist of the compositions of Australians. This requirement has applied since 1956 and increased from the original 2.5% in 1942. It is required also that a license should, as far as possible, use the services of Australians in the production and presentation of programs. For the purpose of the requirement, an Australian is defined as a person who is either born or is ordinarily a resident in Australia.

A further requirement determined by the ABT states that no less than 20% of daily music playing time on radio stations is to be filled by Australian performances. This requirement began with 10% in 1973 and was gradually increased to 20% in 1976. The then regulatory body, the Australian Broadcasting Control Board (ABCB, the Tribunal's predecessor) surveyed the availability of Australian material before introducing and gradually raising the quota. An earlier plan for eventually raising the quota to 30% has not been realized. Throughout the years of operation of the quota, the ABT has, in cooperation with the Australian Performing Rights Association (the organization responsible for the collection of royalties) compiled and published statistics which measure the extent of the station's compliance with the quota.

The Australian performance quota has been the subject of much debate at all stages of its existence. It has been strongly supported by representatives of musicians, recording companies and other industries directly associated with these. It has been opposed by the representatives of the commercial radio stations, which, while supporting the concept of an overall "Australian sound," generally oppose the music quota as a means of achieving this aim. The original aim of the quota enunciated by the ABCB was to build up, in the long term, a characteristic Australian influence in broadcast music, and to advance the best interests of the listeners by using talented Australian performers, composers, arrangers, musicians and technicians; in summary, to develop a healthy and vigorous music industry. Given the assumption that the distribution of newly created music needs exposure through radio, it was intended to use the medium of radio to assist Australian musicians.

Over the years the representatives of commercial stations have argued that the quota is detrimental to the radio industry and obstructs the provision of diversity to the listener. They have argued that much of the Australian material was not of sufficiently high standard to warrant airplay and therefore the few titles that reached this standard needed to be repeated too often, thus alienating audiences.

The shortage of certain types of music produced in Australia, especially "beautiful music," has also been used as an argument against the quota, the claim being that stations using this format were either forced to change their format to comply with the quota, repeat existing material or fail to meet the quota. A crucial argument has centered around the question as to whether or not a distinctly Australian sound exists. Commercial radio stations have consistently asserted that no "Australian sound," as such exists in music played or composed by Australians. Those closely allied with the creation of the music have tended to support the quota by using arguments that have included recognition of an "Australian sound" (however imprecise the concept may be), the need to develop a diversity of musical styles and the need to encourage creative participants within the local scene. It has also been argued by FARB (1982) that the assistance the quota has generated for the music industry is doubtful. Notwithstanding these debates, the stations, with some exceptions (usually those with particular music formats), have fulfilled and exceeded the quota, while appearing not to have lost audiences in the process.

In 1982 the debate culminated in the Tribunal issuing a proposal to repeal the performance quota and seeking public comments on the issue. As a result of the submissions received, most of which supported the quota, the Tribunal held a public inquiry into the matter, which was completed in 1986. In the course of the inquiry the Tribunal examined evidence from all concerned parties and heard the arguments concerning "Australian sound." The report (Australian Broadcasting Tribunal, 1986) concluded that the 20% quota is to be retained. The details of its implementation still have to be resolved. In its report the Tribunal accepted the existence of an "Australian sound," and stated that music qualifies as Australian by virtue of its performance by Australians. The Tribunal also argued that in the public interest, stations should use their privileged positions of licensed access to the community as a means of promoting national culture. The promotion of local musicians was considered an important means of fulfilling this aim.

During the inquiry the effectiveness of the quota in promoting both an "Australian sound" in music and the welfare of artists and other branches of the music industry was debated. Those on the performing side claim that it is still difficult for Australian performers to get exposure on commercial radio and that not only are they accorded no preferential treatment but are often discriminated against by promotional structures, especially if they are signed up by independent record companies with fewer resources. Although distribution of independents' records was mostly undertaken by a major record company, it was claimed that these companies gave preference to their own overseas products in the course of promotion. The strict format adhered to by radio stations was also said to militate against Australian performers. Representatives of the stations, on the other hand, argued that all performers, regardless of nationality, are given fair consideration for airplay.

HISTORY OF MUSICAL DEVELOPMENT

Musical life in Australia never developed for long periods in isolation from overseas influences. For, not only has there been a continuous flow of immigrants from Britain and Europe, but Australia's growth has coincided with the emergence of modern communication technologies. It has been suggested that it would have been difficult for the pioneers to find a country less suitable for the cultivation of a new musical tradition, or a period in history more inauspicious for such a project (Covell, 1967). Thus, although Australia's development has been popularly characterized as occurring within a "tyranny of distance" (Blainey, 1968), it needs to be stressed that in reality the isolation resulting from this distance from other countries has been steadily eroding.

From the outset, imported music was imitated and adapted rather than being radically changed or invented. In the case of songs, such adaptations consisted mainly of the addition of new lyrics which reflected conditions in Australia more appropriately. Throughout the nineteenth century, bush balladeers and music halls played an important part in popular music entertainment. By the end of the century, opera had been popularized as a result of entrepreneurial efforts to import touring companies, and pianos were particularly common in both working-class and middle-class homes.

By this time Australia was becoming highly urbanized and affluent by international standards. These factors, combined with its close ties with other countries, especially Britain, helped sustain a widespread cultural appetite for imported entertainment. The arrival and instant popularity of radio during the 1920s heightened this trend: new kinds of music such as jazz became popular, although listeners and even performers were often unfamiliar with the social and ethnic origins of the music. Another pattern was also becoming established: prospective local musicians usually played only the music of accomplished overseas performers--whatever the style of music. While this was not unusual in itself, within this matrix imported foreign content was constantly overshadowing the fledgling efforts of aspiring Australians, a situation only exacerbated by the ready acceptance foreign performers found with local audiences. By 1942 this problem became a preoccupation for a government committee which in that year initiated the quota system by recommending that 2.5% of music broadcast on radio should be composed by Australians.

Such measures, it could be argued, had little apparent relevance in the early years of rock 'n' roll. For in the late 1950s the idea that local performers could be "stars" preceded attempts by Australian acts to write their own songs. The Australian composition quota did not, at this stage, make provision for Australian performances of overseas compositions. Therefore, in the late 1950s, when local rock 'n' roll acts were becoming stars while performing songs written overseas, there was no existing quota to guarantee media exposure on the basis of their performance--as against composing--activities. As in Britain at this time, America was the main reference point for Australian rock 'n' rollers. Yet Australia's exposure to American rock 'n' rollers was more intense than Britain's, as hundreds of American performers toured Australia between 1955 and 1963 at a time when few were playing to British audiences. America did not remain the focus, however: like America itself, Australia was, by the middle 1960s, in the grip of Beatlemania, a phenomenon fueled by the Beatles' tour of Australia in 1964. In many respects the situation in Australia can be seen as part of a generic Western response: increasing affluence, combined with a large teenage population due to the postwar baby boom, intensified the impact of the Beatles and other groups. And in Australia, as elsewhere, becoming involved in the pop music scene was an experience often linked to a desire to break out from what young people saw as the staid predictability and security of everyday life. In Australia the Beatles were also a source of inspiration for many recently arrived British immigrants to join or to form pop groups. Ironically, two of these, the Easybeats and the Bee Gees, became famous overseas as "Australian" groups.

In Australia both of these groups were at the vanguard of the trend for groups to write their own material. Before them, many groups had gained followings simply on the strength of their ability to imitate the Beatles (the Twilights in Adelaide and the Flies in Melbourne were two such groups). But by 1966 the notion that Australians could be pop stars was gradually accompanied by an acceptance that local acts could also be original and creative. Many groups continued to released "covers" of overseas songs: one common practice was to put out versions of overseas hits before the original recordings were released in Australia.

At the same time, a pop music business was developing that was separate from the entertainment industry. The linchpin of this was the growth of a dance venues circuit across the country: most of the income earned by pop groups at this time came from live performances at these places. Within this matrix, making and selling records became increasingly important for groups; but due to Australia's small population the value of a hit record was realized in the higher fees that successful pop groups could command, rather than through the relatively small royalty payments that accrued even from chart-topping hits--a situation which has generally persisted. If this factor meant that the commercial context of making records in Australia was at variance with those of Britain and America, pop groups in Australia were as keen as their overseas counterparts to gain access to recording and radio airplay. By the late 1960s, after a short-lived boom in the local scene had disintegrated, and as it became clear that groups recording locally could not compete with the technical resources available to bands in America and Britain, the issue of radio quotas resurfaced again. It was during the 1960s that Australia's pop scene began to mature. Although questions like "Is there an Australian sound?" were being asked during the 1960s, the idea that a distinctively local musical flavor had arrived gained particular momentum in the early 1970s with the emergence of the Melbourne group, the Skyhooks. While the view that a uniquely Australian style was at last evident had its proponents, in actuality it was not the music itself that was becoming "Australian," but rather the lyrics. With songs that celebrated Melbourne streets and suburbs--the same places that were famous in England as targets of Dame Edna Everage's acerbic satire--Australian pop music could at last take its local environment for granted. This development paralleled a more broadly based exploration of "Australia" in other cultural areas, and was linked to an emergent self-confident national identity as local iconographies began to gain their own symbolic potency. This resurgence of sentiment for Australian culture was harnessed and fostered by a newly elected Labor government in 1972.

Such changes did not necessarily mean that life was any easier for most pop groups. There was no letup, for instance, in the stream of touring groups that inevitably overshadowed local "support acts," even if the latter were among the local pop elite. And difficulties in gaining airplay continued to undermine chances of success: radio would often play only Australian groups that had already gained large followings in their live performances.

Not surprisingly, then, many pop groups sought overseas success, an aspiration shared with those in other cultural pursuits. In retrospect, the attempts made to realize such ambitions before the middle 1970s can be characterized as suicide missions: groups would leave for Britain or, more rarely, America, with little awareness of the environments they would have to deal with, and with no practical support from the Australian industry. Inevitably most of these groups made little headway, and while beliefs that international success was a logical progression from local stardom started to disintegrate, those groups who had staked all their resources on overseas success split up when such success did not eventuate.

In the late 1970s, however, a more sophisticated approach to promoting Australian groups overseas was spearheaded by Glenn Wheatley, manager of the Little River Band. Wheatley, who as a performer had experienced overseas failure years earlier as a member of the ill-fated Master's Apprentices, pioneered strategies for Australian groups to succeed in America by setting up contacts for the group ahead of its tour. At the same time he stressed that bands could build an overseas following while remaining based in Australia, an outlook which has since been realized by several groups, including the Little River Band.

Meanwhile, the pop music scene in Australia was diversifying. If "art school " groups had been absent in the 1960s, there were several groups by the end of the 1970s that not only wrote their own songs, but were also designing their own clothes and making innovative video clips. Most conspicuous of these were Split Enz from New Zealand, and Mental As Anything. By the beginning of the 1980s the pub circuit, which had come to replace the "dry" dance venues of the 1960s, had spawned a range of different rock music styles within Australia: some, like Midnight Oil, Redgum and Goanna, were unashamedly "political," but to glibly categorize these or other groups is to distract attention from the fact that--in an unprecedented fashion--Australia was now the home of groups with an enormous range of pop music styles. Perhaps the best known of these overseas is Men At Work, and while it would be misleading to suggest that they were bearers of an "Australian sound," they were in an important sense typical of Australian groups in that they had served their musical apprenticeship on the inner-city pub and club circuit.

During the 1970s and early 1980s "bushbands" also revived the traditional music of the nineteenth century. While the performers in "bushbands" are often dressed in traditional costume and play mostly on acoustic instruments, they often perform their own songs which may contain current political commentary. These bands often play in concerts, schools and in pubs.

There is no doubt then that the pop scene has progressed in many respects since the 1950s. The musical results may not be indigenous, yet there has been both originality and creativity in the music produced. An analogy could be made here with the lamington, a small square-shaped sponge cake coated in chocolate and coconut, which is popularly regarded as Australian. Its ingredients are not, of course indigenous to Australia, nor could the lamington be sensibly regarded as archetypal of a national cuisine. Yet the crucial point here is that the arrival of the lamington did *not* depend on such factors. Similarly, the growth of pop music in Australia has had little to do with the use of unique ingredients, or with ideological conceptions of a national style. Its development has, however, been linked to local factors. To push the lamington to its limits, music, like cake, does not simply evolve, but it is fashioned and created.

THE RECORD INDUSTRY

The record industry in Australia is dominated by the major transnational companies. In addition, there are a number of local independents. Detailed financial and other information on the operations of the industry has not been available, but the retail value of the industry was estimated in 1990 to be $448 million.[2] It was then the eighth largest market in world terms. The major record companies are: CBS, EMI, Polygram, BMG/RCA, WEA and Festival, which is the only locally based company. The major activity of the transnational companies is the manufacture, promotion and distribution of overseas recording under license. EMI and Festival have a longer history of producing records by Australian performers, while the other companies have moved into this area more recently.

In 1986 it was estimated that some 70 independent companies also existed, and some examples are Regular, Larrikin, Wheatley, Mushroom, Alberts, Hot, Big Time, Fable, Image and Liberation. Some of these have extended to markets in the United States, Europe and the United Kingdom. The independent companies play an essential role in the discovery of new local talent, but they often rely on the majors to promote and distribute their products. Recently their activities as talent scouts were said to have stimulated some majors to place greater emphasis on seeking out local talent on their own behalf. The growth of the fledgling independent companies received a great impetus in 1970, due to a dispute between the radio stations and major companies. During that year the record companies challenged the previously mutually convenient arrangement between themselves and radio stations. In this arrangement record companies had provided playlist material to the stations, which in turn provided needed promotion for the sales. In 1970 the record companies demanded compensation for the airplay of Australian and British recordings, these being protected by copyright agreement. This dispute resulted in the commercial radio stations banning these recordings from airplay. Since the ban lasted for some six months, and stations were obliged to fulfill the Australian composition requirement, an opportunity arose for smaller independent Australian record companies to have their material played on radio and thus to gain a foothold in the industry. Eventually an agreement was reached whereby radio stations would provide advertising time credits to record companies in return for the use of their material. This arrangement predated the establishment of the commercial FM stations that were not included in the agreement. A new dispute arose with these stations in 1982 which was resolved by the Copyright Tribunal's decision determining that commercial FM stations are obliged to play records of Australian and British origin. To some extent this arrangement can be said to militate against airplay of local content.

The relative success of the transnational companies can be calculated from chart appearances.[2] In the first half of 1985 the two, then American, companies CBS and WEA took the lion's share of chart inclusion. CBS accounted for 31% of the Top 100 singles and 28% of the Top 10, 28% of the Top 60 Albums and 40% of the Top 10; WEA managed 21%, 27%, 24% and 27%, respectively. Added together they took over 50% of all chart entries. The now (post-1987) European transnationals EMI, PolyGram and BMG/RCA between them took 30%, 32%, 20% and 18%, respectively. The slump in the fortunes of the record industry evident in the early 1980s has been recognized to be part of a worldwide slump, and has been in part attributed to the competing entertainment offered by video recorders, which Australians have acquired with enthusiasm, the penetration rate being around 40%. The recovery is seen as a return to music stimulated by new acts, some loss in the novelty value of video recorders and the increasing attraction of compact discs, in spite of their hefty price (around $19, compared with $9 for newly released vinyl albums and $2 for singles).[3] Again, in common with other international trends, the local record industry suffers from piracy in the form of home-taping. In 1982 the Australian Record Industry Association conducted a survey of home taping and on the basis of this survey estimated that some $290 million per year was lost in sales due to home taping of records, prerecorded tapes and radio. A proposal to levy a royalty on the retail price of blank tapes is being promoted.

Sales of vinyl singles and albums fell away during the 1980s. In 1981 22.7 million records were sold, in 1983 15.9 million, in 1985 16.8 million, in 1987 14.5 million and in 1989 13.1 million. Part of the recovery of the industry in the late 1980s was due to the increased sales of cassettes, which had improved in quality and had grown from 9.3 million in 1983, through 12.4 million in 1985, 15.1 million in 1987 to 16.0 million in 1989. Compact discs generated a huge demand, and sales now are only limited by supply. This shortage was alleviated by the commencement of operations by a new local compact disc manufacturing plant during 1987. This was the eleventh such plant in the world and its product was to be aimed largely at the export market, which was greatly assisted at that time by the fall in value of the Australian dollar. Compact disc unit sales started off in 1984 with 0.4 million and rose to 1.1 million in 1985, 3.2 million in 1987 and 9.1 million in 1989.

A major disadvantage suffered by the local record production industry (as well as other industries) is the small size of the local market. To build a profitable local industry, substantial export levels need to be achieved due to the uneconomic levels of sales in the local market. The average cost of the local production of an LP can be in the range of $50,000-$80,0000, although more expensive records can cost up to $165,000. Independents, however, still produce them for as little as $7,000 with skillful use of limited resources. While the importation of foreign master tapes involves a "substantial" license fee (amount not available), this still appears to be a more economical proposition for record companies. The level of risk involved in the release of local records is increased by the competition from records which often enter the country with a history of proven success and with complete promotional material supplied by the exporters.

Further evidence given at the Tribunal hearings indicated that if a locally produced album is marketed only in Australia, sales of 30,000 for records in the lower cost range (around $50,000) are insufficient to achieve a profit. It is possible for a single to reach the top of the national charts and achieve sales of less than 20,000. Record company executives emphasized at the Tribunal inquiry that having taken the risk with the development of a local product it was important to have international distribution rights so that profits could be made in larger markets. This should assist the promotion of worldwide success for Australian musicians.

While much important financial and market information on the recording industry is unavailable, estimates indicate that in general some 20% of records sold are produced by local acts. During its inquiry the Tribunal was given more detailed breakdowns on these proportions by individual record companies whose identities must remain confidential. This data indicated a progressive growth in the proportion of Australian recordings in the total business of record companies. The highest percentage of gross revenue derived from Australian recordings was stated to be 30% for 1982-83. Other companies quoted figures of 28%, 23% and 10% for the same year. Some of these percentages indicate that the figures which applied ten years ago or earlier have increased several fold in 1982-83. Record companies also indicated increased budgets for the development of local records for future years.

During the inquiry, representatives of major record companies indicated that Australian bands were now not only being taken seriously, but were in demand, and record companies were competing to sign them. The Tribunal was told that some overseas companies are willing to bypass their local subsidiaries in attempts to sign up Australian artists directly. Data on the availability of records in Australia need to be complemented by a picture of the activity surrounding the use of records and record-making. Figures from the Australasian Performing Rights Association have shown that the share of radio broadcast fees paid to Australian composers have more than doubled during the years 1974-83, from 9.7% to 21.5%. While the actual dollar amount is not great, the increase in proportion paid out is significant. The earnings of Australian composers from overseas sources have also increased as a percentage of their earnings in Australasia from 1.8% in 1974 to 8.2% in 1983. It should be pointed out that a large proportion of royalties from overseas were earned by a small number of groups, for example, Men At Work (Australian Broadcasting Tribunal, 1986). Meanwhile, success of Australian performers in the charts has fluctuated, quite frequently reaching 20% and occasionally exceeding this percentage. In 1988, 1989 and 1990 the U.K. charts were dominated by two Australian artists--Kylie Minogue and Jason Donovan--they pulled the Australian share of the U.K. market in 1988 to 3.7% of album sales and 6.2% of singles sales and in 1989 to 4.6% and 5.3%, respectively. In 1989 Australian artists came third in the magnitude of their U.K. unit sales beaten only by Americans and the British themselves.

Over the last decade Australian artists have been assisted by the large improvement in recording facilities which have reached international standards, and in recent years performers such as Elton John and Duran Duran have used them. However, due to the shortage of skilled producers and some reputed shortfalls in quality many Australian bands continue to travel overseas to record.

In 1988 the Australian Record Industry Association (ARIA) together with the federal government founded Ausmusic in order to promote and develop Australian contemporary music. It was envisaged that the venture would educate young musicians about the commercial side of their enterprises, provide them with facilities for practicing and playing and open up airplay time to them. In the first two years of its operation it ran 3,000-4,000 people through the master classes, reached 500,000 schoolchildren, hired 400 emerging bands and organized the Australian Music Day.

Radio is clearly an essential mechanism of the promotion of records and therefore of performers, although video clips have become integrated into the promotional structure of the record industry. While often costing $7,000-$10,000, it is generally agreed that video clips are a worthwhile investment. There are a variety of video clip programs on Australian television, some of which give exposure to records which have not yet made commercial playlists. "Countdown," which is screened nationwide on ABC, is the oldest video program at over ten years, and obtains good audiences. The program is reputedly a leader and has provided the debut for many bands. It is accepted as being extremely effective in producing sales and influencing radio play lists. A survey by ARIA has indicated that television exposure motivated 11% of record purchases while radio motivated 38% (Macken, 1982). Australia has a rock press which includes a local edition of the U.S.-based magazine *Rolling Stone* and a range of other magazines, most of which are aimed more specifically at the teenage market, such as *Countdown*, *Juke*, *Smash Hits*, *Ram* and *Melody Maker*.

LOCAL MUSICIANS

On any Friday or Saturday night there are at least 50 rock acts playing in both Melbourne and Sydney. The places of performance range from small rooms in pubs to large rock venues that can accommodate several thousand people. These are the extremes of what might be loosely described as a two-tired live performance circuit. The lower tier is the common denominator of the Australian music industry, and the starting point for almost all rock acts. Normally, groups that play only at small venues are at best semiprofessional: their incomes consist of door-takings which, even after a crowded night, might cover the cost of equipment rental that young groups usually incur.

It is within this environment, however--which has its own hierarchy of groups and venues--that groups seek to establish a following and build both their repertoire and image. It is increasingly common for groups at this stage to release at least one record. Although these are almost always low-budget productions on independent labels that sell less than 500 copies, they can help facilitate exposure for a group via public radio where audiences, though small, are generally enthusiastic followers of the local scene. Similarly many such groups make video clips which are unlikely to be seen on television shows such as "Countdown," might nonetheless reach a target audience on shows with smaller audiences such as "Rock Arena" or "The Noise."

It should be stressed that most groups never graduate from this existence on the edge of commercial success. To do so requires not only luck but also a single-minded commitment which, for groups outside Melbourne and Sydney, means moving to one of those two cities. For it is in these cities that the second tier of the industry is focused: Sydney has both large rock venues and sporting and social clubs and rock TV shows such as "Sounds"; Melbourne is the home of "Countdown "and barn-sized suburban pubs as well as glitzy rock venues.

With their concentration of recording studios and the biggest radio audiences, professional groups can hardly afford to be based elsewhere. Groups that have graduated from the lowest tier--the dress rehearsal stage of a rock career--have normally been living in either city for some time, where many already have experience in recording, video clip production, compulsory encounters with the rock press and television, as well as a following on the live circuit. In some cases, a sustained incubation period on the lower tier is followed by a more dramatic ascendancy within the second tier. Two examples of such a successful transition are the Models and Hunters and Collectors, both groups that formed in the late 1970s in Melbourne. Both groups had achieved "cult" status in small inner-city venues and recorded original records that were largely ignored by commercial radio before releasing albums that not only reached the national Top 10, but also insured them airplay on the most popular rock stations in Sydney and Melbourne. For instance, Hunters and Collectors, which, prior to the release of "Human Frailty" in 1986, had been playing to below-capacity audiences in pubs, were now earning several thousand dollars from door takings for appearances at much larger venues.

Similarly the Models, who were for several years described as "left-field," "alternative," and "postpunk," enjoyed only modest chart success before the release of their album "Out of Mind, Out of Sight." Yet, when both the album and the title track single reached number one in Australia, they, like Hunters and Collectors, could command much higher performance fees. As with other groups, this led to accusations from some of their fans that they had "sold out," but such responses implicitly exaggerate the polarization of the rock scene into "mainstream" and "independent" camps. Certainly it could be argued that both Hunters and Collectors and the Models have become more focused on commercial success. Their respective breakthroughs, however, are the outcome not of transformed ambitions, but of the way in which a career progression has become established within the pop music industry. It is by no means a predictable path, yet it is one that has fostered the development of a range of original music: other groups that have had recent similar career progressions include the Hoodoo Gurus, Do Re Mi, the Johnnys, the Saints and I'm Talking.

During January 1987, a major tour billed as "Australian Made" played to large stadiums across the country featuring many of Australia's most popular rock groups including INXS, Jimmy Barnes and Mental As Anything. One aim of this tour was to showcase the diversity of local talent internationally via MTV and other rock television shows. This, it could be argued, reflects both a more carefully coordinated attempt to market Aus-

tralian rock acts overseas, and a desire to overcome the extent to which local performers have been seen as inferior to overseas stars by audiences, a
factor fueled by promotional practices in the past.

CONCLUSION

The local rock music scene can be portrayed as dynamic and diverse but
continues to compete with a better-financed overseas product. The small
size of the Australian market leaves it very much subject to international
fluctuations, and while the resources of the major record companies tend to
be channelled into the promotion of international products, threatening to
undermine local rock acts, the majors can also be available to popularize
Australian talent on a wider, international scale.

Public policy, as part of a general movement toward the development of
Australian culture, supports Australian musicians through the quota on
radio and the increase, during the last ten years, in the diversity of radio
outlets, which have also led to expanded avenues of entry onto the public
stage. Thus, the formal structures exist whereby "Australian sound" remains
problematic but should not present an obstacle to the fostering and success
of local talent.

NOTES

1. Since this part of the chapter was written, the regulatory system has
changed. This is an on-going process with new proposals for the structure of regulation still under discussion.

2. Source: *Billboard* November 9, 1985 (extracted from performance on the
national Kent Music Chart).

3. U.S. dollars, not Australian dollars, are given throughout this chapter.

BIBLIOGRAPHY

Anon. (1979, 19 July). Tribunal warned of radio formats. *The Age* (newspaper).
    Melbourne.

Audley, P. (1983). *Canada's cultural industries. Broadcasting publishing, records and
    film.* Toronto, James Lorimer & Co.

Australian Parliament. (1942). *Broadcasting and Television Act 1942.* (Incorporating
    amendements by legislation). Canberra.

Australian Broadcasting Tribunal (various). *Annual Reports.* Canberra: Australian
    Government Publishing Service.

Australian Broadcasting Tribunal. (1981). *Notice of proposed amendment to the
    broadcasting program standards.* Sydney.

Australian Broadcasting Tribunal. (1986). *Australian Music on Radio.* Sydney.

Australian Broadcasting Tribunal. (Various). *Estimated resident population. Produc-
    tion Statistics. Import Statistics. Export Statistics.* Canberra.

Baker, G. (1983, 28 May). Australia; music around the world. *Billboard.*

Baker, G. (1985, 9 November). 1984 Market surge helps Australia restore status as major rock nation. *Billboard*.

Batties, R. (1983, 9 April). While the men await their millions. *The Age*. Melbourne.

Beilby, P. & Roberts, M. (Eds). (1981). *Australian music directory*. Melbourne: Victoria.

Blainey, B. (1968). *The tyranny of distance: How distance shaped Australia's history*. Melbourne: Sun Books.

BPI. (1991). *BPI Yearbook 1990*. London.

Caldwell, G. (Ed.). (1977). *Entertainment and society*. Canberra: Australian Government Publishing Service.

Chapple, S. & Garofolo, R. (1977). *Rock 'n' Roll is here to pay*. Chicago: Nelson-Hull.

Copyright Tribunal. (1983, March). *Reasons for decision*. WEA Records Pty Ltd. RCA Ltd. Astor Records Pty Ltd. PolyGram Records Pty Ltd. CBS Records Australia Ltd. Festival Records Pty Ltd. EMI (Aust) Ltd-Applicants. Stereo FM Pty Ltd-Respondent. Sydney.

Covell, R. (1967). *Australia's music: Themes of a new society*. Melbourne, Sun Books.

Federation of Australian Broadcasters. (1981). *Proposed amendment to the broadcasting program standards 1981*. (Repeal of standard 3) comments in support of this proposal.

Federation of Australian Radio Broadcasters. (1982, August). *The Australian commercial radio industry*. A monograph.

Geddes, M. & Thomas, H. (1979, 7 July). Stuck in a groove. *The Age*. Melbourne.

Harbour, R. (1983, 6 May). Bush bands dancing up a storm. *Australian Financial Review*.

Hausman, R.L. (1975). *Australia--traditional music in its history*. North Quincey, Massachussetts: The Christopher Publishing House.

McGarth, N. (1978). *Noel McGarth's Australian encyclopaedia of Rock*. Collingwood, Victoria.

Mackay, I.K. (1957). *Broadcasting in Australia*. Carlton, Victoria. Melbourne University Press.

Macken, D. (1982, 3 July). Video-the changing face of rock 'n' roll. *The Age*. Melbourne.

Macken, D. (1982, 18 November). Tapeworn eats an in. *The Age*. Melboune.

Meyer, H., Garde, P. & Gibbons, S. (1983). *The media : Questions and Answers, Australian surveys 1942-80*. Sydney: George Allen & Unwin.

O'Neill, M. (1983, 15 January). The oils are at home in troubled waters. *The Age*. Melbourne.

Turner, G. (1983). *The day the music died*. Video clips and popular music presented at ANZAAS conference, Perth.

Walls, S. (1983, 9 May). The broadening band of public broadcasting. *The Australian*.

Zion, L. (1982). Pop music and Australian culture: Some considerations. *Melbourne Historical Journal*, 14, 18-23.

Zion, L. (1984). Rock and opera: Selling the product. *Arena*, 68, 31-37.

CHAPTER 2

CULTURE, MEDIA AND THE MUSIC INDUSTRY IN BRAZIL

Nelly de Camargo

CULTURAL INDUSTRY: THE BRAZILIAN CASE

The existence of the cultural industry in Brazil is a function of the country's general process of economic formation and development. It is similar in several aspects to many of the dependent economies in the Third World. As an immediate consequence, Brazil's industrialization process--and the culture industry structure within it--follows the same dependent track. Economic and cultural dependence go back to the discovery era. However, the nineteenth century can be seen as the determinant departure point for the industrial phase of development. The organization of so-called liberal capitalism, noticeably in the most developed areas (United States and Europe), and its expansion to the colonies, allied to the Industrial Revolution, introduced into Brazil new capital-work relationships. The power of the industrialized societies over the nonindustrialized ones was strengthened through processes that ranged from the use of subtle political persuasion to the violent physical destruction of any attempts in independent growth.

On such a base of submission and dependence, Brazilian industry was built--as was its mass culture industry, an industry which has stimulated the growth of needs through the importation, adoption and, in the best cases, adaptation of cultural products and behavior patterns foreign to the Brazilian reality and much beyond the society's acquisitive power. National wealth has had to be channeled to provide for those "needs," instead of being used for indigenous projects which could promote a more adequate social and economic development.

This can be better understood if we realize that Brazil has kept itself relatively stable since its independence in 1822, as far as its structural sociopolitical transformation is concerned. Throughout the first 100 years and more, the few attempts to reach structural changes were isolated ones, originating from movements or groups with no prospect making of a real change in the global structure. Additionally, the clashes between the conservative oligarchies and the liberal progressives were almost always resolved through compromise and concessions from both contenders.

This way of dealing with sociopolitical problems gave rise to a deep respect for upright attractive personalities, and a taste for political rhetoric with discourse on the basic method of persuasion rather than armed weaponry and social revolutions. A partial explanation of this phenomenon is the functional illiteracy of the majority of the population, for whom the printed word has always been strange, who survive through the system of oral communication; the "cultivated" culture of an essentially literary tradition has been maintained at a distance from the masses.

Throughout the first two decades of this century this pattern was maintained. From 1930 onward, due to the acceleration of capitalist relationships, new factors capable of maximizing the social contradictions were incorporated into the sociopolitical reality: greater syndical activities, the rise of nationalism and the weakening of colonialism. General characteristics of the "ethos" of Brazilian society such as the acceptance of a demagogic-populist type of discourse, identification with a particular half-caste nationalism and a peculiar kind of optimism toward the destiny of the country and its potentialities generated other results such as the substitution of the "old Republic" by the "new" one and the appearance of a particular type of mass culture.

In the 1930s, journalistic enterprises expanded as a result of an expanded mass public of the proletarian and urban middle classes. Radio became a national addition with the support of this essentially oral culture. Gradually the economic model of exports restricted to a few primary products and diversified imports gave way under internal products and diversification. The import products and patterns from developed countries grew exponentially. The latter were consumed by the most privileged groups and then filtered down to other strata of society. To these transformations, the 1940s added the reflections of the postwar economic recuperation and expansion of developed countries. This opened the way for the most pervasive medium of the culture industry: television. In 1950 television started working in the country. It brought a new flow of images from the metropolis and consolidated the strong, incipient networks for the dissemination of cultural products. In the 1950s and 1960s the country's most impressive surge of economic development took place. The growth of all markets rose to levels never reached before. The cultural industry system became definitely established and stronger than ever, reaching the whole country. Television, in its ascension, demonstrated its potential for cultural standardization through its processes of conveying patterns, tastes and languages. The 1970s were marked by a slowing down of this process, due to the internal and external economic crisis, as well as to the processes of internal political reorganization. With the decree known as A1-5, strong control over political and cultural manifestations was exerted. Concomitantly, the birth and development of alternative productions, outside the traditional system--questioning the system--took place.[1]

THE BRAZILIAN CULTURAL INDUSTRY:
CONTEMPORARY LANDSCAPE

The Brazilian economy as a whole suffers from the influence of foreign capital: its interests and perspectives constitute important variables affecting activities from the exporting of coffee and iron to the Samba Schools parade in Rio during Carnival. The cultural industry is tied to the same schema. Even though a considerable part of it is not directly associated with foreign capital, as a whole it is subjected to those pressures that guide many of the trends of the economy.

The cultural industry of Brazil may be envisaged, in numbers, as follows: in 1981 there were about, 1,300 radio stations and about 120 TV stations, with a corresponding audience estimated at between 80 and 120 million people for 50 million radio receivers, and an estimated audience of 80 million people for 20 million TV sets. Of the latter, around 20% could receive color broadcasts.

There were approximately 315 daily newspapers, 1,150 weekly and monthly publications, plus 850 magazines of all kinds (from comics to specialized publications). The 315 newspapers had a readership of 5 to 6 million people; only the biggest dailies *O Estado do Sao Paulo*, *Folha de Sao Paulo*, *O Globo* and *Jornal do Brazil* published around 400,000 copies at most. On weekdays the figure varied between 250,000 and 300,000 copies. Monthly and weekly publications had a variable circulation: a weekly information magazine considered good in Brazilian terms, would publish 50,000 to 100,000 copies for a public estimated at 550,000 people; a comic magazine like *Tio Patinhas* (Uncle Donald) in 1978 was the most popular magazine of its type with a circulation of 360,000. The book publishing sector was much smaller. Some 10,000 titles were edited per annum with print runs of about 3,000 copies for both fiction and nonfiction. If a book had good sales prospects, a print run of 5,000 copies was possible, a novel that sold 30,000 copies was considered a best seller. Non-fiction titles rarely had comparable print runs in the first edition. Several editions were necessary to reach the success level of fiction. Jorge Amado, the best-known Brazilian novelist, sells the most books. Up to 1980 he sold a record 1 million copies of a collection of his books published during the preceding 20 years. Compared to other authors he reached an outstanding total; however, in market terms, for a nation of well over 100 million inhabitants, it becomes irrelevant.

With the exception of book publishers and educational broadcasting stations (radio and television), almost all mass media outlets depended on advertising to survive. The advertising space in newspapers was up to 80%. Most of the radio and TV broadcasting companies depended totally in their budgets on advertising revenue.

Managing an amount estimated at $1.5 billion (considered, in 1980, the world's seventh national gross product), the communication media system depended absolutely on its clients and their intermediaries, the advertising agencies. The advertising agencies which were linked to foreign groups (mainly American), took around 40% of the market. The biggest clients of the newspaper and broadcasting companies were multinational companies. Another important client of the media was the government which advertised at federal, state and city levels. In essence the media could not exist without money earned from foreign enterprises and the government. As to the advertising distribution, radio received no more than 8%; magazines an average 12%, newspapers around 20%. Between 50% and 60% went to television, which underlines the privileged role of TV compared to the others, in spite of the fact that the radio audience was numerically superior to that of television. The disparity between audience-reaching and advertisement budget distribution appears to be directly linked to the marked differences in the buying power of the various population strata.

The influence of alternative media (videocassettes, cable TV, etc.) was restricted until recently to a small number of people. However small, the buying power of this group has already produced some changes in the culture industry landscape, mainly in the area of television: there was a rapid proliferation of videoclubs. Even though it has been subjected to specific legislation, the field has become an interesting market for those who can afford it. In the big cities, foreign films (mainly North American), are made available in original or pirate copies, with subtitles or dubbed, months before they are launched commercially in the cinemas or on the television networks. The expansion of sales of videocassettes and the videogames addition can be regarded as the tip of the iceberg that has refreshed all Brazilian programming recently. Little by little more popular, live programs are being shown. Some shows now have millionaire prize distribution to stimulate their audiences. On the other hand, the production of increasingly sophisticated novelas (soap operas) reinforces the most important trend in Brazilian television.

According to existing estimates and in spite of the above numbers and indicators, 10% of Brazilians do not listen to the radio, approximately 30% do not watch television, and around 80% do not read magazines or newspapers. Bookstores reach around 25% of the population with their books (hardback collections and educational books excluded). Strictly speaking, cinema and theatre can not be described as vehicles of mass communication, even though Brazil traditionally had been an important market for foreign films (mainly American). Taking as an example, the city of São Paulo, the greatest population concentration in the country, there are around 100 public cinemas,[2] with an approximate seating capacity of 50,000; there are also about 30 theatres for dramatic plays with a seating capacity in total of 12,000. Considering that there are five daily sessions, a movie will reach a maximum of 250,000 people daily, whereas any television program will reach an audience of 500,000 people in the city of Sao Paulo. Regarding the origin of the films screened, national production only accounted for up to 20% of the premieres each year at the beginning of the 1980s. Since then a new trend has appeared with national productions sometimes being more successful than foreign ones. These particular instances highlighted the need to study audience tastes and expectations in order to cater for them through this specific medium. Foreign investors recognized this trend. Numerous coproductions have taken place, and the press has made much of the offers coming from different foreign film producers.

In the area of film promotion a disparity between foreign and domestic productions is apparent. The foreign product is better launched and promoted, it gets better press coverage and uses better technical and artistic resources.

The audiences for cinemas and theatres have decreased over the past years. It is part of the crisis that has affected all the cultural sectors of society and is the result of the economic problems of the country. For instance, the cost of a movie ticket, in the big cities, is prohibitive for the great majority of people (3% of the highest minimum wage or salary); a theatre ticket costs double, on average, in spite of the heavy subsidies invested by the public sector to popularize theatre. Paradoxically, people will pay many times more than the price of a movie ticket to get a seat to watch a soccer match, while young people will do the same for a seat at a show to listen to popular music.

Shows are also part of the cultural industry. Their mechanisms will be dealt with more extensively as they are intrinsically linked to the main research subject. As far as costs are concerned, shows are inaccessible to the average Brazilian (one ticket may cost more than 10% of the minimum salary), even when one takes into account their infrequency and targeting of taste. The infrastructure needed to stage a show requires huge investment from the producers. This leads to decisions that favor the presentation of only artists who already have a large following: the great idols and their the disciples from 1960s, who have been the greatest financial successes in Brazilian popular music; the new valuable artists, many of whom owe their fame to television. Some assumptions may be drawn from the foregoing information. It would appear that Brazil is still not a society of mass-media communication, despite the existence of a mass-media system which produces and manages large investments emerging from the cultural consumerism of a particular stratum of its population. Income distribution has been the most perceptible variable influencing this outcome: the production planning of the cultural industry is conceived for and directed toward particular classes of people in the South and Southeastern parts of the country, and to a lesser degree, in other regions. Such a consumer perspective generates a cultural product that is diffused heterogeneously over all other classes, for which there are not real but symbolic consumers being offered products made for the minorities.

The consumption of imposed products and the consequent annihilation of the audience's critical capacity, springs from the essentially commercial characteristic of the Brazilian cultural industry production systems, in which the media are tied umbilically to advertising interests. Producers who reject such ties, as some independent theatre, book, record and film producers do, are of minimal economic importance, even though they may be perceived as representative indicators of a positive development in social and cultural terms.

The mass media which are not dependent on commercial rules (educational radio and television), are dependent on the government which subsidizes them.[3] In some cases, in spite of relative institutional independence, as far as options and comments are concerned they suffer constraints and "persuasions," which lead through several mechanisms to transformation into similarities in aims and processes to those operated by the mass cultural industry. However, as they constitute important elements of the political system, these media may change the general pattern, reorienting the mass culture-forming process in the country, insofar as elections and genuine social movements provide grounds for changing the political structure and parameters.

It has been pointed out by communication analysts that the country's economy, global orientation and commercialism are reflected in the culture industry policies, thus leading to a process of content selection of themes, subjects, values and perspectives which are foreign to Brazilian society.[4] Even though such a cross-fertilization process could produce undesirable effects, Brazilian society has been historically open-minded, refusing radicalism as far as intercultural experiences are concerned. Brazilians have always welcomed such contributions, provided that a just measure can be reached and maintained in a balanced dialogue between the traditional forces of Brazilian culture and the new elements and processes of its development. This is not at all an easy task.

CULTURAL INDUSTRY AND INDUSTRIALIZED MUSIC: A BRIEF SYNTHESIS

The setting of the record industry in Brazil followed the traditional patterns of technology transfer from developed to developing countries. Since 1910, there are registers of national record production in Brazil. These records are considered pioneers and belong to the history of Brazilian music. However, they were very few in number and their high cost made them exclusive. The advent of radio in 1922 and the playing of records on it gave musical activities a great boost. Between 1923 and 1925 eight radio stations were inaugurated; from 1926 to 1928 six more came on air. In programming music, radio progressively left its tentative practice of playing classical music only and became the great medium for the diffusion of recorded popular music; from 1930 onward live popular music was presented in all studios and auditoriums.

Auditorium programs were included in the broadcasts and audience seats were highly valued. The 1940s was the decade of the great radio orchestras, conducted by maestros and bandleaders who gave popular music a touch of sophistication by arranging it. This was the golden period of radio when, just to give an example, the National Radio of Rio de Janeiro maintained within its professional staff, 100 musicians and 16 conductors and arrangers, among whom were the greatest names in contemporary Brazilian music. Professional singers became very important, and a whole generation of great interpreters of popular songs led the music panorama for many years.[5] The rise of the idol-singers is a postwar phenomenon. In the 1950s the concert singers had their fan clubs,[6] some of which are still active and successful to this day. In 1950, live concert programs found a competitor in the newly installed medium of television. In the 1960s when television progressively adapted the most palatable radio competitions radio changed its programming. Broadcasting started emphasizing information, soccer commentaries and recorded music. The disc jockeys inaugurated a new era, called by historians "big gramophone."

Still in the 1950s, the cultural expansionism of the North, strengthened by the atmosphere of postwar reconstruction and the cold war policy, exported to the peripheral countries the cultural modes normally associated with youth in those countries. In the movies, rebels like Marlon Brando and James Dean; in music, the rock revolution of Elvis Presley through the paths opened by Bill Haley and the Comets, announced a change in the cultural environment that started with the rupture of the audience's static relationship with music and performers. The old listener became a coparticipant through dance, hysteria and other manifestations. Thus was launched the basis for a growing market which, in the last 40 years, flooded leisure time and developed youthful tastes with numerous diverse music styles: from twist to ye ye yeah, from the samba-canção to the bossa nova, from the protest song to tropicalism, from country to rock 'n' roll.

In spite of the heavy external influences, in spite of (and also as a function of) all the political and social changes, the 1960s have been considered a most fertile decade for Brazilian popular music, from both qualitative and quantitative points of view. The cultural industry, ever alert, technologically and economically developed, absorbed this boom. The music of the previous decade was reissued, records and cassettes became quite popular, and the music of the new era reached the population via radio and TV.

In the middle of the 1950s, the decline of the bossa nova and the rise of the conservative political forces in government created a fertile space for the development of a strongly nationalist, ideologically engaged popular music. To balance this stream, there was the youth music movement (ye ye yeah), similar to the rock and light songs of British and American young people, which introduced new idols to delirious young audiences.[7] At this time the Young Guard and the festivals became national events and gave birth to a very important movement of a new generation of composers dedicated to the re-creation and rearrangement of music that is perennially popular and appreciated.[8] Brazilian popular music strengthened its star-system by involving television and specialized magazines in the diffusion of the images and looks of the new singers and composers. The Young Guard movement was already popular with its stars broadcasting on radio and television and producing records and cassettes.[9] Promoted by the TV stations, little by little the festivals opened up a new space for collective agglutination, political and artistic demonstrations in the presence of the student population, which became extremely important in the process of confrontation with the political regime installed in 1964. As a consequence of this, the possibilities of musical consumption were expanded.

In musical terms, the 1970s started under the shadow of political, social and cultural repression, which caused the most important stars of MPB[10] to withdraw from the scene. The censorship, which tried to extend its influence over the festivals, exerted its power over the lyrics of popular songs. As expected, the lyrics became a form of resistance, very refined and semantically meaningful. These lyrics became one of the most important forms of Brazilian literary expression in the 1970s. They are of such importance that no serious study of that period would be considered complete if it failed to analyze the lyric content of MPB. If, from one side, the protest songs grew rapidly in the 1970s, another rebirth took place: instrumental music, styles that had been forgotten, *chorinho* (softweeping), and the Northeastern rhythms, for instance, came to the fore instead of taking second place. While the struggle with censorship happened inside the country, the invasion of foreign music took place softly and firmed its roots into the market. It was helped by a condescending customs policy toward imported products, and supported by a powerful system of advertising and diffusion through the mass media.

The multinationals of record production created a kind of interesting aberration in market terms with their facilities, which highlighted the nature of the business and interests they represented. While the best sellers (or Top 10) were all Brazilian music, foreign records were the most strongly promoted and diffused through the media. Radio and television broadcast time became more and more restricted and disputed. This was in total contradiction to the elemental rule of "giving satisfaction to popular taste and demand" and, more important, disregarding a special law which required a minimal amount of 50% Brazilian music in Brazilian broadcasts. Most of the disc jockeys broadcast 70% to 80% foreign music in their programs. Since then, there has been a battle over transmission time and, if the media are really influential, the figures may reverse in time. During the whole of the 1980s foreign music was more often broadcast by the media in Brazil, but Brazilian music had higher sales.

At the end of the 1970s the music industry could be pictured as follows:

1. Television, contrary to the trend at the beginning of the decade, shifted the broadcast mainstream from the old variety and singing programs to the "novelas," which attracted large audiences at peak viewing times. Music became an additive to the novela's merchandising, recorded and sold as its sound track. This commonly included an international selection, promoting second-hand canned materials from other producers, who lent tapes to the television enterprises.
2. As a result of this marketing mechanism, an important share of the record market was appropriated by enterprises that relied on other enterprises' contracts, and since they were linked to TV networks, the broadcasting of such selections was guaranteed.

The modern festivals sponsored by the multinationals and stimulated by millionaire prizes were totally controlled by the record industry. They did not produce important contributions in terms of artistic quality and innovation until the 1980s. Lately performers with a scholarly musical education have contributed with electronic instrumentation and produced beautiful new performances which are on the boundaries of classical style and popular tunes and rhythms[11].

Radio, pressured by discotheques and disco music, surrendered to the power of the multinationals by almost homogenizing its broadcasts with music "to jump with" some "made in Brazil" but foreign to the traditional Brazilian musical trends.

Reaction, of course, happens: the university circuits tried to substitute partially for the old festivals, by filling their auditoriums with students who came to listen to the stars of MPB. Here, too, the record industry captured a market share: special records were produced, new styles were created, old accepted ones were reinforced. It also created a place for the new Latin American wave. The short-lived discotheques popular in the 1970s gave way to the *gafieiras*[12] where the samba was recalled, as it always has been, when there is an interruption or pause between genuine music movements. \ generation of female singers, along with composers or *cantautores*[13] formed a new constellation to join the 1960s star system. This group brought together a better organization of singers, musicians and composers to fight for copyrights. Consequently, a more direct confrontation with the hegemony of the large recording companies has taken place and, as would be expected, the latter have retaliated. Concurrently, independent groups have produced and distributed their own records. It was and still is a symbiosis in which the investment is made by the author (or group of authors, composers, interpreters), leasing the equipment from a recording enterprise. In spite of all the difficulties and, many times, as a solution for them, MPB has experienced a genuine growth. Respected names acquired sufficient status within the record industry, to exert a tighter control over their own work, defining their own criteria and style specifications.[14] They also received substantial sums of money. If their contracts run into millions, so do their sales.[15]

In 1986 Brazil was eighth in the world for cash value of record sales, with a retail market worth US $239 million. This is an important indicator considering Brazil's economic situation. Brazil's world ranking dropped since 1979 when it was the fifth largest market. This reflects the deterioration in spending power of Brazilians during the 1980s and also rising costs of record production.

Brazil has a relatively low per capita spending on recordings, $1.73 per head in 1986, a figure that then earned the rank of thirty-second in the world at that time. This illustrates the lack of depth of market penetration through the general population. Another particular Brazilian market variance is the lack of movement found in the developed world from vinyl to other forms of recording presentation. In 1989 the total unit sales of LPs was the highest in the world, with 56.7 million units sold, when only 34.6 million units were sold in the United States and 1.7 million units in Japan, the top two record-selling countries at that time. Additionally the sales of singles in Brazil were the lowest in any major market, at 0.1 million unit sales; cassettes were also relatively unpopular at 17.9 million unit sales in 1989 (446.2 million units were sold in the United States); finally, sales of compact discs, at 2.2 million units, were behind even the smallest Western country. Brazil is the bastion of the long-playing vinyl record.

The industrial production of a long-playing record in Brazil costs around $35,000 which includes the matrix, the material, cover printing and technicians. This same LP is sold at the retail outlet for 70 or 80 cruzados (approximately 12 to 15% of the country's highest minimum wage; i.e., the minimum salary in Brazil could buy eight LPs). This price includes expenses linked to the industrial process and costs linked to the payment of musicians, advertising materials, media diffusion, selling distribution and management. The process of record production is as complex as any other industrialized product, from chickens to computers. An LP is a peculiar product, its characteristics are that it has to compete with some 300 others that arrive on the market each month (3,400 a year). Even though destined for different market segments, each product occupies the same diffusion space and time. As merchandise, a record's selling appeal remains in its own performance. The difficulty of getting broadcasting time in the mass media, allied to the importance of these media as shop windows, defines the degree of complexity and the amount of necessary investment for the promotion of records.

In the Brazilian case, there is another peculiarity in market terms, due to the legislation which protects the production of "cultural goods" by the industries installed in the country. In 1980 records still got physical benefits from the Goods Circulation Tax (ICM): this enabled recording producers to invest monies due to ICM as payment of authors' copyrights, artists' rights (due to interpreters) or connex rights (payment to Brazilian musicians and technicians), from the sales of records. Such indirect exemption appears at first sight as beneficial to national record production; the recording companies use the money to finance records that have little chance of commercial success. However, it also applies to foreign records. The result is that foreign music comes into the country, already prepared at low cost, independent of Brazilian professionals for its production and reaches Brazilian ears and pockets with the ease of a special guest. This is even when it is of an inferior quality. The producer takes double profits: from the sales and from the ICM exemption. The latter is sometimes used to help Brazilian professionals produce the raw materials which will be commercialized by the producers and prove highly profitable for them and their foreign artists. This is to be changed in the near future and new rules are being studied.

MASS MEDIA AND THE RECORD INDUSTRY

In Brazil radio and television reign supreme in the diffusion of music, in spite of several alternative channels ranging from independent recording to the localized diffusion of peasant folk songs. The radio landscape at present is not very different from that of the end of the 1970s. The increased number of radio stations and audience diversification as a consequence of FM diffusion produced some qualitative changes in broadcasting. While the AM stations are almost totally dedicated to clearly popular programming, where most of the music is national, the FM stations have targeted broadcasts according to research findings about audience tastes.

The record promotion system in both AM and FM follows the same pattern: new records are sent by mail (to the back-country stations) to be included in the station's programs. Bigger cities and state capitals receive personal treatment: a representative from the record company pays a visit to the radio stations and/or disc jockeys with the new records. Sometimes the composer and/or singer goes along, or an interview is recorded in order to illustrate the possible presentation(s). This way, the existent stars keep their place and new ones are promoted, the fans are stimulated by phone-ins, letters, competitions for free records or simple requests for favorite songs.

There are also some other characteristics of this business: (1) the *jaba* (payola), a typical expression of radio professionals to designate special kinds of favors, such as the priority of launching a certain record or an exclusive interview with a singer, and other similar mechanisms; (2) the existence of radio networks linked to certain headquarters which are closely related to the recording enterprises from which packages of programs ready for transmission are sent out to their affiliates, and so on.

The so-called specialized critique and music journalists have little influence as far as global sales are concerned, even when enough space is made available in the press, radio and TV to carry their opinions. Moreover, when there is a discussion between critics and artists, it is always in terms of authentic values and opinions. Comments about the economic motives and the behavior of the recording industry are almost nonexistent. The relationship between the critics and the recording enterprises is said to be just cordial. The critics graciously receive the new records, or at least the important ones. The written critique has little possibility of influence. The country reads very little; the possible readers are persons already knowledgeable about music and are almost impermeable to influence from written articles.

Up to 1983 the position on TV was much the same as that of radio. Apart from the broadcasting of traditional sound tracks from the novelas--which would in many cases represent the creation and maintenance of a musical success for six months or more, diffused by all possible media throughout the country--the broadcasting of music on its own was very restricted and a matter of dispute between producers and artists (background music for programs excepted). Just to give a quantitative idea of the position, the most important Brazilian TV network allocated, on average, only 8 hours to music out of 140 hours approximately per week of transmission time. The commercial breaks were included in these 8 hours, as well as the intervals between the performance of the music within the program. [16]

From the middle of 1983 onward a new trend made its appearance. Video clips became more frequent and important in programing. They were used initially as a sort of background or neutral bridge between programs. They then grew in design and production sophistication. The visual and sensual music filled up longer spaces and, in some cases, constituted the main material for special programs. The main production center of these clips belonged to the richest TV network in Brazil. The trend did not last more than three years. Nowadays the few video clips shown on TV are foreign ones. The wave appears to have gone. Records are launched mostly after, or immediately before, live presentations in public theatres; they are well supported by traditional media advertising, radio and TV news, newspaper and magazine advertisements. Direct mail to sell records is small, but it is used to advertise some of the theatrical presentations.

If music, then, seems not to be a high priority for the TV broadcast programmers, the specialized press and magazines do take good care of the audience's information about it. The average consumer buys such publications if stimulated by an event, by identification with the artist or type of music, or by the success of a determined promoter of special national or international events. By 1989 big theatres staged sophisticated productions anchored by new singers or groups.

MEDIATED MUSIC AND THE YOUTH MARKET: CULTURAL TRENDS

Brazil is a young country. More than half of the population is under the age of 19. Without defining what constitutes youth, there is a general appeal from the cultural industry to this pervasive mythical category or word, which may express a kind of weltanschauung, a certain pattern of behavior which stresses love of life, of sunshine, of togetherness, of body expression, of freedom, of generosity, as revealed by research done by the author in

1982, when starting this study.*17* Whatever it may mean, the concept of youth implies a certain flexibility of behavior, a craving for change, that could make it an easy target for the process of homogenization, operated through the media of the cultural industry--mainly radio and TV--and heavily supported by a series of other complementary initiatives.

From specialized publications to show business organizations there is, on one side, a search for the specific motivation/identification processes between youth and its idols; on the other side, there is the young people's search for their own identity, which induces the system to produce events for an ever-growing number of people. In such events, everyone loses or finds himself or herself in the midst of a crowd of fans explicitly assembled for the totemization of the idol, who is felt closest when he or she is most distant. In Brazil, there is no doubt that the idol is really built via Embratel,*18* even though the process seems to be less preponderant when dealing with regional idols, such as the folk and Northeastern singers, who have a captive and faithful audience.

In a country where the per capita income of the great majority results in a low-level pattern of life, television represents the only cosmopolitan type of leisure--the window on the world. That is exactly the point where the mass culture industry engenders its communication processes: through daily idealization and repetition of the same images, television, little by little, invades the minds to insert there the hit of the moment. To illustrate this unique characteristic--and also to face up to it--a significant example can be examined. The most important network in the country has set on a pedestal what has been called "the pattern of quality," through a repetitive appreciation of its own performance. Through this efficient mechanism an unknown singer/composer, who was just a rocky-vedette for over ten years, was transformed in 1982 into a popular star when hired by the recording company which belongs to the TV network holding. The advertising machinery of the cultural industry worked this transformation which produced a jump in sales of one LP from 40,000-50,000 to more than 500,000 records. Some indicators however, show that the mechanisms of star fabrication are still not fool-proof. If it proved its efficiency in the example above, the same did not happen in other cases. The same network tried to make a star out of a soap-opera actor whose screen image was romantic, good tempered, an ideal friend and son. This character had a working musical line very close to that of Latin America's most successful singer of the last 20 years.*19* His image was carried daily through the soap opera's episodes, he became a pop star, but not such a successful one to justify the advertising investments. The comparison would deserve a deeper and more detailed study. Here characteristics of artistic or aesthetic orders were not considered.

In both cases, the focus was on the systematic attempts to promote images through the mass media, which normally do not take such qualitative characteristics into account. Reflections on these facts raise questions about the potential of the cultural industry which exists in the country, and its impact on the various youth strata of the population:

- Does the process or mechanisms of youth star-building change in different times, so that diversified procedures should be used?

- Are the different results due, as sustained by the record producers, to a greater or lesser compatibility/identification process of this or that music promoted with the specific cultural moment, which impacts the target audience?
- What, in reality, affects the young strata of population?
- Would the advertising machinery of the recording industry be limited in its operational capacity by variables prior to its work, such as the artistic quality of the material, or variables which appear late in the process, such as audience permeability?

Many other questions may be formulated after case-studies examination. The interviews conducted during this research with producers, critics and other professionals linked with the recording industry and with audience participants, led to the hypothesis that, in spite of its degree of sophistication, technological and psychological approach, this industry still has not accumulated enough knowledge to predict the magic factor that leads to success.

It is valid to associate the real aspirations and needs of young people and the degree of their identification with the products of the music industry (styles, formats, waves and stars), as seems to have occurred during the past 25 years: the birth and expansion of rock, the world phenomena of the Beatles and Rolling Stones, disco music, the punk movement, the humoristic music of São Paulo and other events like Roberto Carlos' 25 years of success, the revitalization of folk/hillbilly songs for audiences that were not traditionally identified with it. It is also valid to remember that, even though such movements have been commercialized by the recording industry, they were not prefabricated events. Many times, the recording industry and the cultural industry, as a whole, only processed them long after their consolidation with the youngsters and, by extension, with the whole society.

CONCLUSION

Critical theory asserts that one of the first consequences of the cultural industry is the development of a sort of homogeneous society, characterized by what has been called a mass culture, where all the different cultural contributions and components of the social corpus are amalgamated, becoming almost unidentifiable. If so, one can say that in Brazil, the "culture" engendered by the cultural industry has not yet reached the "mass culture" point. It is not really homogeneous.

The previously mentioned differences in income distribution gave birth to a stratified society in terms of consumption. While small groups may absorb all kinds of products advertised through the mass media, a greater number of people maintain their consumption at the lowest level, in a daily fight for survival. Added to this, the effects of the growing difficulties of the economic situation in the last years have restricted the buying capacity of the middle-class population even more. This group traditionally holds a high consumption level of cultural industry products. As a result, the dramatic economic differences have been exaggerated, resulting in inevitable losses for the cultural industry and, mainly, for the balance of the society's structure and the global development of the country.

The musical culture generated in Brazil by these industrial processes is permeated, to a great extent, by elements originating from foreign cultures. This is understandable, since the culture of Brazil has always been wide open to foreign influences and models. Brazil is a country with a comprehensive immigration policy that mixes Europeans, Asians, Africans, people of all latitudes, ethnic origins, religions and languages, with the descendants of old colonial times, which constitutes the basic melting pot for all incoming elements.

In the cultural turmoil of a developing country, native and autonomous manifestations are also strong and important. Such were the Week of 22, the Centers of Popular Culture (growing rapidly from the 1960s onward), the new cinema, the bossa nova, the Theatrical Collective Creation, the Participative Research and others.

A similar process takes place in the recording industry. The diversification of styles ranges from country folk songs (a fast-growing market) to the contemporary instrumental music, all being the products marketed according to their audiences' degree of acquisitive power and sophistication. For the researcher who participates in Brazilian life and culture, there is quite clearly a kind of permanent conflict in the field of the music industry.[20] While the recording industry sells its products--authentic or forged--the specific dynamics of the sociocultural processes in the country create and consume a considerable variety of artistic manifestations.

The forces which operate today in the world reach the whole of Latin America as well as Brazil. Communication of ideas and ideals is part of the feeling that gets stronger day by day about Latin American cultural integration. In such context, music and youth are one entity, which will move in this direction.[21] Brazilian youth is engulfed by an environment of deep and swift transformation of the economic, sociopolitical, cultural and individual orders. Such processes of turmoil have two opposite effects: on one side they give young people a certain fragility in their interaction with the organized powers; on the other side, they confer onto young people a power to justify, confront and rely on their own values, those that can be felt every day, on the streets, in the alternative spaces created by the justification processes, on the university campuses and even inside the cultural industry machinery.

NOTES

1. Nelly de Camargo (1975). *Communication Policies in Brazil* (Paris: UNESCO Press) (see chapter on Alternative Press).

2. In 1980, the country's statistics registered 3,257 cinemas.

3. Federal, state or municipal.

4. Nelly de Camargo (1981). "Communication Policies and the Paradoxes of Development" Rio de Janeiro: Forense Ed..

5. Among the best known, Francisco Alves, Orlando Silva, Carlos Galhardo, sisters Aurora and Carmen Miranda.

6. For Emilinha Borba, Marlene, Gaubi Peixoto, Ivan Curi, Angela Maria.

7. Roberto Carlos, Erasmo Carlos, Vanderleia, Elis Regina and others.

8. Chico Buarque, Edu Lobo, Caetano Veloso, Gilberto Gil, Geraldo Vandre and others.

9. Fino da Bossa, Esta Noite Se Improvisa, Jovem Guarda, and others.

10. MPB = Brazilian Popular Music.

11. For example, Cesar Camargo Mariano.

12. *Gafieiras* started as low-class types of dancing places but now have been upgraded to middle-class ones. They are popular with the advanced, nonprejudiced elite.

13. Composers who normally prefer to sing their own songs.

14. Elis Regina (deceased), Chico Buarque, Caetano Veloso, Maria Bethania, Simone and others.

15. In the 1980s Roberto Carlos sold up to 2 million records annually, Maria Bethania, 700,000, Chico Buarque, 650,000 and a great number of samba singers reached selling standards above 100,000.

16. Data collected in 1983 in Sao Paulo from interviews with broadcasters.

17. Nelly de Camargo, *What is Youth? The Cultural Meaning of Age* (Sao Paulo: 1982).

18. The Brazilian communication network through satellite.

19. Roberto Carlos.

20. As in almost all fields, this is an age of revolution or readjustment in Brazilian society.

21. It has been said that Brazilians are optimists. Being one of them, the author cannot and wishes not to escape from behaving accordingly.

BIBLIOGRAPHY

Caladas, Waldenyr. (1979). *Accorde na Aurora: Musica Sertaneja e Industria Cultural.* Sao Paulo: Comapnhia National.
Camargo, Nelly de. (1981). "Communications Policies and the The Paradoxes of Development." In Amaral et al. *Comunicacao de Massa: O Impasse Brasileiro.* Rio de Janeiro: Forense Ed.
—— (1982) *What is Youth: The Cultural Meaning of Age.* Sao Paulo.
Campos, Augusto de. (1978). *Balanco da Bossa e Outras Bossas.* Sao Paulo: Perspectiva.
Chacon, Paulo. (1981). *O Que e Rock.* Sao Paulo: Brasiliense.
Cohn, Gabriel. (1978). *Comunicacao e Industria cultural.* Sao Paulo: Nacional.
Favaretto, Celso F. (1979). *Tropicalia-Alegoria.* Sao Paulo: Kairos.
Hollanda, Heloisa Buarque de & Goncalves, Marcos A. (1982). *Cultura e Participacao nos Anos 60.* Sao Paulo: Brasiliense.
Miceli, Sergio. (1972). *A Noite da Madrinha.* Sao Paulo: Perspectiva.
Moraes, J. De. (1982). *O Que e Musica.* Sao Paulo: Brasiliense.
Moreira, Roberto S. C. (1979). *Teoria da Comunicacao-Ideologia e Utopia.* Petropolis: Vozes.
Sodre, Mund. (1980). *A Comunicacao do Grotesco-Introducao a Cultura de Massa Brasileira.* Petropolis: Vozes.
—— (1981). *O Monopolio da Fala-Funcao e Linguagem da Televisao no Brasil.* Petropolis: Vozes.

CHAPTER 3

THE ENGLISH EXPERIENCE

Alison J. Ewbank

INTRODUCTION

This chapter is based on the premise that there is a correspondence between musical practices and social relations. This implies that the needs of a society, its institutions, its structures and its people can be reflected in its music. The following cursory glance at this context--the social, economic, political and historical background of English music--is supplied to provide a backcloth against which yet other influences on music making can be considered.

England alone is considered in this instance, although it is only one component of the United Kingdom. The social, religious, economic, political, cultural and musical development of Britain's four constituent countries (England, Scotland, Wales and Northern Ireland) has been somewhat different. Today each area has its own particular characteristics, mores, social mix and values. Although there are many common institutions and there has been much mixing of the populations during the last century, differences remain which are strong enough to lead to periodic debate about a breakup of the Union or other forms of political realignment. In a short chapter such as this, justice cannot be done to the histories, cultures and economic situations of Scotland, Wales and Northern Ireland, so the dominant partner--England--has taken center stage in the early part of the chapter. In the later part, the information available about the phonographic industry and broadcasting systems often refers to the United Kingdom as a whole and so is presented as such.

The geographical position of the British Isles on the western edge of the European continent makes them vulnerable to the westerly population movement of European peoples. Wave after wave of invaders attacked the shores until the latter half of the eleventh century, when adequate defenses could be maintained. Thereafter any disorders and conflagrations were brought about by internal British tensions rather than by external foreign continental forces. This long-term isolation enabled English institutions and culture to evolve gradually and steadily out of domestic necessity rather than from outside imposition.

The immunity from the destruction of the infrastructure did not mean isolation from foreign influence. The English continued to fight wars, but these were on foreign soil. They were fought for religious or imperialist motives, or to maintain the balance of power in Europe. The armies brought home ideas as well as booty. Over the years free trade as opposed to protectionism was the usual government policy. Foreign travel was the norm for the ruling classes. There were few barriers to immigration until very recently. Influence was imported and invited in by choice, but it was exported wholesale only to those parts of the world under its imperial domination.

The economy of the country has always been a demand-led free enterprise one as opposed to a centrally organized command one. Manufacturers endeavor to supply goods that tempt the customers to buy. Entrepreneurs continually search for unsatisfied gaps in the market which it would be profitable for them to fill. Production orders do not emanate from central government economic plans. Consumers expect to be able to choose between competing goods to satisfy any of their needs.

The vast majority of people are well fed and well housed, owning consumer goods and still having some personal savings. The yield from taxation is such that a safety net can be provided to insure that the population is provided with medical care, education, other government services and a minimal income with which to feed, clothe and house themselves. However, deprivation does exist and some people do fall through the net. Looked at from a historical perspective, the economy is at a mature stage of development. Industry and its infrastructure have reached that level which enables advantage to be taken of any relevant new technology which is available.

The numbers of people for skilled and nonmanual jobs are rising, altering the social balance and aspirations of the population. Socially, England has a predominantly urbanized population with a highly developed plural social structure. The class structure can be divided simply into two categories, the working class and the middle class. These two categories have purportedly identifiably differing sets of values. Working-class culture is characterized by the emphasis put on solidarity and current, as opposed to deferred, well-being. Middle-class culture emphasizes individual success and long-term financial security and comfort.

The English consider themselves a tolerant nation but in practice expect immigrants to fit in with the English way of life. This has been difficult especially for recent immigrants who, because of their backgrounds or religions, desire to hold on the their own cultural heritage. Tensions have risen to the boiling point at times.

A whole new race relations industry has come into being in an effort to solve such problems. However, these immigrant groups make up just 5% of the total population. Feelings of alienation from society in the relatively recent past were as likely to have been along age lines as racial, religious, tribal or class ones.

Education for children is obligatory up to the age of 16. There are strict laws to control the use of child labor which limit hours of work for particular age groups. This consequently limits children to the earning of pocket money and does not allow them to be used as financial mainstays by their families. This allows young people to enjoy a lengthy childhood. Marriage takes place, on average, in the middle twenties. The young therefore have an extended period in which to reach maturity without family responsibilities. In their late teens and early twenties they are likely to have the resources to pursue whatever musical interests they may have.

It is voices of the young and especially those from urban working-class backgrounds that have produced the innovations in postwar popular music. The subcultures which developed around particular types of pop and rock have been extensively studied and documented in a qualitative way by Philip Cohen (1972), Stuart Hall (1976), Paul Willis (1977), Dick Hebdige (1979), Stanley Cohen (1980), Dave Rogers (1982) and Ellis Cashmore (1984). From the 1950s Teddy Boys and 1960s Mods through Skinheads, Punks, Rastas, Heavy Metal Kids to Two Toners, New Romantics and Ragamuffin Rap of the 1980s and 1990s, all emerged from the ranks of the young urban working class and gave expression and coherence to the anxieties and concerns bedeviling youth.

However, put in perspective, these subcultures represent the visible, extreme, antisocial, headline-hitting adherents of the pop phenomenon. The majority of young people take their music less theatrically. It has always been difficult to locate more than a handful of sub-culture exponents in randomly selected quantitative studies.

POLITICAL CONTEXT

The British Isles are ruled by a parliamentary democracy under a constitutional monarchy. The monarchy has next to no political powers and does not interfere with party politics. The 700 year old Parliament in London has two chambers, an Upper House, the House of Lords, and a Lower House, the House of Commons. Members of the House of Lords are not elected, but gain their places by nomination, office or inheritance. The Upper House nowadays performs a revisionary task on new legislation and has very limited powers of delaying and amending legislation.

The political power in the country resides in the Lower House elected by universal suffrage at approximately four-year intervals. There are two major political parties with a third party emerging strongly in the last two decades. Extreme legislation on the part of one party can be nullified at a change of government. It is rare that one party holds power for more than two terms of office. The exception to this rule has been the current Conservative government lately led by Margaret Thatcher and now by John Major, which has stayed in power for an unprecedented length of time.

The Lower House of Commons holds the power of the purse over the country as a whole, although local councils--county, district and parish--do raise a small the proportion of their funds themselves. All legislation emanates from the central government, but day-to-day administration and funding of some arts facilities and other services rest with the local councils. These councils are elected by the local communities and are often not of the same political persuasion as the central government. The stability of the democracy is aided by the fact that the armed forces, police, judiciary, civil service (both central and local), and other government institutions are politically neutral, thus providing continuation at changes of government.

Government policy toward popular music could best be described as laissez-faire. The music industry is regarded as just another commercially based industry. At times it is applauded for its export earnings, in the early 1980s for its moral lead in charity work; at other times it is deplored for its lack of taste, potential for debasing its audience and as a possible threat to established order. In cultural terms popular music is not regarded by the authorities as an ennobling spiritual force which needs to be supported and fostered through central public funds. As a result there exist no central directives or sponsorships aimed at safeguarding the English popular music heritage.

Regionally, local government is inadvertently a source of funds for popular music performers. Local councils joined together in the 1980s with the Department of Employment in looking at ways to ease the problems of youth unemployment. As popular music was an obvious activity enjoyed by the young and an activity which offered the possibility of employment, some resources were channelled into music making. The motivation for this action however, arose more from concern for the young people themselves than from concern about their cultural heritage.

Money has been used to set up recording studios and rehearsal space. Local authorities also own gig and concert venues. These can be used on occasion by amateur players. These facilities are unevenly distributed throughout the country, being highly dependent on particular councils' concerns.

Politically, there is a freedom from constraints and censorship and a lack of restrictions on innovation. Conversely there is no political policy or program of encouragement for indigenous music. However, the government does undertake the role of providing a fair trading environment which has been very helpful to the industry in dealing with the piracy problem. There is a legal framework covering copyright, broadcasting and trading practices in general. Its helpfulness was shown when the 1956 Copyright Act was tested through the British courts in 1979 and ended up at the European Court of Appeal in 1982. A judgment was made that it was illegal to import into Britain from outside the European Community, recordings that already had been released there by another company, without that company's permission.

This judgment resulted in stopping the importing of cheap counterfeit recordings. It is policed by the British Phonographic Industry's Anti-Piracy Unit which seizes pirate and counterfeit audio cassettes from markets and street traders. With the cooperation of the police, traders are now charged under the Theft Act charge of: "Going equipped to cheat." Raids on pirate manufacturers are now organized and their equipment seized using the civil rights of owners of copyrights as the legal justification for these actions.

A second Copyright Act came into force at the end of 1988, which gave record producers the right to control the exploitation of their output in "main street" retail outlets. They are able to stop retailers from renting out compact discs to their customers. This has put a stop to their use as inexpensive master discs for copying. No levy was imposed on the sale of blank tape, much to the chagrin of the industry. But the government did ban the importation of apparatus to circumvent anticopying devices which might be incorporated in disc and tape players.

MUSICAL DEVELOPMENT

There are a number of threads which run through the history of music making in England. The most apparent of these is the power of patronage. Chronicled music has appeared to follow money: the English have had a very pragmatic approach to it throughout the ages. This approach led to a pace and type of development rather different from that found on continental Europe. Influences have ebbed and flowed according to patronage circumstances. This is not to say that English music has been immune from outside influences.

On the contrary it has been extraordinarily open to foreign participation. This openness can be said to have been such that native musicians and composers have been underrated at times because of an overwhelming foreign presence. However, foreign musical immigrants, once settled in England, have found themselves conforming to native musical mores. This has led to there being a largely one-way flow of influence *from* the Continent, not to the Continent, since the fifteenth century.

A respect for music and its practitioners was built into the English consciousness from pre-Roman times. The bardic tradition as established by the Celts and Britons before the Roman conquest was shared by the Norse, Danes, Angles and Saxons who kept invading Britain after the fall of the Roman Empire. The bards were held in high esteem and with their narrative singing filled an important place in the social economy of the times. When in 596 the Benedictine Abbott Augustine brought the Roman use and traditions to an England which the Celtic church had evangelized, the secular bardic art was subjugated to the regulated religious art.

There was official recognition of one kind of music being superior to another, because of its technical efficiency and its efficacy in imparting doctrine and in improving morals. These morality divisions have held throughout the centuries and still apply with differential encouragement being given to particular musical genres. The clergy held the monopoly of teaching and learning and so official music, both ecclesiastical and secular, bore the hallmark of the cloister--that is, of pan-European Christian music. However the common people continued to produce their own native music. This developed outside clerical sanction but later came to influence and shape the official order of composition. In the later developmental emphasis from plainsong to polyphony, many minstrel tunes were adopted and adapted for church use.

The twelfth century marked a considerable development of musical interest and an expansion of techniques. On the secular side minstrels were employed in the royal and aristocratic households and by the cities as civic waits (public musicians).

These latter minstrels also played in manor houses, in taverns and at fairs, as did the wandering minstrels who also played for the serfs and peasants in the towns and villages. New instruments were introduced from the East: trumpet, mandola, tambourine, tabor and kettledrum were added to the bowed chrotta, harp, psaltery, cymbals, pipes, organ and percussion instruments in use at the time. In noble households the office of minstrel was upgraded and the art of the troubadour and trouvere was developed to the extent of providing a strong foundation for a cultured secular tradition of song. Toward the end of the thirteenth century, in the reign of Edward I the Confessor, the sacred and secular elements in national life achieved a unique fusion in that there was no conscious division between the two. This was also applied to music. Instruments were used with sacred texts and juxtaposed with secular ones. It is no accident that the symbol of music of that age is the song, "Sumer is icumen in". Two forms of sacred music--rota and rondellus--were combined with secular words to produce a song that can be called neither sacred nor profane. It is a song that expresses a joyous acceptance of life, which by its sheer musical quality can compel the attention of a contemporary audience.

During the fourteenth century, secular and sacred music drifted apart. Within the religious communities stylish perfection was encouraged, indigenous tastes were disregarded and a highly professional pan-European sacred music was produced. The secular scene thrived on its own. The writings of Chaucer illustrate the pervasion of popular music and its preference by the layman over the sacred music of the time. Secular music was open to outside influences. An example of this was shown by John of Gaunt, a member of the royal family, who established his own court of Minstrels in 1381 and five years later brought back a troupe of Moorish dancers from Spain. The practices of these dancers were combined with those of the English fool's dance and provided the basis for the Morris dance which is still performed as a ceremonial May Day dance in some parts of England today.

During the fifteenth century, the proposition that music was a good in itself prevailed in the French, northern Italian and Burgundian courts. Not so in England, music received only such support as was regarded expedient. Nevertheless the court and nobility kept up establishments for religious purposes. During the second half of the century the Kings Henry IV, V, VI were especially aware of the public value of music, they were convinced of its ability to enhance devotional experience and were themselves expert in its practice. The international sacred music produced in the religious communities reached new heights of perfection during the early part of the century. It was the only time in history when English musicians were conceded primacy in Europe, and the works of English composers were sought after by continental connoisseurs. The leader of the English school was John Dunstable. He brought melodic invention, contrapuntal construction, rhythmic diversity, and, above all, harmonic syntax into a state of interdependence, and in doing so gave music a new fluency and richness.

Within the towns and cities the mystery play reached the height of its popularity. In these street plays for holy days, liturgical music took on a new life in a theatrical setting being used for its histrionic and emotional relevance. Music was also encouraged by the municipalities. They continued to use their waits to enhance appropriate municipal functions by producing emotional stimuli and aiding communication. With the enhanced status of the towns and cities, many parish churches came to play a larger role in the field of church music. Organs were mended, stipends raised, professional and freelance singers engaged and altogether the standards were raised in

some cases to those of the great cathedrals. Under the Tudor monarchy in
the late fifteenth and early sixteenth centuries there were ambitions to raise
standards in the court to Renaissance levels. Sacred music was encouraged
and noble patrons employed their own choirs and composers. The practice
of playing music was regarded as a proper and polite recreation. Keyboard
music, other than that written for the organ, made its appearance on the
domestic scene. The music of the Middle Ages had been generally associated
with, or subordinate to, visual display. It was public rather than private
music. Under the Tudors chamber music developed as new styles of houses
and palaces were built. Audiences could at last sit down and listen in a
modicum of comfort as upholstered furniture replaced wooden benches and
long galleries replaced communal halls.

The reformation of the church and abolition of the monasteries in 1536
by Henry VIII put an end to the international genre of ecclesiastical music.
The choral foundations of the English church were on the whole unimpaired
but the church was anglicized. Ritual was simplified and the vernacular became the official language. Religion became subservient to civil authority.
These changes brought about a new view of the function of music in worship. During the reign of Elizabeth I popular music was encouraged. Music,
drama and their pageant progeny spread across town and country, embrac-
ing folk custom and court entertainment alike. There was a universal zest for
Morris dances and jigs, games, mummery and minstrelsy in their various
forms. The strength of Elizabethan music was in the sound and general ex-
cellence of technical accomplishment and the perceptive appreciation of a
largely participant public. The peak of achievement was the madrigal where
the Italian and Flemish antecedents were replaced by English idiom.

Under the Tudors and later the Stuarts and the Hanoverians, the patronage base widened and strengthened to include the squirearchy and the
middle classes. Such were the opportunities that many foreign musicians and
composers were tempted to settle in England. However, those who took up
permanent residence found that they had to adapt their music to suit English mores. They composed and played a wide spectrum of music for their
patrons, which ranged from popular songs and dances through virginals and
lute music to sacred pieces.

During the seventeenth century the future of English music appeared to
have been settled. It was to remain independent, idiosyncratic and conservative. Changes took place when they were in conformity with new phases of
social behavior. There were no stylistic changes coming from theory, only
those that evolved from music publishing and the promotion of public concerts. The concerts lured increasing numbers of visiting virtuosi singers and
composers from all parts of Europe. This enabled the audiences to keep in
touch with musical developments in general and to hear the best performers
from abroad. Concerts were given in the halls of city companies, in dancing
schools and in taverns. At the end of the century, premises started being
adapted for the specific purpose of concert-giving.

In the early part of the eighteenth century a conflict between native and
Italianate styles became acute, leading to a split in taste across social class
lines. The more sophisticated audience of the aristocracy and aspirant bourgeoisie supported the opera, while the rest of the community preferred more
homely fare. In G. F. Handel's lifetime English music was democratized so

that appreciation and practice were probably more widespread than in any other country in Europe. The English form of oratorio that Handel developed was an encouragement to many of the previously musically disenfranchised, to exercise their talents and imaginations. The English choral tradition in its modern form began in the second half of the century. As for ecclesiastical music, a happy accommodation was reached between popular music and hymnody so that it became difficult to distinguish one from the other. In the church, music became separated from the ceremonial and the old metrical psalm was gradually replaced by the hymn.

Toward the end of the eighteenth century instrumental music began to be a thing apart--art music--a polite recreation in no way connected with people's lives. Concert life in the provinces was a second-hand version of that of London. Public subscription concerts with high-brow content like those which had been sponsored by the aristocracy in earlier times became fashionable.

At the same time a different movement was started by the working classes. The churches and chapels of the north had their choirs and bands. From these, numerous choral clubs were started and became the source, not only of musical activity, but of accurate training particularly in sight-reading. Members included handloom weavers, spinners, colliers, public-house keepers, clerks, schoolmasters, parish officials and the occasional village doctor and their wives. These people combined to furnish their communities with the best music that lay within their capacity. This movement carried on the national tradition of participation in music where amateurs took part alongside professionals in performances.

The nineteenth century brought an upheaval in the financing of music. It was the age of self-help and laissez-faire. Employment of musicians by the court, nobility and municipalities gave way to payment by performance. The principle of supporting local and metropolitan music on a professional full-time basis was broken. On the credit side this led to the promotion of popular orchestral concerts at the cheapest price for the greatest number and opened up classical music to a new audience.

The money spent on music was enormous during this period. Organs were built and visiting singers and performers were paid fortunes. But native composers were underrated and starved. They tried to satisfy the potent emotional and intellectual requirements of the respectable and for the first time lost touch with the fundamentals of the art. There was a wish to see the working class able to have and enjoy the same music the upper classes had and enjoyed themselves, so the privileged set about this improvement.

Folk music was seen as a convenient bridge to this, but unfortunately folk music was no longer a reality to most people. There had been a virtual cessation of rural song creation by 1830. In addition to this, by the end of the century the population was to become thoroughly urbanized with only 8% remaining in rural areas. The nation was at the zenith of its imperial career and the exploitation of folk music for emancipator purposes was hardly necessary. The myth that a truly national music must be based on national idiom--that is, the idiom of folk song--did not work in this case and the attempt to create a new music for the underprivileged was unsuccessful.

The working classes managed to provide for themselves. There was an expansion and formalization of leisure time and an improvement in financial status during this period. One result was that in industrial England political balladry and occupational song took on a new lease of life. The work and chapel wind band was replaced by brass bands and a new tradition of folk music was born. The choral clubs developed into choral societies and competitive musical festivals were established in many towns and cities.

Community-based choirs and bands were very much a product of small towns and industrial villages. Music halls came to be centered in cities and large towns and above all in London. There was not merely growth in music making but also diversification.

In the northern industrial city of Bradford in 1840 there were performances of sacred music, chapel choirs, a choral society, a number of music clubs, occasional concerts and singing salons in public houses. By 1900 there were 30 choral societies, 20 brass bands, 1 amateur orchestra, 8 concertina bands, 1 team of handbell ringers, 2 music halls, a number of venues for Sunday evening "Popular Concerts", an annual visit by an opera company and musical comedies. By the end of the nineteenth century something very close to a mass music culture had emerged--a sharing of common taste across a broad social range.

During this century the thesis that music ought to be commercially viable has been replaced by one that "art music" that is, classical instrumental music, opera and ballet, needs subsidy. Popular music, however still has to pay for itself. The invention of the gramophone (phonograph) and the establishment of radio programs and later television have liberated people from reliance on their own resources for entertainment. The electronic media and the recording industry have raised the quality and range of music available to the whole population. Among the range of music broadcast and recorded has been jazz and other types of music from America.

The inflow of early rock 'n' roll music coincided with a surge in the leisure consumption of young people in the 1950s. Rock 'n' roll arrived in England at a time of change in social structures and attitudes which came as a result of World War II. The class system became more fluid and the majority of people's aspirations rose.

As a part of this, young people gained a new prosperity and a wider choice of lifestyle. They became the new patrons of music and a totally new market opened for the industry. Mass entertainment and a new complex of leisure and consumer sectors appeared, specifically catering for the needs and interests of the newly affluent teenagers. These centered on the new pop industry which mushroomed with the rock 'n' roll explosion. Popular music occupied then, and occupies now, a central position in most young people's leisure. And so, from the middle of the twentieth century onward, the popular music industry has successfully developed in size, scale and penetration.

The music has immediate appeal for its young audience, especially in light of adult disapproval. It serves several purposes: peer group identity, the expression of alienation, reaction against prevalent societal conditions, as a survival aid, for escapism, for passing the time, as a background, and also for fun, dancing and courtship. After the initial wave in the 1950s of purely American rock 'n roll, English versions started being produced. EMI, the

British transnational recording company, encouraged and groomed young English performers to produce their own versions of the American music. By the 1960s musicians such as the Beatles and the Rolling Stones were contributing to the musical genre on equal terms with the Americans.

The Anglicization of pop became commercially lucrative and followed the normal English tradition of importing music and changing it to suit domestic taste and circumstances. In this way sounds became integrated, part of mainstream culture, a familiar tool to be used at will with confidence and fluency, which was easily interpreted and appreciated by its audience.

Since the 1960s the bulk of young audiences have not been particularly interested in looking abroad to monitor new sounds. They have been well-served by their own indigenous music scene. This is not to say that they have not supported foreign artists and bought their records, but they have no overriding interest in who is popular or not in other countries. Pop and rock introduced alien elements into the English music scene, notably the emphasis on a beat which stimulates the body as opposed to the brain. This was celebrated by the young and condemned by older generations and the authorities. Another new element was the seemingly fickleness of the audience, which produced meteoric rises to stardom and short-lived reigns. Fashion changes were reported to appear and disappear in a matter of months. Different sounds and styles were shown following each other rapidly in popularity.

One reason for this could have been the result of marketing techniques promoting intentional obsolescence to enhance the profits of the recording industry. Another reason was the disillusionment of the audience with the commercial veneer, which often seemed to clothe each group as it established itself in the national market. An answer might also be found among the audience itself, in its peer group relationships, and in ideas of appropriateness of taste for its self-images. For whatever reasons, changes of fashion appeared to be the norm throughout the early decades of pop music.

Considered with hindsight, it now appears that this was an immediate and simplistic view of the process. Popularity in England is judged by record buying and it disappears when sales of an artist's or group's latest recordings start to drop in volume. No account is taken of the buyer's use of the record. Wober (1984) found that people felt that they remained interested in listening to a new piece of music they had acquired for a matter of months, before they tired of it, rather than for a period of weeks, let alone of days. The younger the respondent the shorter the declared tendency to maintain a long term interest (see Table 3.1).

TABLE 3.1: Length of Time a Record Holds Audience Interest

	Age			
Time	15-24	25-34	35-54	55+
	%	%	%	%
PIECE OF MUSIC				
Week	3	4	4	14
Fortnight	3	11	15	12
Month	31	30	19	12
Six Months	10	5	4	5
Indefinitely	51	51	58	59
GROUP OR COMPOSER				
Week	0	2	7	21
Fortnight	4	4	4	8
Month	19	10	13	9
Six Months	22	11	6	8
Indefinitely	56	73	71	55

Source: Wober (1984).

Tastes in artists and composers appear to be well established for over 70% of the population by the time they reach their mid-twenties. School children are another matter. Wober (1990a) showed that their tastes changed throughout childhood with 7-9 year-olds having a wide range of tastes which became more focused on pop and rock as they got older.

The market for innovation, as expected, would be found among the young. However, another market has been revealed only recently. The introduction of new record-playing hardware has forced fans to replace their favorite recordings and the long-term popularity of certain sounds has become apparent. It seems quite probable now that apart from picking up new fans from time to time there has been a hard-core audience for every variation of sound produced over the years.

Yet another twist arising from the particular circumstances of pop and rock dissemination has been that very few pop stars have been given the chance to hone and experiment with the styles that first brought them to their audience's notice, as in the case of artists in other spheres of the creative arts. Today they are expected to perform their early songs in the same way the did when they were first popular. Their music, or a part of it, is not allowed to mature, although their audiences have.

The culture shock and blatant generation gap of the 1950s, 1960s and 1970s has gradually disappeared as the fans of the Beatles and Rolling Stones have become grandparents. Pop is now mainstream easy listening. The fashions of the truly young are masked by the CD buying habits of the older generation. If new trends are more difficult to detect, the premature demise of older ones has proved not to be the case. It would appear that fans carry their youthful musical preferences through their lives and are prepared to support them throughout adulthood, introducing an unforeseen continuity into the pop/rock business.

BROADCASTING

The airwaves of Britain are dominated by a public broadcasting organization, the British Broadcasting Corporation (BBC), and a federation of commercial broadcasting companies regulated by three authorities. The BBC is financed by license fees, paid by television set owners, at rates set by Parliament. The commercial companies are owned by private or institutional shareholders and raise their finance through advertising. Both sets of broadcasters operate under charters passed by Parliament which lay down rules of program balance, political even-handiness and morally responsible behavior.

None of the broadcasting in Britain is controlled by the political parties. Half the broadcasting services are independent of commercial ties. The commercial television companies had in their formative years no common financial base and so operated independently of each other. The radio stations, on the other hand, have less stringent ownership rules, and, as in the case of the British press, one can find financing companies with interests in more than one station. However, the independent community stations, being nonprofit maximizing projects, are unlikely to attract owners with a great deal of financial muscle. The diversity of financing of the electronic media discourages the monopolizing or manipulating of the airwaves by any single sectional interest group. The plurality of customer choice insures that in the long run viewers' and listeners' tastes are recognized and catered for.

The structure of both sides of broadcasting underwent review during the late 1980s, a process which will continue through the 1990s. Changes to the independent sector were laid down in the Broadcasting Act 1990. The BBC restructuring is expected to be dealt with by the middle 1990s.

Popular music is transmitted by all four television channels; by two of the five BBC national radio stations; by two of the three new commercial national radio stations; by all the BBC and independent radio stations; and also by most of the community radio stations.

Popular Music on Television

Popular music is treated as just another ingredient in the mixed viewing diet transmitted to the public. BBC1 has broadcast a weekly half hour show, "Top of the POPs," since the 1960s. This show has the highest viewing figures of any pop program. It is liked especially by youngsters up to the age of sixteen years. It is a chart-based show, nowadays concentrating on the British Top 40. Experiments introducing American and European charts were disliked by the audience and quickly dropped. Such charts, according to BBC Audience Research,

are almost universally unpopular. Firstly because they are felt to waste precious program time which could be used to play U.K. records, and, secondly because young people are not particularly interested in the chart scene in the States or Europe. They regard the U.K. as leading the pop music world at present and do not look to sources abroad for trends. (BBC, 1986)

Appearances by artists, in the flesh or on video, on this show underline the success of the particular record played and boost sales even further.

The second BBC TV channel, BBC2, also has provided a popular music program slot from time to time. This has been filled by a changing series of programs which have not been overtly chart-based. Initially they were given the brief to cover the whole of the popular music scene apart from the charts, and ghettoized into a late-night slot. Early programs concentrated on the heavy rock scene. Later they were transmitted in prime time, broadcast live and were adapted to a younger audience. The music of artists who had already made appearances in the charts was included together with adult-oriented rock. None of the programs appeared to have made the impact of "Top of the POPs."

The independent companies also provided music program slots from time to time. However the channel (ITV) has not produced a specialist popular music program broadcasts during prime time since its 1960s show "Ready Steady Go." Popular music in the 1990s is banished to the early hours of the morning when only insomniacs are awake. It was found that the companies prepared to pay high fees for advertising on ITV were not interested in the youth market. That is, they did not see a music program selling such products as soap powder. The only advertisers demanding slots within networked music programs came from the industry itself.

Channel 4, the second independent station, transmitted the "Tube" which was for some years the most innovative popular music program produced on television. However, it did not have as high viewing figures as "Top of the POPs." The "Tube" was felt to be disorganized and amateurish by some of its audience. However, it was conceded to be more daring and spontaneous than "Top of the POPs." Its quality was variable as one would expect of a live show which featured unknown groups among its performers. It was in touch with the world of the independent record companies and the fanzines. It featured both star names and up-and-coming bands from all parts of the United Kingdom. It blended live music with archival material, topical interviews, documentaries and out-of-the-ordinary videos.

In 1985 it was transmitted regularly to Canada, Australia, France, Italy, Holland and Sweden, and extracts were shown in New Zealand, Norway, Portugal, Switzerland, Japan and the United States. Since then pop music has become a subject of increasing interest to documentary makers. Live Aid charity concerts are often transmitted in full, live, on one or other TV channel.

Radio Broadcasting Channels

These have been divided by the BBC, since the late 1960s according to musical taste. This was mainly in response to the challenge mounted by pirate radio stations which operated between 1964 and 1967.

These stations eroded the BBC radio audience at an increasing rate until 1967. Then the government outlawed them and the BBC provided a pop/rock channel--Radio 1--to cater for the nation's teenagers. At the same time Radio 2 was established to provide middle-of-the-road music for a housewife audience. Radios 1 and 2 took over the disc jockey system of the pirates, but their contribution to the programming was upgraded in order to compensate for the lack of advertisements. The BBC network of local radio stations was expected to provide a local service for all tastes.

Although they transmitted some popular music, they tended to fill in gaps in their schedules, especially in the evenings, from Radio 2 and 4 (the spoken-word channel). Attempts were made to cover local music scenes, but as these programs were run by the middle-aged, access for young amateurs was not easy. Radio 1 was aimed to appeal to the largest possible audience; the channel was not conceived to make hits or sell records. In theory Radio 1 was a rockin' station, but in practice the emphasis was on easy-listening records--riskless, punchless, familiar.

However, the BBC claims that it has always been its policy to encourage the best new British talent. In 1985 it conducted over 500 different recording sessions of new music for subsequent transmission on Radio 1. The BBC said: "It is thanks to such efforts and the exposure given to new music on the airwaves that the British Music Industry is as healthy as it is today." (BBC, 1986).

In the evenings, the BBC does try to satisfy minority tastes, including both those of teenagers and the youth/student audience. A distinction between "culture" and "entertainment" seems to remain in BBC policy. The music section deals with classical "art" music and the light entertainment section with popular music. Cultural broadcasts are justified by their aesthetic value--Radio 3 broadcasts "good" music at twice the cost of popular music to audiences 7% the size of Radio 1 audiences. Aesthetic criteria are not considered in relation to Radio 1, and "popular" music is defined as "entertainment" and the criteria of success applied to it is audience size. The BBC's aim when programming Radio 1 is that everyone in the mass market hears a record they like when they switch the channel on.

As to popular music program content, the BBC playlists were produced at weekly intervals by a panel including four producers of daily shows. During the 1970s the playlist included a list of 40 singles together with a second page of new releases, oldies and album tracks. Ten numbers from page one and eight from page two were played every hour. The usual rule in making up the lists was that, of the Top 50 chart, every climber was included and every record that had fallen out of the Top 20 was excluded.

This process yielded about 30 to 35 titles, the balance was made up of new releases from chart "certainties"--new records from big stars, follow-ups to big hits. In the 1980s playlists were discontinued and choices left to the individual program producers and presenters. This aimed to produce more individual styles of programs, but the emphasis continued to be on chart-based choices.

The independent local radio (ILR) stations were obliged by their contracts to provide a general service for their listeners. The new 1990s stations are to be allowed to be more specialist in their output. Under the old system they transmitted a great deal of music. The stations used the old BBC pattern of daytime Top 40 playlist with evening and weekend specialist shows.

The playlists themselves were much the same as at the BBC. They were compiled by program directors, producers' panels or DJs themselves, taking some notice of local tastes and sales. The net result of this was a commercial network of localized versions of BBC mass entertainment, with the emphasis more on easy-listening music than on innovative rock.

In the early days of independent radio the record companies hoped they would play the pop music Radio 1 was not playing and help musicians to gain experience and exposure. To this end they backed the stations with advertising and agreed on generously low terms for "needletime". Unfortunately for the companies, because of the speech quotas, the ILR stations found that their audiences were not dominated by the young. Their audience profile was more akin to that of Radio 2--a mainly housewife audience with middle-of-the-road musical tastes. They programmed their music output accordingly.

The record companies were thrown back on reliance on BBC1 for the promotion of their products. Nevertheless, at the end of the 1980s the ILRs became more involved in young peoples' music. Many stations hosted music festivals and claimed that they consistently championed local musicians:

It is a relationship unique to ILR showing its willingness to get involved with music at grassroots and backing its judgment to the tune of millions of pounds over the years. . . . Each of the ILR stations has its own way of identifying local talent. Some simply audition tapes. Others organize local contests, such as Essex Radio's "Band Search '85'". . . . and Metro Radio's "Track to the Top". Strong ties with the local music scene are enjoyed by all stations and home grown talent has a natural way of coming to the fore. (IBA, 1986)

The BBC's interest in successful popular music came to the fore in the introduction in October 1984 of a "Network Chart Show" on Sunday afternoons. This was scheduled in direct competition with Radio 1's Sunday afternoon chart show. With the passing of the Broadcasting Act 1990 licenses for two national commercial channels for music were made available, together with encouragement to expand the numbers of local and community radio stations.

This continues the trend started in the late 1980s toward audience targeting, a process which encourages music specialization. The community and local radio stations are particularly useful for local musicians as they can sometimes provide the first stepping stone to the regional airwaves. The BBC survey (BBC, 1984) showed that British youngsters thought there was not enough of their sort of music broadcast. Mainstream pop and rock were not adequately covered, especially by television. New music and struggling bands did not have their needs of airtime recognized by the broadcasters, in the 1990s provision is yet to come.

The advent of licensed community radio stations has given broadcasting time for specialist sounds--that is, the stations are based on musical tastes or ethnic groupings. Jazz FM, established in Central London in March 1990, is one rare instance; WNK London is another relaying soul and reggae music. It is likely that the vast majority of new groups will still have to find success outside the world of broadcasting and, by that success, force open the doors to the airwaves for their records.

THE MUSIC INDUSTRY

A highly developed, sophisticated commercial industry has grown up over the past 40 years to serve the needs of popular music enthusiasts. There have been changes in the ownership structure of the industry, its technology, its markets, its promotion possibilities and as always in its audience tastes.

In 1989 retail sales[1] of recordings of British popular music reached $1.99 million (BPI, 1991), making the country the third largest market in the world, behind the United States and Japan, with a 10% share. This size was achieved because British individuals bought more records than other nationals. [2]

The British had a higher per capita spending on music products than citizens of any other country. The value of sales fell during the years 1979 to 1982, then gradually recovered to earlier levels by 1987 and 1989.

The technology of the market is going through major changes. In 1989 the total sales value was divided between singles down to 12%, long-playing vinyl records 17%, cassettes 37% and compact discs up to 34%. Over the past few years the market has been subject to a number of pressures and tensions. Some of these arose from innovations and market strategies pursued by the record companies, others from the changes in consumer demand structure.

Compact discs were introduced in 1983 and the discs themselves are still marketed as high-cost, high-margin products. The cost of the CD players themselves dropped in late 1990 to such heavily subsidized levels as $260 for converting a system to CD. This represented a rather late attempt to lock consumers into CD systems before the introduction of newer technology. Further pressure was applied with the announcement by some major record companies that they were reducing the availability of vinyl LPs and singles. After long delay Sony was able to announce the introduction of its digital audio system (DAT) into Britain in 1991. Philips announced that it would be introducing a rival digital compact cassette system (DCC) in 1992. The latter is still not for sale in 1996.

Consumer demand was altered somewhat by a reduction in the size and wealth of the teenage market, due to falling birth rates in the 1970s and difficult economic conditions in the early and very late 1980s. However, teenagers' growing enthusiasm for dancing balanced a loss of 7" singles with increased sales of the 12" versions. The automatic inclusion of cassette players in most new cars sold in the 1980s and the popularity of personal stereo cassette players helped to keep cassette sales buoyant. LP sales remained steady throughout the decade until 1989, when they fell precipitously, volume falling by 24.5% and value by 18%. At the same time, ownership of CD players rose from 9% of households to 14%. A market of affluent adult music enthusiasts who bought CD versions of the music of their youth emerged at the end of the decade.

In the future the fortunes of vinyl, CD, DAT and DCC will depend as always on market strategy. In 1983, 91% of homes in the country were equipped to play cassettes or vinyl, in 1989 14% owned a CD player. If digital tape equipment and the tapes themselves are marketed on a high-sales/low margins basis the scene could change radically, vinyl sales could be marginalised and CD investment could look sickly.

In 1989 the output of the music market in Britain was divided more or less equally between native-born British artists and foreign ones. Two-thirds of the foreign half was taken by Americans and the remaining portion by various musicians from European and some Commonwealth countries. These are all countries with which Britons have had long-term cultural relationships from the days of empire or the days of trans-European culture and warring. There was little sign of less familiar Middle or Far Eastern, Latin American or independent African or Asian influences being widely accepted.

The reverse of historical experience comes when export sales are considered. Unfortunately these have to be deduced from a different base--that of British-based companies rather than British-origin artists. Nevertheless these figures illustrate a remarkable trend. Of an estimated world retail sales market of $2.3 million in 1988, 20%--that is, $4 million--were sales of a British product. With U.K.-based companies selling $834 million worth in their home market $3.16 million was accounted for by exports. Thus, approximately one-quarter of their sales were at home and three-quarters went abroad. It can not be assumed that U.K.-based companies sign only U.K.-born artists or that foreign-based companies have no U.K. signings-- that is patently not the case. However, the differential between foreign and domestic sales of U.K.-based companies is so large that it follows that a great deal of British music is heard outside the country. The tradition of centuries of producing music only for home consumption has been completely swept away in this instance. Artists with ambitions for commercial success simply disregard international boundaries and see the world as their marketplace.

It is an attitude of mind which permeates right through the industry from the large transnationals to small companies with only one or two signings. If artists are judged to have international potential, they are usually signed up by the transnational companies. However, the independent companies have often achieved international success with their artists and their presence in the field is increasing.

All the transnational recording companies run offshoot recording companies in Britain. This obviates the necessity for licensing agreements and enables them to make their own British signings. Their sales accounted for 63% of the singles and 66% of the album sales in the British market in 1990. The Dutch/German group PolyGram, owned by Philips/Siemens, after yet another period of expansion by takeover, having just swallowed up Island and A&M, took 22% of the singles and 22% of the album sales. BMG/RCA (Germany) took 7% and 4.5%; WEA (U.S.) took 10% and 13%; CBS, the world's largest recording company (Sony, Japan) took 11% and 10%; and EMI (U.K.) took 13% and 15%, respectively, of unit sales. Britain traditionally was regarded by these companies as a source of exportable talent rather than as a place to make large profits. However WEA, for one, uses its base in the country to push its sales of its homegrown American signings, which has paid dividends in the late 1980s.

The size and depth of interest of these transnationals can be demonstrated by examining the British transnational EMI, which was established in 1898, when it was called HIMV. It is now a subsidiary of Thorn EMI Plc. It owned 318 overseas companies in 39 countries in 1990, which were located in Western Europe, the United States, South America, Australasia, South and South East Asia, the Middle East, Canada and the Indian subcontinent. In Britain, as well as being a major record manufacturing and distributing company, EMI owns the most substantial record club--World Records--and commands one-third of the rack-jobbing and budget record market with Music for Pleasure.

EMI owns a chain of cinemas and theatres which provides one of the major circuits for promotional rock tours, a chain of clubs, a chain of record and tape shops and is a leading distributor of musical instruments. It also owns a highly successful record shop fitting service, a network of talent and artists agencies, concert promotion companies and ticket outlets. This capital holding of various interests, either by horizontal or vertical integration, is typical of all transnational companies.

In addition to the five transnational companies operating in Britain in 1991 there were another 130 members of the British Phonographic Institute (BPI), the industry's trade association. Of these 130 members, 10 were foreign and a further 29 were not recording companies as such. The remaining 91 represent, in the main, the established, commercially developed side of the British national record industry. These companies accounted for approximately 27% of singles unit sales and 28% of albums in 1990. The strongest companies in the single market were Virgin, Mute, PWL, Factory, Swanyard and Zomba. In the album market they were Virgin, Telstar, Stylus, Dino, Mute and Pickwick. The remaining 10% of the singles and 6% of the album sales were accounted for by small independent companies.

In 1989 there were at least 1,700 registered record companies outside the BPI[2]. The 91 nontransnational British national members of the BPI together with the 1,700 other British companies make up the national independent sector of the industry and together with a further few hundreds of amateur and quasi-amateur recording operations form the springboards for changes in style and new music. These companies are owned, financed and administrated independently. The majority (approximately 95%) are also in no way reliant on the distribution networks originally developed by the transnationals. In the last 15 years there has been a revolution in the distribution of records in Britain and the stranglehold of the major companies has been broken. The independent distribution system is not a national monolithic system as run by the big companies, but is based on a network of geographically dispersed small distributors.

The role of the independent companies of nurturing new talent never looked so commanding as in 1991. Not one of the industry annual awards in the best British newcomer category was a transnational signing. Additionally, in recent years, the normal progression to stardom from an indie label to a transnational one has become less of a norm. Many of the most popular bands such as the Smiths, New Order, Erasure and Depeche Mode did not move on. Many of the late 1980s wave of big-selling dance-rock acts--Happy Mondays, Stone Roses, Inspiral Carpets et al--were all established indie signings. The teenybop favorites of that time, Jason Donovan and Kylie Minogue, proved that the independent sector was sufficiently well-organized and efficient to handle the biggest selling albums in 1988 and 1989. Even the transnationals themselves now use the independent distributor's facilities to handle their minority releases.

Nevertheless, it is essential to realize that if differences in company size and record throughput are taken into account, the distribution picture takes on entirely different dimensions. In turnover terms distribution is dominated by a handful of very large firms. In 1990 the independent sector accounted for 10% of singles and LP distribution. However, in the promotion of innovation and plurality of music, size is of less importance than is existence. The smallest company in the independent network can provide a platform for the start of a career.

The rise of the independent record companies produced a fracturing of what was once a monolithic industry. Recording studios have sprung up all over the country. There is now a 51% to 49% metropolitan to regional split in the location of recording companies. A large number of service companies came into existence in the 1970s to sell advice to the smaller recording outfits. Such professional services as management, legal, radio and concert consultancies, promotion, publicity, security, transport and stage design can be obtained.

Additionally there are song-writing companies, record import/export companies and trade press companies. The independent companies themselves have expanded in different directions according to need, taste and commercial necessity. Virgin built up a nationwide network of retail outlets. Among others Pinnacle, PRT and Rough Trade with their collaborative colleagues in Cartel expanded into distribution. Conifer, Recommended, Lightening, Cadillac Music and Gamut turned themselves into importers.

The industry as a whole provides for a plurality of musical tastes. Apart from the pop-rock genre, which accounted for 69% of market value in 1987, classical music took the largest portion with 10%. Classical music buyers tend to be over 25 years old and most releases of the music are now on compact discs. Easy-listening, middle-of-the-road music took an 8% market share. It is a solid, staid, loyal market made up mainly of people over the age of 35. Its character is changing as more and more pop and rock is reclassified into this category. Country music was the most popular of the peripheral music genres, with 3% of the market. Of the rest jazz, blues, reggae, rap, african music, folk, irish, film and TV soundtracks, big bands, brass bands, children's songs and comedy each accounted for 1% or less of total music sales. Various kinds of black music are imported to satisfy minority tastes--that is, modern, vintage and classical jazz, blues, gospel and swing, together with country and western and folk and ethnic music.

As to the majority category of pop and rock the innovative music is usually home-grown and provided by the independent sector. The transnationals' pop/rock is mainstream compared to the output of the former companies. The flowering of music since punk can be directly attributable to these small companies. They have provided access to the marketplace for innovation and have deghettoized marginal music. The pop and rock music promoted by the transnationals and larger national companies usually has proof of success behind it or shows evident potential for success. It is also not unduly offensive to broadcasters, or the recording establishment. Many bands have been accused of becoming popified on signing or licensing themselves to a large company.

It has taken 40 years for pop and rock to develop into a musical tradition which can be celebrated by the whole community, not one solely defined by age. Over these 40 years the music has developed with cyclical repetition and stepwise innovation. Development has not led to deletion in all cases. Some sounds, on realization, have stayed in their original form to become classic rock. Others once discarded have reemerged at later dates. The development has been akin to the tracks leading to a busy city railway junction. Some particular combinations of sound have originated a long distance away in the 1950s and 1960s; others have come shorter journeys from the 1970s or 1980s; yet others have been minor branch lines for some time before joining the main route. Some tracks have stopped at various points before reaching the city. Often for part of the distance a number of tracks have run alongside each other. Even at more times they have melded into each other or crossed each other's paths. On occasion some tracks have taken big diversions, gotten lost, but reappeared again nearer the city.

To give a few examples; the most obvious case of the latter happening is rock 'n' roll which reappeared for a time in the 1970s after its drop from popularity during the previous decade. Heavy metal electric-guitar-based rock music emerged in the middle of the 1970s to continue unchanged to the present day. Since the early 1970s the young urban West Indians have kept faith with their own reggae, ska and rap developing it to suit themselves and no one else. Others have taken elements from it as in the late 1970s when it was combined with the punk music of the middle 1970s to provide a dance music labeled 2 Tone.

Elements of the psychedelic rock music of the 1960s have appeared time and again in new forms and new combinations over the years. In the late 1980s one emerged from Manchester where their dance-rock bands play high dreamy harmonies, with wah wah guitar histrionics and swirling organ drones underpinned by an acid house backbeat. Innovative music usually emerges from a branch line, whereas teenybop pop appears to have been mainline all the way, regenerating itself by taking from others from time to time in different-sized doses.

Currently the old musical stars' records hold their own against the latest sounds in the Top 10, and their highly professional concerts are sellouts every time. They do not sound old fashioned and appear to have bridged the generations. However, this phenomenon could also be explained by the marketing policies of the record companies, or by the time lag in categorization by broadcasters and the industry. The latest wave of shock sounds with a political edge that has the establishment worried comes from America's black underclass and has been adapted by Britain's first generation of native-born black youth. NWA's album Efil4Zaggin, a chart topper in its native America, was banned from the airwaves and all copies seized.

The British version, Ragamuffin rap, is less stridently violent and addresses British problems such as the subtle racism and the lack of future for young blacks living in inner cities. It fuses reggae with hard-core hip hop beats, rap with live jazz, funk and soul music in a melodic intertwining.

Yet again the English have made the original American beat into something recognizably their own. This, on the surface, has little to do with accommodation to folk song roots or traditional entertainment music. Speculatively, the rhythms of English popular music have been overlaid with other peculiar English characteristics, values and childhood needs and memories. Twentieth-century English popular music incorporates major elements of

fantasy, eccentricity, self-confidence, decadence, threat and, because it origi-
nates from the young, the potential to shock.

LOCAL MUSIC

The most evident innovations in music making at local levels in England are
generated by the young. These are mainly versions of Anglo-American
rock/pop which in the course of development have become, in part, identifiable English.*3* This is not to say that all local music is rock/pop. There are
many ethnic minorities who hold dear their old traditions; emigrés from the
Baltic states; Mediterranean immigrants such as Greeks and Turkish Cypri-
ots; Poles, Hungarians and Germans; European Jews--all with strong music
traditions of their own, who practice their own music as part of keeping
their own identities and heritage. The more recent immigrants from the new
Commonwealth--Indians, Pakistanis and Africans--have also imported their
own music. All these musics, although practiced and listened to by others
have remained in a large part the preserve of their practitioners. The obvious
exception to this has been the music of the West Indies, which has influenced
English popular music, and itself in turn has been changed by the English
social and musical environment. In addition to this ethnic music there is the
English traditional music which can still be heard on the media, at concert
halls, in clubs, in schools and in churches.
    A plurality of music abounds, but still the music of the majority of
young people is popular music. It is their music, played by their peers, which
expresses their feelings and concerns. Usually English children are exposed
to a wide variety of music genres from classical, historical, folk, dance, traditional, regional, religious and choral music to, above all, mainstream pop
and rock music. They emerge into adolescence with ears attuned to music of
various sorts. They have recorders put into their hands at the age of 5, other
more sophisticated instruments at the age of 12, and sing or are sung to from
childhood. However, it appears that a honing in on pop and rock comes
about gradually during childhood, even though they are exposed to music
from a variety of sources. Wober (1990a) found that the mass media were
ever-present in their lives, but in their early years of childhood, learning
from adults was also very important to many of them. Activities such as
singing in school assembly and in church, singing nursery rhymes and songs
learned from parents and singing bits made up by themselves were practiced
by fewer and fewer of his sample the older they were. Conversely, more and
more of Wober's sample sang along with cassettes and chart songs the older
they were. The numbers singing along with tunes, advertisements and music
from TV did not change drastically between the ages of 9 and 15. The expansion of interest was in the area of recorded music.
    The experience of nonpop foreign music, avant-garde and experimental
music or other music not broadcast regularly on the airwaves would have
been limited. Chart music is available on both radio and TV together with a
smattering of avant-garde music. But records give access to a much wider
range of music, both national and international. There are also records
made and distributed on a regional or local basis by the indie companies.
These give access to new music untouched by commercial hyping. Children

are experts on the subject of mainstream pop--that is, international pop music--in early adolescence. They become familiar with innovative peripheral popular music only when they start to attend gigs and concerts and build up collections of their own, usually during their later teenage years.

One of the choices the majority of young musicians make is the rejection of their school musical education as irrelevant to, and restrictive on, the music they wish to play and hear. When asked to consider the influences on their music, it is difficult for young musicians to produce coherent replies. They will acknowledge that they have steeped themselves in popular music from an early age, that they do have their heroes and favorites. They even name a few obscure British bands that they admire. But, for people who are creating their own music, be it ever so mundane, to admit that their original compositions are copies of anyone elses is not possible. Their output is claimed to be totally individual and unique and not for categorization. It seems to me that musical influences become guesswork on the researcher's part. If one does not happen to be a musicologist, one can only judge the presence of influence by availability.

There is a communality of experience between musicians and audience and so the former are able to reflect the concerns of the latter. However, it has been found that young players are not usually ordinary people, truly representative of their contemporaries. To succeed, musicians need to have more than their fair share of ambition and drive. They need to be prepared for hard work and for taking a professional attitude to their work. They need to have great faith in themselves and be highly egotistic individuals. They may have the self-image that they express the values in general of young people, but in actuality they may not share them.

It is quite possible that the innovative music the local groups produce is no more than yet other forms of an international melding of music, and there is little cultural cleanliness in it. However, even if the carrying tune may not have a firm national cultural base, the theme is undoubtedly tied to local or national experience.

The punk explosion in the late 1970s serves as a good illustration of this, when the predominating love song lyrics were displaced by nihilistic themes. At that time many young people liked to think of themselves as rejected by adult society, having experienced unsympathetic authority and irrelevant schooling. More recently the anarchistic themes were in part displaced by more pragmatic ones triggered off by such events as the miner's strike and some of the government's policies in the early 1980s. It was such themes and their expression not only in words, but in the total style of the performers, which then struck chords among young audiences. They emerged directly from shared experiences and were in the most part identifiably British.

As to the musicians themselves, there is a seemingly never-ending stream of new local talent emerging from every large city. In provincial England aspiring musicians often start to form groups to play music while still at school, others join in later, introduced by friends. The interest of these early amateur groups is not necessarily in performing. They play for pleasure, and practice to improve their playing. Most groups compose their own tunes and lyrics instead of trying to imitate current hit tunes.

The latter practice has become a near impossibility due to the sophistication of present recording techniques. In the early days the new compositions tend to be very simple, based on a 12 bar blues sequence. Their originality is constrained by the experience of the composers. It is often formula music with unchallenging lyrics, but still original composition.

As competence progresses the group may start playing to audiences-- that is, to any audience that will listen to them--for which they are paid little or no money at all. Performances are very important in the development of groups as they are the only way to learn how to perform. Once a group feels confident with a few of its numbers it will make a demo disc to send to local record companies, agents, distributors and   radio and TV companies. Groups also sometimes get 300-500 copies of their discs pressed at their own expense to sell at their gigs. They might even make their own videos, as one can hire a video camera for as little as $23 a day. There are recording facilities in all major cities in the country run either privately and/or by local government. The opportunities for performance are not as numerous today as they were in the 1960s when most inner-city public houses (bars) used the services of a rock group. However in Leeds, my home city, in the 1980s live music was still the dominant form of entertainment.

The city's square mile offered roughly 30 venues, these being clubs, public houses and discos. Some public houses featured different clubs on different nights, gate money was taken and each club strived for its own style and identity. Live rock/reggae was predominant, accounting for as many musical events as all other forms together. Benefit gigs and festivals were commonplace, where groups played for reduced fees or gave their services free, allowing all profits to go to a particular cause. Publicity for local music was largely limited to "alternative" channels. Local musicians would deny the existence of any "local sound" as the figment of journalists' imagination. However, local groups know each other. There is intense rivalry between them as well as inter-change of players and camaraderie. Many performers play in more than one band. They go and listen to each other's music to barrack (jeer) or encourage. They are all guaranteed to attend any performance by visiting top class groups or performers. If they cannot afford the tickets, they earn them by giving their labor free to the visitors.

The early playing experience of young musicians, until they reach a good middle level of competence, is mainly confined to their own localities. Interactions are confined to other local groups. If they do happen to travel to a gig outside their locality, they do not integrate with that scene. Very competent musicians fall out of local-level performances. Venues willing to pay reasonable performance fees demand variety and that entails travel for the groups. In addition a wider audience is needed to generate a worthwhile number of record sales Musical contacts become nationwide with a degree of specialization into one genre of music. Performances become tempered to audience needs and venue and media demands.

Gradually, if the band's aims are directed at commercial success the music becomes popified and international. This process loses the group many of its original fans but gives it new ones throughout the world. However, as soon as the music becomes alien to the audience, it loses its commercial value and is dropped by its promoters if it cannot find another audience. The system's in-built pressures on the artists can easily destroy the product thus necessitating the cycle of constant renewal, the search for new talent and sounds. Seemingly elements of cultural integrity are necessary features of success. The greater the choice, the more discriminating and specific can be the demands of the consumers.

CONCLUSION

The foregoing commentary has tried to illustrate the current and historical conditions which have produced a domestic music industry that is highly developed, sophisticated, complex and surviving. Some of the factors mentioned which could have influenced the growth of the industry included the historic political stability of English society; the lack of political or bureaucratic control or censorship over musical development; the highly developed societal structure; the resource availability to invest in music making and appreciation. Added to this is the maturity of the music industry itself, its ability to be self-regulatory and reduce the impact of trading abuses such as chart hyping and piracy, the sophistication and diversity of distribution systems, royalty collection systems and the ability to negotiate play-time agreements with the broadcasting authorities.

Also important is the openness of the English audience to innovation. In short, the country sustains an abnormally high level of musical activity, many opportunities for performers, high rewards and a very wide range of products. This enables a faster rate of technological innovation than would be the case in a less active market, which in turn creates easy access to sophisticated sounds.

NOTES

1. All sales and market share figures quoted were extracted from the *BPI Yearbook* 1991.

2. Data source: Music Master, *Labels List '89*. Hastings: John Humphries.

3. This section was originally written in collaboration with Ray Brown, to whom the author expresses her thanks.

BIBLIOGRAPHY

Abrams, M. (1959). *The Teenage Consumer*. LPE Paper No. 5. London: Routledge and Kegan Paul.

Brake, Mike (1980). *The Sociology of Youth Culture and Youth Subcultures*. London: Routledge and Kegan Paul.

British Broadcasting Corporation (1984). *Young People and Music with Special References to Top of the POPs*. London: BBC.

British Broadcasting Corporation (1986). *BBC Yearbook*. London: BBC.

British Phonographic Institute (1977-1991 inclusive). *BPI Yearbook*. London: BPI.

Cashmore, E. Ellis (1984). *No Future: Youth and Society*. London: Heinemann.

Chanan, M.(1981). "The Trajectory of Western Music or as Mahler said the music is not in the notes." *Media, Culture and Society.* Vol. 3, No. 3, July 1981.

Cohen, Philip (1972). Subcultural Conflict and Working Class Community" *Working Papers on Cultural Studies,* No. 2, Spring. Birmingham: University of Birmingham.

Cohen, Stanley (1980). *Folk Devils & Moral Panics.* 2nd Edition, Oxford: Martin Robinson.

Hall, Stuart & Jefferson, Tony (1976). *Resistance through Rituals.* London: Hutchinson.

Hebdige, Dick (1979). *Subculture:The Meaning of Style.* London: Methuen.

Hutson, Susan & Jenkins, Richard (1989). *Taking the Strain: Families, Unemployment and the Transition to Adulthood.* Milton Keynes: Open University Press.

Independent Broadcasting Authority (1986). *TV and Radio 1986.* London: IBA.

Martin, Bernice (1982). "Pop Music and Youth." *Media Development.* Vol. 29, No. 1.

Murdock, Graham. (1979). *Adolescent Culture and the Mass Media.* Final report to the SSRC University of Leicester: Center for Mass Communications. (mimeo).

Music Master (1989). *Labels List '89.* Hastings: John Humpries.

Radio Authority (1991). *The Radio Authority Pocket Book.* London: Radio Authority.

Rice, J., Gambaccini, R. & Reed, M. (1981). *The Guinness Book of British Hit Singles.* Enfield: Guinness Superlatives.

Rogers, Dave (1982). *Rock 'n' Roll.* London: Routledge and Kegan Paul.

Small, C. (1977). *Music - Society - Education.* London: John Calder.

Walker, Ernest (1952). *A History of Music in England.* Oxford: Clarendon Press.

Watson, I (1983). *Song and Democratic Culture in Britain.* London: Croom Helm.

Weber, M. (1969). *The Rational and Social Foundations of Music.* Trans. D. Martindale et al. New York: Carbondale.

Willis, Paul (1977). *Learning to Labor.* Farnborough: Gower.

Willis, Paul (1978). *Profane Culture.* London: Routledge and Kegan Paul.

Wober, J. M. (1984). *Teens and Taste in Music and Radio.* London: Independent Broadcasting Authority.

Wober, J. M. (1990a). *Children's Musical Lives: Influences from Television and Other Sources.* London: Independent Broadcasting Authority.

Wober, J. M. (1990b). *Interests in Arts on Television.* London: Independent Broadcasting Authority.

Young, Percy M. (1967). *A History of British Music.* London: Ernest Benn.

CHAPTER 4

POPULAR MUSIC AND THE MUSIC INDUSTRY IN GREECE

Fouli T. Papageorgiou

THE BACKGROUND: POPULAR MUSIC
AND FOREIGN INFLUENCES

Greece, by its geographical location, is at the cross-roads between Europe and Asia, between the West and the East. Since ancient times and up to the end of the Ottoman occupation in the nineteenth century, Greece had developed and sustained closer links with the countries at its north and east rather than at its west. The Greek culture of the last 1,500 years has incorporated a large number of Asian and North African elements, which contributed to the remarkable diversity and vividness of traditional Greek art.

Greek music is a mirror of these influences. A rich musical tradition was created by integrating borrowed musical styles or instruments alongside the indigenous ones. Following the revolution against the Turks and the establishment of the new Greek state in the nineteenth century, the picture changed. The new state formed much closer links with the West, as it depended on the Great Powers of Europe politically and economically for its survival. Greece was an essentially rural society until the revolution. After the formation of the new state, the urbanisation process started at an accelerating rate, and soon the first major urban centres and the metropolis, Athens, were established. The cultural shock of urbanisation affected deeply the creation of popular music. Thus, since the beginning of the twentieth century, popular music evolved along two crucial dichotomies: the urban-rural polarity and the West to East antithesis. The former led to the creation of *rebetica*, a greatly original form of urban popular music, distinct from the traditional rural folk *demotica*. The latter determined the mainstream music that was promoted by the music industry, centred on foreign imports or locally created music with Western influences.

The West to East antithesis reflected a deeper social division between the better educated and more affluent elite and the poorer working class masses.

The contrast between the Western taste of the elite and the traditional culture of the masses, with its evident oriental elements, gives the essential background to understanding the structure of the main strands of popular music today and their relationship with the music industry. As a young musician put it vividly during an interview, "Greeks look west with one eye and east with the other. But they cannot decide where their heart is."

For decades, Middle Eastern and Asian influences more generally in popular music were considered as a threat to the culture of the nation. Strands of popular music that incorporated such influences (e.g., rebetica) were banned by the establishment in the 1930s and 1950s as dangerous, regarding the detrimental effects they might have on the young. Even today, music that distinctly recalls Turkish or Indian sounds is treated with caution by the media and there is a reluctance to include it in regular broadcasting of music, particularly by the Athens-based major radio stations public or private. However, such music is greatly popular with the urban working class and the population of rural centres and it regularly features in many provincial station broadcasts.

On the contrary, the threat from Western music is a relatively recent notion, which formed in the mid-1970s, based on two phenomena: first, the strong anti-American feeling created among Greeks during the years of the military dictatorship (1967-1974); and second, the remarkable boom of foreign music, especially Anglo-American, between the years 1975 and 1980 when foreign record sales doubled, bringing foreign popular music on a par with Greek music production regarding market shares. Anglo-American pop music is very popular with the young. The assumed danger stems from the dedication of the young toward a single strand of music that is alien to the Greek culture and that inevitably leads them away from their roots and their tradition. To explore the dynamics of this phenomenon, one has to look into the pluralism of popular music production today and the role of the recording industry and broadcasting.

THE MAIN STRANDS OF CONTEMPORARY POPULAR MUSIC

Rebetica

Rebetica is perhaps the most original and most authentic type of popular music created in Greece during this century. Rebetica has its roots in the traditional folk music of rural areas (demotica) but developed a different form and content which expressed the new conditions of life after the revolution and the establishment of the new Greek state (Annoyiannakis, 1961). Some of the melodies of rebetica were initially brought to Greece by sailors from the ports of the Middle East and were soon spread to the underworld that was connected to the ports and subsequently to prisons. Later, rebetica integrated Byzantine, demotica, island folk and cantata music themes. However, for a long time it stayed away from mass acceptance as fringe music addressed to the underworld and closely connected to pot-smoking.

Following the mass transfer of Greek populations of Asia Minor to mainland Greece in 1922, Athens and the big cities became suddenly surrounded by hundreds of thousands of refugees, who formed a new proletarian class. Rebetica, speaking about oppression, poverty and pain, became adopted by this new class, spreading "like a fire," as a means of primary communication, and evolving further through their refugees' own Middle Eastern culture (Vournas, 1961). As Vournas adds, rebetica "becomes the popular music equivalent to the working masses of urban centres." During World War II, rebetica served the Resistance, carrying messages of courage and freedom through double-meaning lyrics. Later, following the end of the civil war, rebetica expressed the yearning for political freedom and self-affirmation of the proletarian working class, at a time when extensive purges of left-wingers were an everyday phenomenon. At the same time, rebetica enlarged its thematic variations to include love as well as the everyday concerns and values of working people.

Rebetica was never accepted by the elite and never became mainstream music despite its tremendous influence and popularity. With few exceptions, the intelligentsia of the period between the 1930s and 1960s regarded rebetica as decadent music, "un Greek," and because of its Eastern influences it was a threat to the culture of the young and shame for the cultural history of Greece (Holst, 1977). During the 1950s rebetica reached a new peak before starting to deteriorate, overcome by the process of commercialization, consumerism and industrialisation that was introduced to Greek society after the war. However, during the 1950s, rebetica provided the background and the inspiration for two new strands of popular music: laika and the art-popular song.

Laika

Laika, which literally means "popular music," is a simplification of rebetica, meant to be easier to the ear for mass production. Laika often borrowed Turkish or Indian melodies. It is characteristic that the so-called Indian Laika of the early 1960s were based on melodies sung in the Indian films of Narghis which reached Greece and became very popular at the time. The emigration wave, which took millions of Greek workers away from their homes had already started, and laika became associated with the plight of the unemployed and the emigrants.

The immense popularity of laika must be seen in conjunction with two factors. First, the important role the recording industry started to play after the war, which made it possible for popular music to spread widely without the assistance of radio. Second, the fact that laika broke the barrier of working class music, although not because of its value but because of fashion. A large number of expensive nightclubs and tavernas which sprang up all over Athens offering laika sung by star singers became the symbol of this fashion, patronised by the middle classes and the wealthier sections of the working class. Light laika or master's rebetica (*archontorebetica*) were consequently produced to suit the tastes of their wealthier patrons and to comply with the demands of the market which asked for more refined music and more indifferent and innocuous lyrics.

At about the same time, a number of talented young composers used rebetica and folk music as inspiration to create a new strand of popular song, known as the art-popular movement. Manos Hadjidakis and Mikis Theodorakis became the two leading composers within that movement, which aimed to bring quality within the region of popular song inspired by the best traditional music and utilising lyrics written by prominent Greek poets. Theodorakis's music sold the highest number of records ever sold in Greece, creating an amazing boom in the recording market.

Political Song, New Wave

A great part of the work of Theodorakis has been politically inspired. The political song formed a special line within the art-popular movement, appealing mostly to the young. It became a source of identity for young people, a sort of personal and ideological defence during the turbulent period that led to the rule of the military dictatorship in 1967. In parallel to the political song, the new wave ballads of the 1960s were directly addressed to young people, covering another important side of their needs: they spoke about love, loneliness and companionship, values that started to become scarce and threatened in a period of increasing commercialization and political instability.

Rebetica and laika were never promoted by the (state-controlled) radio as mainstream music, but art-popular and new wave were widely accepted as such. Another strand of popular music that has received preferential treatment from the radio is the so-called light music. Light music represents the Western influence on the Greek song from the 1930s up through the 1970s, 1980s and 1990s. A large part of this music was written as dance music, especially between the 1930s and 1960s. Italian, Spanish, Argentinean, French, American and later English music provided the models and the inspiration (Mylonas, 1985). An excessive production of songs characterized this strand, catered by a large number of composers. A characteristic of light music was, in its initial forms, romanticism. Its lyrics almost always talked about love, usually in a trivial and repetitive poetic form. The appearance of the art-popular movement, with its high-quality lyrics and potent musical forms, uncovered the shallowness of the romanticism of light music. However, light music did not disappear from the scene, but was placed at a marginal position, played mostly by dance orchestras in nightclubs. Its revival in the 1980s as the new Greek song was characterized by an effort for innovation in its musical form and lyrics.

Foreign songs, translated into Greek and adapted to the capabilities of local orchestras, have always been a part of light music. Foreign music came to Greece through the cinema and record companies. The opening of the American armed forces broadcasting station in 1959 was also crucial for the wider dissemination of Anglo-American foreign music. Foreign music, since the 1930s, has been popular with the young as dance music. In the 1960s, a small number of groups were formed who played exclusively foreign music (Italian, French, American and English) and sang international hits translated into Greek. These groups also composed their own few pieces along the lines of their international repertoire, always using Greek lyrics, but they never enjoyed a high degree of popularity.

During the years of the military dictatorship, the diversity, novelty and liveliness of popular music came to a halt. The political song, as well as all of Theodorakis's music, were officially banned. Rebetica was excluded from broadcasting. The radio endlessly transmitted rural folk music (demotica), which was judged by the colonels to be the only pure Greek music. In parallel, light music took a prominent position in broadcasting together with foreign Western music, played in much larger proportions of time than ever before. The emphasis on foreign (Western) and foreign-influenced Greek music was part of the junta's effort to prove that Greece belonged to the West politically, culturally and economically. During the dictatorship, the political song went underground while rebetica (which was not officially banned) was adopted by people as a means of covert resistance through music, coming to a new peak of wide popularity. The end of the military regime created euphoria, hope and a great deal of confusion in the musical scene. Initially, the political song, stimulated by large popular concerts in the big stadiums of Athens, reached a great peak, but soon its popularity subsided and eventually disappeared. Apart from the brief revival of the political song, the changeover to democracy created the circumstances for a new order in popular music.

Art-Popular Music

First, the art-popular music strand entered a saturation period, failing to achieve an impressive revival and to arouse the excitement it did in 1969. However, art-popular is still today one of the mainstream strands of music accepted by the media. Contemporary productions of art-popular music often create a short-term interest but rarely speak to the heart of the audience, in the way older productions did. It is claimed that today the place of art-popular music as the people's music has been taken by another revival, that of new laika.

Second, traditional music and rebetica, which were rediscovered during the experience of the dictatorship, became greatly popular across Greece. Old and forgotten original releases of rebetica were reissued by the record companies, thus creating a new, valuable library of authentic popular music that would have been otherwise found only in private collections. More important, the young were sensitized to this type of traditional popular music and groups of young musicians were formed who sang rebetica and the best of laika. These new interpretations of rebetica were met with great commercial success when released on records. The rebetica groups, called *compania*, became very popular during the 1980s. Today, most of them have diversified their repertoire to include, apart from the revived rebetica, more recent compositions in the form of new laika.

The new laika strand is a follow-up to the laika of the late 1950s and 1960s, including strong Middle Eastern elements in their melodic forms and lyrics addressing the everyday worries and concerns of ordinary people. New laika has created its own brand of popular, star singers as it did in the 1960s. A particular variation of laika, nicknamed dog music, borrows Arabic or

Asian themes accompanied by synthesizer or electric guitar. This music is played in expensive nightclubs, often connected with the underworld, which are in a derogatory way nicknamed dog places. Dog music addresses itself to the alienated rural migrants who settled in the metropolis, cannot be integrated, although they inevitably share in the advent of new technology and the consumption models of the big city.

Dog music is considered by both the musical establishment and the big recording companies as an expression of decadence in the field of popular music in Greece. Records of dog music are produced mostly by a large number of small independents, who usually charge the performers for the production of a record. However, this music is greatly popular in working-class areas of Athens and in the regions, disseminated through pirated cassettes of live performances and via local radio stations. There are some students of music who believe that the strand of new laika and the best examples of dog music are the only authentic popular music movements today in Greece. The evolution of dog music in particular reminds one of the initial stages of the development of rebetica in, as far as it reflects, social values of marginal social groups. Transferred to modern reality, this music expresses the low social consciousness, the confusion and the nihilism of a proletarian class which has been taken over by consumerism.

Third, the increased exposure to foreign music during the years of the dictatorship made a lasting impact on the young. Rock groups were formed in the beginning of the 1970s, which created their own brand of pop and rock, following on the traces of the Anglo-American model and sung in English rather than Greek. This was a new phenomenon in the history of Greek popular music, because, as mentioned above, foreign music has always been sung translated into Greek or with new Greek lyrics.

"Greek rock," as this strand was named, did not become very popular during the 1970s, because young people preferred to listen to authentic pop and rock music from Britain or America. Gradually, during the 1980s, some of the Greek rock groups or musicians tried to express a more individual style in their music, by incorporating traditional elements of Greek music in their compositions. They also used Greek lyrics. Lyrics then became very important in this strand of music, perhaps more important than the music itself. Some students of contemporary Greek music believe that Greek rock is the political song of today, because it expresses the cut-off of the young from society, their lack of purpose, their loneliness, their anarchic feelings, their disillusionment with politics, their sarcasm about heroes and radical ideologies, their fears about spreading drug use, their resignation about social corruption (*Eleftherotypia*, 1986).

Greek rock has been for a long time kept out of the recording industry and off the radio, having the status of fringe music, disseminated mainly through live performances in bars, festivals or concerts. In the 1980s, the Greek rock diversified even further to include new styles, in which the influence of Anglo-American pop was more subdued.

The "new Greek song," as the diversified Greek rock has been called, started to claim a place in contemporary popular music during the past ten years. The new Greek song is now being supported by the record companies, after a long hesitation period, performed by star pop singers as well as pop groups. A greater boost was initially given to the new Greek song by the radio, as a new generation of young and open-minded producers have started to make their mark. Today, the new Greek song represents one of the two prevailing genres of popular music (the other being the new laika) claiming a substantial proportion of airtime in all major radio stations.

In its start, the new Greek song gave the impression of "walking in the dark," as it had no clear identity and often sounded foreign enough to the Greek ear. Gradually, it developed into a rather distinct genre, trying to combine traditional melodic forms with the rhythm of modern rock. Undoubtedly, Greek rock and the new Greek song have now become popular with the young. As a record company director put it, the new Greek song gives the young a "roof," something of their own. It is also a means of coded communication between young people. Even the language used in its lyrics is the special slang adopted by youth in their everyday talk, an idiom rather alien to older people. It is true that young Greeks have always had, since the 1950s, a liking for rock music with its vivid beat and antiestablishment connotations. However, living in a country with a strong musical tradition and an enormous diversity of music production gives them the ability to absorb and enjoy a variety of genres and a polyphony of sounds. Results of recent research about music preferences among Greek people (Papageorgiou et al. 1993) show that even the very young (15-19 years old) have a taste for both foreign and Greek music, modern rock and laika. It is also interesting to note in Table 4.1 that as age increases, preference for the rock strands falls, while preference for Greek music goes up, especially for laika and demotica. The youngsters of the 1970s, now in their forties, seem to have outgrown all the dangerous foreign rock influences which marked their teens, to become ardent devotees of the traditional and modern laika and demotica.

TABLE 4.1: Preferences for Different Types of Music by Age Group

Type of Music	Age			
	15-24 N=321 %	25-34 N=328 %	35-54 N=668 %	55+ N=1,702 %
Classical	12.2	15.0	11.5	10.2
Disco	24.0	16.2	9.6	3.2
New rock/pop	37.4	32.0	14.4	5.1
Greek rock/pop	33.3	22.9	14.2	3.1
Classical rock	22.8	22.9	11.1	3.5
Heavy metal	12.2	4.6	1.1	0.4
House rap	19.0	9.5	1.8	0.8
Reggae	11.9	13.1	5.1	1.7
Blues	22.1	18.9	11.4	3.1
Jazz	7.2	12.8	8.1	2.4
Ballads	1.9	3.7	5.2	15.5
Old Greek	16.8	23.8	27.3	39.4
Light Greek	21.5	34.2	36.5	33.4
Art-popular	18.1	22.6	20.1	14.5
Rebetica	11.5	19.2	21.9	27.1
"Light" laika	26.1	41.5	46.2	42.8
Laika	21.2	31.4	33.8	35.8
Greek new wave	16.5	30.5	24.6	11.9
Traditional folk demotica	3.4	12.2	18.0	41.6
No preference	3.7	2.7	5.2	4.6

Source: Surveys in 5 cities (Korydallos, Helioupolis, Kalamata, Sitia, Kilkis), carried out by PRISMA, Athens, between 1990 and 1992.

Today, Greece is a stable parliamentary democracy with a socialist leadership. There are no purges because of political beliefs; there are also large movements of population. There is no social animosity or extreme disparities. There is no political or social cause potent enough and widespread enough to inspire a popular music movement similar to the 1930s or 1960s. The result is a polyphony, a pluralism in the production of popular music, which comes very close to a cross section of the different strands of music that thrived after the war. If we look at the prevailing and most dynamic strands, however, we can see the same model influences as observed throughout the history of popular music in Greece during this century. In the 1990s Greeks still look West with one eye and East with the other.

THE RECORDING INDUSTRY

The recording industry in Greece today is represented by eight major companies and a large number of independents. Six of these companies are branches of multinationals: Minos EMI, PolyGram, Sony Music, BMG, Warner and Virgin. The remaining two are entirely purely Greek-owned: Lyra and Music Box. Between these, only Lyra produces an exclusively Greek repertoire, while Music Box devotes its repertoire, to foreign productions, which it reproduces and distributes under license. About 60 minor companies and independents also operate, according to a survey carried out by IFPI in 1982, but it is likely that this number has substantially decreased in the last five years.

EMI was the first company that got the record manufacturing industry under way in Greece, after a cooperation agreement was signed in 1930, between the British Columbia Gramophone Co. and the Gramophone Company, both of which merged to form EMI in Britain one year later. The company offices and pressing plant were completed within a year and the first locally produced disc appeared in Greece in 1931. At that time, no recording studios were available, and recordings were made in the halls of the larger hotels in Athens. The record market in Greece could justify a working week of only two days for the company.

EMI stayed at the forefront of the development of the Greek recording industry, building the first recording studios in 1936 and introducing magnetic tape for the first time in Greece in 1954. In 1969, EMIAL, as the company was officially named, bought out the Greek shareholder, who ran the branch for a long period and continued its operation as an entirely foreign-owned company. In 1991, EMIAL bought out the pioneer Greek company Minos Matsas and formed Minos-EMI. The company's major labels include EMI, Chrysalis, Capitol, IRS, Liberty, Blue Note and Minos.

Minos-EMI has also incorporated Columbia-EMI, which manufactures records and cassettes on behalf of several record companies and makes exports of Greek, international and Arabic repertoire. Minos-EMI claims about 31% of the Greek market today. This share is split into 65% domestic and 35% international repertoire.

In the 1960s, Helladisc emerged to challenge EMI, especially in the field of international repertoire. Helladisc is 50% owned by Siemens and 50% by Philips. This is the company which brought the Beatles' records to Greece and became later Phonogram (in 1972) and then PolyGram Greece (1982), after the merger of the Philips and Polydor labels. In 1987 Philips became the sole owner of PolyGram having bought out the shares of Siemens. Today, PolyGram is the second largest record company in Greece, holding about 20% of the market. Because of its relatively early inroad to the Greek scene, PolyGram developed a substantial repertoire of indigenous Greek music. PolyGram's major foreign labels include Polydor, RSO, Chrysalis, Philips, Vertico, Mercury, London, Decca, Archive, Deutsche Grammophon, Barclay, Olympic, Fidelity, Fontana, Melophone and Verve. Poly-Gram also has Greek Recording Industries which operates both as a pressing plant and a small recording company. Before the spread of compact discs, 50% of the PolyGram discs were produced in Greece and the rest were imported. However, since 1992 the Greek production was reduced to 30%. Another major multinational Greek Sony, was set up much later. Sony bought the Greek subsidiary of CBS in 1988. PolyGram and its subsidiary claim together 23.5% of the market, split into 50% domestic and 50% international repertoire.

The other two major multinationals operating at present in Greece, CBS and WEA, were set up much later. CBS had started its operations in 1976 producing mostly foreign recordings with only a small Greek repertoire Sony's major labels in the Greek market include Columbia (U.S.), Epic, Jet, Portrait, Aquarius, Vanguard. Sony CBS covers 10.7% of the market, including a substantial output of Greek productions. The sales split between Greek and foreign music is 50/50. Sony-CBS has increased its share of the market during the 1980s very substantially and almost doubled it in 1991. Warner is the current name of WEA records which was set up in Greece in 1980. Until 1987 WEA concentrated almost exclusively on foreign repertoire, but it gradually introduced Greek music since then. WEA has brought to the Greek market the labels Warner Bros, Electra, Atlantic, Asylum, MCA, Atco, Reprise, Sire, WEA. Like Sony-CBS, Warner-WEA has also doubled its share of the market between 1981 and 1991 to claim 10% of the Greek market now. BMG (Bertelsmann Music Group) established a subsidiary in Greece 1989, which is directly managed from the German office. The company includes both Greek and foreign productions in each repertoire with a marked emphasis on the latter. It claims 10% of the Greek market at present. A subsidiary of the British company Virgin was established in Greece in 1984. Before 1984, Virgin was represented in Greece by Poly-Gram. Virgin estimates to have captured today approximately 5% of the market, includes almost exclusively foreign music in its repertoire and has produced a small number of Greek records so far, mostly rock.

Among the Greek-owned companies, we must note Minos Matsas which recently merged a license for labels such as Disneyland, Heavy Metal records, Spring, Mausoleum and others. PolyGram's subsidiary is the oldest and most influential record-producing concern in the history of the Greek recording industry. The company's history goes back to 1925, when its founder started working for the local branch of the Odeon (German-owned) label. As already mentioned, no recording studios were available at the time in Greece, and German engineers and technicians used the prestigious and spacious hotels of the capital to cut the master discs, which were then taken back to Germany for reproduction. The founder of the company, and his subsequent heirs, had a keen ear for new, often-controversial for their time, talents, which almost invariably became great successes in the Greek musical scene. Minos Matsas was the first to realize the potential commercial value of rebetica and was the first to make Greek records of rebetica with Vamvakaris (a great artist of genre) in the 1930s. The company has handed out 12 gold awards (sales of 50,000 records) and four platinum awards (sales of 100,000 records) between 1975 and 1982. Some of its productions exceeded 250,000 copies. The Minos label concentrated on the domestic market of indigenous music and established its success upon the Greekness of the music it recorded. Moreover, since the 1970s, the company has obtained the license for RCA and part of its repertoire became foreign. Minos Matsas has brought to Greece the RCA labels RCA, Tamla, Motown, Magnet, KTL, Jive. The company's share of the market is 16%, split into 85% Greek and 15% foreign. It is estimated that Minos Matsas, prior to its merge with EMIAL, held about 50% of the market of Greek music (records and cassettes).

Music Box and Lyra, the other two entirely Greek-owned companies, were established in the early 1960s. Lyra has built up a traditional and specialised Greek repertoire, earning a reputation for producing quality music and experimenting with composers and performers who were not necessarily classified as commercial successes in the beginning. Lyra produces exclusively Greek music and claims 4% of the market today. Music Box specializes in Greek repertoire for the tourist market or for export, but a large part of its production consists of foreign records, mainly of the disco type, produced and distributed under license from foreign labels such as Pye and Pan Vox. Music Box's share of the market halved in the 1980s, dropping from 4% in 1981 to 2% in the mid-1980s and even less in the early 1990s. Music Box is a very small concern compared to the other companies mentioned above.

Among the smaller, independent companies, which are estimated to cover about 3% of the market in total, we can distinguish three main categories. First are the companies which were set up to support Greek popular music and stimulate the interest in new types of music, new composers and performers, new forms of expression. Some of these companies produced new records of older Greek music, concentrating mostly on re-issues of authentic rebetica and demotica or first issues of unknown works in the same strands. A second category concentrates on Greek rock, especially the type of rock that uses foreign lyrics, which has not at all attracted the interest of the big companies. A third category deals exclusively with laika and in particular with the so-called dog music. The records produced by these companies are of very poor quality and often are cut-to-order for individual singers, who also pay the costs, in order to be taken by the artist for sale in provincial tours of live performances.

Table 4.2 shows in detail the market shares of the major recording companies in 1981, 1985 and 1991. As shown in this table, the only companies which substantially increased their shares are Sony-CBS and Warner-WEA. Substantial falls in their shares are shown for EMI (which eventually merged with Minos Matsas) and the Greek companies Lyra and Music Box. Remarkable is the share achieved by the new company BMG in a short period of time (1987-1991).

TABLE 4.2: Market Share of Recording Companies

Companies	% 1981	% 1985	% 1991
EMIAL	16.5	13.0	
Columbia - EMI	8.9	7.8	31.0
Minos Matsas & Sons	15.6	16.0	
PolyGram Records	16.6	18.5	
Greek Phonographic			19.6
Industries (PolyGram Sub.)	4.4	4.9	
Sony-CBS	8.8	10.6	16.7
Warner-WEA	4.5	5.4	10.0
BMG	-	-	10.2
Virgin	-	5.0	5.5
Lyra	5.6	6.2	4.0
Mysic Box	3.5	1.8	
Others	15.6	10.8	3.0

Source : International Federation of Phonographic Industries (IFPI) for 1981, 1985 data, Greek Association of Phonographic Industries for 1991 data.

In total, the market is roughly divided in half between foreign and Greek music, for the sales of both records and prerecorded cassettes. However, this dichotomization of the market is a recent phenomenon, which occurred after 1976. Between 1976 and 1980, the international share of the market doubled, soaring from 25% to 50%. There is, however, a significant difference between the indigenous and foreign music shares of the market. Records and cassettes of Greek music sell very large numbers per release; while the international releases, being far more numerous than the Greek ones, sell relatively few units per item, in comparison. This is reflected in the fact that there are 2-3 gold disc awards every month for Greek records but only 5-10 such awards per year for foreign records. As a rule of thumb, record retailers consider a foreign release to be a hit if over 10,000 units are sold; but a Greek record is labelled as a success only if it goes past the 30,000 units mark, which gives it a gold disc award.

A study of new releases in 15 European countries, including Greece, carried out by PolyGram for its own product, vividly illustrates this situation. In 1982 PolyGram released in Greece 15 new LPs in its Greek repertoire and 300 LPs in its international repertoire. The proportion of total sales of these releases was 55% for Greek music and 45% for international music. Another example is provided by the Greek company Minos Matsas, which also has the RCA license. In 1985, it produced approximately 100 foreign and 50 Greek music records, which in terms of sales provided 15% and 85% of the company's income, respectively.

Recent statistics of the production and sales of recording companies illustrate the different market values of Greek and foreign music. In 1991 PolyGram brought out 28 Greek records, 110 foreign records and 36 classical music records. However, its sales were split evenly between Greek and foreign music (around 45% each) with a 10% share for classical music. In the same year BMG circulated 15 Greek records, which achieved a 30% sales share and 150 foreign, including classical music, which corresponded to 70% of the total sales. However, we must note that the foreign record market is doing much better now compared to the situation ten years back. Thus, in

1982 PolyGram released 15 new LPs in its Greek repertoire and 300 LPs in its international repertoire. The proportion of total sales of these releases was 55% for Greek music and 45% for international music.

Although these figures give a general picture of the structure of the foreign music market in relation to Greek records, there are exceptions which show the popularity foreign music may achieve on occasion or the effect of clever advertising. In 1985 a record by Dire Straits sold 70,000 copies and another hit of Tears for Fears sold 35,000. Another five or six records containing collections of big hits by several groups, advertised intensively on TV, sold about 70,000 copies each. Earlier, "The Wall," by Pink Floyd, had sold 100,000 copies. There is a tendency now for the record companies to aim to 20,000-30,000 copies as a satisfactory sales figure. Among the Greek repertoire, the highest sales figures are achieved by laika. Art-popular music is kept in general below the 50,000 mark, while Greek rock moves at the same levels as foreign music and the 10,000 mark is definitely considered a success. As a rule, star singers, coming from the strand of laika, sell large numbers even in the few occasions that they change strands and sing a different type of music (e.g. art-popular).

The current trend among multinational companies, as shown in Table 4.1, is to increase their share of the market. The main reasons why multinational companies try to increase their international repertoire are known and described accurately by Wallis and Malm (1984): the international repertoire is readily and cheaply produced locally from master discs and a large percentage of the profits can be exported as copyright dues. In Greece, the increasing costs of domestic recording are coupled with the headache of copyright, an issue that is not yet settled by legislation. However, after the 1975-1980 boom of foreign music sales, the situation seemed to have been stabilized in the 1980s, keeping the relationship between Greek and international repertoire sales roughly to 50/50. Besides, an interesting development has taken place in the 1990s: practically all multinational companies entered the production of Greek music, which sells large numbers of records per issue, while at the same time they managed to increase the sales volume per issue of foreign music. The vast majority of records sold in Greece are produced locally in three pressing plants. As mentioned earlier, one is owned by EMI and another by PolyGram. A third plant is owned by a Greek concern and was developed to break the long-standing monopoly of EMI in the business. There are also six major recording studios in the country. A small proportion of Greek records is exported, mostly aimed at the Greek communities abroad. An equal small number of records is imported. All records that are marketed in Greece are 12".

Distribution is undertaken by each of the major companies for their own product and the most usual method is direct manufacturer-to-retailer distribution through company representatives. Some of the major companies, like EMI, also distribute a number of independents. Distribution via wholesalers accounts for a smaller but appreciable part of sales volume and is particularly valuable to the smaller retailer.

Publishing in Greece is undertaken by subsidiaries of the five major recording companies only as far as their foreign music productions are concerned. The copyright interests of Greek composers and performers are looked after by two independent companies. The older of the two, AEPI, is a private company, created in the 1930s with French capital. AEPI has come under severe criticism recently, concerning its excessive profits and the exploitation of artists. The second company was created in 1978 by the Composers and Lyric-writers Union (EMSE) as a cooperative. In addition, the three pressing plants act as publishers for those artists who do not wish to subscribe either of the two publishing organizations. All publishers collect copyright dues from the record companies on the basis of record and cassette sales, but only AEPI collects neighboring rights, deriving from playing its members' music in nightclubs or other public places either live or from discs. The collection of neighboring rights, however, is a very fuzzy business and is done on a small scale.

Cassettes have been dominating the market since the early 1980s but they are themselves dominated by piracy. There are four cassette/cartridge manufacturers in Greece, who produce 4.5 million blank cassettes out of the 12.0 million units that come on to the market. The remaining 7.5 million units are imported. A large part of Greek cassette production supplies the Arab marketplace. EMI alone in 1982 supplied 95% of the legitimate Arab cassette market, although this in itself is only a tiny proportion of the total Arab market, because the bulk is pirated product. However, exports to Arab countries have fallen drastically since 1985. Regarding the domestic market, cassettes have risen from one-third in 1981 to one-half in 1985 of all legitimately produced records; but if the volume of pirated cassettes is taken into account, it is estimated that cassettes account for 80% of all sales and records for only 20% (*Billboard*, November 1983).

However, the picture was changed drastically in the 1990s with the introduction of the compact disc. In 1990, compact discs sold in Greece accounted for only 7.3% of the total recorded music volume, against 58% for records and 34.3% for cassettes. In 1991 the share of compact discs rose to nearly 21% at the expense mostly of cassettes, whose share fell to 25%. Table 4.3 shows the evolution of sales between 1981 and 1991.

TABLE 4.3 : Sales of Records, Prerecorded Cassettes (Legitimate) and Compact Discs

Year	Records		Cassettes		CDs	
	No.	%	No.	%	No.	%
1981	3,498,000	66.5	2,772,000	33.5	-	-
1985	5,653,000	50.0	5,435,000	50.0	-	-
1990	4,985,000	58.4	2,929,000	34.3	629	7.3
1991	4,657,000	54.3	2,149,000	25.0	1,777,000	20.7

Source: IFPI. London and Athens branches.

Prices of records and tapes are relatively high. The average price for an LP or prerecorded cassette is Drs 3,000 ($12). Compact discs are far more expensive, costing 5,000 Drs on average ($20). The breakdown of the cost of a phonogram is shown in Table 4.4.

TABLE 4.4 : Breakdown of Recording Costs

Cost Analysis	%
Cost of manufacture	3.0
Cost of cover	8.0
Copyright royalties for author/composer	5.0
Royalties for artist/conductor	7.5
Cost of musicians, orchestra, recording changes	9.5
Profit for record company	27.0
Profit for dealer	35.0

Source: Greek Association of Phonographic Industries.

Some 0.1% of the total monthly expenditure of the average Greek family goes for records and tapes, but this is rising. For Greek standards the cost of legitimate recordings is high and is increasing constantly following a 20% annual rate of inflation. Consequently, piracy had an ideal ground to develop, given also the lack of prohibitive legislation.

Piracy became a major problem for the recording industry in Greece during the 1980s. Cassette piracy reached enormous proportions in 1982: out of an estimated 10 million cassettes sold, 8.5 million (85%) were pirated, and only 1.5 million (15%) were legitimately produced. The recording companies started a long and intensive campaign against piracy. In 1982 they established a vigilante force which raided shops suspected of selling pirated cassettes and confiscated their goods and equipment. They were also helped by a number of court decisions which equated piracy to forgery and fraud and imposed sentences up to six and a half years in prison to retailers of pirated products. One year later, in 1983, all companies reported increased sales of prerecorded cassettes up to 35%. In 1984, pirated cassettes accounted for 64% according to IFPI. This figure, however, has risen again in the 1990s to the region of 80-85%.

Advertisement of new discs is undertaken through the media (radio, TV, periodicals) by conventional methods, or via video clips shown on television. Most conventional advertising concerns albums, new singers or new releases of star singers of laika. Music video clips, which in 1981 were considered by many companies as a potentially successful new line, have proved very unpopular so far. The record companies believe that the demand for video clips, especially from the international repertoire, is covered by television through its weekly foreign pop shows.

BROADCASTING AND POPULAR MUSIC

Broadcasting in Greece is undertaken by the public broadcasting organization Hellenic Radio-Television and a host of private organizations which operate a large number of radio and television stations. Until 1987, all broadcasting in Greece was dominated by the government-controlled public broadcasting organization, with only a few pirate radio stations operating in Athens or in the regions for limited periods of time. In May 1987, the municipality of Athens started its own radio station, Athens 9.84, having previously failed to obtain a legal license for it. The municipal radio of Athens marked a new era in broadcasting of quality and diversity unknown until then because it ended the monopoly of Hellenic Radio-Television, forced the legitimization of private broadcasting and literally opened the air waves to all interests, talents and concerns. By the end of the 1980s, Greece had experienced the snowball effect in broadcasting, as hundreds of radio stations mushroomed all around the country.

The Hellenic (public) Radio Company (ERA) operates four stations, which are meant to reach all Greek regions. Besides ERA, there are about 65 private radio stations in the Athens area alone, twelve of which are the most popular (Sky, Antenna, Flash, Ellada FM, Klik FM, Galaxy, Pop FM, Geronimo Groovy, Melodia, Rock FM, Athens 9.84, Kiss FM). Most of these stations broadcast to the regions, too, either directly or via local stations. An undefinable number of local stations operate in all towns and cities around the country. Many local authorities have also set up their own radio stations either separately or in groups. A central feature of radio broadcasting after 1987 is specialization of radio stations. A few stations have kept the all-round style of the pre-1987 days, placing an emphasis on news and current affairs. Many stations broadcast exclusively music and a few are devoted mostly to sport.

Following the breakup of the monopoly of state-controlled broadcasting, the national (public) radio stations lost a large part of their influence in favor of local (independent-private) stations. In the Athens area, the three ERA stations occupy positions below the fifteenth, regarding audience ratings (scoring 2.0%, 1.2% and 1.1% respectively) and the fourth station is placed below the thirtieth position. The two top positions are occupied by a station devoted mostly to news and current affairs (Sky with 42%) and a mixed-program station with emphasis on entertainment (Antenna with 19%), followed by two rock music stations (Klik FM with 10% and Geronimo Groovy with 9%) which appeal mainly to the young. The relative advantage of ERA is that it operates a national network and can therefore bring its programs to an audience far wider than that of the local stations. Among the public radio stations, ERA-1 has adopted an educational-informative profile, dividing its program between news/current affairs/documentaries and music by a proportion of 60 to 40. The music program of the station is evenly divided between all types of Greek music and a large variety of the international repertoire.

ERA-2 places emphasis on entertainment, devoting 70% of its airtime to music. The rest is evenly divided between prose and news/current affairs. The station gives priority to Greek music, both contemporary and older (70% of music broadcasts) and also devotes some time to foreign music for young people, mostly of the pop and rock type, both older and contemporary (30% of music broadcasts). ERA-2 has a policy to promote the contemporary Greek song and since 1991 has organized a yearly "Week of Greek Song" which tries to present via interviews and reviews the state of the art of Greek popular music. ERA-2 is the only radio station in the Balkans which has established zoning of music, including specialist zones for laika and light songs as well as zones for foreign pop.

ERA-3 broadcasts mostly classical music. It devotes 90% of its airtime to music and the rest to educational or informational programs about music or the fine arts. Two-thirds of music programs consist of classical music and one-third of traditional music from all over the world, including traditional Greek music. Selected jazz programs are also included.

ERA-4 (or ERA-sport as it has been recently renamed) places emphasis on entertainment and sports. A large part of its program (62%) consists of music, another 30% is devoted to information (mostly about sport) and a small part (8%) is prose. The main part of its music program (75%) is devoted to Greek music and in particular to the new Greek song, including largely new releases. The rest is devoted to foreign pop and rock hits and new releases.

ERA-1, 2 and 3 transmit in medium waves via a 150 KW transmitter and in FM via 17 FM-centres around Greece, ranging from 3 to 10 KW each. ERA-1 also borrows the medium waves of the "Voice of America," which operates in the north of Greece and in the Aegean via two 500 KW transmitters, for four and a quarter hours every day. Regional radio stations operate under a network system, transmitting the programs of central stations. In addition, regional stations produce on average six hours of local programs every day. Apart from three powerful transmitters of 100-150 KW, situated in the north and south of Greece, the remaining stations use transmitters of 1-5 KW. ERA-Sport transmits also in medium waves via a national network of transmitters ranging from 1 to 200 KW and has installed a powerful FM transmitter of 100 KW in Athens. The station is very poor in terms of facilities. ERA-Sport used to be the official armed forces radio station until 1982, and although it has completely changed its profile since the changeover to national radio, it still has buildings and equipment that remind one of a military camp. Its integration to ERA was expected to upgrade its profile.

ERA stations can be received almost everywhere in Greece, although not always clearly, either in medium waves or FM. When ERA-1 is networked on the "Voice of America," it can be received clearly in Africa or the Soviet Union and most of this time is given to news. The current policy of the government is to help the regional stations to develop and acquire better facilities (studios, cameras, etc.). The facilities of the central stations are satisfactory and they have recently been modernized to a large extent.

Advertizing of recording companies on the public radio stations is forbidden. The companies send their new productions to the stations and it is up to the program makers to decide which songs will be broadcast. However, until 1981, one public radio station was to a large extent devoted to advertising of the record companies.

The predecessor of ERA-2 (called Radio 2 at the time) offered 80 hours per week to record companies, which could buy several half-hour slots to broadcast the music they wished to promote. This produced a revenue of $2 million for Radio-Television, in return for handing over total control of Radio 2 programming to the record companies. As expected, the more wealthy of the companies dominated Radio 2, promoting their foreign repertoire and Greek laika, mostly of the dog music type.

After the change of government, following the general election of 1981, the wholesale music advertising system of Radio 2 was stopped and the station started normal operation on the basis of a program designed and run in the same way as the other two stations of the network. The impact this change had on the sales of foreign music was dramatic. Sales dropped overnight to minimum levels and most of the record companies panicked; but it took them only a year and a carefully designed advertising campaign, through other media, to recover their old sales levels. This campaign consisted of TV advertising, promotions through discos, concerts and rock clubs. Advertising in pirate stations was also used, but on a more limited scale. Unfortunately, the new system encouraged corruption in broadcasters, especially during the initial period, when some cases even reached the courts.

Following the advent of independent, mostly private, broadcasting and the dramatic fall in audience ratings of the public stations, this problem lost its significance. The major record companies prefer now to advertise their productions via video clips shown on television, or by commercials on the radio. At present there is no official system in Greece that defines the Top 10 of either the Greek or the international repertoire. *Pop and Rock*, a monthly review, publishes a list of top-selling records in Athens on the basis of information provided by selected record shops. However, the reliability of these lists is doubted by both the broadcasting organizations and the record companies. The current Top 10 lists of the U.K. and U.S. markets are regularly presented on the radio.

Since the mid-1980s, the profile of the radio stations and their contribution to the development of contemporary Greek music has been an ongoing discussion theme in the daily and specialised (music) press. In May 1986, the periodical review *Defi* devoted an issue to the "Greek Song on State Radio" which started an open discussion on this really controversial topic. Since 1981 the main issues concern the "elitism" of the radio in its treatment of popular music and the role it plays in promoting foreign music. The policy of ERA-1 has been clearly stated since the change of government in 1981. As far as Greek music is concerned, the emphasis has been put on "quality," which in practice meant that large proportions of airtime were given to the art-popular strand, older and new, while laika was almost excluded from broadcasting despite its popularity.

Regarding foreign music, especially of the modern pop and rock type, there was initially a policy to minimise its broadcasting. However, gradually foreign music came back on the radio in increasing proportions every year. This was, in a way, inevitable, as more and more foreign records were released by the recording industry and more demand for this music became evident among the audience and especially the young. It is indicative of the attitude prevailing in the mid-1980s among the staff of the public broadcasting organization that the controller of one of the stations declared in a publisher interview: "If foreign music programs attract large audiences, that's the audiences' fault." The picture changed drastically after the introduction of independent/private broadcasting. Public radio had been criticized as being out of touch with popular culture, imposing a strict censorship on the music strands not approved by its top executives.

It is characteristic that none of the public radio stations ever used audience research data. The private stations have to use such data in order to seek their revenue and secure their viability. Inevitably the private stations have become very sensitive to audience taste and preference, shaping their music programs accordingly. However, the national policy still supports Greek music by enforcing its broadcasting, through the inclusion of such an obligation to the license of the private stations. At present, in the wider Athens area, seven of the major private stations broadcast exclusively music, intersected only by very brief news bulletins. Among these, two broadcast exclusively Greek music, while the remaining five broadcast mainly foreign pop and rock. Five more major independent stations broadcast a mixed program of music and news/current affairs, in which the Greek songs prevail.

Music does not feature systematically on television and does not occupy significant slots in most channels. As on the radio, there are both public and private television channels. The state-run Hellenic Television operates three channels, two of which are based in Athens and one in Salonika. All three channels are visible throughout Greece. There are also seven major private channels which broadcast from Athens and can be seen in some regions too, as well as a large number of smaller Athens channels and regional channels with a limited radius of broadcasting. Moreover, satellite TV is accessible to most homes, allowing good reception of the main European channels and CNN.

Among the major Athens-based channels, two broadcast music on a daily basis. The first, Geronimo Groovy TV, broadcasts foreign music on a 24-hour basis, in a background of video clips. The second, Seven X, broadcasts foreign music for 11 hours every day (from 8:00 p.m. to 7:00 am.) through a satellite connection with the French channel MCM, including a half-hour interval of Greek music. An additional 6-16% of its program consists also of music. Both channels address the 18-25 age group. The two most popular TV channels (Mega and Antenna, with 42% and 38% audience ratings, respectively) devote very little of their time to music. Mega devotes four hours per week on regular slots, divided 50/50 between Greek and foreign music; Antenna devotes only two regular slots of one hour each per week, both to foreign music. The three national (public) channels (ET-1, 2, 3) broadcast exclusively Greek music on a regular basis and are the only channels to include the traditional type (demotica). ET-1 presents daily programs which account for 3-8% of its airtime; ET-2 includes ad hoc music programs which cover 6% of its airtime; and ET-3 devotes 5-10% of its daily program to the Greek song.

Overall, in its diversity, the broadcasting of music in the 1990s reflects closely enough the market of the recording industry. The policy of the state-controlled media still favors Greek music, both on radio and television, but it has been forced to adapt to the tastes of the audience to a large extent since 1987. Private broadcasting, on the other hand, responds more closely to the market forces by its diversity and by promoting specialisation of its products. Thus, the 1990s saw the emergence of radio and television stations which cater exclusively for the musical tastes of the young by offering endless hours of international pop. However, the most popular radio stations are dominated by Greek music, reflecting the preferences of the majority of the audience. The only significant difference in the makeup of the music broadcasts before and after the advent of private broadcasting concerns the promotion of the different strands within the popular Greek song. Before 1987, the prevailing of an elitism which excluded laika set the scene of broadcasting; after 1987, elitism has been replaced by the domination of the market forces. In the 1990s the question of the palpable demand has emerged among the dozens of radio and television channels.

OTHER MEANS OF POPULAR MUSIC DISSEMINATION

Popular music is also disseminated through nightclubs, discos, music bars and restaurants, festivals and concerts. Nightclubs are crucial for the dissemination of laika, as already has been mentioned, with reference to dog music in particular. Music bars and concerts are important for Greek rock and the new Greek song. A large number of concerts take place all the year round, with a special peak in the summer when various festivals are organized across Greece. Pop concerts, especially of visiting foreign groups, attract huge numbers, but so do concerts of the popular star singers of laika. There is no government policy for the promotion and support of popular music of one kind or another. The Secretariat of Youth has started a small-scale effort in 1984 to encourage Greek rock and to give opportunities to young people who make up the rock groups to play their music in front of an audience. The Secretariat also encouraged setting up a musicians cooperative, called Mousinca. The cooperative consists of four rock groups at present, based in a music bar. This gave the opportunity to 90 new groups to play their music, within the period of three months. The Secretariat of Youth also organized a rock festival called "Sounds of Winter," which gave the opportunity to 20 groups to present their music, and supports a number or rock concerts in provincial towns. In the past, competitions were held once a year, supported usually by the national broadcasting organization. These competitions gave the opportunity to new talent to come to the fore, helping greatly the development of popular music. Many of the best composers of the art-popular movement of the 1960s had become known through such competitions. This practice, however, has greatly declined in recent years, and although a government-sponsored competition still takes place once a year in Salonika, participation is far from representative of the present music strands and the results are generally poor.

CONCLUDING REMARKS

To understand the components of contemporary popular music in Greece, it is essential to follow the historical development of Greek music, understand the social and political conditions which formed its environment and take account of the role of broadcasting and the recording industry in promoting mainstream and commercial music. This chapter has tried to give an outline of these components. It has also hinted on the main dilemmas that have determined the development of popular music: The West-East dilemma, concerning foreign influences on Greek music; the dilemma of authenticity and aesthetics, which mainly presented itself as a gap between crude working class music and refined elite music; the dilemma of whether radio should reflect the taste and culture of the majority or should endeavour to set high standards of musical quality and educate people according to these standards; the dilemma of no consistent government policy vis-a-vis a transactional recording industry which imposes its own policy through the market or other less direct or transparent methods. These dilemmas accompanied the development of popular music in Greece since the 1930s, and reflected a diversity that always characterised this development and explained, to a certain extent, its peaks and troughs. But what is the future of popular music now? Are we in front of a peak or a trough? The pessimists declare that there is a crisis in Greek music today, reflected in its triviality and lack of musical value. The pragmatists claim that music reflects its time and this is an era of videos, fast motorcycles and snapshot human relationships which have made their mark on how people choose to express themselves. The optimists believe that Greek music has always shown the strength to deal with contrasts and to express social change and crises through pluralism and diversification.

BIBLIOGRAPHY

Annoyiannakis, F."About Rebetica," *Art Review* (Epitheorisi Technis), July 1961.

Defi, "The Greek Song on State Radio" (special issue), Vol. II, No 3-4, edited by S. Elleniadis, May 1980.

Eleftherotypia (daily newspaper), 20-23 January 1986. "The New Greek Song," a research by F. Apergis.

Holst, G. (1977). *The Road to Rebetica*, Athens: Denise Harvey.

Mylonas, K. (1985). *The History of Greek Song*, Vol. I and II. Athens: Kedros.

Papageorgiou, F. et al. (1993a). "Culture and Leisure Needs in Korydallos." Athens: PRISMA.

Papageorgiou, F. et al. (1993b). "Culture and Leisure Needs in Helioupolis." Athens: PRISMA.

Papageorgiou, F. et al. (1993c). "Employment and Free Time in Sitia." Athens: PRISMA.

Papageorgiou, F. et al. (1993d). "An Exploration of Leisure Time Needs in Argyroupolis." Athens: PRISMA.

Vournas T. (1961). "Contemporary Laika Songs," *Art Review* (Epitheorisi Technis).

Wallis R. and Malm, K. (1984). *"Big Sounds from Small People: The Music Industry in Small Countries."* London: Constable.

Other Sources of Information

A large amount of the information contained in this chapter has been obtained or verified through a number of interviews conducted by the author. The persons interviewed include: Executives of ERA-1, ERA-2, ERA-3 and ERA-Sport; executives of independent stations : Sky, Antenna, KLIK, Geronimo Groovy; executives of Poly-

Gram, Minos-EMI, Sony, BMG, Virgin, Warner; an executive of IFPI, London; the President of the Greek Group of IFPI; a member of the board of the Greek Association of Recording Companies; two senior members of staff of the Secretariat of Youth, with responsibility for music promotion; a journalist and writer of Greek popular music.

CHAPTER 5

A BRIEF HISTORY OF MUSIC PRODUCTION IN HAWAII

Elizabeth B. Buck

INTRODUCTION

Eighteenth-century European imperialism, nineteenth-century American colonialism and twentieth-century postindustrial political and cultural economies have reshaped the sounds, production and meanings of Hawaiian music.

Throughout Hawaii's history, music has been an important part of social, economic and political social structures. Prior to the fateful arrival of Captain James Cook in 1778, chant and *hula* were the most important forms of social representation and expression. The poetry of the chants and the accompanying dance of the hula constituted the ideological nucleus of a very hierarchically organized society. Their cosmological and genealogical accounts of Hawaiians and their history celebrated and legitimized the political-religious power of the highest ruling *ali'i* (chiefs) and the social relationships among the ruling chiefs and their families, lesser *ali'i,* the priesthoods, and the *maka'ainana* or commoners.

The discourse of the early explorers such as Captains Cook and Vancouver described Hawaiian chant and *hula* as exotic practices of an exotic Pacific culture. Their descriptions, both in written and painted renditions, were avidly consumed by Europeans at home. In the 1820s, a few decades after Kamehamela I had unified the islands and the traditional practices of Hawaiian religious and political structures had been undercut both by Kamehamela's restructuring and by Western influences, American missionaries established church missions throughout the islands. Within a decade they had become influential with the ruling Hawaiian *ali'i*. Practicing and preaching a particularly harsh and ascetic form of Calvinistic theology, the missionaries saw chant, and particularly *hula*--with its obvious celebration of sexuality--as pagan licentiousness to be contained and eliminated.

Through the first half of the 1800s, as the Hawaiian social structure was increasingly eroded by Western and, more particularly, by American-influenced structures and forces of power, religion and rationality, traditional chant and *hula* lost much of their religious and political meaning. By the late 1800s, only a hundred years after Cook's landing, the Hawaiian social structure had been ruptured and reformed to such an extent that chant and *hula* existed only on the margins of island society, primarily in rural areas of Oahu and the neighboring islands. When the Hawaiian monarchy was overthrown in 1893 and a territorial government was set up by the United States, power was formally wrested from Hawaiian hands.

Throughout the 1900s Hawaiian music was transformed into cultural commodities that could be marketed to and consumed by mass audiences. The combined forces of radio, recording technologies and tourism have continued to change the forms, production and meanings of Hawaiian music.

Still Hawaiian music is for many Hawaiians the most vital element of their culture. Since the "cultural renaissance" of the 1970s, Hawaiians have reappropriated all styles of Hawaiian music as sources and markers of their identity as a people. Ancient *hula* and chant are avidly studied and performed, and the beautiful *hula* of the King Kalakaua period are still danced. Even some of the *hapa-haole* music of the Territorial Period (1898 to 1959) has been incorporated into the body of "traditional" Hawaiian music, played at local *luaus* and parties. Equally important, contemporary Hawaiian musicians are composing songs that combine various styles of popular music, including pop, rock and reggae, with Hawaiian words, themes and instrumentation. Today the local music industry comprises all of the people, organizations and communication channels that are involved in producing and selling music, including local composers and performers; record producers, music publishers, distributors, retailers and promoters; radio and television broadcasters; music critics; hotels and nightclubs that are the main commercial venues for music; as well as music consumers, both tourists and local residents. The local music industry, including Hawaiian music performance and production, functions within the broader context of the national and international music industries. These large entertainment industries set professional norms and the legal and commercial frameworks within which the local industry operates. Therefore, the practices of music production as well as the music produced by the U.S national and the larger international industries are major influences on local musicians, producers and music consumers.

The local music industry is organized to exploit two primary markets: the more than 6 million tourists that come to Hawaii each year, and the permanent residents of the state, which now number over 1 million. The majority of both markets have only limited interest in and appreciation of locally produced music, including Hawaiian music. A relatively small proportion of local residents are *active* consumers of locally produced music of any kind; most of their music money is spent on recordings produced and distributed by the mainland music industry or on live performances of touring musicians. A larger proportion of local residents are *passive* consumers of Hawaiian music, watching the occasional Hawaiian music program on television, or tuning in from time to time to KCCN, the all-

Hawaiian music station, or occasionally buying a locally produced cassette or disc.[1]

THE INTERTEXTUALITY OF CONTEMPORARY
HAWAIIAN MUSIC

The total body of Hawaiian music is an intertext of traditional and modern musics (*hula* and chant, hymns, jazz, rock 'n' roll, reggae); of different cultural expressions and experiences (Hawaiian, Western, Asian and other cultural regions of the world); of myths about Hawaii (Hawaiian and ad-agency created); of various economic motivations and constraints; and of contending political ideologies (ancient Hawaiian, modern global capitalism, and Hawaiian political consciousness).

In a Barthean sense, Hawaiian music is an intertext woven out of the past and the present (Barthes, 1981). It is a continuous production of significance where history, social context, composers and performers, audiences and consumers create and recreate meaning through musical forms and practices (Barthes, 1981). As successive social structures have come and gone in the islands (Hawaiian hierarchical, American colonial and neo-colonial, tourist-dominated postindustrial), Hawaiian music has changed its instrumentation, style and content. More important, it has changed in its definitions of what is Hawaiian music and who performs it, and in its ideological tasks and motivations.

However, to speak of the Hawaiian music as intertextual is not to see that production as resulting from a plurality of equal forces and influences. Some of the threads in the woven text of Hawaiian music have been severed; other threads are discontinuous, reappearing in muted or transformed styles. Throughout the history of this production of forms and meanings, contending forces of power have shaped the musics of the islands.

This intertext of contemporary Hawaiian music is the result of different types of cultural interaction. Wallis and Malm's (1984) categories of cultural exchange, cultural domination and cultural imperialism are evident in the musical fabric of the islands.

Cultural exchange, where cultures interact and exchange cultural styles and forms of expression on more or less equal terms, is seen in the Hawaiians' adoption, adaptation and incorporation of the guitar and the *ukulele* into Hawaiian music. The guitar was introduced by cowboys who came in the 1800s from Mexico and California. Hawaiians developed their own unique style of guitar playing, *ki ho'alu* or "slack key." The *ukulele* was brought to the islands by the Portuguese in the 1870s, and it also became an integral part of Hawaiian music (Kanehele, 1979). Both instruments were creatively integrated into the production of Hawaiian music. Hawaii, in turn, contributed the steel guitar, a mechanical modification of the guitar, to American country and western music.

The second type of cultural interaction, *cultural domination,* occurs when a more powerful culture is more or less systematically imposed on another culture. During the 1800s, cultural domination was evident in the missionaries' heavy-handed prohibition of *hula* and their enthusiastic instruction in hymn singing--a new technology of expression that the Hawaiians readily embraced, along with literacy. Later American settlers tried to Westernize and Americanize the by then diverse population of the islands, partly by establishing cultural organizations and events such as music schools, opera, choral singing and music clubs.

The third pattern of cultural interaction is *cultural imperialism*. This takes place when domination is accompanied by the transfer of money and/or resources from the dominated to the dominating culture. This was most evident in the economic practices of mainland record companies in appropriating and marketing Hawaiian music, or what was passed off as Hawaiian music, to mainland music markets. Very little of that money went to local musicians and composers. In contemporary music production, the situation is more complex because of the extensive interchange of musical styles, codes and forms from all over the world, as well as the rapid changes taking place in the technologies of audio and video reproduction (Robinson et al, 1991).

TOURISM AND HAWAIIAN MUSIC

Tourism has been an important economic force in the islands since the 1920s. With statehood in 1959 and the beginning of large-scale tourism in the early 1960s, tourism became the major industry of the islands. In 1964 the visitor count was 564,000; in 1967, 1.1 million; in 1982, 4.2 million; and in 1990, 6.9 million. Tourism accounts for 40 percent of Hawaii's gross state product (Otaguro, 1991).

Tourism has played a major role in redefining Hawaiian values and practices. The perceptions that outsiders have of Hawaiians, and to some extent the self-perceptions that Hawaiian have of themselves, have been affected by stereotypes created by the tourist industry and further disseminated by advertising and recording media throughout the world. These stereotypes are used to promote Hawaii as a place peopled by beautiful, exotic *hula* maidens, *ukulele*-strumming musicians, friendly beach boys, funny tour guides and happy-go-lucky Hawaiians sleeping under coconut palms or riding surf boards (Brown, 1982).

During the territorial period, tourists came by boat and stayed in a few big hotels such as the Royal Hawaiian and the Moana. These hotels had their big bands, such as the Royal Hawaiians and the Moana Orchestra which played swing music along with *hapa-haole* music,[2] such as "Sweet Leilani", "My Little Grass Shack", and "Hula Blues."

In the 1960s, tourism became big business. Now, tourists, primarily from the U.S. mainland and Japan, come in large tour groups. To entertain them, Hawaiian music and dance, supplemented by other Polynesian music and dance, is packaged into shows prebooked by tour agents back home or by local agents in local lobbies. These big tourist shows have star entertainers like Don Ho, Al Harrington and Danny Kaleikini, or feature luau-type shows. These shows present a commercial pastiche of Pacific music and entertainment--a little bit of Hawaiian *hula* and singing, along with Samoan knife and slap dances, Tahitian shimmies, Maori poi-ball twirling and Fijian fire dances. Between numbers, the emcee tells "visitor" jokes, announces anniversaries of those present and asks where tour groups are from. These almost-nightly shows are expensive, costing approximately $55, more or less, for a dinner-and-show package or $25 for a cocktails-only show.

The most enduring model of how Hawaiian music is exploited for commercial purposes is the Kodak *Hula* Show. It has been a constant of Waikiki tourism-oriented entertainment for more than 50 years. The show, staged outdoors in a public park at the edge of Waikiki, constitutes for most tourists their only exposure to Hawaiian culture and history. It is heavy with tourist mythology, mystifying and obscuring the history of Hawaii and distorting Hawaiian culture.

Commercial forces dominate the music of Waikiki and other tourist areas in the islands. One of the ironies of the Hawaiian music scene is that with a few exceptions (for instance, Alfred Apaka in the 1950s and the Brothers Cazimero in the 1980s and 1990s), the best Hawaiian musicians--those respected by local lovers of Hawaiian music--are the ones least likely to make it or want to make it in Waikiki. When they do perform there, it is often in small lounges, or as background music for dining or during the day when hotels hire "old time" Hawaiian musical groups to provide Hawaiian atmosphere. In short, the value of music in Waikiki is based either on its ability to sell itself directly to tourists (what they will pay to go to) or, indirectly, to give the tourist experience a semblance of contact with authentic Hawaiian culture.

A type of symbiotic relationship exists between tourism and local music, with tourism providing venues and jobs for local musicians and a market for the local recording industry. In turn, music provides a cultural resource that enhances the lure of Hawaii as a tourist destination and entertains tourists once they're in Hawaii. Although the relationship of tourism and music is symbiotic, power resides with the tourist industry.

The unequal relationship that exists between those who own and manage the hotels in Waikiki and local musicians who work there is a function of the social and economic relationships that characterize Hawaiian tourism. While the jobs of entertainers are less menial than those held by most tourist-industry workers, they are poorly compensated and even more insecure. With the exception of big-name entertainers, it is impossible for most musicians to make enough money to adequately support a family in Hawaii. Even with a union, musicians are in a no-win situation: if the musicians' union pushes salary scales higher than the hotels are willing to pay, jobs are eliminated or performances are cut back, with the results that more musicians join the ranks of the unemployed or underemployed. Because entertainment cutback and start-up costs for hotels are minimal, entertainers have little bargaining leverage. In other words, the entertainment demands of the tourist industry are based on the ups and downs of the numbers of tourists coming to Hawaii, but the supply of musicians is more or less static. As a result, most local musicians depend on other jobs for their main source of income.

Fortunately, not all live Hawaiian music is devoted to entertaining tourists. There are a few places where the best of contemporary Hawaiian music is offered to appreciative local audiences, Hawaiian and non-Hawaiian. Throughout the year there are also events (fund-raisers, family *luaus,* special gatherings, songfests, chant and *hula* competitions) where the very best Hawaiian musicians, singers and dancers (some of the same ones who entertain in Waikiki) perform for people who love Hawaiian music in all its now-existing forms.

THE MUSIC INDUSTRY

Most of the popular music heard in Hawaii is produced, distributed and promoted by the large national and international music industries. With the exception of a relatively small section devoted to Hawaiian music, the bins and racks of local retailers are stocked pretty much like music stores on the mainland. Only one local radio station devotes itself to Hawaiian music; other local radio stations offer the same formats as mainland stations. The major rock acts come regularly to Honolulu. Hawaii, however, is different from the rest of the United States in that it has maintained and continues to fashion a musical tradition and style of its own, and it has a relatively independent local music industry.

The recording industry in Hawaii goes back to the early 1900s when, following annexation, Americans became interested in anything Hawaiian. Record-making started in Hawaii in 1905 with the arrival of the Victor Talking Machine Company (Hopkins, 1979). In one year Victor recorded and released 53 records. Five years later, Columbia began to record Hawaiian music--both companies recording at this time primarily for the local market. A Hawaiian music craze swept the mainland (as well as much of Europe) as a result of the appearance of Hawaiian musicians at the Panama-Pacific International Exhibition in 1915 in San Francisco and the great hit of Broadway in the 1920s, *Bird of Paradise. Hula* dancers were regular features in mainland floor shows and on vaudeville.

The pace of recording was intense as record companies tried to capitalize on the international fad for Hawaiian music. Composers and performers who had never even been to the islands began writing, performing and recording "Hawaiian music." Many of Hawaii's musicians also performed on the mainland during this era.

The first locally owned recording company began in 1936 as part of the operations of KGU, the first local radio station, which was owned by the Honolulu *Advertiser*. At first records were just transcriptions of live radio programs for use by other NBC affiliates. In time, however, Hawaiian Transcription Productions began to release singles for the Hawaiian market--residents and tourists. The first local record company to dominate the local market was Bell Records which began in 1944. Bell produced the first solo recordings of Alfred Apaka, Andy Cummings and Gabby Pahinui. At the end of the 1940s, Bill Fredlund, the owner of Bell, claimed he was selling "tens of thousands of 78-rpm records each month, most of them in Hawaii" (Hopkins, 1979, 328). When Bell sold out, 49th State Records, owned by George Ching, a Honolulu record store owner, took over as the largest local record producer, putting out a large number of Hawaiian records, mostly *hapa haole* hula music for the tourist market. Most of the music of 49th State Records has been rerecorded on long-playing discs and is still available. In the 1950s several new local labels were started: Waikiki Records, Tradewind Records (which stressed "authenticity" and released albums of *ukulele* and slack key guitar music), Hula Records (also with a more traditional orientation), and Music of Polynesia, the company of Jack de Mello which, more than the other local record companies, geared its music to the tourist market. Performers like Don Ho and Kui Lee were popular nationally and internationally.

During the 1960s rock and roll dominated popular music in Hawaii as it did everywhere. By 1969 the U.S. recording industry's interest in Hawaiian music had declined to the point where Decca and Capitol, the two largest national producers of Hawaiian recordings, dropped the Hawaiian category completely ("Music Seen as Potential", 1972). Even the local record companies had little motivation to record since the market for Hawaiian music seemed to be limited to tourists and old-timers--both groups happy with rereleases of already-recorded music. Still, Hawaiian musicians like Marlene Sai and Kahauanu Lake continued to record Hawaiian music.

However, with the political and cultural revitalization of Hawaii in the 1970s, the local recording industry took off. Local musicians began performing in small clubs and restaurants, at open-air concerts, at protest rallies, and at local luaus and fund-raisers. Many new local recording companies were started, such as Lehua, Makaha, Sounds of Hawaii, Poki Records, Pumehana, Mountain Apple, Seabird Sound, Paradise Records and Panini. It was the latter which "rediscovered" Gabby Pahinui, mentor and inspiration for many young local musicians who were rediscovering the slack key guitar. Just as on the mainland, many contemporary musicians started their own labels so that they could have more control over the production of their music and also receive more of the proceeds. However, with only a few notable exceptions (e.g., Peter Moon), the artist-controlled labels have not been as successful as the larger record companies, primarily because they lack the capital and the means to promote and distribute their recordings.

During the 1970s the production and sale of local recordings were very strong, with some albums selling 50,000 to 100,000 units, where previously 5,000 or even 3,000 was considered a successful release. Contemporary musicians like Peter Moon, the Brothers Cazimero, Palani Vaughan, the Beamers, the Pahinui family, Olomana, and Cecillio and Kapono (C&K), who created a new sound that combined folk, rock and Hawaiian music with added amplification and more instruments were extremely popular as concert performers and as recording artists. Some, like Gabby Pahinui and C&K were picked up by mainland recording companies. Whereas only five Hawaiian albums were released in 1975; in 1977, 53 were released (*Na Hoku Hanohano*, 1987).

In 1978 the local music industry started its own association called *Na Hoku Hanohano* (The Stars of Distinction). It gives annual music awards in various categories including contemporary Hawaiian Album, Haku Mele (Hawaiian Language Song or Chant), Traditional Hawaiian Album, Contemporary Albums, and Album of the Year as well as recognising best male and female vocalists, liner notes, engineering, graphics and so on. 1978 marked the peak of recording activity: 110 albums were released--an average of eight to ten recordings a month (including some singles). An estimated total of 250,000 units were sold, generating a revenue of from $1 million to $6 million for the local industry.[3] "Honolulu City Lights" by the Beamer Brothers sold more than 50,000 copies in its first year alone. Locally produced records accounted for about 20% of total record sales in the 1970s with about half bought by tourists (*Hailono Mele*, 1980; "Multi-million Dollar Business," 1979.

Through the 1980s the local recording industry cooled off, with the number of albums dropping to 59 in 1979, 51 albums in 1981, 37 albums in 1982, 41 albums in 1983, and 53 albums in 1984 (*Na Hoku Hanohano*, 1987). Recording activity appears to have remained at approximately 35 to 45 albums per year through the 1980s and into the early 1990s. With a tighter local market for locally-produced music, local releases have to compete with recordings produced on the mainland, which means matching the technical and professional quality of the large record companies. The necessity for high-quality recordings has increased the cost of production for local musicians. The tighter music market has also shaped the style of music produced, with musicians selecting music for their albums that will attract the widest possible market of local and tourist buyers.

For instance, the recent albums of Peter Moon, one of the most successful of the local artists not working in Waikiki, offers a musical mix that will have a wide appeal: jazz, reggae, restylizations of old favorites, and several new songs in Hawaiian and/or about Hawaiian themes by local composers. Moon and his band have recorded an album a year for the last 11 years under his own label, Kanikapila Records. According to Moon, strictly ethnic Hawaiian music doesn't reach a broad enough market to sell well anymore. He and his band record primarily to enhance their local audiences because it is from performing on weekends on Oahu and the neighboring islands, as well as giving two or three major concerts a year, that they generate most of their music income (Jacobs, 1990). The Brothers Cazimero are perhaps the only Hawaiian music entertainers that combine Waikiki commercial success with a strong local following. This they do through their annual recordings of traditional and contemporary Hawaiian music, their Christmas and May Day concerts that are marketed primarily to residents (many of whom cannot afford or do not want to frequent the Monarch Room of the Royal Hawaiian Hotel) and their demonstrated knowledge of and respect for the traditional Hawaiian chant and hula and the Hawaiian language.

The local recording industry tries to balance the different components of the music-buying market: local residents, tourists and limited markets outside of Hawaii, primarily the West Coast of the mainland and Japan. It has not been easy to do. One of the most successful of local musicians in gaining attention on the mainland for contemporary Hawaiian music has been Henry Kapono, who combines rock, reggae, African and Hawaiian sounds in a "world beat" style. Other local musicians like Glenn Medeiros have been signed by mainland labels, but for mainstream pop or jazz styles, not for island-style music ("On the Record," 1988).

CONCLUSION

Hawaiian music is an intertext of many different histories, elements, forms and codes. Most notably, in the second half of the twentieth century, the production of local music has been shaped by the structures, practices and motivations of capitalist music production. Although much of Hawaiian music has been shaped and reshaped by outside cultural and commercial forces, it still expresses an alternative and, to some extent, oppositional culture.

The 1970s saw a resurgence of interest in chant and hula and in contemporary Hawaiian music. This musical activity was part of a larger renaissance of Hawaiian culture, a politics of culture movement that expressed a new consciousness of Hawaiian identity, history and political interests. Through the 1980s and into the 1990s there has been a relatively steady fare of nontourist-oriented Hawaiian music at local clubs, restaurants and concerts, but not at the same level of activity as during the 1970s. Also, the explicit political nature of Hawaiian music has been less evident than in the 1970s, although the recent emergence of "Jawaiian" music (a combination of Jamaican reggae and contemporary Hawaiian music) has been, like Reggae, a vehicle for political messages.

Hawaiian music is many things, used many ways, serving different myths of Hawaii. The same forms and styles of Hawaiian music, even the very same chants and songs, are appropriated by competing myths of what Hawaii is, and what it should be. The now-dominant myth of Hawaii appropriates Hawaiian music as a signifier of a harmonious and alluring paradise. The alternative myth, that projected by Hawaiians seeking to regain their history and identity (as well as those who see in the recent Hawaiian movement an alternative to the overdevelopment of Hawaii), has reappropriated Hawaiian music as a signifier of a culture that before contact with the West was complex and elaborate, of a history of destruction and domination after contact, and now of a culture that is challenging the dominant structures of power in late-twentieth-century Hawaii.

Concerns have been raised about the future of the local music industry and its relationship to the mainland market, the growing market in Japan and how these commercial forces affect the production of Hawaiian music and its relation to contemporary Hawaiian culture and the constantly changing social context of the islands. In some ways Hawaii's local recording industry is an example of what other countries would like to achieve: a locally owned industry that serves as an outlet for the traditional music of the past from precontact to the recent past, offering contemporary musicians a structure within which to produce their own music. However, the music industry of Hawaii also illustrates the danger that a capitalist mode of music production holds for any subculture that must operate within the context of the larger international and national entertainment industries.

The large systems of production and marketing exert a centralizing pull on marginal cultural production. Since the mid-1880s, Hawaiian music has been under constant tension vis-a-vis the hegemonic culture of the United States. It remains to be seen if Hawaiian music, as a symbol and expressive channel for Hawaiians and an alternative culture for others, will continue to survive as an active and creative force in Hawaii.

NOTES

1. The term "music of Hawaii" includes all the music produced in the islands; the term "Hawaiian music" is used for music that has some characteristics identifiable with Hawaii, whether it be Hawaiian language instrumentation or just being

about Hawaii.

  2. *Hapa-haole* music is part Hawaiian and part American. It literally means "half foreign."

  3. As in other places, it is difficult to get accurate figures on record production and profits. Many individually produced cassettes may not come to the attention of the association that tries to keep track of locally produced music. In addition, privately owned music companies do not have to and are often reluctant to publicise information on their profits and losses.

BIBLIOGRAPHY

Barthes, Roland (1981). In Robert Young (Ed.), *Untying The Text: A Post-Structuralist Reader*. Boston: Routledge and Kegan Paul.

Brown, Desto (1982). *Hawaii Recalls: Selling Romance to America: Nostalgic Images of the Hawaiian Islands 1920-1950*. Honolulu: Editions Limited.

Buck, Elizabeth B. (1984). "The Hawaii music industry." *Social Process in Hawaii*, 31, 137-154.

Hailono Mele (1980, January). Honolulu: The Hawaiian Music Foundation.

Hopkins, Jerry (1979). "Record Industry in Hawaii." In George's Kanahele (Ed.). *Hawaiian Music and Musicians: An Illustrated History*. Honolulu: University Press of Hawaii.

Jacobs, Ron (1990, October). "Peter Moon," *Honolulu*. 25, No. 4, 46-54.

Kanahele, George S. (Ed.) (1979). *Hawaiian Music and Musicians: An Illustrated History*. Honolulu: University Press of Hawaii.

"Multi-Million Dollar Business." (1979, December). *Hawaii Business*, 26-28.

"Music Seen As Potential New Industry." (1972, March). *Hawaii Business*. 39-44.

"On the Record." (1988, December 7). *Honolulu Advertiser*, B1, 8.

Otaguro, Janice (1991, August). "Tourists: can't live with 'em: can't live without 'em." *Honolulu*, 26, No. 2, 43-45, 147-152.

Robinson, Deanna Campbell; Buck, Elizabeth B.; Cuthbert, Marlene et al.; and the International Communication and Youth Culture Consortium (1991). *Music at the Margins: Popular Music and Global Cultural Diversity*. Newbury Park CA: Sage.

The 1987 Na Hoku Hanohano Awards. (1987). *Overview*. Honolulu: Hawaii Academy of Recording Arts.

Wallis Roger and Malm, Krister (1984). *Big Sounds from Small People: The Music Industry in Small Countries*. London: Constable.

CHAPTER 6

MUSIC IN INDIA: A LOOK AT SOMETHING DIFFERENT

Usha Vyasulu Reddy

INTRODUCTION

Much has been written about Indian culture and civilization. Much more remains to be written. To a foreign eye, Indian culture appears to be a jigsaw puzzle in which the pieces do not quite fit but give an illusion of coherence and reality; to the Indian, this illusion is the reality. As for any other Asian civilization, it is necessary for one to be born here or to have lived here for several years to scratch beneath the surface and understand the complexity and diversity that is India.

Any attempt to interpret India in light of Western theories and norms can be both erroneous and compromising to the integrity of a scholar. Indian culture must be interpreted in terms of its own perspective, as must Western cultures, for to the Indian, all of Western civilization seems essentially common (again, a mistaken notion).

In this chapter an attempt is made to look at music within the framework of the culture of which it is a manifestation--that is in terms of the environment in which it is embedded, and the influences upon its production and distribution resulting from the technological changes which appear to be leading toward a global village. The special focus of this study is on the interaction between modern music and national music as a part of international communication flows. To undertake this, the chapter will proceed through an examination of the economic, social, cultural and political contexts of music in India, to an examination of the music industry in this country and, finally, to an exploration of the effects of present-day information technologies upon the production and enjoyment of music among various sections of the population, in particular youth. The author wishes to alert readers to the fact that since this chapter was written, the state of mu-

sic and mass culture in India has been in such a state of flux with the introduction of cable-based and satellite transborder services that the current
picture is not clear and yet there is a renewed insistence on the
"Indianization of Pop Music" in a debate led by the film-based music industry.

HISTORICAL AND SOCIAL CONTEXTS

Music is an important part of the development and regulation of human
kind and its emotions. No human society is complete without music and no
society worth its name neglects it. Music is considered the hallmark of culture and refinement, and the pulse of India throbs in the music and dance of
the country--from the shepherd's cry in the forbidding Himalayas to the
rhythms of the Southern tip of the subcontinent. It is as spontaneously a
part of all festivals, feasts, weddings, births and deaths as it is a form of
worship in the temples and of pleasure and enjoyment in the courts and
durbars (formal receptions). If the Indian cities have the sounds of film music blaring from loudspeakers in restaurants, village India has a vibrant
musical tradition as part of folklore. There are both modern rock 'n' roll
beats and ancient ragas developing and growing side by side without any
apparent conflict and as equal partners in cultural development. To com-
prehend this complexity, let us look at the historical development of music
in India, before placing it within a modern sociopolitical context.

Archaeological evidence points to the existence of music, instruments,
dance and drama from very ancient times in India, although an impression
is often gained that the origins of Indian music is in the Vedas (early Hindu
sacred writings). From the excavations at Mohenjodaro and Harappa, to
the discovery of pottery vessels found in the Deccan, from the drawings and
reliefs in the rock paintings at Bhimbetka in Madhya Pradesh, it is clear that
music and dance predated even Vedic times.

Music treatises trace the origins of Indian music to the Samaveda, saying *samavedadidam gitam samjagraha pitamahah,* or that the science of music, *Gandharvaveda*, is the upaveda of the Samaveda. The Samaveda is itself
the musical version of the Rigveda, where the hymns of the Rigveda are
used as libretto or *sahitya*, or *yoni* for the melodies. From the Vedas there
arose a body of songs, called marga or gandharva, in the form of praises of
Siva sung in jathis and which form the precursors of the ragas.

The end of the ancient and early medieval periods witnessed the writing
down of texts (until this time a largely oral tradition existed) on stagecraft
such as the Arthasastra, and on dance, drama, and music like Bharata's
Natyasastra.

If the ancient times provide one of the roots of Indian music, the second
phase is the period of the Middle Ages, which began with the invasions of
the Mongols and Arabs and ended with the establishment of British colonialism in India. This period is important, for the patronage extended to
performing arts by imperial rulers and music grew in brilliance as composers
and singers flowered. The influence of Muslim culture on Indian society was
such that Muslims became devoted to music and *gharanas,* or schools of

music, developed.

During the British rule, Indian music underwent a decline except in the South where, under the patronage of enlightened kings, there was a great resurgence of art. Barring a few, the British for the most part did not understand or appreciate the nuances of a highly developed art form, poured scorn on it and took an interest in promoting Western culture. Aping their rulers, the Indian middle classes in general looked on music as frivolous and immoral and discouraged their children from pursuing the art.

In the first half of the twentieth century, it was eminent poets and philosophers like Rabindranath Tagore in Bengal and Rukmini Devi Arundale in the south who gave a new respectability to Indian art, both music and dance. But respect of Indian music did not by itself remove the obstacles in the way of progress for Indian music. It is to the credit of modern Indian musicians like Pandit Ravi Shankar, Bade Ghulam Ali Khan, Bismillah Khan, Vilayat Khan, M.S. Subbalakshmit and Dr. Balamuralikrishna that Indian music has found belated recognition in the West and subsequently in India.

With the coming of Independence in 1947, three factors were to influence the development of Indian music. The film industry (which predates independence but is a popular entertainment medium in India), began to use music, particularly playback singers, as a major component of films, and introduced a new popular form of music which has since dominated the music industry in the country. The second major factor was the growth of All India Radio and the introduction of music on radio and later on television which changed the face of music, both by giving music a much needed lift and also by setting down limits of time and broadcast requirements for musicians.

The third major factor, political independence, introduced a new society blending the three roots of Indian history into a single constitution and culture. Indian ethos today is reflected in the polity and has its roots first in the traditional past, a continuous history, civilization and philosophy of more than 3,000 years, during which many living traditions evolved. The Aryans brought their culture to the Indo-Gangetic plains. Alexander and the later Mughal emperors left their mark, while Christianity was introduced by one of the apostles of Christ. There was no serious conflict between the Indian ethos and these new entrants. The adaptability and pragmatism which insured the continuing vigor of all these unbroken traditions derived from an all-encompassing philosophical vision, which reconciles opposing concepts by evolving a synthesis that transcends the limitations of opposing philosophies (Kapoor, 1985).

The second major origin of present-day Indian culture comes from the colonial experience. The chronologically recent influence of the West, especially during the British rule, brought with it educational, industrial, and political structures and institutions, and created the modern elite--the small but dominant cultural group in the country today.

The third source of Indian culture comes from India's aspirations for the future with material and economic well-being as goals for the people. The materialistic thrust forward is not at odds with Indian spiritualism, which divides the temporal from the intellectual.

This is the Indian culture of today, diverse in form and language, full of contradictions where the individual's link is to family, caste and locality without a strong sense of overall society. There is a sense of otherworldliness, a belief in a world beyond the temporal, in myths and superstition. There is also a sense of nationality, a general hungering for Western materialism and no apparent conflict between the two.

A brief look at the political and economic systems is essential here. The Indian political system is a federal one, with a strong central government and 22 states and several union territories; the working democracy is based on the British parliamentary tradition. With three branches of government-- a bicameral parliament of which the Lok Sabha (House of the People) is directly elected, an executive with an elected Prime Minister as Head of government and a President as Head of State--India is the world's largest functioning and stable democracy. Freedom of thought and expression is a fundamental right, with the broadcast media of radio and television currently the only media under direct government operation and control. Both the press and the film industry are privately owned and practice freedom under Article 19(i) of the Indian Constitution. There are, however, laws relating to the regulation of the media, dealing most of all with management and not with content. A uniqueness of this policy is the constitutional protection granted to minorities for the exercise of religious and personal freedoms.

The Indian economic system is that of a mixed economy with private and public sectors competing with each other in the economy. While the public sector is to some extent protected and pampered, this sector still has to meet standards of quality in order to survive in the economy. Protective laws to shelter Indian industry from competition abroad are fast disappearing, and India today ranks among the top 25 developed countries in the world (on the basis of GNP alone) but among the Fourth World in terms of GNP per capita.

As for the music industry, it must be stated that like any other industry, it is governed by the laws of India relating to multinational corporations, and there is no specific law relating to the quantum of national vis-a-vis international music that is produced by the industry or broadcast by All India Radio.

Since music is a reflection of culture, it comes within the purview of the areas of education and culture in the society. Both these subjects are on the list of concurrent subjects according to the Indian Constitution--that is, a subject dealt with by government at both central and state level. There are Ministries of Education and Culture with the purpose of protecting, overseeing and promoting the cultural development and heritage of the society. This includes music, and the government has defined policy so as to include classical, traditional and folk forms for special attention. Popular music, defined as film music in India, does not come within the purview of government promotion.

Through its Ministry of Culture, the government provides opportunities for musicians to perform, scholarships for training new talent and travel grants and other subsidies through the Indian Council for Cultural Relations. Through organizations like the National Film Development Corporation, the government has funded the production of films on the lives of great composers and performers in order to popularize classical forms of music among the citizens.

Indian cultural policy is concerned with the preservation and promotion of classical, semiclassical and folk music, against the onslaught of Indian popular music as produced by the music industry and distributed throughout the country. International music forms a negligible part of this picture because it has a very limited elite audience, restricted only to the major cities of the country and among the rich and Westernized segments. Before concluding this section, it is important to emphasise that there are two Indias existing within the same country. One is the urban India, represented by the middle class and the elite in the major cities, and constituting about 20% of the population. The other is rural India, consisting of 80% of the population, living in the villages, and the gap between the two is wide, following divergent paths. Another major characteristic of Indian society is its linguistic and cultural diversity, making it impossible to speak of any pan-Indian popular culture. Therefore, when we examine the music industry, it is with an understanding of Indian culture and ethos and with the humble acceptance of the complexity of culture and cultural expression, and we search only for the common threads which bind the music industry together.

INDIAN MUSIC

Indian music today can be classified into the following genres:

1. *Indian Classical Music:* Music which is based on the classical structure of raga and tala, in its purest form, which has not changed much in substance from ancient times. Examples are the music of Pandit Ravi Shankar or M. S. Subbalakshmit; included would be both Hindustani and Carnatic music.
2. *Semiclassical Music:* Ghazals and Geets, instrumental and classical music, which have been modified and molded to fit popular taste.
3. *Indian popular music:* Indian film music, which has come out of the classical structure but which is from the sound tracks of popular films, incorporating rock 'n' roll, jazz and other Western forms with Indian instruments and lyrics.
4. *Indian folk music:* The folk songs and rhythms of the villages in the different parts of the country, sung at times of festivals in rural India.
5. *Western popular music:* All forms of Western music, barring the classical as defined internationally.
6. *Western classical music:* Western classical music as defined internationally.

All this music is on sale today on records and prerecorded cassettes, and prerecorded music has taken the place of live music performances throughout the country. It is because of this phenomenon that an examination of the music industry assumes importance. The music industry in India is a parasite of the film industry, depending upon and catering to the largest film industry in the world (900 feature films and 2,000 short films each year). Compared with the gigantic music businesses abroad, the Indian music industry appears minuscule, as is apparent from Table 6.1.

Table 6.1. Music Business Abroad and in India (in millions $ U.S.)

Countries	7"	LPs	Cassettes	Total Value	%
United States	246	2,113	1,261	3,623	48
Japan	n.a.	755	401	1,156	15
United Kingdom	n.a.	568	166	734	10
France	n.a.	n.a.	n.a.	880	11
West Germany	n.a.	n.a.	n.a.	1,200	16
India	4.4	11.1	1.5	17	not relevant

1982 figures as available.

The industry looks tiny internationally, but this image has to be related to various dimensions, whether it be the production of reproducing equipment (record players and tape recorders) or the channels of distribution, (the conduits of communication content).

Figures about this industry are very hard to find. They have to be inferred from other available information, and the trade magazines have a very limited circulation. Still, figures for the latest years show that this is a rapidly growing and changing industry and the number of cassette recorders (two-in-ones) available in the country is anybody's guess. However, it can be argued that in a developing country with a low per capita income, demand for recording and playing equipment is generally low on the list of household priorities, limited by the low purchasing power of the middle and poorer classes, who use radio as their main channel of information and entertainment.

However, the decade of the 1980s witnessed the fastest growth of the television system, the effective deployment and use of many satellites, the mushrooming of the electronics industry which created the electronic boom and, most recently, the de facto invasion of the urban areas by private cable channels linked to satellites beaming foreign programs and, yes, MTV has come to India through its satellite-based STAR TV network. Indian policy (or the lack of it) has resulted in opening up a market which even the most liberal government can no longer ignore.

As the hardware of the culture industry has grown, the picture for the software production feeding the system is changing beyond recognition. Production of programs to feed the system has grown with both the major film industry and the fly-by-night operators fighting for a fair share of the market. One can only conjecture at the size of the industry if we take into account outright piracy of culture products and the recording of music off the air.

The implication of the growth rate of the technology in this field is clear. With a hungry market able to absorb almost anything that is produced, it is not the record players/CD players which are important, but the audio-cassette industry. Although still prohibitive in cost, video has begun to make a dent into the urban and semiurban areas of the country. International media have entered the Indian media market.

The music industry has been unprepared to meet the challenge of cassette recorders and international broadcasting. This lack of preparedness

has been compounded by its inability to check cassette piracy in the subcontinent. Though piracy in one form or another is a worldwide phenomenon, in the West the problem centers around home taping. But in South
East Asia, as in India and Pakistan, it is an organized racket, and Hindi film
music, in particular, is one area in which this kind of operation has bur-
geoned. On a very conservative estimate, at least eight out of every ten music cassettes sold on the Indian market are pirate products (nearly 20 million
blank cassettes are sold in India every year). Though recording quality is
poor, the pirated cassettes are at least 25% to 30% cheaper than the higher
priced original cassettes. The Indian Phonographic Industries Association,
of which all the major music companies are members, has taken steps to
combat piracy in India, but not with any notable results. The laws are difficult to enforce because many of the pirates are fly-by-night operations.
Some are quite prosperous and are actually willing to spend money to bend
the law.

What, then is the repertoire of the records and cassettes in India? As already stated, it is heavily loaded in favor of the film industry, with some
other forms of music taking a backseat. Figures from all of the record companies show that 70% of the music is film music, 20% is classical or folk and
international (popular, Western, and classical) music comprises a mere 10%
of music products.

THE INDIAN MUSIC INDUSTRY, YESTERDAY AND TODAY

The history of recorded music in India is the story of the Gramophone
Company of India (Gramco or HMV as it was known). Until 1968, Gramco
was a fully owned subsidiary of EMI of the United Kingdom and dominated the market almost as a monopoly. It is symptomatic of the very limited market in which recording companies operate that it took ten years for
Polydor (backed by PolyGram International) to find a place in the sun.
Even with the rapid growth of the recording industry in the 1970s, Gramco's
market share continued to be about 75% with an estimated turnover of Rs.
19.5 crores (one crore = 10 million rupees).

Polydor was started in 1969 the Indian Record Company (Inreco) in
1973, CBS/Tata in 1982, and Supercassettes in 1982. So the base of competition was broadened from a monopoly operation to a very limited oligop-
oly. However, because of the law regulating business and foreign investments in India, laws such as those relating to monopolies and restrictive
trade practices, no recording company can claim to be a fully owned subsidiary of any transnational corporation. Indian investment in the company
is normally 50% and there is an export obligation to fulfil to the government.

Let us now look at a profile of the major recording companies in India:

Gramco: Started in 1907 as a small unit, the first stereo recording was
made by Gramco in 1931 after the first film sound track appeared on records in 1930. Since then, the history of Gramco is closely linked with the
Indian film industry and it dominated the market until 1968. It has since
become an Indian company with more than 50% of its equity being held by

Indian investors. In spite of spirited competition from newer companies, Gramco continues to have the largest share of the market.

Polydor: Started by a local tycoon with movie-world connections in Bombay with the backing of PolyGram International in 1969, the majority of shares are also owned by Indians. The first five years for the company were tough going, as it had to avail itself of a distribution network fostered by Gramco and also of the exclusive dealership clauses with record retailers.

Inreco: The first wholly Indian-owned Indian Record Manufacturing Company-was started in Calcutta by the owners of the Hindustan Label in 1973 and had its first year of production in 1976. It grew to account for about 4% of the market share.

CBS/Tata: CBS Gramophone Records and Tapes (India) was incorporated in 1982, and has been jointly promoted by CBS Records International (holding 40% of the share equity) and the Industrial house of Tata (with 50% share). The balance of 10% is held by an Indian who was a senior executive of CBS worldwide. Because this company has an export obligation, feeding the markets in Eastern Europe, Africa and the Far East, only the residual portion of the company's output is available for the Indian market.

Supercassettes: Established with an investment of US $80,000 in 1982, Supercassettes plant and equipment are now worth $16 million. Supercassettes earned $65 million in 1987, of which $20 million were from prerecorded music cassettes. About 80,000 cassettes a day are produced using state-of-the-art Japanese technology, and are marketed under a T-Series Label. One of this company's sales methods is to make copies of recorded music (hits of the day) and sell them at a very low cost. The tape thus purchased is good for playing about 30 to 40 times before it begins to deteriorate. It is the market strategy of this company that a hit song will be heard only about 30 times before a new hit comes along. Such a tape is priced at less than one third of the amount Gramco would charge for a cassette, so T-Series is rapidly capturing the market.

INDIAN MUSIC ABROAD

India is different from other developing countries and is probably the only developing country involved in the export of national media products. India's export turnover in films amounted to Rs. 99.2 million in 1980 ($10 million), but this figure has grown with the introduction of videocassettes (although figures are not available readily). Recording companies have an export obligation and are exporting to countries where there are Indian settlements of substantial size--to Africa, West Indies, United States, United Kingdom, Canada, and more recently to the Arab world. Predominantly, the music exported to the other countries consists of popular film music and sound tracks of films. In terms of imports, hardly 25% of international media products are imported and the import and consumption of international music is also less than 25%, consumed mostly by the urban elite, the Anglo-Indian minority and the armed forces in the country.

MUSIC AND COPYRIGHT

The Copyright Act of 1957, which governs all creative work, including the works of the music industry, is enforced for public performance of records by Phonographic Performance (Eastern) Private Limited (PPE), which is an arm of the Indian Phonographic Industries Association (IPIA). While broadcasting, about which IPIA has a separate agreement with All India Radio and Doordashan (TV), falls into a category of its own, all other public performances in which a commercial element enters require permission from the PPE. The exceptions are the playing of music during religious and other public festivals, in clubs or other nonprofit-making societies, and in piped music provided in hotel rooms. In all these cases, it is assumed that music is being played for noncommercial purposes. If records or cassettes are played in restaurants or in the lobbies of hotels, then a license is required, for which a fee must be paid.

The IPIA currently has about 16 members and the only qualification needed for membership is a live catalogue and a serious intent to carry on business. The one main preoccupation of the IPIA has been to combat cassette piracy, for which a special fund has been set up. However, since violation of copyright is not a cognizable offense under the law, the IPIA first has to go to court for a warrant so that the law enforcement authorities can take action. This legal procedure is time consuming and also means that the pirates can close their shops overnight if they get wind of the operation.

The problem is also compounded by piracy which takes place in neighboring countries, notably Pakistan and Bangladesh. IPIA is a signatory to most international agreements regarding copyright of recorded music but the neighboring countries are not, and if piracy takes place in these countries, the Indian companies are helpless.

The copyright conventions that govern film music, the most popular music, are also unique. Usually, the copyright is owned by the film producer who adequately compensates the lyric composer and the music director. The producer then transfers the copyright, for a price, to the company that makes the records. The record company then becomes owner of the copyright for the music in these records, for a period of 50 years from the release of the film. Version recordings can be made in payment of a consideration. Unfortunately, such version recordings are rare, unlike in Western countries where the publishing divisions of recording companies make substantial contributions to incomes from this source. Broadcasting (All India Radio), which is a major distributor of music, has separate agreements with the recording companies and merits a separate examination.

THE BROADCASTING SYSTEM IN INDIA

Radio's influence in the transmission of popular culture is second only to the movies in India, and in many homes, radio sets are switched on from early in the morning to late at night. All India Radio (AIR) is a government-owned and -operated service which started with radio clubs in Calcutta, Bombay and Madras as early as 1923. Taken over by the government in 1930, it was run by the British Indian government until Independence in 1947. Since then, it has been used for informational and educational services, along with some light entertainment until 1957, when Vividh Bharati service was introduced as an alternative to the competition provided by Radio Sri Lanka. A commercial service was started in 1967 and at present the commercial service of light popular entertainment is broadcast from 32 centers for 13 hours a day. The content of the programs consists mostly of film music, humorous skits, short plays, and features. Income from the commercial service is a approximately Rs. 105 million, making the service self-sustaining.

Since the reach of the commercial service is restricted to the urban areas, there are 86 radio stations for other services, with a reach of over 90% of the land area. On these other stations are broadcast special programs for women, children, youth, students, rural folk, industrial workers and the armed forces.

A major part of the broadcast time from AIR stations is devoted to programs of music which include classical, folk, light, devotional, film and Western music. The weekly national program of music, the Annual Radio Sangeet Sammelan and the weekly concerts are designed to provide listeners with the best classical music in the national genres. In the national program of music, well-known exponents of music including old masters are featured, as are popular and eminent music artists. AIR stations also broadcast programs of folk music with the objective of bringing to the listeners the variety and richness of the folk heritage of the country. A monthly program of regional and light music on the national hookup is also provided. If measured in percentage terms, international music is broadcast less than 10% of the time. Table 6.2 shows the breakdown of the program composition, and Table 6.3 the music component of All India Radio.

Table 6.2. Program Composition (Home Service) of All India Radio

Type of Program	Hours	Minutes	%
Music	155,869	57	36.11
News	95,869	30	22.17
Spoken word	180,085	52	41.72
	431,823	139	100.00

1982 figures as available.

Table 6.3. Breakdown of the Music Component of AIR Broadcasts

Music of Type	Hours	Minutes	%
Classical Music	52,143	42	36.46
Folk Music	16,100	41	10.34
Light Music	33,265	46	18.57
Devotional Music	21,927	58	14.06
Film Music	21,150	58	17.42
Western Music	4,920	52	3.15
	149,865	297	100.00

Figures as available.

The most important competition for All India Radio comes from Radio Sri Lanka, a commercial service which is heard on shortwave in India and consists primarily of light entertainment oriented popular music from Indian films.

Television is a fast-growing medium in the country, perhaps the only challenge for the film industry in terms of reach, and as a promoter of Indian culture. With the introduction of commercial television on a large scale throughout the country, the revenues from advertising alone are Rs. 200 crores approximately.

Television came to India 25 years after its introduction as a pilot project in 1959. Over a span of 24 years, Indian television (called Doordarshan) expanded its coverage to include a system which introduced satellite-based television broadcasting through low power transmitters and through direct receiving sets to far-flung villages. While the express purpose of television is informational and educational, highlighting the processes of development and integration, over the past two years, Doordarshan has introduced a variety of entertainment programs, consisting of slapstick comedy, soap operas, news and feature-based programs and sports.

Programs of music have been introduced on Doordarshan, including the film based program, Chitrahaar, featuring songs from Indian films broadcast for half an hour twice a week; Chitramala, songs from regional films, broadcast for half an hour once a week and special programs of Western music, notably rock 'n' roll (called Hot Rock, and Aid Bhopal Concert) broadcast once every two weeks. The Aid Africa Concert was televised for the urban audiences as were the Grammy Awards--both broadcast as part of late-night programs. Doordarshan also has a conscious policy of promoting classical and folk culture and a regular weekly feature consists of a Kavi Sammelan or Mushaira (meeting of poets who recite poetry to studio audiences) and a National Program of Music (broadcast once a week and featuring the classical musicians of the country).

LOCAL MUSIC CULTURE

Three things must stand out in this description of the local music cultures and environment in India. First, diversity of music styles and of the cultures is bound to be reflected in the music in the research community under question (Hyderabad) so much so that even music from another part of the country may not be "local" in the strict definition of the term. The second major aspect of local music production is that, although Hyderabad is a major city in the country, much of the music production is concentrated in the cities of Bombay, Madras and Calcutta, which are the centers of a thriving movie industry. This aspect in itself restricts the discussion of music production in the local environment. As for the country itself, the size and composition of the music industry has already been described. This music industry, dominated by the film medium, is itself a cause for worry among the musicians who find that their avenues for production are severely limited. A third major aspect of Hyderabad is the unique cultural and historical background where there has been a blend of the Hindu and the Muslim cultural patterns, where each citizen speaks at least two languages and the different religions survive side by side but never blend in a melting pot.

Let us now systematically look at the findings of the survey of the local musicians to obtain a picture of the local music environment. A narrative account is given to describe the environment as perceived by the musicians who compose, produce and perform in the twin cities of Hyderabad and Secunderabad.

Most of the musicians are mature, between the ages of 35 and 50, and have been performing for more than ten years, usually since the age of about 15. They are at the very least high school or college graduates. Much of their training has been from professional music teachers for payment in the traditional *gurukul* system--that is, becoming students of well-known maestros. Two kinds of musicians have influenced their styles well-known exponents of classical music and, for the more Western-oriented young musicians, pop groups such as the Beatles, Crosby, Stills & Nash, Simon & Garfunkel and so on.

Predominantly male, the musicians are of two types: those performing as soloists and as parts of groups; and those who perform as accompanying artists. The structure and cohesion of a band is not necessary in India, given the nature of Indian music, a sitar player can perform as a soloist and also as an accompanying artist for different singers. A tabla player, on the contrary, can play only as an accompanying artist, unless he or she has achieved the measure of recognition to perform as a soloist.

The instruments played by Indian musicians range from the sitar, tabla, mrigangam, veena, flute, violin (traditional Indian instruments) to the harmonica, electric guitar, keyboards and synthesizer. A musician usually plays more than one instrument. Most of the musicians play Indian classical or semiclassical music and, to a lesser extent, popular music from Indian films. Very few, mostly amateurs, play Western popular music or Western classical music.

Most of the musicians are professional but do not depend upon music as their prime source of income, less than 25% of which is derived from their musical performances.

Recognition as a musician usually comes in the form of a gradation by All India Radio. Although licensing is not necessary in India, recognition by All India Radio enables musicians to perform for radio and television, two major avenues of exposure. Most of the musicians are recognized artists of All India Radio.

Most of the artists do not know of a musicians' union existing in India. No information is available about any such union in any of the major music production centers in the country. Musicians are ambivalent in their views about the need for such a union; some feel that it would permit musicians to exchange views and share experiences while preventing the musicians from falling prey to unscrupulous practices. Some of the younger musicians feel that there is no need for such unions, which become political and ego-oriented in nature.

Almost all kinds of Indian music are popular in the research community; there is an audience for each kind of music, and one form is not displacing any other. The identified genres of music for this region are Carnatic music (South Indian classical), Hindustani (North Indian classical), film music and, among the young elite, Western music--mostly rock 'n' roll, country and Western.

Less than 20% of the music performed are original compositions by the musicians; most play music by other composers. The organizations which provide outlets for performances by musicians are predominantly radio and television and cultural associations which arrange performances for their members. The musicians organize their professional engagements themselves, through friends or through cultural organizations. There are no agents to act on behalf of the musicians and most of the musicians see no need for such agents. The musicians also see no need for legal help in dealing with professional matters relating to their performances; they feel it is not necessary.

All India Radio and television are the highest levels of professional recordings made by the musicians; copyright for this music rests with the All India Radio and Doordarshan.

Music is not a means of livelihood, although the opportunities for performance exist in the research community. Therefore, musicians do not depend on music alone for their income. Some of the professional musicians also teach in the government music colleges. By virtue of such employment, they are forbidden to perform professionally; this is observed more in the breach than in implementation. It does not make a substantial difference in terms of the income earned from music performances, so even those who teach in music colleges perform through available outlets. Since each form of music has its own audience, the musicians feel that they do not normally have to compromise between the music they play, although they sometimes modify it to meet audience preferences and tastes.

Music performances are widely covered by both local and national media, mostly in the form of reviews, but it is through the various programs of All India Radio and Doordarshan that musicians feel they get the widest coverage of the country. Thus they look forward to performing for radio and television.

About the most important aspect of transcultural music, the professional musicians feel that while the introduction of Western music elements and electronic sounds into India is not harmful *per se,* it should not be as a substitute for the purer sounds and should not lead to the destruction of national music and culture. Many have experimented with instruments such as electric guitars, keyboards and synthesizers; some have pointed out that the placement of contact microphones has altered the sound and tonal quality of the instruments. Western music as influencing Indian popular music is strong, but the musicians feel that if the music has an effect upon other values of Indians, it could be harmful in the long run. Some of the older musicians, especially those who perform predominantly classical music, feel that the influx of popular music is harmful to the youth, who do not learn to appreciate the finer aspects of Indian classical music.

Government and other organizations can do much to encourage Indian music by promoting talent competitions, developing more music colleges to teach music, by arranging concerts and incentives for young musicians. One such organization is the Society for the Promotion of Indian Music and

Culture Among Youth (SPIC MAOAY) which is a nationwide voluntary organization whose primary function is to introduce the youth to an appreciation of Indian music styles.

There are also many music festivals in India organized by both government and voluntary groups. Jazz Yatra, a festival of music held annually in Bombay, has its own important following among the elite. But in other cities it is the small cultural organizations which are responsible for concerts for musicians. International groups also perform in India, under the aegis of the various cultural missions of different governments. Thus, Indians are exposed to many forms of musical styles and rarely does a concert or performance go without a full attendance.

IN CONCLUSION

What all the data point to is a continuous but lingering doubt in the study of the music scene in India. One continuous aspect forms the recurring theme of discussion, whether it be of Indian music or Indian culture. What Indian culture are we talking about? Are we talking about a front-line metropolis like Bombay or Delhi where the influence and penetration of Western culture and ethos are deep, as shown by the growing number of discotheques, fast-food outlets, budding musical bands and rock stars and open air concerts? Or are we concerned with the music styles of the second-level cities such as Hyderabad, where many forms of music exist side by side; where commercial radio promotes Indian film music all day--what we can call Indianized rock 'n' roll? Or are we talking about the major part of the population which lives in Indian villages where folk songs and classical forms dominate the music scene.

To research and write about any of the three different levels in isolation is to reflect a distorted view of the country's music scene; to attempt to describe all three is to point to a picture of contradictions.

This chapter has tried to identify and describe the music scene in a second-level city which has both the modern and the traditional living side-by-side and where the dent made by modern music styles is still restricted. If there has been any major conclusive finding at all, it is that diversity and resilience of this Indian ethos is such that there is a demand and a market for all kinds of music in India, reflective of the Hindu view of life, which will ultimately find an emerging synthesis.

BIBLIOGRAPHY

Beeman, W.O. (1980). "The Use of Music in Popular Film" *International Center Quarterly* 8, 1: 77-88.

Deva, I. (1981). "Popular and Folk Culture in Contemporary India." *International Popular Culture 2*, 1: 12-21.

Gidwani, I. (1978). "Record Industry: Mass Production Vital." *Economic Times* (July 8): 5.

Goew, M.S. (1977). *Indian Youth: Process of Socialisation.* New Delhi: Viswa Yuvak Kendra.

Kapoor Satish C. (1985, September). "The Hindus and Their Isms: Contemporary Relevance." *Seminar*, p. 30-37.

Kirpal, P. (1976). *Youth and Established Culture.* New Delhi: Sterling Publishers.

Philipose, P. (1978). "Record Companies: Stuck in a Groove." *Time of India Magazine* (March 12): 13.

Reddy, V.E. and Bhat, K.S. (1977). *Out of School Youth.* New Delhi: Sterling Publishers.

Sequeira, I. (1981). "The Study of Popular Culture in India: a Frontier Situation." *International Popular Culture* 2, 1: 6-11.

Sequeira, Isaac (1991). *Popular Culture: East and West.* New Delhi: B.R. Publishing Company.

Singhal, Arvind and Rogers, Enereti (1989). *India's Information Revolution.* New Delhi: Sage Publications.

Srivastava, P.C. (1981). "Impact of Mass Communication on Adolescents." *Indian Journal of Criminology* 9,1 (January): 51-55

Sud, A. (1982) "Threat of Piracy." *Commerce Supplement* 145 (3718) (September 11): 8-9.

CHAPTER 7

THE ISRAELI MUSICAL ENVIRONMENT: CULTURAL HERITAGE AND SOCIOCULTURAL CHANGE

Hanna Adoni

INTRODUCTION

Patterns of production and distribution of popular music and its central function in the lives of young people were investigated and discussed as early as the 1930s and 1940s by Frankfurt School scholars (Adorno, 1976) and later by major American social scientists (Riesman, 1950; Mendelsohn, 1964). The last decade has witnessed renewed interest in this subject and growing recognition of its significance in the study of mass culture and its effects (Shudson, 1987; Lewis, 1980). Empirical studies on related subjects were conducted mainly in the United States (e.g. Lull, 1985; Clarke, 1973; Denisoff & Peterson, 1972; Peterson & DiMaggio, 1975; Hirsch, 1971) and Great Britain (Frith 1978, 1983, 1988; Martin, 1982; Brake, 1980; Willis, 1980) and referred mainly to the musical environment within the social context of the countries where the major share of the modern popular music originated and was produced. Recently, however, a growing interest developed in the musical environment of small countries which depend on foreign sources for the production and supply of the greatest part of their popular music (Blaukopf, 1982; Ala et al. 1985; Adoni, 1986; Wallis & Malm, 1984; Wicke, 1985; Roe, 1984; Roe & Carlsson, 1990; Adoni & Kama, 1991). In my study of the Israeli musical environment, my main objective was to investigate the dynamics of the interaction among the components of the Israeli musical scene within this particular sociocultural context including its dependence on foreign sources (Robinson et al., 1991).

On the institutional level I was concerned primarily with the intrinsic tension within the creative milieu, namely composers, performers and the various organizations which produce, distribute and broadcast popular music, either commercially or as a public service. In terms of quality and musical genres, I relied on recent research concerning sources of modern, Israeli popular music (Cohen & Shiloah, 1985; Regev, 1986; Benski, 1989; Ben-Porat, 1989) and focused my interest on the impact of imported, foreign music on locally produced material.

This chapter is based on information derived from three main sources: (1) data available from ACUM (Society of Authors, Compositors and Editors of Music in Israel) concerning the consumption trends during the last 5 years; (2) a series of semistructured interviews conducted with people associated with the Israeli Broadcasting Authority (IBA) and the major recording and distributing companies active in Israel; (3) semi-structured, in-depth interviews with 13 well-known, popular Israeli singers and musicians. These interviews were based on questionnaires which included both closed and open questions about the musicians' personal background, professional history and status and various sources of influence. I should like to emphasize that this group is not a representative sample of Israeli musicians. Also, they were not chosen according to either any systematic evaluation of their popularity or the quality of their work. The main condition for including them in our study was that they are well-known in Israel and are either currently enjoying popularity to varying degrees or have enjoyed it in the recent past.

These particular musicians were interviewed primarily because they were available at the time the study took place and because they agreed to give a personal interview and devote about 2 hours of their valuable time to academic research with no professional publicity attached to it. Although the number of interviews is rather limited, I would argue that the information they provided can give us a fairly good idea what it means to be an established popular musician in Israel. By describing their attitudes, feelings and difficulties, as well as the main characteristics of their careers and work, these musicians have given us an insight into their particular musical milieu. It would be impossible to achieve the objectives of this study without presenting the reader with a short description of the social and political context in which Israel's popular music is created, produced, distributed and consumed and I therefore begin the next section with a short and sketchy portrayal of Israeli society.

SOCIAL AND POLITICAL CONTEXT

Israeli society abounds with contradictions. It is a young state, established in 1948, possessing many characteristics of a developing society; at the same time it is the homeland of one of the most ancient cultures in the world. It is a small country with a population of approximately 4 million, yet it is regarded as a national center by million of Jews living in other countries. It is a society which is undergoing a rapid process of modernization and secularisation, yet the minority religious segments of the population are politically powerful and constantly exercise their influence in matters of education, culture and leisure.

The State of Israel was established in 1948 after World War II and the Holocaust in which about 6 million European Jews perished as a result of Nazi persecutions. The most important function of the Jewish state was to provide a homeland for Jews from all over the world. During the 30 years of its existence, Israel has absorbed more than 2 million Jews who have emigrated from various countries. Many of them were refugees, either from postwar Europe or from traditional Arab countries which were already at war with the newly established state. Nowadays, Israel is absorbing a new flux of immigrants from Russia and Ethiopia who are bringing along their rich and unique cultural heritage.

During the first years after the establishment of the state, there was a tendency to favor West European culture as represented by the Ashkenazi Jews of European and Anglo-Saxon origins. Since the 1970s there has been a powerful movement to reassess the role of Oriental Jewry in the social and political systems. As a result, the present trend is toward a pluralistic society in which various ethnic groups are equally valued. Governmental and other cultural agencies have devoted serious attention to ensuring equitable distribution of resources among the different ethnic groups.

The objective of these relatively recent cultural policies was twofold: to guarantee the preservation of various Jewish cultural traditions and to foster creativity of young people from various ethnic groups. On the political level, participation of people from Oriental backgrounds is now encouraged by all political parties. Nevertheless, the situation is still far from optimal; there is constant tension among various ethnic groups concerning the distribution of economic resources and opportunities as well as political power. Israel's central problem, however, is its conflict with the Arab world. It is a well-known and much regretted fact that relations between Israel and most of its Arab neighbors, excluding Egypt, are hostile. Since the establishment of the State of Israel in 1948, the country has been involved in three major wars: Six-Day War, Yom-Kippur War and Lebanon War; in several more limited military operations; and in uncountable, almost daily acts of hostility and terrorism.

The political tensions and conflicts between Arabs and Jews in Israel and the areas which are termed "the territories" have become more tense, severe and violent since the beginning of the Intifada in 1988. In January 1991, Israelis experienced the traumatic experience of missile attacks from Iraq, even though they had neither joined the Allied Coalition forces nor retiliated for the recurring missile attacks and continuous threats of chemical and biological warfare.

Regime and Government

Israel is a sovereign parliamentary democracy. It was established by proclamation on 14 May 1948 as the culmination of a long historical process which started in Europe in the nineteenth century with the rise of the Zionistic movement. Its ideal was the reestablishment of an autonomous Jewish community in its historical homeland, Palestine, known since Biblical times as "the Promised Land." The nation's first prime minister was David Ben-Gurion and one of the first laws adopted was the Law of Return, guaranteeing the right of immigration to Israel for all Jews. The supreme political authority of Israel is the Knesset (Parliament), whose 120 members are selected by universal suffrage for a period of four years, on the basis of proportional representation of the political parties. The president (the constitutional head of the state) is elected for a five year term of office by the Knesset; his functions are mainly symbolic. The cabinet takes office after receiving a vote of confidence in the Knesset, to which it is responsible. Israel is divided into six administrative districts. There are 31 municipalities (including two Arab towns), 115 local councils (46 among the Arab and Druze) and 49 regional councils (one Arab) comprising representatives of 700 villages. The municipal authorities are elected simultaneously with Knesset members.

Education and Language

There is free and compulsory education from 5 to 16 years of age (and one may continue free education until 18 years of age). The State Education Law (1953) established a unified, state-controlled elementary school system, providing for special religious schools as well. The Ministry of Education and Culture issues a standard curriculum for all elementary schools. It is possible to add supplementary subjects comprising no more than 25% of the total syllabus. Many high schools are maintained and directed by municipalities or teachers' cooperatives of trustees. There are also a number of private schools maintained by religious foundations--Jewish, Christian and Muslim. (*Israel Government Yearbook*, 1986). The official languages of Israel are Hebrew and Arabic. About two-thirds of the population speak Hebrew, including most Jews. About 15% of Israeli citizens, including Muslim Arabs, speak Arabic. Many European languages are also spoken. Among the Jewish population, the older immigrant generation speaks a wide variety of languages. Among the young there is a notable tendency to speak only Hebrew, even the compulsory study of English from the 4th grade on is somewhat problematic for many youngsters.

Economy

Most of Israel's population is urban and employed in services and industry. Agriculture is highly developed in various types of rural settlements such as moshavim and kibbutzim. Absorption of millions of immigrants followed by rapid economic development resulted in an unstable economy and a high rate of inflation. The constant and heavy burden of military defense also contributed to this unhealthy economic situation. Currently, the situation is somewhat stabilized, but most of the fundamental problems remain to be solved.

MUSICAL ENVIRONMENT IN ISRAEL:
BACKGROUND AND ORIGINS

There are several musical traditions which influence the present musical environment. They are closely interwoven with the history of the Jewish people in the Diaspora and the recent history of Jewish settlement in Palestine and the struggles for independence. Classic European music, the heritage of the European-emancipated Jewery since the seventeenth century, holds a central place in Israeli culture. The establishment of the Israel Philharmonic Orchestra (IPO) 50 years ago by Bronislau Hubermann was a major musical event in then British-governed Palestine. The new orchestra attracted many famous musicians and conductors and provided an artistic home for Jewish musicians who fled from Nazi-dominated Europe. Since then the IPO has become one of the renowned orchestras of the Western world. Under the leadership of the famous conductor Zubin Mehta, the IPO performs with the finest musicians and records with the best international companies. It has a loyal audience in Israel as well as abroad. The Young Philharmonic is composed of young Israeli musicians (aged 12 to 24) who come to Tel Aviv regularly from all parts of Israel in order to practice and play. The importance attached to music education is characteristic not only of the urban population: the kibbutzim also give their young people the highest level of musical education. There are Academies of Music in both Jerusalem and Tel Aviv, which grant academic degrees and several other music schools.

Though classical music is not the main subject of this chapter, it is important to note that the long tradition of classical music appreciation and education certainly influences the musical potential of the young, fosters their creativity in all musical genres and enhances the degree of critical consumption of popular music. The roots of Israeli folk music are rich and diverse and can be traced to different regions of the Diaspora. Both geographically and culturally, these were wide apart. There are two main large categories of folk music: Jewish-European and Jewish-Oriental. The first category comprises musical types created and practiced in the Ashkenazi Jewish communities in Eastern and Central Europe, among them Russia and Poland and includes different types of Hassidic music. The second category consists of the vast variety of Oriental and Sephardic music of Jews dispersed throughout North Africa, the Middle Eastern countries, Greece, Turkey and the Balkans. This is of course a heuristic division into two large general categories. Even the short and incomplete list of regions and countries mentioned above implies the diversity of musical styles within these main categories. Research on traditional Jewish folk music focuses on the differences between the musical instruments, musical styles and levels of sophistication.

In the context of this chapter, it is not necessary to present the findings of these studies. However, in describing the Israeli musical environment, it is imperative to mention that the two types of folk music are still very much alive, both in the traditional religious ceremonies of various communities and as contemporary popular music written in Middle Eastern or Hassidic style.

There are, in fact, special contests and festivals to encourage the composition and performance of Oriental and Hassidic-style music. These traditional music types, which also define two major ethnic groups of Israeli society, constitute a major factor in the dynamics of Israel's musical environment. The development of popular music in Israel has to be understood against this background. Contemporary Israeli popular music comprises three main genres: songs of Eretz Israel, international pop music and Israeli Middle Eastern music.

The songs of Eretz Israel consist of songs composed by Israeli poets and composers, stemming from what can be defined as Israeli folklore prior to the establishment of the State of Israel in 1948. These songs, which are often considered as the "classic" repertoire of Israeli music, are a blend of Russian, East European and Hassidic melodies, sometimes with a strong hint of Oriental sounds and rhythms. Their composers were consciously striving to build a new culture and develop a new musical style which will express the principal values and way of life of the Zionist pioneers. Many of these songs deal with the love of the country and communal ideas of the first half of twentieth century (Cohen & Shiloah, 1985). Many of the lyrics of these songs were written by major Israeli poets and are included in the canonical corpus of modern Hebrew poetry (Ben-Porat, 1989). I would like to emphasize that many of the modern Hebrew songs composed in the 1980s and the 1990s are defined as songs of Eretz Israel. The major messages are still the love of Israel and its nature as well as the common and often difficult history of its citizens. There are, however, also songs of this type which deal with love and passion, hopes and fears, happiness and pain common to all human beings.

The Israeli pop-youth music genre is comprised of local versions of all different genres of this music such as rock, hard rock, new wave and experimental jazz (Adoni, 1983; Adoni & Kama, 1991).

The third popular genre is the Israeli Oriental music (*musika mizrakhit*), which is an unique blend of Arabic, Middle Eastern, North African, Yemenite, Greek and European rhythms and tunes. This musical genre developed during the 1960s and the 1970s and as in other cases of cultural subcultures (Hebdige, 1979) fulfilled a central function in defining and strengthening the social identity of Oriental social groups in Israeli society. All types of Oriental music have flourished since the beginning of the 1980s and in this period became an important part of the Israeli musical soundscape (Regev, 1986).

These three types of popular music are associated with distinct social groups in Israeli society (Benski, 1989). International popular music is associated, as could be expected, with young people. As in other Western countries, some of these, the so-called 1960s generation, are still fans of the Beatles and Elvis. However, there is also the second generation, in their teens and twenties, the fans and the composers of Israeli rock and up-to-date pop. The Oriental music is associated with Israelis of Middle Eastern, North African, Yemenite, Persian, Turkish and Greek origin (Halper et. al. 1989). Most of the Israeli Oriental music is in fact composed by Sephardi musicians, although lately there are some instances of popular Oriental songs written by Ashkenazi Israelis. Since the period of the early years of the State of Israel, the "Oriental" communities were characterized by lower social status, income and level of education and their music was also considered to be inferior when compared with Western standards.

Various types of Jewish Oriental music were similar to Arabic music, which was foreign and monotonic to the ears of the European elite, a fact that caused a further alienation on their part. An exception to these generalisations was the Yemenite music, which was adopted as a kind of authentic ancient Jewish folk music. In contrast, the songs of Eretz Israel were associated with the Ashkenazi elite, the old-timers who "built the country" and fought for it. These songs are also associated with the national consensus, implying the love of the Jewish people for its homeland.

It is important to stress that this study is not dealing with the musical characteristics of different genres of Israeli popular music. Each of these three main characteristics has numerous subcategories which are beyond the scope of this chapter. Also, I am not trying to determine the degree of authenticity of each one of the genres, since it can be argued that it is impossible to do so for the definition of the concept is too ambiguous. Cohen (1988) suggested that "authenticity" is a socially constructed concept and its social connotation is "negotiable." He argues that the possibility of a social negotiation leads to the process which can be termed "emergent authenticity" during which the cultural product that was "invented" for various commercial or social reasons acquires new meaning and becomes an "authentic expression of the culture." Applying these notions to the analysis of the three main categories of Israeli popular music, it was suggested elsewhere (Adoni & Kama, 1991) that they all underwent a process of "emergent authenticity."

Songs of Eretz Israel were in many cases invented by Zionist poets and musicians who were consciously trying to invent "authentic" Israeli folklore and can be seen as a phenomenon of "invention of tradition" which occurred in many societies and cultures (Hobsbawm, 1983). International pop music was composed and distributed at least to a certain extent for commercial reasons, and Israeli Oriental music is not equivalent to the original music brought from various countries of the Diaspora. All three main categories of Israeli popular music are fusions of different styles and influences, and therefore in the context of this study I was equally interested in all three types and in particular in the intrinsic tension related to the foreign-indigenous dilemma.

RECORDING INDUSTRY: PATTERNS OF
PRODUCTION AND DISTRIBUTION

Research on culture in society has shown that one of the main questions regarding cultural environments concerns cultural products as commodities. Patterns of production of books (Escarpit, 1971) and records (Peterson & Berger, 1975; Peterson, 1976; DiMaggio, 1975) and their distribution patterns have been shown to be a decisive factor in the development of culture and its social functions for society, subcultures and individuals. One of the major directions of our research, therefore, was a survey of organizations which deal with the production and distribution of music. However, at this stage of our study, it has to be emphasized that a deficiency in statistics about the operations of the record industry is a worldwide problem (Wallis & Malm, 1984) and at times compels researchers to rely on estimates. In Israel there are 12 recording companies of note with an estimated annual output of about 700 releases. Six of these are major companies which during 1988 sold over 100,000 records (CBS, Hed Artzy, Phonokol, Eastronics, Israphon and Hataklit) and another six are medium-sized companies which sold during the same year between 15,000 and 38,000 records (Helikon, Galron, Kinereth, Reuveni and CDI). In addition there are several smaller companies which record about one or two records per year.

The majority of these records are of locally produced music, but about 25% include music purchases from international recording companies, usually British and American. There is almost no production of singles, but almost exclusively full-length albums. Each recording company has its own recording policy. The differences between them can be examined according to several criteria: (1) the extent of recording and/or printing of jazz and classics in comparison to pop music; (2) the extent of recording and/or printing of Israeli music in comparison to foreign, imported music; (3) the extent of importing foreign records (recorded and printed abroad); and (4) promotion techniques and policies. According to our sources, popular music constitutes the major output of all the companies, yet most of them also record jazz and classical music. There are, however, some differences among the various companies. Galron's production can be divided almost equally in half: one part classical music and jazz and the other recent pop music. Hed Artzy records mainly popular music, but an estimated 20% of its output is classical. At both Helikon and Eastronics, pop music is the dominant genre, yet they too record classical music and jazz.

These same companies also serve as importers and distributors of foreign records. The music which Galron supplies to the Israeli market is about 30% local music (including all the different genres), another 30% consists of foreign music purchased abroad and recorded in Israeli studios and about 40% is imported records. Most of their imports, both records and recording copyrights, are from small British companies. About 20% of Hed Artzy's output consists of foreign records or tapes imported to Israel, about 40% foreign music (both popular and classic) recorded in Israeli studios and about 40% music both written and recorded in Israel. Hed Artzy is connected with the American firm WEA (the three companies Warner, Electra and Atlantic). Hed Artzy also deals with the American-German company Ariola Artista and purchases pop and reggae music from a British company, Island. Eastronics recording company deals with foreign music. About 60% of its output is foreign music recorded in Israel; the remaining 40% is imported records. This company is the Israeli representative of several international companies such as RCA and Arto (which supply most of its classical music) and Motown and Pablo (which supply pop and jazz).

Promotion policies differ regarding local and imported music, though there are no significant differences among the companies. Local material, including all the major genres of popular music (i.e., Oriental, Eretz Israel and Israeli rock and pop music) is promoted by interviewing local musicians on radio and television. All the companies which record local material regularly send DJ discs to the relevant radio channels and a video clip, if available, to the television programs devoted to pop music. Most of the companies report that it is not commercially worthwhile to make a special video clip for a record which is to be marketed only in Israel. There is very limited promotion of imported records. Not all music shops carry these records, which are much more expensive than the local ones. Foreign music recorded in Israel is advertised by sending DJ discs to radio stations and, frequently, by purchasing the video clip from abroad. Helikon, the youngest recording company, has two public relations departments, one responsible for local records and the other for foreign material. They start their campaigns about a year before the records are expected to be on the market.

According to the 1990 Yellow Pages, there are over 100 stores in the three major Israeli cities which sell records, cassettes and videocassettes. In Greater Tel Aviv area, with its population of half a million, there are 80 music stores, in Jerusalem there are 14 and in Haifa 11 such establishments. Of course there are also music stores in smaller towns and special sections in all the big department stores and university shops. In 1988 nearly 3 million records (i.e., LPs, music casettes and CDs) were sold. This sales figure includes all the records produced in Israel: both original productions recorded by local artists and foreign productions reproduced in Israel in accordance with agreements between local and international companies. These figures did not include records imported directly by privately owned stores, of which there are no official accounts. The same is true of many Oriental musicians who record at home and do not normally participate in the royalty system.

The comparison between sale charts of the ten most popular records of either Israeli or foreign artists bears evidence of high degree of popularity of Israeli musical fare. The top local record sold about 2% of the entire 1988 sales volume while the top foreign record achieved a mere 0.75%. Furthermore, the ninth record on the local chart sold slightly more than the first one on the foreign chart. Taken together, the ten local artists had a share of approximately 13% of the total volume of sales versus 5% shared by the top ten foreign records.

The composition of these two sale charts is also of interest in the context of this study. The Israeli chart includes three pop singers, four rock numbers and three artists singing songs of Eretz Israel. Occupying first place is Gali Atari, an exemplary middle-of-the road pop singer; second and third places on the chart are held by Rita, a rock singer, while Yehuda Poliker is in fourth place on the chart on the strength of a record containing an unusual mixture of Holocaust-related texts with rock-adapted Greek tunes. On the foreign chart the picture is much more homogeneous: eight records in the chart are "mixes" of various artists that represent current hits and prevalent genres predominated by disco.

The picture that emerges from these data portrays a music market consuming a lot of imported music yet an even greater quantity of various genres of Israeli popular music. To do justice to Israel's recording companies, it must be said that they are aware of the problematics of the situation and consciously foster local talents. Two-thirds of their output consists of Israeli music; nevertheless a major share of the music supplied to the Israeli public still consists of either imported records or imported music; the copyrights are purchased from large foreign companies and then recorded by Israeli recording companies. This is true for both classical and popular music, yet approximately 70% of the imported records and/or music consists of international youth music composed and produced in Britain and the United States. For foreign recording companies, there are four main methods to penetrate the local market: (1) by having Israeli representatives who function as distributing agents; (2) by selling records to Israeli distribution companies; (3) by selling copyrights to their music; (4) by regularly supplying new records to Israeli radio. As has been shown, most Israeli recording companies participate, at least to some extent, in three of the methods mentioned above for importing foreign popular music to Israel. In the next section, while describing the main characteristics of the Israeli broadcasting system, I shall demonstrate how the fourth method works within this system.

BROADCASTING AND THE PRESS

Television

The Israeli Broadcasting Authority is a public broadcasting organization responsible for both radio and television broadcasts and financed by license fees paid by TV set owners. Established upon the BBC model, the IBA operates according to the Broadcasting Authority Law, which states that the Broadcasting Authority is a public service and its main functions are determined by the needs of Israeli citizens and of Jews throughout the world. Its main task is to provide educational entertaining and informational programs in Hebrew and Arabic as well as in several other languages. These programs have to deal with all domains of social life: politics, economics, welfare, science, art and culture. In addition, the law ensures equal and balanced exposure of various political viewpoints and fosters various expressions of Jewish culture and folklore. After a long public debate, the Knesset recently passed a law licensing the Second Channel, which is financed by commercial advertising and which recently started to broadcast on a regular basis.

On the First Channel of Israeli television there are two weekly programs featuring mainly pop music. On the Second Channel there are also several weekly programs covering both the Israeli and the foreign, mainly British and American, musical scenes. The bulk of each program is devoted to video clips of the latest hits in Israel and abroad, but there are also live interviews with Israeli musicians and foreign guests as well as live music performances of aspiring new bands. In addition, both channels broadcast many special programs devoted entirely to jazz and pop and rock music as well as the newest videoclips, which serve as "fillers" between various programs. The gradual introduction of Cable TV to Israeli households, since 1990, marks the beginning of a new era both in television viewing and in the exposure to popular music, since MTV is one of the most popular channels among young Israelis.

There are also many programs devoted specifically to indigenous Israeli music, which fall into two basic categories. The first features a sing-song with one or several popular musicians. These are usually recorded live in the dining room of a kibbutz or in a big hotel. Singing together--around a campfire or indoors--has always been popular with Israelis and in recent years there has been great revival of this activity. All generations are usually represented--from the very young to the senior members of the community. However, it must be stressed that the most active participants are in the large 30 to 60 age group. Younger Israelis do not particularly like the public song feasts; they prefer various genres of popular youth music.

The second category of TV programs dedicated to local music features one or several well-known singers and musicians who present a solo evening or a shared program, which is generally focused on a specific subject. For example, a program in honour of famous Israeli poets, such as Alterman or Rachel, will present only the songs written to the lyrics of their poems. On national and religious holidays, television programs feature songs and music celebrating various aspects of these holidays. It is important to stress that these programs are presented on the evening of the holidays, when the religious segments of the population do not turn on their television sets. The repertoire of these programs mainly includes the songs of Eretz Israel, which very often give expression to collective national experiences such as the history of the Jewish settlements in Palestine, love of country (its history, archaeology and nature) as well as the traumas of wars and longing for a better, more peaceful future. Naturally, there are also songs which deal with the individual's emotions, fears and hopes. The educational television programs in the afternoons also feature well-known singers and musicians who present various programs for children and teenagers. These programs combine educational and informational material with Israeli songs which are very similar to their American and English counterparts.

Radio

IBA's radio station "Voice of Israel" (Kol Israel) operates six radio channels which vary in their target audience and consequently in the composition and character of their programming. Channel 1 primarily broadcasts serious, informative programs and magazines dealing with history, culture, literature and politics. Of its 18 daily broadcasting hours, about two and a half are devoted to music. This channel gives priority to Israeli music, mostly Hebrew songs, but also includes interesting programs on the folklore and native music of other countries. Channel two broadcasts light informational programs, many magazines and interviews, entertainment programs, games and advertisements. About 40% of its total 19 hours of daily broadcasting time is devoted to music, either solely in musical programs or as combined with other types of programs. It is important to note that on this channel the time is equally divided between foreign and Israeli music. The foreign music is mainly pop and international rock music, but there are also slots for Greek, South American, Middle Eastern and other types of music. In addition, Channel 2 has "request programs" for songs chosen by listeners.

In our study, Channel 3 or "Reshet Gimel" is the most important one. It was established in the late 1970s with the clearly defined objective of catering for young audiences. Channel 3 broadcasts only musical programs and advertisements. Its hours are from 6 a.m. to 1 p.m., seven days a week. Channel 3 features imported music, but Israeli songs and other local music also appear, generally Israeli versions of international youth-music genres. About 45% of the programming time is devoted to local music, 55% to the imported fare. There are times that the channel broadcasts imported music only, when a whole week, for example, is devoted to the British or American hit parades. On other occasions a whole day may be devoted to the hit parade of Israeli songs. Three hours daily out of the channel's 19 hours are personal programs presented by three popular disc jockeys; they spend about 60% of their time on music. On Channel 3 there are at least 6 hours of uninterrupted music every day and about two-thirds of all the musical fare is imported.

Channel 3 stays on top of everything that happens on the pop scene in London and New York. The connections between the IBA and the American and British recording industries are very close and the information flow is highly efficient. Israeli radio is updated about three or four days after the release of a new record. The large companies such as CBS and Philips regularly send free samples of their new singles and albums to Israel. Israeli recording companies supply about 8 to 20 copies of each record to the IBA for a nominal fee. The more popular the record, higher the number of samples supplied. It is important to note that due to the relatively high price of records, Israel's hit charts are not based on record sales but rather on postcard "votes" sent to the radio.

Three weekly programs on Channel 3 keep young listeners informed of the latest news in the world of pop. These programs are timed specifically to reach young audiences. Immediately after they come home from school at 2 p.m., youngsters can listen to the "Tonny Fine Show" featuring all the newest hits from London and New York. When a song enters one of the Top 50 places in English or American charts, a single is immediately flown to Israel and Israelis can listen to it the following day. "Tonny Fine" is a daily program with a total of seven broadcasting hours weekly. There are another two programs devoted to the British and American charts--one daily from 5 to 6 p.m., the other weekly from 6 to 9 p.m.--presenting the Israeli hit parade of foreign recordings. The IBA`s Channel 4 the "Voice of Music" station (Kol Hamusika), broadcasts only classical music--including live transmissions from concert halls--and informational programs on related topics.

Besides the IBA`s radio channels, there are also two channels of Galei Zahal, operated by the Israeli Defense Forces (IDF). These channels function as the military spokesperson and deal with the particular needs of Israel's military forces. Consequently they combine informational programs on military matters with educational programming on the history, geography and archaeology of Israel and intersperse these with popular music. Since most Israeli soldiers are young (boys are drafted at 18 for three years, girls for two) Galei Zahal channels broadcast popular youth music to insure their listening and participation. They broadcast 24 hours a day and many soldiers tune in during the hours they are on duty.

IBA's channels 5 and 6 are geared to foreign countries and Arab audiences and are not directly relevant to this study. However, as Regev (1986) pointed out, Arab music is an important part of the Israeli musical "soundscape." This phenomenon is also enhanced by the transmission from Arab countries' radio stations. In summing up the managerial attitudes and policies at the IBA, it should be noted that they are aware of their problematic relations between imported and local music. People responsible for the musical programming on different channels stressed that they try to balance the two while satisfying the needs and interests of their audiences. Music show presenters who were interviewed were also conscious of this issue and made an effort to present their audiences with well-balanced musical selections. This issue of imported versus local popular music is by no means the only dilemma confronted by IBA policymakers.

As was mentioned in the introductory section of this paper, the tension between Israel's major ethnic groups is one of the country's central political and social problems. A sense of social inferiority and deprivation prevaded certain segments of the Sephardi-Oriental community, extending to cultural as well as other spheres of social life. In the early 1970s, for instance, a heated and prolonged public debate arose concerning the low proportion of popular Oriental music heard on Israeli radio. It was claimed that Sephardi composers and performers had less access to popular music programs, particularly to the hit parade of the Hebrew songs.

Some disc jockeys were even accused of "ethnic discrimination." Political and social changes in the late 1970s and early 1980s changed this situation to a great extent, with two major results in the cultural domain. The first was a reassessment of the intrinsic nature of Jewish Oriental tradition and culture by both ethnic groups. The Ashkenzai populations became more open to Jewish culture as developed in Middle Eastern and North African countries, while the various Oriental communities became increasingly proud of their cultural heritage. The second important consequence was the application of this new social awareness in cultural policy making. Today Israeli radio is fully open to Oriental music and Israeli musicians with Oriental backgrounds. In fact, about two years ago the country was swept by a wave of popular songs in Oriental style composed and performed by musicians from all the ethnic groups. These songs were enthusiastically received by both young and not-so-young audiences. Currently, Greek music and Greek-style Israeli songs are most popular. Some of the singers who only a few years ago performed at nothing but weddings have become major stars, recording full-length albums of songs that have clearly entered the mainstream of Israeli music.

Shlomo Bar's musical group "Habrera Hativit," whose members play and compose exclusively Oriental music and have been the pioneers in enhancing the reception of Oriental sound by general audiences, is one of the most prestigious and esteemed musical groups in the country. The list of Israeli hits in 1988 consisted of 31 of the international pop music category, 16 songs of Eretz Israel and three Oriental songs. The first two places on this chart are rock songs by Rita with 384 and 370 airplays, respectively.

Third place is occupied by Yehuda Poliker's Eretz Israel song (340 times). The first of the Oriental songs, by the now world-famed Opfra Haza, is in thirty-seventh place with 175 airplays. In comparison, in first place among the foreign hits was "Yeke Yeke," the African ethnic rock song played 202 times during 1988; the second place (169 times) was occupied by an Eddie Grant reggae hit. After these two songs the remainder of the list includes an array of Anglo-American hits varying from Sting to Pet Shop Boys, the only exception being one French song which placed fifteenth with 133 airplays during 1988. All three of the Israeli musical genres enjoy precedence over imported musics in airplay time.

In 1988 the number one on the chart for imported music was played only as often as a song by Shoshana Damari, a veteran singer since the mid-1940s, which was number 22 on the Israeli chart. These findings are supported by data accumulated by ACUM between 1985 and 1988 which reveal a trend toward a quantitative equality between local and imported music. This trend suggests the emergence and strengthening of the local popular music. Table 7.1 contains the percentages of broadcasting time of local and imported music out of the total music hours broadcast by all Israeli radio stations.

Table 7.1. Broadcasting Time of Local and Imported Music (percentage of total hours of music broadcasting)

Year	Local	Foreign	Total Hours	
1985	48	52	16.297	
1986	46	54	12.297	*
1987	46	54	15.547	**
1988	50	50	16.595	

* Because of a change in data-gathering procedure, 1986 was a nine-month "year."

** This sum is relatively small due to a strike of IBA employees during almost 2 months in 1987.

Press

Almost all the daily newspapers have weekly columns devoted to popular music. Most of the popular weekly and monthly magazines cover the popular music scene in Israel and abroad. There is one magazine which is devoted exclusively to the local and international pop/rock scene. There are also special columns in local weekly newspapers which are financed through advertising and distributed free of charge. Highly popular, these throw-always reach every segment of the population and all age groups.

Maariv Lanoar, a weekly for the young reading public, which is issued by the major evening paper *Maariv*, naturally devotes special attention to everything connected with youth music. It is interesting to note that *Ba'Machane*, the IDF weekly, also has wide coverage of new records and recording stars, disco club openings and other aspects of the local and international pop scene.

ISRAELI MUSICIANS: A GLIMPSE INTO THE CREATIVE MUSICAL MILIEU

Personal and Professional Backgrounds

Among 13 interviewees there were 7 women and 6 men, in age from 28 to 43. In comparison to some foreign superstars this is definitely not a young age group. All of them had finished at least high school, and some also had higher education. Most of our respondents had musical influence in their immediate environment since early childhood. In many cases, at least one parent and in several cases both parents were performing artists. When asked where they had received their musical training, the subjects reported several ways of learning music in their childhood and youth. Family influence was apparently very strong--most of the musicians got their early musical training from their parents and relatives. They also mentioned self-training, learning at private lessons or in small groups. Most of the musicians were encouraged by their parents from the very start of their musical careers. Parents encouraged their children by taking an active interest in their playing, by exposing them to music and by actually teaching musical skills and paying tuition for training.

Several of the musicians were members of military musical groups, considered to be an excellent start for a professional career. After highly competitive professional examinations, young musicians (18 years old) are accepted in these troupes as part of their military service. The interviewed artists have a great deal in common regarding their professional backgrounds. Since in Israel there is no musicians' union, they all belong to the Israeli Union of Performing Artists (IUPA). Most of them do not work in nonmusical jobs. All the musicians compose music which is recorded with Hebrew lyrics. In about half the cases, they themselves write the lyrics. Most of them compose music which is performed mainly by themselves as well as by other musicians.

Eleven of the musicians are singers and they usually sing alone. Some musicians are accompanied by groups of young, usually unknown, singers or attractive female dancers. Nevertheless, these are not "groups" in the American or English sense, as they do not work or create together. Recently, however, several such groups do perform in Israel and enjoy a high degree of popularity. In the majority of cases there are no "stage names": musicians generally perform under their own names. Most of the interviewed musicians are also instrumentalists: one excels in four instruments, two play three instruments, another two play two instruments each and six of them play one instrument.

Eight of the musicians claim that in order to continue supporting themselves solely from their music, they need only to continue what they are already doing. However, four among them feel that they will have to make some artistic compromises and pay more attention to audiences' tastes.

The majority of the group believe that their music represents the Israeli culture, both present and past. Four of them believe that their music mostly represents contemporary culture. Moreover, most of them report that their work emphasizes specific cultural and political themes, yet two of the most popular musicians, Shlomo Artzy and Nurith Galron, noted that their music is highly personal and not representative of any larger cultural trends.

Most of the respondents compose "danceable" music but they do not believe that this is an essential ingredient of their music's popularity among young audiences. All of them feel that in Israeli society musicians have higher status than film stars, yet they all agree that government agencies do nothing to encourage local popular music.

All musicians record in professional studios and most of the recorded songs have Hebrew lyrics. Eleven of these musicians have recorded at least one album with a major recording company. One has produced his own single record; another has had an album produced by a small recording company. They all have arrangements with distributors; none is personally involved in record sales. Their records are distributed by recording companies and sold in record stores. The majority reported that they did not have to compromise between the type of music they would like to record and what they have been able to record. Five made some compromises; they believe that as a result of the limited size of their audience in Israel there is a demand for constant change and innovations which constrain the country's musical scene. As a rule, these musicians have formal contracts with their recordings companies and in most cases lawyers represent the interests of all the participating parties. In six cases the copyrights of their recordings are held by the musicians themselves or the recording group. In other cases the producer retains the copyright. The interviewees were not willing to supply information on the exact number of their records sold: either they did not know or were not willing to provide details of their incomes. In Israel there is no difference between "local" and "national" media coverage.

There are no local television or radio channels; like newspapers, they are all nationwide. The local throwaways, mentioned previously, are the only exceptions. The interviewed musicians reported that their recordings, performances and other musical events are all covered by all types of print media: magazines and daily papers, local newspapers and small local bulletins and schedules.

The majority of our respondents believe that radio and television promoted their music on both national and international levels. All the respondents believe that Israeli television is the single most influential factor in increasing their popularity and record sales. The introduction of TV in 1967 is perceived as a crucial point in the development of local popular music.

Sources of Influence

The musical sources which the interviewees felt had influenced them were quite diverse.

In analyzing the sources of Israeli music, Sassi Keshet talked about the Russian music and early Israeli "shepherd songs" which had dominated the country's music until the late 1950s. In the past, he felt, Italian, Greek and French music had been significant, but today they have given way to the stronger British and American musical presence. Several musicians, including Yehudit Ravitz, Ricki Gal and Yael Levy emphasized the fusion of various cultures and music types--Russian, middle-Eastern, Eastern and international music. Oshik Levy, in his turn, pointed out the combination of Ladino songs (Jewish Sephardi music) and East European music, alongside the Beatles and Rolling Stones.

Both Chani Livne and Shula Chen felt that International Western music currently exerts the strongest influence in Israel, while Shlomo Artzy singled out the Beatles and several Israeli singers as his most important sources of influence. The musical sources which influenced the respondents' personal styles were even more diverse and it is thus difficult to sum them up in any general way. Yehudit Ravitz was influenced by different types of rhythmic music--American, South American and Oriental--and by the work of Israeli artist Matti Caspo, She particularly likes soft rock, such as Elton John's.

Classical music, cantorial chants and the scores written for movies and musicals influenced Sassi Keshet's development as a singer-actor. His personal inclination is toward the romantic--"a combination of Neil Diamond and Elton John," but he also likes French chansons, jazz, blues, swing and various types of rock and roll. Nurith Galron was particularly influenced by Israeli musicians Yael German and Chava Alberstein and also in her early stages by Hassidic melodies, Her family's German background and especially Kurt Weill's music left a mark on her early musical development. Jazz and music by Billy Holliday, Duke Ellington, Janis Ian and Joni Mitchell rank as her favorites.

A curious combination of classical and gypsy music influenced Chani Livne's musical personality. She likes Tina Turner's style and the sincerity of her lyrics and the songs of Janis Ian and Carole King. Ricki Gal's taste tends toward various modern rhythms, such as Brazilian and Latin music. She likes rock-theatre, soul and Bette Midler. Midler was mentioned also by Shula Chen, who also recognized in her own style the influences of Elton John and the Beatles. She particularly likes French chansons "where the lyrics are important" and the singing of Dolly Parton, Barbra Streisand and Esther Opharim (an Israeli living in France). Oshik Levy was greatly influenced by a 1967 performance of Tom Jones in New York and by Frank Sinatra and Elvis Presley. Last but not least, Shlomo Artzy acknowledges Paul Simon's stylistic influence.

This rather detailed information on musical sources of influence has been presented here in order to illustrate, on the one hand, the powerful effect of Western-international music and on the other, the wide and rich frame of other musical references. It is worth noting that 8 of our respondents revealed that the most dominant influence on their style was a foreign artist whom they do not know personally. In fact all these musicians admit that they have been heavily influenced by international Western music.

When asked to single out a significant event which influenced their decision to become professional musicians, nearly all mentioned a rock or a pop concert they attended in the United States. However, they also claimed that they have been influenced by Jewish musical traditions and by the Israeli contemporary scene. Hence, even when their music does have a distinct international sound, its roots are pronouncedly indigenous. And by and large, they all believe that their music represents contemporary Israeli culture as well as the old Jewish traditions.

The musicians did not feel that foreign popular music had a deleterious effect on their creativity or technical skills. On the contrary, they felt that a particular blend of various musical types was emerging through their own and their colleagues' musical output. All of them also stressed the great improvement in the technology of recording that enables them to work under conditions that enhance and promote better sounds.

The audiences of the interviewed musicians cover a whole range of social segments in the Israeli society. Four of the interviewed musicians--

Artzy, Ravitz, Keshet and Gal--envisage their audience as anywhere between 18 and 50 years of age. Shula Chen's audiences are mainly young children and adolescents. Chani Livne sings primarily for young adults. Oshik Levy claims that his audience comprises very large segments of the population: he performs in kibbutzim and moshavim and in the big cities, for youth and adults alike. Several of the musicians emphasized that they prefer audiences which are intelligent, open, interested in their music and able to provide serious feedback. Ravitz stressed that it is important to listen to her lyrics.

Keshet seeks listeners who share his interests; and Galron prefers an audience which resembles her, intellectually and emotionally. Artzy is not interested in people who do not understand his music and cannot give feedback. Yael Levy wants to make contact with her audience through her music and therefore looks for audiences who display sensitivity and identification with her work.

COMMENTARY AND CONCLUSIONS

In this chapter I have attempted to describe and analyze the components of the Israeli musical environment while locating it in its historical, cultural and socioeconomic contexts. This holistic approach stemmed primarily from the cultural trend in the study of mass media and culture (Bourdieu, 1974, 1980; Foucault, 1977; Lewis, 1978; Robinson, 1985; Robinson et al., 1991; Shudson, 1987). The composite which emerges from our various data sources is complex and often ambiguous. For better or for worse, Israel is a culturally open society characterized by highly efficient and effective communication with other societies. Each year hundreds of thousands of tourists visit the country and Israelis themselves travel abroad frequently. (Note, for example, that all the musician interviewees have attended major musical events in the United States or Great Britain). Under these circumstances, it is virtually impossible for Israel to remain culturally isolated and immune to foreign influences. Furthermore, as a small country facing constant external and internal tensions, Israel is simply not able to supply all the cultural needs of its heterogeneous population.

One of the many consequences of this situation is that the Israeli musical market is to some extent dependent on a foreign supply of recordings of popular international youth music. However, I would like to emphasize that there does exist a dynamic, thriving musical scene in Israel: a proportionately high number of musicians composing in diverse genres; a high recording level and large audiences eager to hear "made in Israel" music. In other words, there seems to be a modus vivendi between imported music and that which is indigenous and/or locally produced in terms of production, distribution and consumption of musical fare, a situation compatible with McCormack's (1969) "additive" hypothesis according to which local culture is a semiautonomous cultural domain and thus can exist side by side with mass culture.

The main issue in the context of this commentary is to what extent does Israeli music environment permit genuine creativity on the part of local artists? Or is the imported culture so powerful that it dominates the local one to the extent that it will eventually destroy it and any spark of artistic creativity will be doomed to result in second-rate imitations? On the basis of this research, I would suggest that this need not happen and that there is a type of interrelation which may be termed the absorption hypothesis. According to this hypothesis, interrelations with foreign popular music may under certain social conditions encourage innovative musical creation. The Israeli musical scene might be a convincing illustration of this possibility, not only because foreign and local music exist here simultaneously, but also because of evidence that the musical imports foster the production and distribution of local music in several subtle ways.

This may be seen first in the technical level of performance. The very fact that imported music is recorded on such a high professional level constitutes a challenge to local composers, musicians and performers. Every musician who participated in our study mentioned the influence of electronic instruments, the high performance level and the innovative techniques of making music and also video clips by British and American musicians.

Another positive influence is obvious on the stylistic level. Young Israeli composers are influenced by musical genres such as rock, hard rock and black music, and by various modes of expression such as protest songs. These can be adapted to Israeli social context and musical traditions without necessarily making Israeli music a mere imitation. The musicians interviewed in this study were well aware of this type of influence, yet their final products reflect many other musical sources as well, so that the most talented among them clearly create music with an authentic personal signature. Granted, the relation between representatives of imported music and those of the local scene are not idyllic and tension-free; Israeli performers were very open in discussing their problems on this score. However, the representatives of both the recording industry and the Israeli Broadcasting Authority see a cultural imperative in preserving the balance between local and foreign music and have promulgated measures to insure its continued existence. This intervention is positive and essential as fostering a cultural policy which responds in a healthy self-defense to a flood of foreign music and imported records.

The music critics and the radio music-program editors who were interviewed in this study unanimously agreed that the Israeli musical arena has been significantly changed during the last decade. This change had been taking place through social dynamics in which popular music influenced by Anglo-American rock and pop encroached on the songs of Eretz Israel and, eventually and suprisingly enough, took dominance over the imported foreign materials from which it had originated. On the other hand, songs of Eretz Israel as well as Oriental music have gone through profound change as they accommodated both external and internal influences. Songs of Eretz Israel adopted electronic and electric instruments and recording devices. Oriental music has been undergoing marked changes as well, such as refinement of lyrics and better recording techniques resulting in improved sounds.

In sum all the genres of popular music have enjoyed in recent years an efflorescence that has no precedent in the history of Israeli popular culture. In fact, the conclusions of this study are quite similar to those of Robinson et al. (1991), who suggested that the "one-way flow" of international music "has not homogenised world music" and that "popular music . . . has evolved via a process of continuous cultural exchange" (p. 259). A longer time perspective and an ongoing compilation and reevaluation of data will be required to understand the implication of the present trends to future developments. At this point, however, we may conclude that the Israeli musical scene shows no symptoms of stagnation or decadence.

On the contrary, it is thriving and innovative, particularly in its syntheses of the modern international popular music with various Jewish musical traditions. I would argue that the current trend is toward functional coexistence between imported and local music (Adoni, 1983, 1986). In terms of young audiences, it may be hypothesised that, on an aesthetic level, imported music satisfied the thirst for postmodern, sophisticated sound at the highest performing level. On the societal level, this music possibly enhances generational consciousness among young people, of both their own youth culture in Israeli society and their invisible bonds with other young people throughout the world. Local music remains an essential ingredient of cultural life as it fulfils two seemingly contradictory, but in fact complementary, functions on the macrosocietal level. On the one hand, it preserves ethnic, religious and other social identities, this being a central sociopolitical need of Israel's pluralistic society. On the other hand, it includes cultural elements which are critical in fostering social integration and the creation of an authentic Israeli culture.

BIBLIOGRAPHY

Adoni, H. (1983). "Youth and Music Industry in Israel." paper presented to a Wing-spread Conference on Youth and the International Music Industry, Racine, Wisconsin.

Adoni, H. (1986). "Popular Music in Israel." *Critical Studies in Mass Communication.* September, 369-371.

Adoni, H. & Kama, A. (1991). "Something Old, Something New, Something Borrowed: Emergence of New Interrelations Between Foreign and Indigenous Popular Music in Israel." Unpublished monograph.

Adorno, T.W. (1976). *Introduction to the Sociology of Music.* Trans. E.G. Ashton. New York: Seabury.

Ala, N.; Fabbri, F.; Fiori, U.; & Chezzi, E. (1985). "Patterns of Music Consumption in Milan and Reggio Emilia." *Popular Music Perspectives,* 2.

Ben-Porat, Z. (1989). *Lyric Poetry and the Lyrics of Pop.* Tel Aviv, Tel Aviv University (in Hebrew).

Benski, T. (1989). "Ethnicity and the Shaping of Musical Taste Patterns in an Israeli Urban Community." *Social Forces,* 67(3), 731-750.

Blaukopf, K. (Ed.) (1982). *The Phonogram in Cultural Communication: Report on a Research Project Undertaken by Mediacult.* Vienna: Springer-Verlag.

Bourdieu, P. (1974). "Cultural Reproduction and Social Reproduction." In R. Brown (Ed.), *Knowledge, Education and Cultural Change.* London: Tavistock.

Bourdieu, P. (1980). "The Aristocracy of Culture." *Media Culture and Society* 2(3), July.

Brake, M. (1980). *The Sociology of Youth Culture and Youth Subculture.*, London: Routledge and Kegan Paul.

Clarke, M. (1973). "The Skinheads and the Study of Youth Culture." Birmingham: Center for Contemporary Cultural Studies, No. 23.

Cohen, A. (1972). "Social Control and Subcultural Change." *Youth and Society* 3, 259-276.

Cohen, E., & Shiloah, A. (1985). "Major Trends of Change in Jewish Oriental Ethnic Music in Israel." *Popular Music*, 5, 199-223.

Cohen, E. (1988). "Authenticity and Commodization in Tourism." *Annals of Tourism Research*, 19(3), 371-386.

Cohen, S. (1980). *Folk Devils and Moral Panics.* Oxford: Robertson.

Denisoff R.S. & Peterson R.A. (1972). *The Sounds of Social Change.* Chicago: Rand McNally.

DiMaggio, P. and Useem, M. (1978). "Social Class and Arts Consumption: The Origins and Consequences of Class Differences in Exposure to Art in America." *Theory and Society*, 5(2): 141-161.

Escarpit R. (1971). *Sociology of Literature.* London: Frank Cass.

Foucault, M. (1977). *The Archaeology of Knowledge.* London: Tavistock.

Frith, S. (1978). *The Sociology of Rock.* London: Constable.

Frith, S. (1983). *Sound Effects: Youth Leisure and the Politics of rock 'n' Roll.* London: Constable.

Frith, S. (1988). *Music for Pleasure: Essays in the Sociology of Pop.* Oxford: Polity Press.

Halper, J., Seroussi, E. & Squires-Kidron, P. (1989). "Musica Mizrakhit: Ethnicity and Class Culture in Israel." *Popular Music* 8(2), 131-141.

Hebdige, D. (1979). *Subculture: The Meaning of Style.* London: Methuen.

Hirsch, P.M. (1971). "Sociological Approaches to the Pop Music Phenomenon." *American Behavioral Scientist*, 14(3), 371-389.

Hobsbawm, E. (1983). "Introduction: Inventing Traditions." In E. Hobsbawm and T. Ranger (Eds.), *The Invention of Tradition.* Cambridge: Cambridge University Press.

Israel Government Yearbook 1985-1986. Jerusalem: 1986.

Lewis, G.H. (1978). "Trend Report: The Sociology of Popular Culture." *Current Sociology*, 26(3).

Lewis, G.H. (1980). "Taste, Culture and Their Composition: Toward a New Theoretical Perspective." In E. Katz and T. Szecko (Eds.), *Mass Media and Social Change.* Beverly Hills CA: Sage.

Lull, J. (1985). "On the Communicative Properties of Music." *Communication Research*, 12(3): 363-372.

Martin B. (1982). Pop Music and Youth." *Media Development* 29(1).

McCormack, T.W. (1969). "Folk Culture and the Mass Media." *Archive Europeennes de Sociologie*, 10(2).

Mendelsohn, H. (1964). "Listening to Radio." In L.A. Dexter & D.M. White (Eds.), *People, Society and Mass Communication.* New York: Free Press.

Murdock, G. & R., McCron (1976). "Consciousness of Class and Consciousness of Generation." In S. Hall & T. Jefferson (Eds.), *Resistance Through Rituals: Youth Subcultures in Postwar Britain.* London: Hutchinson.

Murdock, G. & R., McCron (1976). Youth and Class." In G. Mangham & G.A. Pearson (Eds.), *Working Class Youth Cultures.* London: Hutchinson.

Peterson, R.A. (1976). "The Production of Culture: A Prolegomenon." *American Behavioral Scientist,* 19.

Peterson, R.A. & D.G. Berger (1975). "Cycles in Symbol Production: The Case of Popular Music." *America Sociological Review,* 40.

Peterson, R.A. & P. DiMaggio (1975). "From Region to Class, The Changing Locus of Country Music: A Test of the Massification Hypothesis." *Social Forces,* 53.

Regev, M. (1986). "The Musical Soundscape as a Contest Area: Oriental Music and Israeli Popular Music." *Media, Culture and Society*, 8, 343-55.

Riesman, D. (1950). "Listening to Popular Music." *American Quarterly*, 2 (4).

Robinson, D.C. (1985). "Youth and Popular Music: A Theoretical Rationale for an International Study." *Gazette* 37, 30-50.

Robinson, D.C.; Buck, E.; Cuthbert, M. et al.; and the International Communication and Youth Culture Consortium (1991). *Music at the Margins: Popular Music and Global Cultural Diversity.* Newbury Park, CA: Sage.

Roe, K. (1984). *Youth and Music in Sweden*, Lund: Lund University, Report 32.

Roe, K., & Carlsson, U. (Eds.) (1990). *Popular Music Research: An Anthology from NORDICOM-Sweden.* Goteborg: NORDICOM.

Rosengren, K.E. & Windahl, S. (1978). "The Media Panel: A Presentation of a Problem." *Media Panel Report,* No. 4 Lund: Lund University, Department of Sociology.

Rosengren, K.E..; Roe K.; & Sonesson J. (1983). "Finality and Causality in Adolescents' Mass Media Use." Paper presented to ICA Convention, Dallas.

Shudson, M. (1987). "The New Validation of Popular Culture: Sense and Sentimentality in Academia." *Critical Studies in Mass Communication*, 4(1), 51-68.

Wallis, R. & Malm, K. (1984). *Big Sounds from Small Peoples: The Music Industry in Small Countries.* London: Constable.

Wicke, P. (1985). "Young People and Music in East Germany: A Focus on a Scene." *Communication Research*, 12(3): 319-325.

Willis, E.P. (1980). "Symbolism and Practice: A Theory for the Social Meaning of Pop Music." Birmingham: Center for Contemporary Cultural Studies, No. 13.

CHAPTER 8

LOCAL MUSICIANS IN JAMAICA: A CASE STUDY

Marlene Cuthbert & Avonie Brown

BACKGROUND

In 1494, Christopher Columbus landed in Jamaica and found a clearly defined culture of Arawak Indians. Though he was credited with the "discovery" of the New World, it is now known that the indigenous peoples of the New World settled the region, possibly as much as 20,000 years prior to Columbus' landing (Black, 1958). Subdued by the military strength of the Spanish, the native population was subjected to forced labor. The encounter proved disastrous for the Arawaks, who were eventually rendered extinct by the Spanish conquerors, who were themselves replaced by the British with the signing of the Treaty of Madrid in 1670. With the native population eliminated, the British turned to West Africa and the importation of Africans to provide slave labor. In 1834 the slave trade ended, a trade that had facilitated the enslavement of over a million Africans by the British Empire.

Emancipation did not change the pattern of domination of African-Jamaicans by Europeans. Furthermore, indentured laborers from India and China were introduced to the island's continued unequal social and economic construct, which was still defined by the European minority. The resulting population is over 75% African, 20% brown mixtures such as Afro-European, Afro-East Indian and Afro-Chinese, about 2% East Indian and Chinese and 1% white. One significant feature of the postcolonial era in Jamaica is the continued connectedness of race with the definition of class. While there are exceptions, the upper class is often white or lighter skinned and the lower class is populated by the black majority.

The country's total dependence on Britain continued until 1944, when the activism of trade unions and protest movements in Jamaica contributed to the granting of universal suffrage and, in 1962, full independence. Jamaica, as Carl Stone (1989) states, is an anomaly in the Third World because of the relative stability of the two-party system fashioned after British parliamentary traditions (p. 20). The Peoples National Party (PNP) and the Jamaica Labour Party (JLP) are outgrowths of the vibrant trade union struggles for change. The PNP under the leadership of Michael Manley is now identified with the democratic socialist policies he tried to institute in the 1970s, while the JLP led by Edward Seaga has a more conservative capitalist agenda.

Situated in the northern Caribbean, 90 miles south of Cuba and a one-hour flight from Miami, the island has a population of more than 2.5 million people in an area of 11,000 square kilometers. The population growth rate is 1.3% with a life expectancy of over 70 years. Some 80% of the population is literate and nearly all children are enrolled in primary schools. GNP per capita is US $1,070 compared with that of United States at $19,840 (Thorndike, 1990, 32).

The labor force is heavily concentrated in the service industry (47%) with direct and indirect linkages to the tourist industry . Other areas of concentration include agriculture (35%) and the manufacturing (18%). Jamaica remains a primary exporter of raw material: bananas, bauxite, alumina, sugar, citrus fruits, rum, cocoa and coffee. Unemployment figures are very high with nearly a third of the labor force jobless, and income distribution is highly unequal with the richest 5% having 32% of the national income (Thorndike, 1990).

Jamaica's economy remains defined by dependency. Since political independence in 1962, its economic dependence has shifted from European imperial powers and succumbed to the neoimperialism of the United States. Jamaica, like the rest of the Caribbean and Latin America, has been disparagingly classified as a region in the "backyard" of the United States. The close proximity to the United States and a shared official language, English, have helped to ensure that the island remains a U. S. client state. Nearly 25% of export income goes to service the immense World Bank/IMF debt acquired since the late 1970s.

MUSICAL DEVELOPMENT

The culture of resistance is a dominant feature in all colonial encounters, and music is one element of cultural resistance. Music--drumming, singing and dancing--is central to the communal lifestyle of Jamaica. The culture of music extends to all aspects of life, including work, funerals, religious and cultural celebrations. Faced with a colonial society that reinforced European cultural hegemony, the African majority developed a complex, unique and often underground cultural network of games and rites that provided a vehicle for self-expression. Music has maintained this essential characteristic, expressing the identity of the majority (Cuthbert & Wilson, 1988, 3).

Mento, the first stage in the development of reggae, evolved out of the music and dance of slaves. This was a musical form concentrated in rural communities. But with increased urban migration from the 1940s to the 1960s, the rhythms of mento and religious cults were brought to the urban areas. The increased number of radio sets in the urban areas resulted in increased access to popular music in the United States (Cuthbert, 1985, 382).

As the popularity of American rhythm and blues (R&B) grew, so too did its impact on Jamaica's music. Musical instruments such as the electric guitar, organ and bass were included in local music creations. There were several stages in the development that were facilitated by both internal and external influences. Mento combined with R&B led to the blue beat, the jazz influence led to the development of ska, later to rock steady and finally to reggae in the late 1960s (Cuthbert, 1985, 383).

The development of reggae was also influenced by the distinctive drumming of Rastafarians. Both reggae and Rastafari were products of the ghetto of western Kingston and as such share a common theme of protest, giving voice to oppressed peoples. Reggae has also shared some of the religious philosophy of the Rastafari religious movement, which originated in Jamaica after Ras Tafari was crowned as Emperor Haile Selassie of Ethiopia in 1930. Rastafarians believe that Selassie is divine and his crowning the fulfilment of Old Testament prophecy and of the pronouncement by Jamaican National Hero, Marcus Garvey: "Look to Africa when a black king shall be crowned, for the day of deliverance is near" (Augier et al, 1960, 2). Rastafarians were also influenced by Marcus Garvey's Universal Negro Improvement Association and helped to define the Jamaican culture of resistance to colonialism, imperialism and racism. Reggae became a vehicle for expressing these views.

The strength and increasing popularity of reggae music since the 1970s has not stifled the flow of imported music. The close proximity to the United States means that satellite dish receivers, shortwave radio owners, as well as residents of the North Coast, are able to tune in and directly access Unite States television and/or radio stations.

In a 1983 survey of 300 Jamaican youth, Cuthbert found a strong correlation between socioeconomic status and musical preference, where the higher the socioeconomic status, the greater the preference for foreign over local music. Respondents from the upper class said that imported rock music reflected the way they dress, act and talk. In contrast, respondents from the lower socioeconomic class more readily identified with and were affected by reggae's message, highlighting the situation of the poor and oppressed. But the popularity of foreign music among the social elite has not changed the essential musical environment of the poor in Jamaica (Cuthbert, 1985, 390).

To provide greater access to reggae music, the sound systems and the dance halls remain essential alternatives to the broadcast media. They are fundamental to the strength of reggae music in Jamaica because they expose their audiences to the fullness and variety of the music. The music played is dictated by the taste and immediate responses of the audiences. They are outside the governmental and nonformal censoring of reggae music common at radio stations. These structures are illustrative of the characteristics of Enzenberger's (1974) "Emancipatory Use of Media" which include: decentralized program, each receiver a potential transmitter, mobilization of the masses, interaction of those involved (feedback), a political learning process and social control by self-organization (p. 113).

Reggae music, once classified as the music of the subculture, is now the dominant musical culture of Jamaica. The upper classes, with their continued white bias, once dismissed the music as militant, extreme and fanatical. By the 1980s they began to recognize the power of this popular expression and made attempts to exploit its wide public appeal. However, certain critical strains of reggae remain a tool for empowerment and a product of the lived experience and realities, both negative and positive, of Jamaica's working class.

THE MUSIC INDUSTRY

Inadequate regulations and documentation make access to information on the music industry difficult. Jamaica's recording industry began production during the early 1960s under local ownership. Between 1976 and 1980 the growing popularity of reggae attracted many international producers and artists to record in Jamaica. Local artists also began to be subcontracted to international labels. Advancements in technology such as digital and multi-track recording meant increased sophistication and costs of production. The increased expense of production also meant a restriction on the number of producers and artists.

After his election to office in 1980, Prime Minister Edward Seaga introduced deregulation and divestment policies with the intention of assisting the economic growth of critical areas in the economy. The effect on the recording industry was to create an oligopolistic enterprise. The few local companies that controlled the industry until then entered into joint contracts with international companies such as CBS, Capitol, Island, and EMI. Deregulation also meant that production and distribution costs increased dramatically. In 1983 the American transnational corporation CBS bought into Dynamic Sounds, one of Jamaica's leading recording companies/labels, after having been refused permission by previous governments (Cuthbert & Wilson, 1988, 10).

Transnationals are in a position of power because they have greater access to and control of advanced technology, as well as financial and distribution networks. How does this technological and economic control affect the creative control of reggae artists? One consequence of the internationalization of reggae is a "softer" sound to suit the tastes of foreign audiences and radio programmers. However, the strength of the musical tradition allows for divergent musical strategies, most of which are able to maintain the commitment to the language and culture from which reggae comes.

The international appeal of reggae in the 1980s meant an increase in its export. To adequately promote an artist internationally, large distribution companies are necessary. Many musicians have also migrated to the United States, Canada and Britain to access much larger audiences as well as better technical facilities. But while more structural facilities are available abroad, some artists have returned to Jamaica to produce their music because of the cultural "vibes" that are essential to making quality reggae music.

In large enclaves of Caribbean migrant communities in Toronto, Brooklyn, NY, Washington DC, and Brixton, England, small promotion companies are a growing phenomenon. With direct ties to the musicians in Jamaica, but being outside of the formal structures of the industry, they have become an essential element in the promotion and distribution of reggae artists in those communities.

CASE STUDY OF LOCAL MUSICIANS

Between February and August 1986 Cuthbert and two research assistants conducted interviews with 26 musicians in Jamaica. A judgmental sample was used because any kind of representative sampling of Jamaican artists is impossible since there is no available sampling frame from which one can select systematically.

The Jamaica Federation of Musicians (JFM) has only a partial listing of artists, consisting mainly of those who want protection because they play for the tourist trade and/or those who are financially successful enough to pay the membership fee. Hence musicians were selected from the three most distinctive music areas of the country: Kingston, which is the heartland of reggae (19 musicians), the North Coast tourist areas of Ocho Rios and Montego Bay (4 musicians) and the rural areas of Mandeville and May Pen (3 musicians).

Most interviews lasted between two and three hours, and many were conducted in two different sessions. The musicians consisted of 20 males and 6 females, and they ranged in age from 20 to 53 with approximately 28% (7 people) in both their twenties and forties, 42% (11) in their thirties, and one man age 53. Table 8.1 shows the breakdown by age and sex.

Table 8.1: Jamaican Artists by Age and Sex

Age	Sex		Total	
	F	M	F	M
Under 20	0	2	0	0
20 - 29	2	3	7	28
30 - 39	3	8	11	42
40 - 49	0	7	7	28
Over 50	0	1	1	4
Total	5	19	26	102

Note: Percentages do not total exactly 100 due to rounding.

Of the 26 respondents 14 were members of groups. Some 35% of the musicians were featured singers with their group, 27% singing as part of the group only, 19% singing by themselves and 15% not singing at all.

All but two artists played at least one instrument, nearly 50% of these playing at least two, and nearly 40% played three or more instruments, with one musician listing six instruments and another listing nine instruments. The guitar was the instrument played by the most musicians, followed by drums (usually acoustic but also synthetic, bongo and conga drums), and the saxophone (usually alto, but also the tenor sax). Other instruments played by more than one musician were the keyboard, acoustic piano, trumpet and autoharp. Table 8.2 lists the numbers who played these and other instruments.

Table 8.2: Instruments Played by Jamaican Musicians

Kind of Instrument	Number
Acoustic drums	8
Guitar	7
Electric bass guitar	5
Acoustic piano	5
Alto sax	4
Keyboard	3
Trumpet	2
Autoharp	1
Bongo drums	1
Conga drums	1
Synthetic drums	1
Electric lead guitar	1
Electric rhythm guitar	1
Tenor sax	1
Synthesizer	1

Virtually all instruments were owned by group members but in one North Coast venue the club owner/band manager supplied instruments. The amount of money invested in instruments was estimated for seven of the bands as follows: US$ 40,000, $20,000, $13,600, and four groups had spent about $4,000 each. The instruments of ten of the bands were financed from personal funds of individual members, two bands used a combination of personal funds and profits, while one band bought instruments entirely from profits.

Purchasing instruments is a major investment. While there is minimal local production of musical instruments, instruments of the highest caliber are imports and come with a correspondingly high cost. By any standards these figures are high, but coupled with a poor local economy--the Jamaica dollar is valued at approximately $8 US--the effects are even more severe for performers, especially those whose sole income is dependent on the fluctuating music industry.

Only 30% of respondents were working at a nonmusical job: three were self-employed, two were skilled service workers, one each held white-collar, skilled trade and unskilled worker jobs. Only two musicians earned all their 1985 income from these jobs, while two relied mainly on family and friends and two had also used savings. Thus the majority of musicians made most of their income, limited though it was, from musical activity.

Early Musical Formation

Most artists developed an interest in making music from a very early age, some from before they can remember. Over a third were showing interest in music by the age of 5 and almost a third more by the age of 10. Oftentimes musical instruments were available at home and/or the family was musical. Some musicians, to whom instruments were not readily available, made their own. One made a little guitar and two used a bamboo as a reed instrument or fife; another made drums from buckets and a pot; another made a guitar using fishing wire and a chocolate box, and one musician set up tins tied to the top of a barrel, cut a pair of sticks and taught himself to play on this drum. Need and desire led to a total expression of their multifaceted creativity.

When asked to identify the sources of their musical training, it became obvious that these musicians took the initiative, accepted help and took advantage of any available source. The majority of the artists (16) indicated that they were self-taught. Several received free lessons from friends or other musicians, a school band or cadet corp, a father or other relative. Another four received paid private or small group music lessons, and one attended a specialised music school.

Their musical development was encouraged by other events and circumstances. The primary factor was the artist's own appreciation of music, as indicated by seven of the respondents. Others were encouraged by a combination of their own innate ability and the support of relatives, and three received their support from friends. Other encouraging factors include: teachers, attending live performances and seeing other bands perform, winning a talent contest, purchasing an instrument as well as the prospect of making money.

The musicians interviewed were all fairly well educated. Half of the artists have at least some secondary school education with five and two having gotten a secondary school and a technical college diploma, respectively. Five others received eight years of primary education and only three had less than a primary level.

Cultural Roots

Artists were asked to describe the culture of their childhood, and their responses show an intimate identification with the typical majority of Jamaicans. Six of them described their childhood as traditional, five as cosmopolitan, three as urban, and two others said religion was an important value. They defined themselves as a part of the poor working class and economically depressed yet hard-working masses of Jamaica--in the words of one musician, "Strugglers, people who want to do something and somehow they go out and find a means and a way to do it!" Rural culture was mentioned by some artists. One artist described this as "the section of Jamaica that has not been spoiled or influenced by modernization."

Four mentioned their connection to an African culture, one older musician saying that he felt like a "displaced African who still wants to go home and feels alien in Jamaica. "The other three, however, while seeing Africa as

an important part of their heritage, felt a need to celebrate the diversity that
has created a unique Jamaican culture, and one of them said: "In Jamaica
you have cultural pockets from different groups who've come to the island.
I have to identify with the people I come from. I eat curry goat (African),
masha (Jewish), bammy and fish (Arawak culture). Even the culinary part is
mixed. It's difficult to say what Jamaican culture is; we use pieces of all of
these."

When asked whether their music was more reflective of their past or
present culture, most musicians (17) thought that their music reflected both
cultures, while four felt no connectedness with either, and one felt the music
was reflective of the present culture only.

Cultural or Political Themes in Music

Musicians were asked if their personal music or that of their group em-
phasised any cultural or political themes: 12 replied that the music did not
while 10 musicians said their music did have cultural/political themes, and
they explained as follows:

- We sing about cultural unity.
- We sing about religion, lifestyles, the good that mankind should do.
- Antiracism, antiimperialism, antistupidity.
- Lyrics in some songs deal with some of the political scene in Jamaica, comment-
  ing seriously.
- You have to sing about oppression, the difficulties your brothers and sisters are
  facing, and your dreams--what you would like to happen.
- The motto of our group is "unite we must." We sing about social and political
  problems of African people, the disunity of people and international political institutions.

There was consistency in the perspective of all the musicians, in that
whether the focus was cultural or overtly political they dealt with issues
pertinent to the African diaspora and oppressed peoples generally. The tendency was to articulate the condition of the oppressed, and then make a call
for unity to affect positive change in the situation.

Music and the Larger Culture

The encompassing focus of their musical message was more explicitly
cited when musicians were asked if there were ways that their music also
represented a larger culture: 2 musicians said no and 20 said yes. About half
of the respondents characterised their music as international in some way:

- Love is international, social problems exist everywhere.
- My music is a universal message.
- I'm singing to oppressed people, not just in Jamaica alone, like Bob Marley.
- My music represents the international unification of races, cultures and people on
  the whole, that we are trying to bring about.

Two artists said their music represents the larger culture of the Caribbean only, and offered the following comments:

- My music represents the West Indian culture, Caribbean flavor.
- My music is influenced by the imposition of imported music. Jamaicans aren't rock and roll people by nature. Jamaicans are basically calypso and metro-influenced, and country music (the roots of rock and roll) is influential.

In response to whether their own personal music or that of their group has been influenced by internationally distributed music, 3 respondents said no and 19 said yes. They explained how this influence worked:

- As an entertainer, you are influenced by others. You must be exposed to all and you absorb influences.
- Whatever you hear is an influence on music. It is incestuous. Whatever you hear gives you ideas.
- It's got to rub off. Even reggae has gone international; the influence goes both ways.

Influences on Popular Music in Jamaica

Interviewees were asked to name major events or circumstances that they thought had affected the development of popular music in Jamaica since the beginning of rock in the 1950s. Six people believed ska music of the 1950s and 1960s was the most important development insofar as it led to the development of reggae by the 1970s. Several specifically named the Skatalites group as the most influential. This group, featuring world-renowned trombonist Don Drummond, was the chief exponent of ska, the forerunner to reggae (Cuthbert & Wilson, 1988, 5). Ska was mentioned in conjunction with R&B, mento, and rock steady in the 1960s with such key personalities as Alton Ellis and Hopeton Lewis. Other Jamaican "greats" mentioned were Sonny Bradshaw, Prince Busta and the Skatalites.

Six people thought Bob Marley's music was the major development. One person said Marley carried reggae music to the international scene in the 1970s and another complimented the better use of female backup singers by Marley's arrangements with help from Chris Blackwell. Bob Marley is indeed the international symbol of reggae music. Like reggae he came out of the ghetto of western Kingston. Though the thematic structure of reggae has changed throughout the years, Marley made visible the element of protest and, as a Rastafarian, incorporated the religious/philosophical expressions of Rastafari.

Comments also included other social and political influences such as "Marcus Garvey's response to the colonial experience, culminating in the birth of Rastafari, reggae and Bob Marley in the 1970s." One of the well-known Jamaican musicians outlined developments as follows:

In the late 1950s the attempt to reproduce foreign music resulted in the creation of a new sound. Jamaica's political evolution and independence resulted in our music being taken abroad in the 1960s, and it expressed our experiences during the political changes. World political changes in the 1970s including protest movements provided a context for Rasta protest and world changes in the 1980s lead to frivolity in this era.

Some artists commented mainly on negative circumstances:

- We have become more broad-minded musically. Up to a few years ago you had to play reggae. Jamaican music now is not as good as in the 1970s with Marley, Jacob Miller and Peter Tosh. It's stagnating now, the same chord structures are used over and over. Jamaicans aren't as willing to experiment with reggae as foreigners are, but are sticking to the same thing and it can't sell. They say foreigners are stealing our music but that's stupid because music is for everybody.
- There are adverse effects from radio playing soft soul and disco from the 1970s--artists here have lost imagination and all the recent music sounds "DJ--canned " in style.
- People talk about Bob Marley but in the country we didn't hear him on radio. He was performing in Kingston but was not appreciated until he went to America and got very hot and got lots of dollars. Here in the country we seldom hear him on radio, and its only by radio broadcasts we know what is what.
- Because of the corruption of DJs, the demand for good music lessened.

Influence on Personal Music

Respondents were asked to name up to three major events in their lifetime that affected their musical tastes/composition. Specific major events named were: the Beatles (2 artists), prominent foreign jazz musicians and Jamaican jazz musicians who were living abroad coming to Jamaica to play, growing up with funk in the mid-1970s and rock in the 1980s and changing with the times. The main effects of the major events were that they changed the respondent's musical perspective (in 6 cases) and that they were music ally inspiring (in 4 cases).

Other events and influences affecting respondents' personal music were: hearing Hugh Masekela; hearing Western heavy metal guitar for the first time; attending a United States music school and learning the nuts and bolts of modern music; hearing the classical guitar sound mixed with pop sounds; obtaining a "rhythm box "in 1984 which allows more scope and life to playing compositions; playing the congos which provides a better sense of rhythm and hearing the drums and percussion with steel bands.

Music and Influential Musicians

The kind of music which each artist personally preferred to play or sing indicates a vast range in musical genres. The types of music in order of preference are reggae (13), pop ballads (6), soul (4), pop (3), rock, hard rock, jazz (2), funk, ska, gospel, mellow, easy rock, neo-African, Latin jazz, romantic ballads, R&B, heavy metal, crossover reggae, country, punk, blues, tango and bolero (1 each).

Respondents were asked who was the single individual who influenced them most, but most could not isolate only one influence and those who attempted to do so ended up naming two people or groups. Their responses were equally divided between national and nonnational influences. Americans chosen as the most influential were: George Benson, Lou Rawls, Robert Davies, the Coasters, Al Jarreau, Joe Pass, Prince, Aretha Franklin and Sun Ra. British groups in this category were the Beatles and Bee Gees; Hugh Masekela of South Africa was also chosen. Jamaican musicians included Tommy McCook, Don Drummond, Black Uhuru, Byron Lee, a father (2), Robert Davies and Shelter, and Grace Thrillers.

Styles of Music

While most of the artists openly admit to external influences, we wanted to find out if these influences were explicitly discernible in the styles of music played and/or recorded by these musicians. Most artists had two or three types of music on their recordings. Only five respondents, about 20%, said that their only style of music was reggae or hard reggae, rockers, roots reggae or rap.

Four others described a combination of reggae and other forms: reggae with country and western, fusion reggae, reggae (semi-funk) and reggae/ska. Two others played/sang reggae as well as other styles of music: gospel, R&B, jazz, Latin jazz, African-oriented, up tempo, rock, hard rock, new wave, and soca/calypso.

Two musicians insisted that their music was "original" or "unique" and that they could name no model. Half of the musicians felt they had to compromise between the type of music they would like to record and what they were able to record. The main reason was economic. As one musician expressed it, "You divert the music in a way to gain popularity."

Compromise

Respondents were divided on the issue of compromise: 10 felt that they had to compromise on the kind of music they would like to play while 12 felt there were no pressures to compromise. Of the 10 who answered in the affirmative, the most common reason for compromise was the demands of the marketplace, cited five times by the respondents.

They indicated that they were forced to compromise to make the music marketable, or to satisfy the audiences' desires. Sources of pressure to compromise were sometimes distributors, promoters or the band manager. The following comments explain how the pressure to compromise works:

- Some places don't want the sort of music we project--there's economic pressures.
- Tourists like a mixture of music, and you can't get a job unless you perform what they like.
- You're told or asked to play certain selections. Sometimes being hired is based on your compliance.

Jamaica Federation of Musicians

There is no licensing of musicians in Jamaica. Some respondents perceived that the Jamaica Federation of Musicians performs some functions of a union: protecting the rights of the musicians, securing increased income and $J10,000 worth of insurance protection. Over 60% of the musicians interviewed belonged to the JFM for periods ranging from one to twenty-five years. Eight of the groups were unionized and six were not.

Local Production: Expenses, Contracts, Copyright and Sales

Most of the musicians interviewed had done some level of production. Nineteen artists had made a record or album, and three others had produced a tape. Five of these musicians had produced an album or albums with a major recording company, two had major-produced singles, four had produced with a small company, and four each (15%) had either a small-company-produced single or a self-produced single. In addition, two had professionally produced demo tapes, and one had made only a nonprofessional self-produced tape. Only four artists had not made any recording.

The costs of the master recording, when known, were J$200, J$700, J$5,500 and J$13,000. The copyright to the recording was owned in three cases by the producer, in two cases by the group or the interviewee, in one case by the song writer and in another case by the songwriter and manager. Groups had produced on each of the following labels: their own label, a regional label, a national label and an international label. Labels were owned by CBS, Sonic Sounds, Dynamic Sounds, Chris Blackwell's Island Records, The Little Pub Complex, and All Gold.

To fund recordings which were self-produced, musicians had usually used personal funds of group members or a combination of personal funds and music profits, two musicians had had financial backing from outside parties, one had all three of the above, and one relied entirely on profits from music-making activity.

Of the artists who recorded, 42% did not make a profit. Two who made a profit were paid a flat fee by the producer of J$500 and another received $3,500. Four artists were paid from 20% to 65% per copy sold and two had other arrangements. In one case where the group members were the producers, the profits were equally divided, and in another case of a self-produced single, the artist made a profit by selling 1,000 records, mainly at performances. One artist said she was paid for her full contribution pluses all release rights.

The infrastructure of the Jamaican music industry provides very little protection for its musicians. The level of accountability is such that artists often receive little or no compensation for their creations. This problem is pervasive because of the absence of effective copyright legislation in Jamaica. To date Jamaica still adheres to a 1991 Copyright Act that does not reflect the technological sophistication and the issues facing the modern music industry. While there is no local protection, there is also no international protection of Jamaican artists because Jamaica has not participated in any international copyright conventions (Cuthbert & Wilson, 1990, 73).

However, on February 1, 1991, after much debate, the final draft of a Copyright Bill was delivered to the parliamentary secretary in the Information and Culture Ministry. The draft was to be sent to the Legislative Committee for parliamentary approval. To ensure that Jamaica becomes a signatory to international conventions, thereby providing international protection, the bill has to have final approval by the World Intellectual Property Organization (WIPO).

Nearly three-quarters of the musicians did not know how many copies of their recordings were sold. Among them was an artist who said, "I don't have an accounting but my song was number two on the British charts." This artist received no royalties. Of those who did, the sales figures stated were 100, 300, 1,000, 1,500, 2,000, 10,000 and 50,000 copies sold. One artist needed more copies but couldn't afford to press any more.

Publicity

The music industry in Jamaica relies heavily on radio promotions. This is the most effective medium because it is able to reach the largest number of Jamaicans. For many years Jamaica had two major radio stations, JBC-AM and FM and RJR-AM and FM. However, on October 1, 1990, the government granted a license to Independent Radio Company (IRC) to operate a national commercial radio station. IRC is owned by a consortium whose shareholders include Radio Jamaica and the Gleaner Company, publisher of two of Jamaica's three daily newspapers.

Because of the competition in accessing radio, artists have been forced to resort to alternative means to get their music on stations' playlists. As Cuthbert & Wilson's 1990 work shows, bribes and payola were options explored by the respondents. Respondents admitted that disc jockeys have been paid as little as $J20 and as much as a $10,000 car. Through it all artists have become their own sales representative, taking their records around to radio stations and disc jockeys, hoping to leave a lasting impression that will translate into air play.

Jamaica has no cable television so television was limited to one channel, until recently, the Jamaica Broadcasting Corporation. But in 1990 a local consortium, CVM-TV, was granted a license to operate Jamaica's second television station. With the advent of video production, television is increasingly becoming an important medium for musicians. However, television in no way matches the audience penetration of radio, and video production is an added cost that most musicians cannot afford.

To assess the practical use of television for the promotion of their music, the musicians were asked about the accessibility of television for local artists: 46% thought local music was played on TV several times a week, 27% thought it was played every day and nearly 20% thought it was played only once a week or less.

Just as for radio, artists used a variety of alternative approaches to gain access to television. Over 40% (11 artists) said they got their music on TV by taking the record to the station, seven said they did so by making a video and taking it to the station. Two artists each got music on TV through contacts ("knowing someone") or by invitation, and one artist each said they did so through their promoter or manager, bribes and payola and by the station recruiting them to perform. Only one group had ever bought TV time.

Six groups had made a video, one at a cost of J$20,000 and another at a cost of $15. The video production was paid for in two cases by the group's promoter, in two cases by national TV, in another case by members of the group and in the final case by a 50/50 split between the manager and a video company.

Print media coverage of local music was considered to be fairly good by most musicians. Local newspapers were the first or second choice of 70% of artists, while local free bulletins and schedules were the first or second choice of 65% of artists. Tourist papers were another source of publicity for North Coast musicians.

Performances

There are several potential venues available to the musicians. The types of places at which the groups most frequently played are nightclubs, bars or pubs, outdoor concerts, concert halls, private parties and dance halls. Performances are done at "benefits, weddings and other events, often at hotels," and for what band leader Ainsley Morris called "VIP performances" as he has played for Ronald Reagan and Jesse Jackson, among others.

Of the 14 bands, 6 travelled only locally to perform and some of these had long term contracts with a particular hotel or club; 4 bands each said they travelled regionally and nationally, and 3 bands travelled internationally. Of the 14 groups, 12 were paid for performances via an amount agreed upon in advance, and one group was paid 50% in advance. Most interviewees would not or could not state the group's approximate income. However, two groups had incomes of US $2,700 and $7,500 respectively. Groups' music making expenses for 1985 were given by two artists as US $3,000 and $50,000.

Does Government Encourage Music?

Fourteen respondents thought that the government does not do anything to encourage local or national popular music making, while six respondents said the government does help by funding contests and festivals. The consensus was that the government did not consistently play an active role in enhancing local musical talent. There are "various talent contests with prizes of recording contracts and musical education," as one respondent indicates, administered by the Jamaica Cultural Development Commission (JCDC), but they occur infrequently. The yearly song festival competition was the most prestigious, but that too came under attack by the respondents who saw a constant decline in standards.

One respondent proposed four guidelines that the government should take to raise the standards of music in Jamaica.

1. A government copyright law is the most important thing for government to do just as in England and the United States to protect the rhythm as well as the

lyrics.

2. Upgrade the standard of the Festival Commission.

3. Emphasize music in schools.

4. Equip groups to do demos and produce their first record. Equip major parishes with a small studio. A person wins at the parish level and it's left there. The Festival Commission should do some promotion. Then charge a fee after the first record to provide funding. Government pays an officer to work for the commission all year, but they only seem to work close to festival time. They should be planning shows, raising money, etc. all year--be more involved.

Another respondent highlighted the government's own exploitive role and the unequal access to adequate training. Except when government wants to win a campaign and says "come play an when dem win, dey don't know you again." They aren't doing anything at all. There's the Jamaica School of Music but if you don't have $500, there are no scholarships. The standard of Jamaica's music is very low; there's little formal training." The pessimism exhibited by this and other artists is directed at the government's lack of support, financially or through legislation, for the continued development of quality music that is reflective of the people. Artists are understandably angry at the inadequacy of a system that continues to exploit their artistic, financial and emotional commitment to music. Their resilience and ingenuity are remarkable in light of the varied obstacles they must overcome to get their music heard.

CONCLUSION

Consistent with the model of interaction outlined in the introduction to this book, Jamaica is currently at a stage of integration. However, since the indigenous Arawaks were wiped out by colonialism, Jamaica's culture has evolved from many sources. Consequently, mento, ska or any of the early musical traditions outlined in this chapter are not originally indigenous, but are a part of Jamaica's cultural evolution. Jamaica's musical tradition is born out of a process of adaptation to the social and cultural milieu defined by colonialism. It is in fact an amalgamation of foreign musics to create a new "indigenous " sound that has at its base the distinctiveness of the African cultural heritage.

Having described the process by which the traditional music was defined, we can now discuss the continued integration of a variety of musical forms with reggae. The latest phenomenon in reggae music is dance hall DJ music, which has many parallels to the rap sensation in the United States. Both musical forms are a blend of rhyme, rhythm and heavily synthesized music that is sometimes critical of the social and economic conditions of blacks but oftentimes focus on sex and a misogynic view of women. They take an apolitical stand and are preoccupied with "slackness" (lewd and overtly sexual music). However, some dance hall DJs are currently reviving and incorporating folk and spiritual songs; they continue the tradition of reggae music by using the Creole language of the people and rejecting the official language, standard English, in their cultural expression.

External influences, as outlined above, are openly embraced with little fear of negative repercussions on the local musical form. On the contrary, the strength of reggae has spread its influence externally. In 1984 reggae was added as a category in the Grammy Awards, the highest award for musical achievement in the United States. White working-class and black youth are attracted to the radicalism and counterhegemonic underpinnings of the music.

Foreign groups in Africa (Alpha Blondy), England (UB40), United States (KRS-1) as well as Japan and elsewhere are adapting and performing reggae. But what price is Jamaica's cultural expression and emancipation paying for this popular phenomenon? Jamaica does receive an immense influx of foreign musical products, giving rise to the suggestion of cultural imperialism. But while the international communications industry is structured in such a way that developing countries are kept in a state of dependency, the term "cultural imperialism" belies the strength and dynamism of local cultures.

Jamaica is open to external influences and has an inclusive and democratic approach to them; however, it does not imitate, but *transforms*. External influences are redefined to take on the distinctiveness of a Jamaican cultural expression. Jamaica's music, from mento to dance hall serves as part of the cultural resistance to the recolonization of the nation, arising from the hegemonic influence of its neighbor to the north, the United States Despite the exogenous cultural influence, there continues to be a rejection of Eurocentrism and a celebration and pride in the indigenous cultural life and expression. While foreign musics may have aesthetic appeal and influence, reggae continues to express and reflect the reality of the majority of Jamaica.

BIBLIOGRAPHY

Augier, Roy; Nettleford, Rex; & Smith, M.G. (1960). *The Rastafari Movement in Kingston, Jamaica.* Kingston: Univerity of the West Indies.

Black, Clinton (1958). *History of Jamaica.* London: Collins Clear-Type Press.

Cuthbert, Marlene (1983). "Cultural Synchronization and Cultural Autonomy: A Jamaican Case Study." Paper prepared for the Windspread Conference on Youth and the International Music Industry, Racine, Wisconsin.

Cuthbert, Marlene (1985). "Cultural Autonomy and Popular Music: A Survey of Jamaican Youth." *Communication Research,* 12, 361-393.

Cuthbert, Marlene (1989). "Reggae Tells What Life Is Really Like." *Group Media Journal* (Munich), 8: 4, 10-12.

Cuthbert, Marlene & Wilson, Gladstone (1988). "The Recording Industry in Jamaica." Paper prepared for International Communication and Youth Culture (ICYC) research team.

Cuthbert, Marlene & Wilson, Gladstone (1990). "Recording Artists in Jamaica: Payola, Piracy and Copyright." In John Lent (Ed.), *Caribbean Popular Culture* (pp. 64-78). Bowling Green, OH: Bowling Green University Press.

Enzenberger, H. (1974). *The Consciousness Industry.* New York: Seabury Press.

Robinson, Deanna Campbell; Buck, Elizabeth B.; Cuthbert, Marlene et al .; and the International Communication and Youth Culture Consortium (1991). *Music at the Margins: Popular Music and Global Cultural Diversity.* Newbury Park, CA: Sage.

Stone, Carl. (1989). "Power, Policy and Politics in Independent Jamaica." In Rex Nettleford (Ed.), *Jamaica in Independence: Essays on the Early Years* (pp. 19-54). Kingston: Heinemann Caribbean.

Thorndike, Tony (1990). "Jamaica." *New Internationalist,* November, 32.

White, Garth (1982). "Reggae--A Musical Weapon." *Caribe* 6 (1), 21-25.

CHAPTER 9

INTERACTIONS OF IMPORTED AND INDIGENOUS MUSICS IN JAPAN : A HISTORICAL OVERVIEW OF THE MUSIC INDUSTRY

Toru Mitsui

BEFORE WESTERNIZATION

The earliest music imported into Japan was *gagaku*, an upper-class art music which came from continental Asia. It was assimilated between the fifth and ninth centuries. The first European music to which the Japanese were exposed, though only a limited number of them, was the ceremonial music of Christianity which was first used in Japan by the missionary Francisco de Xavier in the early 1550s. However, a decree proscribing the Christian faith was issued in 1587, with the result that the implanted Christian vocal music only survived in secrecy, in a somewhat adapted form, among a small number of crypto-Christians (Ebisawa). In the late 1630s Japan closed its doors to all foreigners. It was not until the mid-1850s that the country was finally forced to open its ports to the United States and then to some dominant European countries. However, the ensuing unequal trade treaties eventually led to the Meiji Revolution in the late 1860s. Conscious of Japan's relative underdevelopment in terms of industrialization and democratization, the new postrevolutionary government accelerated the Westernization of Japan. The indigenous music of Japan had been unaffected by foreign music--especially Occidental music--for such a long time that an American visitor made the following comment in the early 1900s:

To Occidental ears Japanese music, set, as it always is, in a minor key and abounding in discords, seems unworthy of the name of music. To characterise it as merely: "strummings and squealings" because it does not conform to our ideas, is however, an unfair aspersion. (Clement, 1903, 231)

The person criticized here is obviously Basil Hall Chamberlain whose aversion to Japanese music he demonstrated in 1890 in his book on Japanalia. Despite his good understanding of Japan, he did not modify his opinions in the second edition (1904). The observation on Japanese music made by the British scholar begins with a sentence: "Music, if that beautiful word must be allowed to fall so as to denote the strumming and squealings of Orientals, . . ." (Chamberlain, 1904, 339).

On the other hand, the Japanese people must have had a similar reaction to Occidental music, particularly to "refined" types. The Westernization encouraged by the new government included the promotion of military brass bands with their own repertoires and the adoption by schools of Scottish, Irish and American melodies, which appeared in contemporary American textbooks of music, for singing in schools with Japanese lyrics. Nevertheless, as Chamberlain admits, "Dislikes are apt to be mutual. Of all the elements of Europeanization, European music is the one for which the Japanese have been slow to evince any taste" (Chamberlain, 1904, 343). Even around 1930 Western music seems to have been physically disturbing to many Japanese, as a theatrical director described in his reminiscences. He said that when his mother, presumably in her late thirties, heard the recorded music of Beethoven, her brains reeled, her face turned pale and she nearly fell into a swoon (Takechi & Tomioka, 1988, 65).

STYLIZED INDIGENOUS MUSIC

Government policy led to a growing appreciation of this alien Western music, although this was not reciprocated in the West by appreciation of Japanese music. The historical development of this process of Japanese musical acculturation, conspicuous in the field of popular music, and its relationship with the music industry as a whole, will be sketched out in chronological order later.

It should be kept in mind, however, that the various stylized forms of indigenous music have never been seriously threatened per se by the impulse of Westernization. Despite the active introduction of Western music, many stylized forms of indigenous music have survived with established repertoires, coexisting with Western music as well as with manifold mixtures of Western and Japanese musical elements. The conventional forms of Japanese music include *gagaku* used in the imperial court and shrines, *shomyo*, the Buddhist vocal music, *nagauta*, the accompaniment to *kabuki* and *kabuki* dances, and the professional singing of folk songs, which was developed many years after the Meiji Revolution. (This coexistence of stylized indigenous forms with new development is a cultural phenomenon which is also found in literature (e.g., *waka* and *haiku*), fine arts (e.g., *nihonga*), theatre (e.g., *noh* and *kabuki*) and other cultural realms (e.g., *sado, kendo* and *sumo*)). Thus the amazingly spiteful prayer of Chamberlain offered more than a century ago has never been, and will not be, realized: ". . . may be turned into firewood to warm the poor, when--if at no previous period of their existence--they will subserve a purpose indisputably useful!" (Chamberlain, 1904, 344).

This conventional indigenous music, generically called *hogaku*, has been enjoyed more as live performance than in recorded form, but its tenacity can be seen by the number of new record releases of the music: 535 out of 14,586 (the sum total of all domestic recordings released in 1989). This is comparable to the number of new releases by Japanese artists of Western classical music, which was 424 (JPRA, 1990).

Out of the remaining number of the 1989 new releases recorded by Japanese performers, 11,260 were recordings of popular music and 2,367 were "educational & children's songs," "music for animation films" and others. All of these displayed Western influences to one degree or another, though many of the Western elements had been absorbed for so long that they were not always felt to be particularly Western. On the other hand, the huge number of foreign records released in Japan--that is, discs and cassettes of foreign origin--should be noted as a reflection of the continuous Japanese infatuation with Western musical culture. The sum total of the releases of such foreign records in 1989 amounted to 10,265 in comparison to the 14,586 released by domestic performers. Out of these 10,265 releases, 6,515 were of popular music, including movie music, and 3,750 were categorized as classical music (JPRA, 1990).

THE RECEPTION OF WESTERN CULTURE AND
THE TAISHO DEMOCRACY

In terms of the Japanese music industry, attempts to adapt Western musical elements to Japanese taste were first noticeable in the linkage of theatre and gramophone recording, when Matsui Sumasko[1] sang "Kachushano Uta" (Kachusha's Song) in 1914.

There had already been quite a few recordings by Japanese performers, even since the days of the cylinder in the late nineteenth century, but most of the music recorded was the stylized indigenous music mentioned above. The rest were mostly *hayariuta* (fashionable ditties) (later called *shoseiuta* (student ditties), which were first recorded in the early 1910s.

They were topical, satirical and humorous songs in the tradition of *enka*, which were political protest songs in the mid-Meiji era, though this *enka* should not be confused with a hard-core type of modern *Kayokyoku* with the same appellation. Musically, this genre, whose heyday lasted until the late 1920s, was characterized by a Japanese traditional five-note mode, a traditional vocal style, which sounds rustic to modern ears, and a violin accompaniment in unison, the performing style of which was raucous. The violin was a new adoption from the West as was the piano which was sometimes used along with the violin at recording sessions, but its performing style by people who were musically untrained self-accompanists was anything but refined.

The whole rustic effect engendered by these musical characteristics can be compared to such Anglo-American folk music as is heard in the 1923 recordings of Fiddlin' John Carson from Atlanta, Georgia. (In that respect, one may well wonder how Chamberlain would have reacted to the traditional singing and fiddling of British folk music).

The Birth of a Hit Song

A newer kind of song with much more appeal first appeared in one particular theatrical presentation. The play was *Resurrection* adapted from Leo Tolstoy's novel, and performed by Geijutsuza (the Art Company), one of the troupes in the theatrical new wave which began performances under the influence of European drama in the late 1900s in opposition to the indigenous forms of drama. Songs had been used in plays before since 1910 but had been of a more conventional type (Kurata, 1979, 170). The innovative "Kachusha's Song" from *Resurrection*, sung by Matsui Sumako, who already enjoyed a good reputation, attained popularity in the course of a month and a half after Geijustuza began touring in March 1914.

The lyrics about the pain of lovesick parting written by Soma, Gyofu, were a precursor of poetry in a colloquial style, and were set to an original melody composed by Nakayma Shimpei, who was a young graduate of Tokyo College of Music, a national institution wholly oriented to Western music. Shimamura Hogetsu, the leader of Geijutsuza, made a comment on musical composition, according to Nakayama when he was interviewed by a Tokyo newspaper reporter in 1935 (Nishizawa B., 1990, 3003-3004) to the effect that Japanese musicians should make music which is identifiably Japanese, instead of imitating Western ways. He suggested Nakayama should aim at a hybrid between a Japanese indigenous ditty and a Western "lied" as a song to be sung by a housemaid in the play. (It should be noted that "music" was an imported conception, and therefore musical composition must have been understood as a new field). The result was an enjoyable tune in a compromised pentatonic major scale (the fourth and seventh notes "lacking") which sounded readily appealing to the Japanese. Nevertheless the unaccompanied singing of the song recorded during the tour for Orient in Kyoto sounds utterly amateurish to our modern ears (truly realistic as a casual performance by a housemaid). But this musically underdeveloped Westernization in pitch and vocalization must have sounded refreshing to the contemporary audience, along with the song itself, as a blend that retained an identifiably Japanese substance.

The record, entitled "Fukkatsuno Uta" (Resurrection Song) but later known as "Kachusha's Song," increased the song's popularity, particularly as Shimamura played it at a lecture meeting that preceded a run of successive performances in each city during the tour, which boosted the audience's anticipation (Kurata, 1979, 176). The sale of the record attained some 20,000 copies, making it the first hit in the history of the Japanese record industry. This was before the invention of electrical recording and when the price was not moderate (¥1.5 when an initial salary paid to an elementary-schoolteacher was ¥12 to ¥20 (Nishizawa B, 1990, 3007). Meanwhile, the touring of Geijutsuza ran on well into the next year, 1915. A Tokyo cosmetic manufacturer commercially parodied the song lyrics in a newspaper advertisement, making it one of the earliest advertising jingles (Kurata, 1979, 173).

The Taisho Democracy

That the core of the audience were students is apparent from various quotas from contemporary newspapers, such as "Students are singing this song enthusiastically. Those who are not singing aloud are singing under the breath" (Kurata, 1979, 173). These students were obviously attracted in the beginning by a new age suggested by the name of the play's original author and his latest novel, which had been translated into Japanese in 1905, five years after the original publication. Behind this intellectual thirst was a certain *Zeitgeist*, which was named the Taisho Democracy long afterward (Taisho is the period which began in 1912, when the newly crowned Emperor Taisho succeeded the deceased Emperor Meiji, and lasted until 1926). The Taisho Democracy, which roughly covered the Taisho period, refers to a growing democratic and liberal tendency in Japanese politics, society and culture in general. It was caused, among other things, by an easing of strained relations between Asian nations after the termination of the Russo-Japanese War in 1905 and the awakening to political and civil liberty of the urban middle and unpropertied classes, which grew up in association with the rapid development of capitalism after the same War (Heibonsha, 1985, Vol. 8, 1267). It was this period that produced the first commoner premier in Japan, Hara Takashi, who promoted the Japan-U.S. cooperation in foreign transactions before he was assassinated, in 1912, three years after assuming office. On the other hand, many poets ardently admired Walt Whitman in this period, whose work was first introduced in 1892.

Nakayama scored more hits recorded by Matsui thereafter, elaborating his compositions in pentatonic major and minor scales. Even after Matsui committed suicide following the death of Shimamura, her lover, from sickness, Nakayama's songs continued to be successful, making him a leading composer of popular songs in the Taisho Period. In particular, "Sendo Ko'uta" (Boatman's Ditty) was successful with its mood of despair and pessimism (lyrics by Noguchi Ujo) emphasized by the typical minor-inclined pentatonic scale, which touched the heartstrings of the Japanese more intimately than his melodies in the similarly typical major-inclined pentatonic scale. The song was not only recorded by several singers in 1922, but its popularity was further accelerated by a successful film which jumped on the bandwagon--an early example of the mutual benefits from interrelated media.

The Asakusa Opera

The period of the Taisho Democracy was also characterized in musical terms by an adaptation of Italian opera which enjoyed a vogue in the field of show business as a new popular theatrical art. The first performance of opera in Japan was in 1903 when the graduates and students of Tokyo College of Music played Gluck's *Orfeo ed Euridice* in Japanese translation under the direction of European structures (Masui, 1990, 47-9). And in 1912 Giovanni Vittorio Rossi from Italy began giving full-scale lessons at a newly formed theatre. After this proved unsuccessful, some of his pupils formed troupes of their own to perform in several theatres in Asakusa, an old entertainment district in Tokyo.

The age of the Asakusa Opera began in 1917, and its success was caused by transforming such operas as Verdi's *Aida*, Biset's *Carmen*, and Suppes *Boccacio* into the style of Japanese entertainment. The original works were ivariably reduced to operettas by being abbreviated, and the arbitrariness of the abbreviation was reflected in the way in which the lyrics were flexibly translated. Thus the Asakusa Opera was a popular entertainment in which "the stage and audience were happily united" (Miyazawa, 1990, 1). It should also be noted that this phenomenon was nationwide because the troupes often toured around the country. It can be argued, therefore, that the Asakusa Opera contributed to the modification of the musical sensibility of the Japanese by exposing them to refined musical idioms from the West. On the other hand, skill in adapting Japanese lyrics to Occidental melodies was unmistakably honed by the people who were involved in the performance of the operettas.

The Asakusa Opera, which put on everybody's lips such songs as "Hab ich nur deine Liebe" (translated into Japanese) from *Boccacio* sung by Taya Rikizo), which came to an end in 1925 due to the effects of the great Kansai earthquake two years before. However, the opera served as a breeding ground for many talented people who were later actively engaged in various fields, including Fujiwara Yoshie, who led a full-scale opera company Futamura Teiichi, a successful recording artist; Enomoto Ken'ichi, a high-spirited comedian; Sasa Koka, a proficient songwriter; and Iba Takashi, a popular playwright.

The Takarazuka Revue

At about the time when the Asakusa Opera was coming into vogue, there emerged, also in the field of show business, a musical revue which was again a Japanese modification of a European model. With their first show in 1914 and the establishment a decade later of Japan's largest theatre (a seating capacity of 3,000), the Takarazuka Kagekidan (the Takarazuka Revue Company) was formed by Hankyu, an electric train company, as the chief attraction in a hot spring resort town, Takarazuka, which is located near Osaka, the second largest city in Japan. The all-women or, more properly speaking, all-girl Takarazuka theatre has been characterized by its luxurious spectacle and girlish romanticism, featuring male protagonists played by starmembers to create an image of idealized men or safe male beauty. Significantly, the Takarazuka is still going strong as a theatre which "presents a pastiche of styles derived from European and American musicals and juxtaposes these against a variety of Japanese theatre and dance traditions" (Brau, 1990, 80), and many of the accomplished foremost actresses in Japan graduated from this company, which has its own training school of dancing, singing and playing for girls.

Dance Band Music and Jazz

Meanwhile, jazz was introduced to Japan also in the period of the Taisho Democracy. In fact, it seems to have been introduced to the Japanese audience before 1917 when the first recognized recordings of jazz music were released in the United States by a white quintet, the Original Dixieland Jass (or Jazz) Band for Victor and Columbia. Japan participated in World War I on the side of the allied forces and established diplomatic relations with the United States. Passenger and cargo liners crossed back and forth over the Pacific Ocean, importing and exporting commodities in abundance, includ-

ing records. An aged music journalist remembered that American gramophone records by white dance bands were often played in modish, namely
Western-styled, coffee houses, which were called "milk halls" (Noguchi,
1976, 7). Moreover, it is known that the Hatano Orchestra, consisting of
five graduates of Tokyo College of Music, used to buy sheet music of
popular dance music in San Francisco from 1912 to 1918 when they were
employed by a Japanese steamship company to perform for the passengers
on their regular liner. After leaving the steamer, this orchestra led by
Hatano Furutaro worked as an intermission band in theatres which featured American films, playing short classical pieces, pre-jazz dance music
and some jazz. Then they performed at Kagetsuen in Yokohama, which was
the first commercial dance hall ever opened (1920) in Japan. On the other
hand, in the 1920s, some American house bands for passenger liners, with
some jazz orientation, often performed in hotels in Yokohama and Kobe,
the two largest international seaports, when their ships were lying in harbor
(Uchida, 1976, 16ff).

THE FLOWERING OF THE RECORD INDUSTRY
AND WARTIME

In 1923 the great Kansai earthquake badly affected show business in general as well as the record industry in particular. On the other hand, the first
Japanese broadcasting station, JOAK, came into service in 1925. This Tokyo station and two more in other large cities were combined into one as
NHK, the Japanese equivalent to the BBC, in the following year (which
marked the end of the Taisho period and the beginning of the long Showa
period). The popularity of broadcasting can be inferred from the rapid increase in the number of receiving sets: in just one year, ownership rose from
5,455 sets to 338,204 (Kawabata, 1990, 26). The record industry feared the
competition, as a matter of course, from this new entertainment medium,
but eventually it turned out that the two industries operated to their mutual
convenience.

The Formation of Joint Ventures

In order to raise economic conditions, in 1924 the government promoted the production of domestic goods by passing a bill to impose customs
duties on imported luxury goods. Being regarded as luxury items then, imported gramophone records were liable to a duty of 10% tax levied on them
(Morimoto, 1985, 15). The record companies and dealers which had the
selling rights of specified foreign records were thus obliged to find a means
of pressing records in Japan, instead of importing them from the countries
of origin. This necessity compelled Japanese companies to form new organizations in which they invested jointly with foreign firms. The oldest and
largest record dealer, Nicchiku, formed a subsidiary, Japan Columbia, together first with British Columbia and then also with American Columbia,
in early 1928. Anan Company formed Japan Polydor, in May 1927, with
German Gramophone, with which Anan had had a sales agreement. Japan
Victor was also formed in July 1927 as a joint venture with the Fraser Com-

pany in Tokyo and American Victor. Surprisingly, the domestic pressing by these joint ventures made it possible to have their records priced at one-half to one sixth of the amounts charged for imported discs (Kurata, 1979, 315).

At the same time, the new companies set about producing records by Japanese artists with the newly introduced technique of electric recording. The first such hit by a Japanese artist was, however, a disc recorded overseas originally for overseas audiences. This record pressed anew in Japan was a coupling of "Debuneno Minato" (Sea Port) and "Debune" (Outgoing Ship) sung, with a piano accomaniment, by Fujiwara Yoshie, a tenor singer who was trained in the Asakusa Opera. Fujiwara, born the child of a Scotsman and a Japanese woman, had been invited to record the songs as an artist for Victor's prestigious "red label" in 1927 at Victor's studio in Camden, New Jersey (Spottswood, 1990, Vol. 5, 2545); while he waited for his session, a renowned violinist, Fritz Kreisler, was recording (Daicel, 1990, 4). The song-poems Fujiwara recorded were born out of a movement to create new "folk songs" among a new generation of poets, and the equally pseudo-traditional music was composed by Nakayama Shimpei, who first succeeded in composing songs for Matsui Sumalo.

Encouraged by the success of the record, Japan Victor pressed and released another song in the same vein by Fujiwara, "Habuno Minato" (Port of Habu), recorded in Oakland, California, in March 1928. The song was also recorded in Tokyo by Sato Chiyalo, a female soprano who was also trained in Western vocals, and these two versions released in May 1928 sold some 160,000 copies to the surprise of the staff of Japan Victor: "We little dreamed that a record would have such a great sale" (Daicel, 1990, 5).

Apart from pressing records from foreign sources, the newly formed firms undertook to make domestic "cover" versions of original records, including such hits as "Valencia," "Barcelona" and "Ramona." The most successful among the earliest covers was that of "My Blue Heaven" (Gene Austin and Paul Whiteman, 1927; Nick Lucas and others, 1928 [Whitburn, 1986, 39, 284, 450, et al.]). released in November 1928 simultaneously by Japan Victor and Japan Columbia in different recordings (Daicel, 1990, 7). Both versions were sung by Futamura Teiichi, a former Asakusa Opera singer, whose vocals were characterized, to our present-day ears, by straightforward, unsophisticated delivery. The words were translated by Horiuchi Keizo, one of the first in the field of the translation of jazz lyrics, who was also in charge of arranging the music for the Japan Columbia Jazz Band. The arrangement for the Japan Victor Jazz Band was made by Ida Ichiro, a pioneering Japanese jazz-band leader. Both records were respectively coupled with "Sing Me a Song of Araby," translated by Horiuchi and sung in duet by Futamura and Amano Kikuyo, which also became very popular on its own in contrast to the obscurity of the original record.

Hits Produced by Newly Formed Companies

As to popular song records autonomously conceived and produced by Japanese record companies with the intention of creating a hit rather than taking up already-existent songs, the first successful attempt was "Kimi Koishi" (Yearning for You) released by Japan Victor in January 1929. It was one of the songs planned in response to a proposition made by their first president, B. Gardener, who remarked that, in the United States, popular songs were produced monthly and placed on the market (Uchida, 1976, 80). The light-hearted music by Sasa Koka in the conventional minor pentatonic scale tinted with a hint of jazz or American contemporary popular music was combined with the languish-in-love lyrics by Shigure Ottawa and sung happy-go-luckily, again by Futamura Teiichi with the arrangement by Ida Ichiro and accompaniment by the Japan Victor Jazz Band. This great hit was also a precursor of what was called "jazz songs," an appellation used for a group of songs newly composed and performed as composites of Japanese sentiments and American modernism.

"Kimi Koishi" was soon followed by another great success by Victor, "Tokyo Koshinkyoku" (Tokyo March), composed by Nakyama Shimpei to the lyrics of Saijo Yaso, professor of French at a Tokyo university, who, in his own words, "verbally caricatured some scenes of "modern" Tokyo life" (Morimoto, 1985, 28). The song, actually not "a march," again in the conventional minor-pentatonic scale, was sung by Sato Chiyako and released in May 1929 with a backing arranged by Ida Ichiro, whose work was characterized by its jazzy flavor. It is noteworthy that, while "Kimi Koishi"was followed by a film with the same title in March, "Tokyo March" was produced from the beginning as the theme song for a film version of a novel, *Tokyo March*. It was, however, still in the days of silent films, and this song was a theme song in the sense that it was performed during an intermission at cinemas. Naturally, after the introduction of talking pictures, there appeared many successful theme songs for films which were widely heard and sung.

Thus record companies established themselves as business enterprises to produce as many hit songs as possible while they established a new type of Japanese popular song called *ryokoka* (fashionable songs), a hybrid of modified vernacular expressions and adapted Occidental and American idioms, which mirrored social and cultural changes in Japan. To systematize their hit-making machinery, the record companies made an exclusive contract with a lyricist, a composer and a singer, and whereas singers were given royalties, payment to lyricists and composers was made on a nonroyalty basis until the early 1960s when the exclusive contract practice was invalidated. At the same time, there emerged many companies which were financed domestically such as Taihei, Nitto and Tsuru, which stimulated the whole industry.

A Widening Spectrum of Ryokoka

In 1931 a Japanese cover version of "Sous les toits de Paris" by Taya Rikizo, a former star of the Asakusa Opera, became a hit. The song was taken from one of the first talkies with the same title directed by Renı Clair, which had become popular among students and young urban intellectuals. In October of the same year appeared an epoch-making song entitled "Sakewa Namidaka Tameikika" (Is Wine Tears of a Sigh?) with which the composer, lyricist and singer all made their debut. The guitarist-composer, Koga Masao, whose success would soon exceed that of Nakyama Shimpei, composed it with the intention of creating "something that is intermediate between 'jazz song' and '*dodoitsu*'" (Morimoto, 1985, 46), and the record became an instant hit, representing the despondent feelings of the people in those hard times. (*Dodoitsu* is an old colloquial love-ditty form perfected in the mid-nineteenth century). The song was sung to an accompaniment of violin, cello, guitar and ukulele, in a school-trained but crooning voice by Fujiyama Ichiro. The singer enjoyed thereafter a happy combination with Koga, producing continuous hits which were not only in the conventional gloomy minor-pentatonic scale but also in the conventional jolly major-pentatonic one.

To make the record more distinguished, its flip side was also successful with "Watashi Konogoro Youtsuyo" (I'm Feeling So Down These Days) as a substantial debut song for Awaya Noriko, who was also trained but was severely reproached, as in the case of Fujiwara, by the authorities of the institute from which she graduated for singing *ryokoka*. Starting with this sorrow-stricken song of self-abandonment, she developed her career, the first successful period of which was in the late 1930s when she became "the queen of the blues"with such "blues," composed by Hattori Ryoichi, as "Wakereno Blues" (Farewell Blues) (1937), "Ameno Blues" (Rainy Blues) (1938) and "Tokyo Blues" (1939). These blues, which were established as a loose genre of *ryokoka*, were slow-tempo songs in minor keys with melancholic lyrics without musical affinity with the blues proper.

On the other hand, the hard times popularized a rollicking dance song, "Tokyo Ondo" (Saijo Yaso and Nakayama Shimpei) sung by Katsutaro (later Ko'uta Katsutaro) and Mishima Issei, and released in July 1933. A kind of collective Japanese folk dance and song with indigenous rhythm emphasized by response refrain sung in chorus, *ondo* was reinvigorated with a new melody and lyrics in traditional style performed with basically Western orchestration which featured traditional drums and *samisen*. Beginning with this big hit, many occasional and regional *ondo* have been produced successfully, establishing a solid genre in Japanese popular songs. Meanwhile, Katsutaro was the first of many *geisha* (a traditional song-and-dance woman entertainer for customers at a feast) to become popular recording artists. They especially contributed to *ryokoka* by incorporating *ko'uta*, a short piece of *samisen* song standardized in the mid-nineteenth century. On recordings new *ko'uta* were performed with an orchestral accompaniment, but the arrangement retained the traditional elements which were complemented by the typical murmur-like vocalizing in which *geisha* were trained along with their own *samisen* accompaniment.

While the domestic song forms, *ondo* and *ko'uta* were adapted for effective use in the field of recorded popular song, early 1934 saw the emergence of a new song type with lyrics about popular historical heroes or tales before the Meiji period or Westernization. The first hit of this kind, "Akagino Komoriuta" (Lullaby of Akagi), which was the theme song of a film based on a well-known story of a wandering gambler who died in 1850, and sung by the pioneer of this song type, Shoji Taro, sold as many as 400,000 copies. The combination of his clear, modulated voice, conventional minor-pentatonic scale and Japanized orchestration with heroic or tragic tales of domestic legendary figures was successfully repeated with many songs in the 1930s and the early 1940s, and served as a model for other lesser-known singers. As has been conjectured by an historian, the appearance of these romanticized retrospective songs might well have been designed by record

companies as a counterplan to cope with governmental censorship on recorded songs (Nishizawa A., 1990, 10). Indeed, in August 1934, the Ministry of Home Affairs began to impose record censorship.

Censorship, Jingoistic Songs and Wartime Pressure

The instability of social conditions caused by the international distur-
bance stemming from the Manchurian Incident, which began in September
1931 and the Shanghai Incident in January 1932, led to enhanced activity by
both extreme rightists and leftists. This triggered action by the special political police who set out later in 1932 to suppress political offenders. Accordingly, they kept a close watch on various publications as well as broadcasting and films, and eventually found that extreme leftists had begun to use
gramophone records for propaganda purposes. This prompted the Ministry
of Home Affairs to begin to regard records legally as another kind of publication (Kurata, 1979, 408). In a newspaper article the following year, it was
made clear that the authorities took offence also at excessive amorousness in
expression, reminding us of the demand made by the organization of music
teachers, namely those educated in Western classical music. Three years before, the organization presided over by the head of Tokyo College of Music,
had offered a proposal to both the Ministries of Education and Home Affairs for legislating censorship on sheet music and records to eliminate
"indecent" and "decadent" popular songs (Nishizawa A. 1990, 8).

An amendment of the publication law to place censorship within the legal framework was passed in March 1934 before being put into operation in
August (Kurata, 1979, 409). It emerged that the affected recordings were
those with critical references to the government or the military authorities.

Then the outbreak of the Sino-Japanese Incident in July 1937 caused the
governmental issuance of nation-wide mobilisation which affected every
aspect of civilian life. Thereupon, record companies began releasing, in conformity with state policy, such songs as "Sen'ninbari" (Thousand-stitch belt)
and "Jugono Tsuma" (Wife in the Home Front) to raise the morale of civil-
ians, and others like "Tate! Kogun" (Rise, the Imperial Army) and "Sorawa
Wagamono" (Having the Air at My Will) to encourage soldiers (Kurata,
1979, 430). The production of these songs was designed possibly to take the
edge off the censorship, but the continuous release of amorous ditties became subject to more stringent censorship.

Meanwhile, in September 1937, the Public Information Section of the
cabinet took the lead in inviting the public to join in a prize contest for
writing "Aikoku Koshinkyoku" (Patriotic March) in order to consolidate
unified thought (Kurata, 179, 443). This governmental adoption of the kind
of contest favored by newspapers since 1932 urged record companies, will-
ingly or not, to give more priority to morale-raising policy, and numerous
martial and jingoistic songs were produced. Their orchestrated music was
either heroically major-pentatonic or sentimentally minor-pentatonic with
public preference for the latter.

In 1940 the Ministry of Home Affairs issued orders for the singers with
such stage names as Dick Mine,[2] Miss Columbia and Ama Ryllis to change
them into appropriate Japanese ones on the grounds that they were words
used in hostile countries. Furthermore, after Japan entered the Pacific War

in late 1941, even record companies with such foreign names as Columbia, Victor and King were forced to have their names replaced with Japanese phrasing (Kurata, 1979, 437, 457-458). The joint ventures had not been run under joint management since 1938, when foreign parent companies withdrew from the business (Kawabata, 1990, 27).

Immediately after the beginning of the Pacific War, the Public Information Section and the Ministry of Home Affairs gave instruction to the public that American and British music should not be performed either in recorded form or live.

Then, in 1943, vexed at the general disobedience, the section listed in its official weekly all the catalogue numbers of records which should not be played, asserting that they were a disclosure of nationalities characterized by frivolity, materialism and paying high regard to sensuality. Arbitrarily, the songs included not only such Tin Pan Alley songs as 'My Blue Heaven' and "Alexander's Ragtime Band," but also "Annie Laurie," "Home on the Range," and all the imported Stephen Foster songs (PIDC, 1943). It should also be noted that in October 1940 the government had ordered all the dance halls to be closed, which numbered 52 on the four main islands, throwing the dancers and musicians out of employment (Nishizawa A., 1990, 16).

Needless to say that the quota of such material as shellac for record companies had been cut because of its indispensability for manufacturing weaponry. Steel, which was even more indispensable, had ceased to be allocated to gramophone manufacturers in 1938 (Kawabata, 1990, 27).

POSTWAR RESUSCITATION OF THE MUSIC INDUSTRY

In August 1945 the war ended in the defeat of Japan with the result that people suffered from hunger and despondency on the destroyed land under American occupation.

The New Development of *Ryokoka* or *Kayokyoku*

The first postwar hit song, "Ringono Uta" (Song of an Apple), appeared late in 1945 as a theme for a film, *Soyokaze* (Breeze), sung by Namiki Michiko. The song has left an indelible impression in the memory of the people who lived in the postwar period. First sung on stage, broadcast live by radio, finally recorded for Japan Columbia in late December and released in January 1946, this sunshiny, carefree ditty about a symbolic red apple served immensely to invigorate disheartened people all over Japan. The melodious tune had appealing mirth despite its minor scale, and the fact that the scale was fully diatonic saved the song from possible gloominess and crassness caused by the conventional pentatonic minor.

Then, six months later, King Records was revived with a great hit, "Tokyono Hanuri Musume" (Flower-Girl of Tokyo). Sweetly sung by Oka Haruo in medium tempo backed by an orchestra with syncopated rhythm, this depiction of a postwar street scene in Tokyo in a moderately melancholic major tune was also cheerful enough to divert the minds of the people from care. Released at the same time by Japan Columbia, "Asawa Doko-kara" (Where Does the Morning Come From?) was similar in its high-spiritedness, though more homely rather than worldly. The mixed duet (Anzai Aiko and Okamoto Atsuo) backed by female chorus contributed to the innovative and positive qualities of the performance.

While melancholic songs in the conventional pentatonic minor made a come-back, especially early in the next year (1947) by the King's "Nakuna Kobatoyo" (Don't Cry, Little Dove) sung by Oka Haruo, more characteristic of the postwar period were morale-boosting songs. The tendency was underlined by a series of songs in boogie-woogie rhythm sung by a sprightly female singer, Kasagi Shizuko. Composed by Hattori Ryoichi, who had tried his hand in the late 1930s at boogie-woogie tunes before the time was ripe for them, the first of the hits to burst on the postwar scene was "Tokyo Boggie-Woogie" released in December 1947 by Japan Columbia. The lyrics, by Suzuki Masaru, were also vivacious with *ukiuki* (buoyant), *zukizuki* (throbbing) and *wakuwaku* (thrilled) rhyming with "boogie-woogie." Thus the prevailing depression and sense of humiliation under American occupation was swept away, if only temporarily, by the adoption of an Afro-American rhythm imported as a jazz element. Meanwhile, the monthly record output by five existing record companies in late 1947 amounted to about 900,000 which was one third of the average monthly product before the War (Kurata, 1979, 481).

The Korean War, which began in June 1950, gave economic benefits to Japan through a munitions boom, while the United States concluded a treaty with Japan in 1951, putting an end to the occupation days, though a certain number of United States bases were kept operating. The consequent easing of social conditions made the public more receptive to relaxed lyrical songs. At the same time, a singing prodigy, Misora Hibari, developed her extraordinary talent. The 12-year-old girl had her first big hit, "Kanashiki Kuchibue" (Plaintive Whistle) released as her second single in September 1949 and followed this up with a succession of hits, including "Tokyo Kid" and "Watashiwa Machino Ko" (I'm a City Girl). Solidified by "Ringo Oiwake" (Apple *Oiwake*) (*oiwake* was a traditional packhorse-driver's song) a release in June 1952, her stardom never waned until her death in 1989.

Then, from the mid-1950s on there emerged a large group of successful homesick songs reflecting the influx of young rural workers to large cities, which was caused by the general switchover of Japanese industries to heavy and chemical industries. "Gokigensanyo Tasshakane" (How Are You, Are You All Right?) (1955) by Mihashi Michiya with nasal tenor which was reminiscent of his background in professional folk-singing; "Wakareno Ipponsugi" (Solitary Cedar by Which We Parted) (1956) by Kasuga Hachiro, who had made himself extremely popular with "Otomi-san" (Miss Toni) (1953), a convivial song about a character in a well-known *kabuki* play, and "Tokyodayo Okkasan" (Here We Are in Tokyo, Mamma) (1957) by Shimakura Chiyoko with her grief-stricken crying are simply examples of many hits of the kind. Along with these nostalgic songs invariably in the conventional pentatonic-minor scale, the late 1950s also saw, as the other side of the coin, quite a few hit-songs which affirmed urban life, in full minor melodies performed with sophisticated orchestration and crooning. They included such self-explanatory titles as "Tokyo Gozensanji" (Tokyo 3.00

A.M). (1957) and "Yurakuchode Aimasho" (Let's Meet in Yurakucho) (1957) by Frank Nagai, who had made a debut as a jazz singer with a Japanese version of "Lover, Come Back to Me," and "A Tokyo Nightclub" (1959) sung in duet by Frank Nagai and Matsuo Kazuko.

Broadcasting and Popular Music

It should be noted that those popular postwar songs were disseminated to a majority of people mainly by radio, which was the predominant audio entertainment for people with restricted lifestyles and no record players.

When it was formed in 1926, NHK of the Japanese Broadcasting Corporation, was supposed to play the part of cultural leader, and the music broadcast was classical-oriented with refined Western and Western-style music as well as stylized indigenous music. The popularity of recorded *ryokoka*, however, made it increasingly difficult for NHK not to play the records. Then in 1936 they started, under government control, a program entitled *Shin Kayokyoku* (New *Kayokyoku*), in which 'wholesome' *ryokoka* were deliberately selected and the use of the word *ryokoka* avoided (Sanseido, 924-5). The usage of *Kayokyoku* as the term referring to *ryokoka* began with this program before being popularized with liberated postwar programming and gradually superseding *ryokoka* with its less respectable connotations, though the term continued to be used for some time.

The postwar contribution of radio to the popularity of *ryokoka* records was largely made by the Nodojiman Shiroto Ongajukai (Amateur Singing Contest), which NHK started in January 1946, six months after the end of the war, as a weekend live show. How the program was of use to record companies was illustrated at the beginning by the fact that, in February 1946, "Ringono Uta" proved to be the favorite song among the contestants (Kurata, 1979, 480), boosting the popularity of the record released a couple of weeks before and played on the radio. This barometer effect long characterized the program, and hit songs were inadvertently publicized for the benefit of record companies. Long-lived *Nodojiman* was eclipsed with the increase of other entertainments in parallel with the general affluence, but the phenomenon of amateur singers gleefully imitating their favorite recording artists in public predicted in retrospect the emergence and popularity of *karaoke* in the 1970s.

With the opening of commercial broadcasting stations in 1951 and the inauguration of television service in 1953, more record-playing programs and amateur singing shows appeared as well as visual live performances by popular singers. The TV shows visualized not only the facial expressions and gestures of singers during their delivery, but the reaction of the audience, with such techniques as panning and zooming, transformed the ways in which artists performed popular songs and, consequently, the way in which the audiences responded. 1953 was also the year when the annual New Year Eve's show, *"Kohaku Utagassen"* (Singing Battle Between 'Red' and 'White') started concurrently on radio and television as a remodeled program which used to be broadcast on New Year's Day. This contest-festivity featuring an array of exclusively domestic stars of popular song became a national event, boasting an extremely high audience rating. Even when its popularity finally began to decline in the late 1980s due to various reasons, including generational change in musical taste, the rating was more than 50%. Thus the whole music industry has been sensitive to the annual select list of participants in *kohaku*, which yearly reflects the popularity of singers.

It was at this time that the first music publisher was formed along with the removal of the nonroyalty system for songwriters who were under an exclusive contract with a specific record company. The Japanese Society for Rights of Authors, Composers and Publishers (JASRAC) had just become domestically functional after a long period of insubstantiality since its formation in early 1940.

Infatuation for American/European Music and Occupation Forces

By means of the radio, people were also exposed to a great amount of recorded Western music, which was largely American popular music, especially after the opening of commercial stations in 1951. In fact, Japanese interest in Western popular music was rekindled, this time into even larger flames, with the overnight introduction of American democracy and the exclusion of militarism. Newly implanted democracy looked dazzling with images of freedom, positivity and affluence, promoting an infatuation for music from the West among the young Japanese, which overlapped with the postwar development of *kayokyoku*.

It was in August 1948 that American hit records began to be pressed one after another from the original masters, which were imported under a royalty contract between Japan Columbia and U.S. Columbia. This was done with the permission of the general headquarters (GHQ) of the occupation forces to whom application had been made by U.S. Columbia. In the following year, another international contract was concluded between Japan Victor and U.S. Victor (Kawabata, 1990, 30).

Indeed, the Japanese preoccupation with American popular music was inseparable from the presence of American occupation forces. Significantly, a station, Far East Network (FEN) was started in September 1945 for these 400,000 soldiers. The service, with playlists of the latest releases of popular music, was easily accessible to Japanese people with enough interest to tune in and living in the vicinity of the many U.S. bases stationed all over Japan. The first song put on the air was "Smoke Gets in Your Eyes," which gave the defeated Japanese a refreshing surprise with its bright and sweet melody, initiating a yearning for American culture among younger people (Sanseido, 1991, 792).

Furthermore, the demand for live music to be performed at recreational facilities at U.S. bases, both for the ranks and officers, led the GHQ to employ many Japanese musicians, who cultivated their skills in playing American popular music to cater to the tastes of the soldiers. The musicians, including those who had been active since prewar days, former military-band members and music-school students, played mostly contemporary jazz band music, though there were a limited number of younger performers who formed country and western bands. This kind of self-apprenticeship produced talented jazz musicians, who became active in the newly evolved Japanese jazz scene in the 1950s, such as Matsumoto Hidehiko, George

Kawaguchi, Nakamura Hachidai, Shiraki Hideo and Ono Mitsuru. Aki-yoshi Toshiko and Watanabe Sadao were involved with more progressive tendencies and later studied in the United States, but were also schooled at the bases. The GHQ contributed to the development of a Japanese entertainment agency as well by ordering the government to supply a variety of entertainment, including not only music, plays and some sports but also exhibitions of such Japanese martial arts as judo, kendo and karate. To cope with this order, a great many new agencies were organized, which would eventually form a basis for the subsequent expansion of the agency industry accompanying the growth of television and the reinvigoration of show business. Additionally, dance halls were reopened in 1945 to entertain American servicemen before the opening of their doors to the Japanese public in 1947 (Sanseido, 1991, 590), which led to the later development of go-gos and discotheques.

The mostly favored form of imported popular music that the Japanese listened to and performed themselves was what was called jazz or main-stream American popular music. The popularity of country music, which had been called hillbilly music until the early 1950s, was largely owed to the taste of stationed American servicemen, among whom even non-Southerners enjoyed the music because of its nostalgic quality. The Japanese interest in Hawaiian music dates back to the 1920s when a strong sense of affinity had been engendered by Japanese-Hawaiian performers who were active in Japan (e.g., Haida Katsuhiko and Bucky Shirakata). Having also been imported before the Pacific War, tango was revived with Fujisawa Rango as the female leading spirit and chansons came back with conservatory-trained Japanese chanters and chanteuses, who accentuated the romanticized image of Paris. In the mid- and late 1950s, Afro-Cuban mambo and cha-cha merrily reverberated from the records by Perez Prado and the performances by Japanese Latin bands as well as rockabilly songs shouted against a background of strummed guitar by late-teen converted country and western stars who posed as Elvis Presley, Gene Vincent and Paul Anka, among others.

In the meantime, beginning with the Gene Krupa Trio in April 1952, there were a handful of foreign artists/groups visiting Japan every year throughout the 1950s, apart from those who were sent on an entertainment mission from the United States for exclusive performance in the bases. The former included such a variety of acts as the Xavier Cugat Band, Louis Armstrong (1953), Josephine Baker (1954), Johnny Ray, Perez Prado, Yvette Giraud (1955), Benny Goodman & His Orchestra (1957), Paul Anka (1958), the Jack Teagarden Sextet, Charles Trenet, Carlos Montoya and the Golden Gate Quartet (1959) (Nakamura, 1988, 454-456). From 1962 on the number of visiting artists/groups has continually increased in proportion to Japan's economic growth, particularly jazz musicians at first and then later rock musicians.

DIGESTION OF IMPORTED MUSIC AND NEW DOMESTIC MUSIC

The 1950s can be labeled as an adoration and imitation period for those who were involved in performing cover versions, both on TV and on records, of imported music. Whereas the lyrics of prewar covers were exclusively Japanese, these covers sandwiched original verses between translated ones and were sung in a style closer to that of the home soil, as can be heard in such successful records as Eri Chiemi's "Tennessee Waltz" (January 1952) and Koshiji Fubuki's "C'est Si Bon" (November 1952). This cover practice, which was in vogue until the early 1960s, survives now in the field of adopted musicals as exemplified in the Japanese version of *Cats* in the mid 1980s.

Japanese composition in the idiom of imported music was also attempted as in the case of successful boogie-woogie by Hattori Ryoichi, quite a few tango songs both in prewar and postwar periods, some chansons and a couple of country and western songs (e.g., "Wagon Master"). However, such undertakings were not enduring or supported enough to establish genres.

On the other hand, quite a few performers who started their careers as imitators of imported music tried their hands at, or often converted to, Japanese music, especially *Kayokyoku*, with the introduction of some foreign elements. The Dark Ducks, the Duke Aces and the Bonny Jacks are long-standing male quartets in dinner jackets, who have been strong in Russian folksongs, Negro spirituals and children's songs, respectively, with an additional repertoire of school-taught Japanese songs and some jazz songs, in which they specialized when they were formed in the mid-1950s. Some Hawaiian bands and Latin bands became successful with *Kayokyoku* composed for their musical format in which a male chorus and the steel of requinto guitar was featured.

Likewise, jazz singers won renown by singing successful *Kayokyoku* as was the case with Frank Nagai mentioned above and Peggy Hayama, whose name has been closely associated with "Nangoku Tosao Atonishite" (Leaving Tosa, My Southern Home, 1958). Even the rockabilly singers who achieved success were those who were provided with *Kayokyoku* songs, with Mizuhara Hiroshi as the most distinguished example, whose "Kuroi Hanabira" (Black Petals, 1959) was widely enjoyed. This songwriting team of this song, Nakamura Hachidai and Ei Rokusuke, also composed "Ueomuite Aruko" (1962) for another converted rockabillian Sakamoto Kyu, which was an international hit known as "Sukiyaki." Though the record retained some of the indigenous feel of *Kayokyoku*, it represented a move away from the confines of the genre, but this innovative sound failed to catch on.

Rock Music

As an extension of the rockabilly craze, the Ventures who visited Japan in May 1962 sparked off among young people what was called "elec boom," which was characterized by a skilful display of electric guitar performance. This instrumental-oriented music was combined with vocals influenced by the Beatles and other British beat groups. Promoted by evolving artist agencies, beat groups consisting of four to seven male singing members who played electric guitars and drums in uniforms and with their hair worn long become a phenomenon called "group sounds." They initially modeled their own compositions on the British groups as well as copying them, but successfully released songs which were composed by professional songwriters as a compromise with *Kayokyoku*. The fad headed up with the Spiders" "No No Boy" followed by the Blue Comets" "Aoi Hitomi" (Blue Eyes) in 1966, the year when the Beatles performed in Tokyo. In the following year, when the Blue Comets succeeded with another great hit, "Blue Chateau," many more groups going in diverse directions emerged, including the Tigers, the Golden Cups, the Jaguars, the Carnabeats and the Tempters.

It is perhaps significant that in late 1967 the yearly consumption rate of imported music (records pressed from imported mastertapes) was less than that of Japanese music (records originally recorded by Japanese artists) in the proportion of 46.2% to 53.8% (that of the preceding year was 50.8% to 49.2%) (Kawabata, 1991, 335). Since the GHQ had permitted international dealings in 1948, imported music had dominated the sales, but now for the first time in 20 years domestic music outsold imported music, reflecting a change in the market and the popularity of group sounds. (The ratio in 1989 was 35.3 to 46.2). 1967 was also the year when the Japanese government decided to free foreign investment four years after Japan joined the Organization for Economic Cooperation and Development, and in the following year CBS Sony, the first of several powerful joint ventures in the record industry, was formed. It should also be noted that in the late 1960s and early 1970s quite a few music publishers as well as firms which produced records for record companies were formed one after another.

Manipulated by the music industry which was basically interested in promoting the groups pretty-boy image for teenyboppers, group sounds rapidly died away in 1970. However, it contributed to the musical sensibility of young Japanese with music which emphasized beat and vocal harmony, and the idea of music for youth by youth which was first conveyed by rockabilly was further underscored.

Some talented former members turned to what was called art-rock and psychedelic music with a time lag of two or so years after the United States, forming such bands as the Flower Travelling Band, Power House and Blues Creation. The most influential in the early 1970s was Happy End, which contributed to the expansion of the scope of Japanese rock with experiments in sound and style, including, among others, adherence to Japanese lyrics. In terms of the antiestablishment, Zuno Keisatsu (Brain Police) and Murahachibu (Ostracism) were more representative of hard-rock bands who spoke for young dissenters. The commercial success of Japanese rock bands first achieved in the mid-1970s by Go Die Go singing in English to a Japanese sound and the Sadistic Mika Band singing in Japanese to a British sound was reinforced in the late 1970s by Carol, who specialized in early rock 'n' roll, and the Downtown Boogie Woogie Band armed with Japanese boogie-woogie songs. On the other hand, while the Yellow Magic Orchestra succeeded with its electronic instrumentation and the Southern All Stars with "Itoshino Ellie" (Ellie, My Love), which was later recorded by Ray Charles, the early 1980s saw the appearance of many indie labels for obscure bands which emerged under the influence of imported punk and new wave music.

Contemporary Folk

Running parallel with group sounds, Japanese contemporary "folk" music evolved, when the American folk revival was introduced to Japan. It had nothing whatsoever to do with indigenous folk music. In the early and mid-1960s an interest in such pop-folk groups as the Kingston Trio, the Brothers Four and Peter, Paul & Mary, produced "college folk." This vogue of sing-it-yourself acoustic music was not commercially very remarkable except for "Baraga Siata" (Roses Are Out), a gentle song a la pop folk composed by Hamaguchi Kuranosuke and sung by Mike Maki in 1966.

What was more durable was the tendency, engendered among the followers of Bob Dylan and other singer-songwriters, to perform to one's own guitar accompaniment songs of a socially and politically committed nature. Though the songs were in the style of American models, the words, which were often ill-fitted to Western melodies, were a deviation from the conventional *Kayokyoku* tradition in their rhythms and vocabulary, and to compose one's own songs was in itself a positive aspect of this movement.

This somewhat underground school of amateurish singers surfaced commercially when "Kaettekita Yopparai" (Drunkard Returning from Heaven) became a seller of a million discs in 1967. Sung and independently produced by the Crusaders, a group of Kyoto students, this humorous and ironic song about a drunkard who died in a car accident opened the door to socially-politically oriented singers, including Takaishi Tomoya who made a debut with "Jukensei Blues" (Student Examinee's Blues").

This school then led in the early 1970s to the emergence of a more cultivated group whose introspective style was typified by songs of daily life, as exemplified by Yoshida Takuro, Garo, Kaguyahime and Tulip.

New Music

Developing out of the music of singer-songwriters as well as early 1970s rock, there arose the loosely defined "new music" with Arai Yumi (later Mattoya Yumi) as its precursor. Her first album *Hikokigumo* (Vapor Trail, 1973), displayed her urbane sophistication and eclecticism, causing the critics to hail her as neosensualist. Supported by other musicians such as Tin Pan Alley, her kind of music prevailed among young audiences and was soon grouped together with the newly developed music of such singer-songwriters as Yoshida Takuro and Inoue Yosui, whose careers slightly preceded hers, and also with that of newcomers, including Nakajima Miyuki, a gifted poetess who made a debut in 1975. Hence the appellation, "new music," which appeared in the same year, was originally given to what was difficult to designate under the existing terms "folk" and "rock" but eventually the borderlines became blurred and the term "new music" fell out of use. In fact, the usage was directly opposed to *Kayokyoku,* a conservative music produced in a hit-making system in which the singer, lyricist, composer and recording orchestra are separate instead of all these roles being combined for fuller self-expression.

It should be noted here that this self-composing and performing, which was first encouraged by beat groups and then by contemporary folk singers, had much to do with the growth of the Japanese manufacturing industry for musical instruments. The manufacturing of such musical instruments as piano, harmonica, acoustic and electric guitar, electric organ and synthesizer, has long flourished, popularizing these instruments among many Japanese, and this prosperity has involved an amazing expansion of music-lesson classes. Yamaha and Kawai, the two largest manufacturers who made Japan the world's leading piano producer in the 1970s (Kobundo, 1991, 636), formed their nation-wide network of music-lesson classes in 1954 and 1956, respectively, which were to expand to accept more than a million trainees in the 1970s (Kobundo, 1991, 121).

These classes served as the cradle for aspirants to a musical career, and to encourage them, the manufacturers sponsored talent scout contests, including the Yamaha Popular Music Contest which started off the careers of such folk groups as the Akai Tori (Red Birds) and Off Course in 1969, as well as such solo singers as Nakajima Miyuki.

The relative sophistication of new music can be partly explained by the fact that advertising agencies cooperated with record companies from the mid-1970s on in making many new music songs successful by using them as the soundtrack for suave TV commercials, in which manufacturers of such goods as cosmetics, whiskey and coffee invested.

In 1980 the sales of new music singles finally exceeded those of *Kayokyoku* in the proportion of 50% and 42% (the rest, 8%, being singles pressed from imported mastertapes) (Kobundo, 1991, 589).

Idol *Kayo*

In the meantime, there appeared in the early 1970s a type of *Kayokyoku* for young people who found it difficult to identify with the kinds of music based on imported idioms such as adapted rock and folk. With three young male singers in the early 1960s as predecessors, including Funaki Kazuo who first succeeded with "Koko San'nensai" (The Twelfth Grade), this trend called "Idol *Kayo*" arose from the popularity of another set of three young male singers among teenyboppers, Noguchi Goro, Saijo Hideki and Go Hiromi. However, it soon became more feminine with three girl singers, Minamai Saori, Mori Masako and Koyanagi Rumiko, who made their debuts at around the same time and established an image of pure and innocent looking female teenage stars. The success of this visual image was instantly proved by another trio of three females singers who had independently of each other won in a talent scout TV show, *Star Tanjo* (Birth of Stars), which had begun in 1971 and was followed by two other similar shows.

In the middle to late 1970s Idol *Kayo* underwent changes when Yamaguchi Momoe and the elaborately choreographed performances by two girl groups, the Candies and Pink Lady, added an element of sexuality. Moreover, Matsuda Seiko, who replaced Yamaguchi as the leading star in the 1980s, stressed her feministic lifestyle while retaining her assumed innocence. At the same time, boy idols were revived in the form of trios with the emergence of groups such as the Tanokin Trio and the Hikaru Genji.

These changes were in parallel with musical deviation from *Kayokyoku* conventions, as is significantly suggested by a book entitled *Dorobo Kayokyoku* (Stealing *Kayokyoku*). This fully annotated list of 190 songs said to be partly copied from American and European originals, consists of "compositions" of new music, folk, rock and group sounds as well as many Idol *Kayo,* though all are put under the umbrella of *Kayokyoku*, the comprehensive usage of which is avoided in this chapter (Datahouse, 1987).

Enka

In the early 1970s *Kayokuoku* was given a fresh impetus. Mainstream *Kayokuoku* had remained active during the 1960s with Record Awards, which were founded after the Grammy Awards in 1959, and with some TV shows which emphasized conventional singers and songs in contrast to others which catered for younger and urban tastes. However, it was also true that many people who were not young enough to feel comfortable with rock, folk or Idol *Kayo* demanded their own type of music. What filled the void were a series of hits in the early 1970s beginning with Fuji Keiko's "Keikono Yumewa Yoruhiraku" (Keiko's Dream Unfolds at Night, 1970), which was labelled as *enka*. The despairing sadness and self-denying forbearance which permeated these songs harked back, in terms of both lyrical and musical characteristics, to the extremely popular song composed in the early 1920s, "Sendo ko'uta," which can be seen in retrospect to form the hard core of ryokoka and the *Kayokuoku*.

Enka has been connected closely with drinking as is suggested by the emergence of *karaoke* in bars in the early 1970s with *enka* as its main repertoire, and also by the fact that *enka* was often popularized by cable radio. The music programs of this new medium, which began its service in the early 1960s, were so enjoyed by bar customers that record companies eventually tied up with cable firms to boost their new *enka* singles. Thus *enka* continually became the mainstream of *Kayokuoku*, even though the popularity of *Kayokuoku* began to be relatively eclipsed by pervasive new music since the mid-1980s. The reversal of the ranking was also reflected in the changing preference of songs by *karaoke* consumers due to natural generational renewal and to the introduction of the "*karaoke* box." The box is substantially a separately constructed small room hired out to small groups. This allows *karaoke* singing to be exclusively available to an intimate group as well as easily accessible to females and minors who are not much interested in drinking.

New Ethnic Music

Meanwhile, the recent "world music" phenomenon has indirectly awakened the Japanese younger generation to the popular and folk music of Southeast Asian countries and, on a smaller scale, to the indigenous music of their own land. This arose out of interest in ethnic music, particularly African popular music, which was in itself another fad imported from the West. However, it, along with the Japanese economic invasion of Southeast Asian countries, helped to give young Japanese an impetus to their interests in the music of Indonesia and Singapore, among others. In the 1990s, for the first time, foreign popular music is being imported by a non-American or non-European route.

Largely as an extension of this interest, many young Japanese enjoy the modernized music of Okinawa, a Japanese prefecture consisting of small islands located far from the mainland in the subtropical zones. This "exotic" music is performed in the local dialect by a limited number of bands, including the Rinken Band, with synthesizer and electric guitar as well as *jabisen* and local drums. The music emerged recently as a reinvigoration of the kind of music experimented with in the early 1970s by the Champloos, who can be compared to Fairport Convention in England or, more closely, to Alan Stivell and his band in Brittany. As to mainland musicians, Shan Shan Typhoon is popular with its hybrid of Asian, Japanese and Western elements, and Ito Takio with his own interpretation of Japanese folk songs. The limited but growing interest among young Japanese in the forms of stylized indigenous music as well as such musical experiments as combining *shakuhachi* (Five Hole Bamboo Clarinet) with Western idioms will possibly generate in the next century more musicians who are less Westernized.

It is uncertain how much this kind of music will be appreciated overseas, but a few critics have a premonition that the twenty-first century will be a century of the East as a final reaction to the domination of the West. Anyhow, it is practically certain that this new ethnic music will be exported, along with other kinds of domestic music, to Western countries, particularly through such companies as Sony and Matsushita who now own CBS and MCA, respectively. It should be pointed out that the international market for domestic artists has already been opened up by more than a dozen New Age musicians such as Tomita Isao and Kitaro.

NOTES

1. The names of Japanese people are written in the Japanese style of the family surname, preceding the given name throughout this chapter, except the name of the present author below the chapter title.

2. Where Japanese person has adopted a Western Christian name, the names are in the order of Western style. This appears in the stage names of such people as Dick Mine, jazz singer, and Jimmy Tokita, a country and western singer.

BIBLIOGRAPHY

Brau, Lorie (1990). "The Women's Theatre of Takarazuka." *TDR* (The Drama Review), 34 (4. Winter), 79-95.

Chamberlain, Basil Hall (1904). *Japanese Things*. New edition, Tokyo: Charles E. Tuttle, 1971. The first edition (1890) was entitled *Things Japanese*.

Clement, Ernest W. (1903). *A Handbook of Modern Japan*. Chicago: A.C. McClurg & Co.

Daicel (1990). *Nihonno Ryokokashi Taikei* (A Chronological Collection of Japanese Popular Songs). A book which accompanies a 66-CD set with the same title. Tokyo : Daicel Chemical Industries.

Datahouse (1987). *Dorobo Kayokyoku*. Tokyo: Datahouse.

Ebisawa Arimichi (1983). *Yogaku Denraishi* (A History of the Introduction of Western Music into Japan). Tokyo: Nippon Christkyodan Shuppankyoku.

Heibonsha (1985). *Heibonsha Daihyakkajiten* (Encyclopaedia Heibonsha). 16 vols. Tokyo: Heibonsha.

JPRA (Ed). (1990). *Japanese Record Industry*, 1990 ed. Tokyo: Japan Phonograph Association, April.

Kawabata Shigeru (1990). *Record* Gyokai (The Record Industry). 6th ed. Tokyo: Kyoiku-sha.

Kawabata Shigeru (1991). "The Japanese Record Industry." *In Popular Music.* (Cambridge: Cambridge University Press), 10 (3), 327-345.

Kobundo (1991). *Taishobunka Jiten* (Encyclopaedia of Popular Culture). Tokyo: Kobundo.

Kurata Hoshihiro (1979). *Nihon Record Bunkashi* (A History of Phonograph Culture). Tokyo: Tokyo Shoseki.

Masui Keiji (1990). *Asakusa Opera Monogatari* (A Story of the Asakusa Opera). Tokyo: Geijutsugendaisha.

Miyazawa Juichi (1990). Foreword to *Asakusa Opera Monogatari* in Masui Keiji. Tokyo: Geijutsugendaisha.

Morimoto Toshikatsu (1985). *Onban Kayoshi* (A history of *Kayokyoku* on records). *Kyoto*: Shirakawa-shoin.

Nakamura Toyo (1988). "Rainichishita Artisttachino Sokusoki" (Visiting foreign artists). *In Music Guidebook 88* (Tokyo: Music Magazine), pp. 456-461.

Nishizawa So (1990a). *Nihon Ryokoka Taikei: Ryakushi* (A Chronological Collection of Japanese Popular Songs: A Brief History). Supplement to Nishizawa. S. *Nihon Kindai Kayoshi* (Tokyo: Ufusha).

Nishizawa So (1990b). *Nihon Ryukoka Kayoshi: Ryakushi* (A History of Modern Japanese Songs). Tokyo: Ufusha.

Noguchi Hisamitsu (1976). "Nipponno Jazz Popularno Ayumi" (A Historical Sketch of Japanese Jazz and Popular Music). In a booklet to *Nihonno Jazz-Song* (Japanese Jazz Songs). 5 volumes (Nippon Columbia Sz7011-15), pp.6-9.

PIDC (1943). "The Expatriation of American and British Music." In *Weekly Bulletin* (The Public Information Section of the Cabinet), No 328. (27 January).

Sanseido (1991). *Sengoshi Daijiten* (Encyclopaedia of Postwar Japan 1945-1990). Tokyo : Sanseido.

Spottswood, Richard (Ed). (1990). *Ethnic Music on Records.* 7 volumes. Urbana: University of Illinois Press.

Takechi Tetsuji & Tomioka Taeko (1988). *Gendai Geijutsutowa Naninanoka?* (What is the Traditional Art?) Tokyo: Gakugei Shorin.

Uchida Koichi (1976). *Nihonno Jazzshi* (A History of Jazz in Japan). Tokyo: Swing-Journal.

Whitburn, Joel (Comp). (1986). *Pop Memories 1890-1954: The History of American Popular Music.* Menomonee Falls, WI: University of Wisconsin.

CHAPTER 10

THE PROBLEM OF OUR TIME: CULTURE OR INDUSTRIAL CULTURE? MUSICAL CREATION OR INDUSTRIALIZED MUSICAL PRODUCTS? THE SPANISH CASE

Blanca Munoz

INTRODUCTION

The greatest problem we face when trying to determine precisely the characteristics and functions of Spanish mass culture and its musical industry appears when we try to answer the question of what type of cultural form it creates and in which cultural model the latter can be included. Culture can be defined, in general terms, as a group of values, norms and institutions which, at a certain historical moment, establish symbolic and significant forms of expression for a collective or human group. That is to say, culture evolves historically into specific cultural forms. This can be clearly seen in the evolution, during the twentieth century, of a specific cultural structure which has created a mass culture distributed and transmitted through powerful technical systems of communication: the mass media.

The recent appearance of such a cultural form, and of its channels of transmission, has led researchers to pose a number of questions which represent a vast field of study. Such questions are focused basically on the cultural and social functions of mass communication. In this sense, the study of the meanings and effects of these new cultural norms is a very complex subject.

To be precise, one the most determining effects of the formation of a new type of industrialized culture has to do with the profound problem of *national cultures* and their transformation through the influence of international influences.[1] The case of cultural industries, such as the music industry, allows for a detailed study of the changes which are taking place within the specific musical--or cultural--forms of a country. In this way, the analysis of the Spanish case not only reveals the present state of the Spanish case but also provides a better understanding of the cultural problems which the conversion of culture into industry creates at the international level. Throughout this study the following aspects will be considered: the economic, social and political conditions that influence, and have influenced, the evolution of Spanish music; the historical and contemporary musical development of the country; and finally, the levels of activity of Spanish national music. The analysis of these aspects will reveal the level of interaction that exists nowadays between local Spanish music and the imported music of Anglo-American origin.

The Spanish state was formed in its earlier periods--in antiquity and the Middle Ages--by the union of diverse cultures: Christian, Moorish and Jewish. Thus, cultural domination was not imposed by a foreign culture, but rather was the result of a synthesis of different cultures. So, with the appearance of the modern state, under the regime of the Catholic monarchs, Spain attained a hegemonic position which would expand during the sixteenth and seventeenth centuries. Nevertheless, this exterior hegemony did not have a parallel within the inner social and economic conditions. The literary picaresque portrayed better than any political treatise the reality of the country and its people. The eighteenth and nineteenth centuries signified the disconnection of the Spanish state from the industrialization and modernization of the other European societies. Crises followed one another and peasant and labor conflicts became acute at a time when the nascent bourgeoisie retained a conservative ideology without a foreseeable future. This situation did not allow for the development of an industry or technology which would make possible Spain's independence from outside forces. Despite all these crises, a cultural vitality was always present. Literature, painting and architecture embodied the renovation which neither politics nor economics could undertake. It can be said that Spain always renewed its superstructures and remained shackled with slow and heavy infrastructures which did not allow for originality or renovation.

In short, Spanish society is characterized by a long historic path, which in times of political and social crises--such as the end of the hegemonic empire in the seventeenth century or the crisis of the end of the nineteenth century--encouraged the emergence of strong cultural movements, such as the golden age or the literary generation of 1898. We are speaking, about a country in which history and art have lived in constant contradiction. The dominant elite have little in common with the rest of the population.

The famous Spanish art--by Diego Velazquez, Francisco Goya, Federico Garcia Lorca, Antonio Machado--is always inspired by popular themes. This is why we can speak of a "dual" society. A society in which there exists a constant tension between geographic centers and the periphery, above all, in the Basque Provinces and Catalonia. There is also tension between social movements and governing classes, and between tradition and modernization with the result of a technological and industrial secular delay. With all these contradictions the twentieth century appears as the moment in which all the conflicts converged: the conflicts accumulated from the end of the eighteenth century, Spain's disconnection from the progressive ideals of the Enlightenment and its isolation from Europe. This isolation together with the loss of the colonies and the Cuban War in the nineteenth century brought about the social, economic and political processes which crystallized in the Civil War of 1936.[2]

Yet, to completely explain the relationship between music and society, as is the purpose of this study, we have to take into account the social and political conditions of Spanish culture and society from the beginning of this century to the present time.

In Spain, the collective social movements are a determining factor for understanding the process of cultural creation. The intellectual world with which the nineteenth century closed fluctuated between a renovation of its values--modernism as a spirit of a liberal bourgeoisie, or the Catalan Reinaxenŋa, which tried to recover the national memory--and Traditionalism--Jaine Luciano, Balmes, Donoso Cortes--which returned to church doctrines as a defense against the arrival of industrial society. The passing to the twentieth century occurred with the Generation del 98--Miguel Unamuno, Ramon Maria del Valle-Inclan, Azorin, (Jose Martinez Ruiz) Manuel Machado--and the intellectual renovation of the Institucion Libre de Ensenanza (directed by Francisco Giner de Los Rios), planned with the goal of connecting Spanish culture with European culture.[3]

Nevertheless, these cultural attempts were maintained within some very narrow social limits, represented by the middle classes who had no contact with the peasant and proletarian social groups. It was within this disconnection that the cultural integration of Spanish society presented its most serious problems--problems that only during the period of the duration of the Second Republic would find means of rapprochement. Thus, the Generation del 27 would be a type of cultural bridge between the groups pertaining to the bourgeois and middle strata and the popular and social sectors. Authors such as Lorca symbolized more than any others this approaching of authentic popular folklore. Lorca would receive from the true and creative spirit of popular tradition (Andalusian) the vitality of a latent culture within the people not tied to commercial links. The evenings in the Residencia de Estudiantes in which Salvador Dali, Rafael Alberti and others were present is well known. In these Lorca cheered up his companions with songs which were from the collective memory.

Popular culture, as will be seen later on, as opposed to the elitist consideration of Jose Ortega y Gasset, of being *una ganga plebeya y vulgar* (a plebian and vulgar windfall) that gravitates over all the Spanish arts, is, nevertheless, that which has impregnated all of the truly creative manifestations which Spain has brought to high universal culture. From Miguel de Cervantes to Lorca passing through Goya, the characteristic element of all of them is their connection with the vitality of a people that has created an entire artistic vision of the cosmos apart from the control of the ruling sectors. And to give an example, in the case of the most cultured Spanish classical music, the work of Manuel de Falla, Isaac Albeniz or Enrique Granados, cannot be understood without understanding the component of inspiration in a tradition which is born directly from the people, both in the compilation of musical forms and its themes.

This same vitality of Spanish popular culture can be seen in moments of conflict as serious as the Spanish Civil War. Even during the long period of

Francoism--from 1939 to 1975--this culture would survive underground in spite of ideological, political and social controls. At this point we will center our analysis on the cultural reconstruction that slowly took place after the armed conflict. The introduction of cultural industries and above all of the music industry during the regime of General Francisco Franco deserves a systematic and detailed study.

THE DEVELOPMENT OF CULTURE AND OF MUSICAL CULTURE FROM 1939 TO 1975

The era of General Franco, which extended from 1939 to 1975, saw the creation of the political and social apparatus in which were mixed aspects coming from many distinct places. In the political realm there was a clear inspiration in Benito Mussolini's Italian Fascism. In the economic, the traditional oligarchies and the middle classes sought security in not having to contend with the powerful syndicalist and workers' movement of the decade of the 1930s. The church, the army and the falange constituted the nuclei upon which the new regime was built. But it was within the cultural realm that Francoism tried to elaborate a logical model of values without fissures or contradictions.[4]

This cultural model revolved around some official norms in which there were constants, which were repeated in their creations. These goals were:

1. There should be an exaltation of traditional values in which family and the Catholic religion were privileged.
2. The rejection of exterior influences caused an ideological component centerd upon a definition of the Spanish, which could be traced to the reign of the Catholic monarchs with the discovery of America being celebrated. But, within this component of Hispanization, Andalusian culture became a basic element in the appearance of the pseudopopular culture crystallizing specifically in music.
3. In Franco's cultural model, populism--typical in authoritarian political regimes of this type that based themselves on the state apparatus--was encouraged in both cinemagraphic productions and music dedicated to mass consumption.

The first decade of Franco's regime coincided with the outbreak of World War II. The war between the Axis and the Allies left Spain with a political isolation and an economic autarky which lasted until the changes which took place between 1951 and 1962. Economic stability and the end of isolation came with the pact signed with the United States in 1953. The visit of President Dwight Eisenhower consolidated Franco's regime. Moreover, the incorporation into the government of technocratic ministers stabilized the economy, which, at the same time, facilitated the entrance of foreign capital--in 1950 the Export-Import Bank granted a credit which alleviated the situation of the country--while the emigration of the Spanish labor force to other European countries began. The entrance of Spain in the United Nations in 1955 implied international recognition for Franco's regime. Within this group of circumstances is located the formation of the first cultural and musical industry dating from the decade of the 1940s.

As has been pointed out, with the Second Republic intellectual and cultural activity witnessed an extraordinary development. This activity was not only in sectors of "high culture"; "popular culture" also experienced a great renovation. It is precisely in the development of music where we can better appreciate this collective transformation. Popular musical tastes preceding the Franco regime fluctuated between the *cuple* and the popular song which later would be called *cancion espanola*. The *cuple* dominated Spanish popular music in the first decades of our century, having its origins in the music-hall developed at this same time in Europe. From a sociological point of view, the *cuple* which is the partrimony of theatres and show palaces, expresses frivolous and picaresque intentions, very much in agreement with the general state of satisfaction that up to 1925 extended itself through industrialized societies. Notes of spicy sensuality described a world in which there was a mutation of traditional values and a larger invasion into the restrained sections of the middle classes. But, above all, we witnessed the first attempts at the appearance of a cultural industry that would have its symbols and its myths. Josephine Baker created a sense of mass entertainment that would powerfully influence the following decades.

In Spain, Raquel Meyer and her *cuple el "Relicario,"* but also La Argentinita (who collaborated with Lorca) or Imperio Argentina and Pastora Imperio, made up a first and very precarious record industry--an industry that during the Second Republic joined itself with a newborn cinema industry in which the film starring Imperio Argentina, *Morena Clara,* was an authentic success of musical cinema with its theme completely inspired by Andalusian folklore and by popular sentimental comedies. The opening of the Rialto movie theatre in Madrid in 1936 converted this film into an industrial landmark as its projection occurred throughout the Civil War, on both the Republican and National sides.[5]

The inheritance that the Franco regime received from the cultural and musical tendencies of the Second Republic was transformed in function with the ideological diffusion of the apparatus of the new states.

If the *cuple* was the representative popular music of the first decade of the twentieth century, a new *cancion espanola* took over the most representative commercial circuits. But let us view this process in a more detailed form.

The consolidation of the Franco regime needed a certain apparatus for the diffusion of the new ideology through which the exaltation of traditional values, which characterize the Spanish, could be collectively disseminated. In this way, a type of musical creation grew defined as *cancion espanola* which was a mixture of music and themes whose contents were inspired in a topical manner which could be considered as specifically Andalusian. But, it was not the suffering Andalusia of "flamenco," but rather a stereotyped Andalusia, that gave birth to a type of melodic song in which passionate feeling were expressed and elevated to an entire social cosmos. With these themes, Francoist Spain tried to transcend the reality of misery and shortages, and throw itself into passionate dramas--always punished when they exceeded the reigning morality--or into the expression of a sentimental charge that celebrated the fact of having a milking cow that "was not just any cow because it gave condensed milk." The mixture between this *cancion espanola* and the light melodic song became more and more representative of the popular music of the Franco regime.

The *cancion espanola* had already developed in the decades previous to the dictatorship. Figures of great status such as Imperio Argentina, Concha Piquer or Estrellita Castro had sung the lyrics of quality writers. Manuel Machado (brother of Antonio Machado), Serafin and Joaquin Alvared Quintero or later Manuel Quiroga and Rafael de Leon created a type of copla that mixed the poetic with the ordinary and the universal with the particular. Nevertheless, when the regime broke out of its isolation and evolved toward an economic and political stabilization in the decade of the 1950s, the *cancion espanola* that had dominated the musical panorama of Spain was, little by little, accompanied by the introduction of a light song of clinging rhythm and simple lyrics. The melodic song that in the decade of the 1950s extended throughout Europe and which had in the Festival of San Remo one of its foci of creation, also arrived in Spain at a moment in which the government of the old Falange was being substituted by new technocratic ministers more in agreement with the international recognitions encouraged by the United States from 1953 on.

Thus, in the decade of the 1950s there was a gradual change produced in the symbolic structure of Spanish culture and Spanish musical culture. Without entering deeply into the new panorama that was being created, but rather as an annotation about what is experimental in literacy creation, there appeared new styles with names such as Celaya, Cela, Delibes o blas de Otero. But it was the beginning of a mass culture, together with an incipient industry; the phenomenon connected the country with foreign international influences, with the effect of the music industry being most apparent.

After the end of World War II, the means of mass communication accelerated a transculturization which consumer society converted into the specific characteristics of postindustrial capitalism. The cultural industry and above all that of consumer music were the carriers of the new mass phenomena, in which identification with idols and stars who frequently appeared in the massmedia promoted one of the most important productive structures: fashion and its temporal creation of supply and demand.

Within this panorama, the record industry, which after the World War II needed new investments, consolidated once again. During the decade of the 1950s an exceptional protagonist appeared on the international scene: the teenager. Adolescents entered into the market of new music industries with their own identities and with values that were no longer those of the austerity that the war years had consecrated as dominant.

The population of the societies that took off economically after the war economy looked for idols that reflected the rupture with the past and the psychological rebellion against the previous generation typical in a society that begins to be opulent and satisfied with itself. Rock 'n' roll was the musical phenomenon that best expressed the eruption of the adolescents as a sociological process of the twentieth century.

International economic growth also acted on Spain. The national music industries, which began to feel the development of the international record industry, elaborated a line of melodic song that at the same time mixed itself with a type of music with Latin American and Caribbean influences, such as *boleros* or more *alocados* rhythms such as the *Cha-cha* and the *mambo*. Antonio Machin in this class of music, los Cinco Latinos--recreating the dwop-dwop--or Luis Mariano with his *Ole torero* in 1951 initiated a certain opening against the domination of the Spanish Copla. The world triumph of Elvis Presley was counterattacked with the type of music dedicated to youth, but a youth integrated into the system and without the least doubt of its political position Jose Luis and his guitar with a rancid song entitled *Mariquilla* is the best example of this.

The 1960s were thus the culmination of a certain national record industry. While in the panorama of the foreign industry the Beatles and the Rolling Stones triumphed, in Spain musical youth groups appeared with "decaffeinated" themes, trying to imitate the foreign groups. The Mustangs, the Sirex and, above all, the Brincos and the Bravos played a rock in which the international influence of the Anglo-American music industries could be observed.

The economic growth of the so-called *desarrollismo* (development), due essentially to the foreign capital that arrived in the country and the remittances that were sent by immigrants and the income from tourism, between 1962 and 1973 caused the Franco regime to consolidate some ideological processes of modernization through the action of mass media and its industries.[6]

In this situation, the representative current of the consumer music industry can be classified in the following:

- The survival of the *cancion espanola* but complemented with a "pseudo-Andaluzation" that tried to provide a more modern vision of Spain. This music was destined for the consumption of the working classes and the lower middle classes. It had Manolo Escobar as its most characteristic figure.
- Pop music was inspired by that coming from England and the United States. The victory of the singer Massiel in the 1968 Festival of Eurovision in London was celebrated as a national victory. This triumph, exploited by the regime, was presented as almost a reversal of the disaster of the Invincible Armada in the era of Philip II. But apart from this anecdote, pop music in the decade of the 1960s permitted record companies such as Hispavox to compete with multinational record companies.
- Rock triumphed in Spain with groups of strong national accent. The Brincos tried to create a synthesis between Spanish contents and rhythms coming out of Great Britain. Moreover, the paradox arose from the use of the English language preeminent as a rock language. The Bravos, with their warlike name got tied to the epoch and their German singer Mike Kennedy represented the most elaborate attempt to find a connection between the national music industry and the international music industry.

Finally, in these categories of music and the Spanish consumer industry in the 1960s, one cannot leave out a movement that reflected better than any other the political problems that General Franco's regime would have during these years of development. The singer-songwriters made up a movement of "testimonial" content which was projected from the peripheries, fundamentally Catalonia, to the geographic center of the country. With the *Nova Canco*--Raimon, Joan Manuel Serrat, Lluiss Llach, Maria del Mar Bonet--

the reaffirmation of the existence of nationalities with their own language was proclaimed in a firm way.

The Calatan Gallero, and Eusquera languages along with the testimony of a real Spain against the official one, with authors such as Paco Ibanez, the Andalusian Manuel Gerena or the Asturian Victor Manuel, converged parallel to the strengthening of political opposition to Franco's regime on the part of the universities, the workers and the rising liberal bourgeoisie, for which Franco's dictatorship was an obstacle to Spain attaining the economic and political order of the Occidental countries. The hardening of the last years of the Franco era--with the assassination of Admiral Carrero Blanco in June 1973, claimed by ETA (Basque Nation and Liberty), definitely ended Francoism, although we cannot speak of the end of the regime until after the Franco's death in 1975--responded to this growing demand for openness toward the exterior.

The last two years of Franco's life (1974 and 1975) moved between the death agony of Francoism, with the execution of three militants of FRAP (Revolutionary Popular Action Front) and two of ETA, and the rise of the opposition joined in the Junta Democratica, with a strong Spanish Communist Party (1974) and the Platform of Democratic Convergence, with the Spanish Socialist Workers' Party (1975) as the principal protagonists of the change toward a representative monarchy.

It can be said then that the epoch of development--from 1962 to 1973-- had an effect on the consumer music industry, planting the bases of the music industry of our time. In this sense, the most important processes can be summarized in the following manner:

- The constitution of a national record industry created a market for Spanish artists who adapted, to the circumstances of the country, the melodic song, pop music and rock.
- The economic growth of the decade of the 1960s saw the arrival of multinational capital and business, among which those of the music sector would grasp wide quotas of the market.
- The introduction of Anglo-American transnational record companies was, at the same time, the agent which spread among the youngest generations the attitudes, norms and values of the consumer society. This diffusion ideologically molded wide social sectors. The English language and the "American way of life" were consolidated, through the continual action of the mass media, as forms of social elevation.

As a result, the inheritance left by the Franco regime in the formation of a mass consumption industry as an escape for the collective desire of social transformation developed fully with the establishment of the parliamentary monarchy.

The stabilization of the political reform placed Spain in both the international economic and representative political institutions of the industrial countries of Western Europe. At this point, the music industries of mass consumption begin to follow a parallel and similar path.

SPANISH MUSIC EVOLUTION

Spain is a country with strong musical traditions. From prehistory, signs of representations of dance in cave paintings have been found. But it was the Roman Marcial who described the *puelle gaditane*, the dancers of Cadiz, as representatives of a culture in which music and dance were in their genesis. 7

If we center ourselves in the field of cultural music in the Middle Ages, Spain was distinguished by an exceptional activity. The activity which carried the synthesis from the Orient to the West (Cordoba) was, in the year 711, the center where Oriental music was melded with the musical forms that developed in the Middle Ages. The *cantigas* of Alphonse the Wise, composed between 1221 and 1284, were a collection of 400 songs that created an entire style of religious music without liturgic character and which, at the same time, were sung in an autochthonous language: Gallero.

Not only were the *cantigas* of Alphonse a monument to medieval music, but also from the thirteenth century examples of profane music have been conserved--the *cantigas* of Martin Codax and court music of the Provenηal and Catalan troubadours.

It can be said that from quite early the vitality of music, in what later became the Spanish state, was a reality. A reality that became more concrete with works as important as the *Codice Calixtino* (or Pseudo-Calixtino) and the *Llibre Vermell*, works which from the twelfth century to the fourteenth century established the polyphonic field and the evolution from the *ars antigua* to the *ars nova*.

The existence, moreover, of sacred dances in the codice *Llibre Vermell* was a unique phenomenon in Europe, the Iberian Peninsula was a cultural reception center and a synthesis of traditions.

The Spanish musical Renaissance, in the transition to the sixteenth century, is best shown in religious polyphony. Cristobal de Morales, Francisco Guerrero and Fernardo de Infantas are a few of the names that stand out in this polyphonic field. Nevertheless, with the *Tres Libros del Delfin de musica* and *El Maestro* of Alonso Mudarra and Juan Mila, respectively, the music of the *vihuela* dominated throughout the sixteenth century until slowly the guitar became the preeminent popular instrument. The most representative figure of the era, nevertheless, was Antonio de Cabezon, who created *el tiento* as a new musical form.

The seventeenth and eighteenth centuries were moments of great creativity. Through the influence of the theatre--Lope de Vega and Pedro Calderon de la Barca--a type of dramatically adapted music developed which later on would lead to the genre of the *zarzuela*, an authentically Spanish genre because of its music and content. The arrival of Domenico Scarlatti and Luigi Bocherini influenced the birth of an Italianized type of opera which little by little took on characteristic Spanish elements.

On the other hand, throughout the seventeenth century, a school of organists and clavichordists renewed with relevant pieces the panorama of the nation; Antonio Soler, in the first group, and Narciso Casanovas, in the second, were two of the most representative artists.8

Once again, the role of the population was the star in the musical evolution of Spain. Opposed to opera, which assimilated the ruling sectors, the people cultivated the *zarzuela* and the *tonadilla* as a genre that related episodes of the daily life of the epoch. With the nineteenth century and the development of musical nationalism, the zarzuela took over with an extraordinary force. Francisco Asenjo Barbieri, who lived between 1822 and 1894, was followed by Francisco Chueca, Tomas Breton, Ruperto Chapi, authors among many other dedicated to the so-called *genero chico*; that is to say to the renovation of the zarzuela, a genre which in the nineteenth century must be understood as a sociological phenomenon given that its characters came from popular culture--above all from the nascent urban proletariat--and was the best reflection of the customs and social usage of the Spanish population of the nineteenth century.

The freshness and vivacity of the zarzuela situations as well as the authentic quality of the music, as good as the Italian opera, offered an esthetic renovation that produced a type of nationalistic music, in which the protagonist was assigned to the popular masses. Isaac Albeniz, Enrique Granados, Joaquin Turina and, fundamentally, Manuel de Falla gathered the new European tendencies, but adapted them to a country that had always been set apart by the force of autochthonous folklore. From the *jota aragonesa* or the enormous richness of the Andalusian rhythms and *cantos--fandangos*, *bulerias*, *malaguenas*, *martinete*--the variety of Spanish popular music is such that the development of contemporary music cannot be understood without underlining the perseverance of a type of music and song intrinsically inserted in the folklore. The shared existence of a sophisticated Anglo-American music industry with a Spanish song of flamenco style define the significance of the force of the folklore traditions, in spite of their ideological utilization by the nation.[9]

It is important to underline the radical separation that in our time takes place between "cultural music" and "music for the masses." The tradition of a serious music (a reflection of daily life such as is the zarzuela) disappeared in the global manner, and after the Civil War models were slowly introduced into the country coming first from France and Italy and later from England and the United States. The implementation of industrialized music would play an ideological role of the first magnitude.

Taking up again the evolution of the music of the mass in Spain from 1975 to the present, it can be said that in spite of the political and social changes which have taken place--consolidation of the parliamentary monarchy, the constitution of a consumer society with goals of reaching the "American way of life," membership in the international organizational institutions such as NATO and the European Parliament--one can continue speaking of permanent styles in the tradition of Spanish popular music. These styles can be classified in the following way: the Spanish song and the flamengo-related song (with an extraordinary variety of types and singers) continue to be the most popular styles among the middle and lower classes. Their contents refer to topics like the "Spanish soul": jealousy, unrequited love, punishment to the woman who has gone outside the collective moral norms and in general an unending line of prejudices in the sense of the concept given by Pareto. Singers such as Manolo Escobar, El Fary, Rocio Jurado, who were already present in the preceding epoch, continue such a tradition, although there have been some attempts at critical renovation--for example, those realized by the Andalusian singer Martirio during her first epoch on the stage.

A phenomenon connected with this line would be the emergence of a very commercialized type of Andalusian folk song the *sevillanas*. This dance music has become very popular due to the arrival of the Socialist Party whose principal leaders are from Andalusia. Thus it can be stated, from a sociological point of view, that this folk song has been utilized in a political way, giving a stereotyped image of the Andalusian-Spanish with a strong component of Spanish nationalism targeted toward tourism, which at the same time is the source of millionaire profits by creating international musical consumption of high-volume sales.

The "eternal" Spain is transmitted adapting to the times and generations. And this pseudo-folk song overtakes the true flamenco that was born from the poor and tragic world of the Andalusian universe, such as was collected in the 1930s by authors such as Lorca, or as has been studied by intellectuals such as Felix Grande. Thus we have Spanish songs and flamenco songs elaborated by the commercial record circuits, and distributed by the large transnationals of the sector, not only in Spain but also in Latin America.

The limits between the Spanish and the easy listening songs at times remain badly explained. The "light" Spanish songs for the consumption of a large sector of the population, places itself within the molds of the music industry. Raphael, in the 1960s, created a style of singing and of "light" songs that had a great influence within the country but above all in the Hispano-American market. Julio Iglesias, being a product elaborated for the middle classes of a consumer mentality, and with certain touches of the "authoritarian personality" analyzed by M. Horkheimer and Theodor Adorno, represents a continuity between the national, the Latin American and the U.S. Chicano markets. Nevertheless, the renovation of the light song moves in different directions. On one hand, it is a type of song dedicated to the professional classes with lyrics of higher quality and a theme with some, though not many, social hues. Ana Belen in this sense would be a paradigm of this renovation. And on the other hand, the light song is dedicated to the rural and lower-middle classes, and its contents present an almost nonsensical elementary simplicity.

Pop music, as opposed to before-mentioned styles, is a product for wider consumption. Foreign influences dominate this sector. The multitude of groups and soloists is extraordinary, with Mecano being the group best known and most representative. Adolescents and the juvenile sectors are the consumers of a type of product in which the *amoroso-meliflua* theme, with large doses, at times, of bad taste stands out as an inequivocable aspect.

Rock, at the same time, is a product absolutely dependent on the Anglo-American culture. Here, nevertheless, one has to enter into specific hues. Standard and commercial rock, accepted and spread though the mass media, is made up of numerous groups that change each year with the typical velocity of the market, in which novelty is the determining factor in sales. But at the same time, there is marginal rock, not spread through the means of mass communication and which as opposed to the typical standard rock record, appears to live in public and for a determined public. In this area there is a nationalist rock, above all in the Basque Provinces which reflects the tension and contradictions of a marginalized and rebellious youth. Like hard rock, marginal rock offers more politicized messages, with a generalized protest,

not only using political aspects but also with lyrics of rupture against habit-
ual social conventions. Kortatu and Barricada are two of the most representative names of this type of rock of national or critical characteristics.

A phenomenon that cannot be left out of the panorama of the contemporary Spanish music industry is that which we can define as
"pseudocultural music." The consumer society, with its specific logic studied
by authors such as R. Barthes, J. Baudrillard, T. Adorno and Umberto Eco,
carries with it the rise of a new middle class which tries to approach culture
as a sign of status. But its approach is superficial; thus, a new form of musical industry appears that tries to bring great musical creations to this consumer. But this "bringing to" is done through a mediation which simplifies
the process, themes and effects. Thus the industry creates a group of idols
who superficialize their art and who put it at the service of this economic
process. Luciano Pavarotti, in the international panorama, is the greatest
exponent of this tendency, but in Spain an authentic explosion of this type
of serious "pseudomusic" has come forth. Placido Domingo, Jose Carreras
and Alfredo Kraus have entered into this market singing items from Argentinian tangos to old operatic arias which are well known and very easy to
understand. The slave chorus of *Nabuco*, the quadrille of bull-fighters from
Carmen, or "Nessum Dorma" of *Turandot*, are repeated as decaffeinated
refrains. Luis Cobos, within pseudosymphonic music, follows the same path
of converting to the marketplace pieces and fragments of classical musical
works. From Beethoven to Strauss or Dvorak, determinant works of human
musical evolution have suffered the cutting up and conversion into fragments adapted for an average public. The aforementioned zarzuela, a genre
that reflects the spirit of a vital people in transformation, has also fallen into
the circle of industrialized pseudocultural music. As can be observed, consumption and cultural creation are usually rather incompatible aspects.

The appearance in the last years of a type of Latin America music,
which is a transfer of rhythms and contents of the Hispanic populations,
cannot be left out. *Salsa* arrived in the Spanish music market with an un-
heard of force. The antecedents of this transfer from Latin America to Spain
and to Europe must be searched for in the *bolero* and in its derivations. But
this *salsa* is based on a synthesis of rhythms with strong caribbean folk song
components. Nevertheless, the themes of the songs contain an erotic and
danceable standard adapted to the summer season, this being understood as
a time of vacation and adventure. In reality this type of Latin music cannot
be considered as representative of the specific folk song of South America,
but rather as one more product of the transnational music industry which
stereotypes once again musical forms and contents.

Within this context it is necessary to place the "health of indigenous
music" for domestic consumption in Spain. But the level of introduction of
Anglo-American music is of such influence that it is necessary to make a
concrete analysis dedicated to this effect. As a result, we are going to consider in detail the domination of Anglo-American music and its consequences.

The decade of the 1960s meant the domination of rock and of Anglo-
American music in the world panorama. This domination, which increased
throughout the 1960s, spread in the decade of the 1980s in a variety of substyles which changed without interruption, as the consequence of a continu-

ous search for fashion. In this way, breakdancing, hardbeat, acidhouse, acidbeat, hip-hop, punk, rockabilly and streetmusic make up a plurality of substyles launched by the record companies which take over the national markets, creating at the same time influences and social effects that deserve a detailed commentary.

In effect, all these musical substyles are directed at young people who assimilate ideological values centered on a consumer system and on its classifications of the world. Nevertheless, these substyles establish cutting distinctions between youth groups by reason of their social class and their consumption level. For example, heavy metal, rap or break dancing reflect a type of street youth whose vehicles of expression are graffiti and music, given that undoubtedly these youth--blacks and Chicanos--are those excluded from the incentives of the system. Opposed to this group, the new waves are directed at the young professionals who escape from their work alienation looking for cathartic experiences and rites of initiation in discotheques, whose entrance prices already are a selective brake. In both cases there is a connection between music, drugs and cosmos; that is, this industrial music generates values and youthful reactions in which sex and experiences taken to the limit are the most significant nuclei.

From garbage music to radical dance, we find ourselves faced with the determining fact, that the diffusion of these substyles (which become archaic within a month) develops in the youth sections of the population. This is a paradoxical situation of the growth of an enormously idealized nihilism through cultural norms in which social Darwinism is reborn with incredible force--a Darwinism which has the discotheque as its ritual temple. The discotheque is the center of a group therapy in which one "drinks, dances, shouts, tells all and relates battles," as a famous disc jockey has stated. This release nevertheless moves fabulous economic volumes. The most modern Spanish discotheques compete among themselves to offer the music and the records that both in New York and London are best-sellers. In this competitive fight to be "on the edge," forms of life are also imported in which fetishism and alienation are important axes.

The psychological and sociological effects, thus, of this importation of Anglo-American music on national cultures are not encouraging given that it socializes a large sector of the youth into a very distorted perception of reality.[10] But, at the same time, there is an entire underlying culture of drugs tied, to a large extent, to all of these musical substyles. The problem, in consequence, will not be solely in the assimilation of exterior musical forms but, above all, in the introduction of the other types of consumption that have little to do with the strictly musical. The sociological phenomena that surround the interaction between national and transnational music should become the center of analysis of the effects that the importation of industrially elaborated music carries with it. Not only should the strength of national musical traditions be studied, but we have to study, at the same time, the sociological and cultural strengths of those groups which directly receive the influence of contemporary musical products.

THE MUSICAL INDUSTRY OF CONSUMPTION
IN THE SPAIN OF OUR TIME

The introduction of transnational record companies since the middle 1960s, followed a similar process to that which occurred in a greater part of other Spanish industrial sectors. The companies of Electrical Musical Industries (EMI), Phonogram, Philips, CBS, RCA, Polydor and Barclay entered Spain both as producers and distributors. This entrance into the Spanish market can best be seen in the lists of gold and platinum record obtained, not only by the artists, but fundamentally by record companies. An analysis of the evolution of the lists from 1986 to the present gives us an idea about the companies that govern the market, and at the same time, of the capacity of those companies (see Table 10.1).

Table 10.1. Gold and Platinum Disks Awarded by Record Company, 1986 to 1989

Record Company	Gold 1986	Platinum 1986	Gold 1987	Platinum 1987	Gold 1988	Platinum 1988	Gold 1989	Platinum 1989
Ariola	1	1	19	9	7	7	7	5
EMI Odeon	8	3	14	3	7	7	14	13
Hispavox	2		9	4	8	6	9	9
PolyGram	14	2	12	6	4	6	17	
RCA	3	2	6	1				
Virgin	2		4	1	1		4	1
WEA	6	1			7	4	11	8
CBS	2	4			12	10	10	12
Blanco Y Negro					10	1		
BMG					7	5	1	5
Ariola Eurod.								
M. Horus					7	5	1	2
Grab. Acid			1	1	1	1	1	1
Prod. Twins			1	1	2	1		2
PDI			2	1		1	2	1
Sanni Records							3	
Zafiro								3
Serdisco			2					
Total	**38**	**13**	**70**	**27**	**73**	**54**	**80**	**62**

National Companies: Gold discs= 88   Platinum discs= 59
International Companies: Gold discs= 173   Platinum discs= 102
Gold discs= 50,000 copies,   Platinum discs= 100,000 copies

Source: Asociacion Fonografica y Videografica Espanola (AFYVE), 1986-1989.

In the year 1988 there was a slight drop in the number of copies sold by the dominant companies in the market, against a small increase in the companies dedicated to the national industry. The explanation for this would have to be sought in a certain revival of Spanish music during this period. If one observes the listings of records, there was a strong tendency toward the launching of local authors and a revitalization of the flamenco song--the rumba--targeted at the youthful sectors. This tendency, nevertheless, changed in the following year. In 1989, one can observe the triumph of a pseudoclassical type of music--Pavarotti is its maximum international exponent and Luis Cobos in the national market. But, again, transnational record companies impose their supply on the Spanish market.

The imposition of transnational companies upon the Spanish music industry is a phenomenon that is growing. And despite the fact that, within the national market, some authors and groups have a strong drawing power, the truth is that one cannot doubt the domination of Anglo-American groups and singers. The same occurs with record companies, thus CBS, EMI and WEA Records, reign in a market that moves an incredible amount of profits as can be verified in the quoted statistics (see Table 10.2).

Table 10.2 Origin of Principal Singers and Groups by Record Company, 1986 to 1989

Record Company	Spanish				Anglo-American				Latin American				Others			
	1986	1987	1988	1989	1986	1987	1988	1989	1986	1987	1988	1989	1986	1987	1988	1989
Ariola	6	7	9	6		7	6	4	1					1	1	
EMI Odeon	5	6	6	9	8	8	2	9						3		
Hispavox	7	11	9	14		4	1	1						1	3	4
PolyGram	10	2	1	6	9	8	8	12						1		3
Virgin				1	3	2	1	6								
WEA	1	4	4	4	3	8	9	14								
RCA	4				4											
CBS	2			9	4			15								1
Blanco Y Negro		3	5			8	4							2	2	
BMG		3	3	1		9	10	9								
M. Horus		7	9	3												
Grab Accid		2	2	2												
Prod. Twins		2	2	1			1									
PDI		2	1	1												
Sanni Records								3								
Zafiro				3												
Total	35	49	51	60	31	54	42	73	1					8	6	8

Source: Asociacion Fonografica y Videografica Espanola (AFYVE), 1986-1989.

The Anglo-American music industry in Spain, then, acts as a great monopoly which unites, at the same time, the big circuits of diffusion and controls the majority of the music transmitted by radio and television. Thus, a kind of communicative cycle of music with a strong parasitical character is produced, fundamentally of youth, of values foreign to their own culture. This distortion, as is proven by Umberto Eco in *La cancion de consumo* and, Rene and Ford, in *Les vedettes de l'ecran*, underlines, through commercial and publicity strategies, an ideological framework of the exaltation of the American way of life, opposed to the cultural scheme of our national context. The position, then, of musical transnationals in European countries, and concretely in the case of Spain, confers on the North American culture a world hegemony for its products. Products that follow a double path; that is, on the one hand the transnational companies are introduced into the different countries through groups and singers produced through techniques of market analysis. But national record companies also try to adjust themselves to the tastes created by the transnationals, with which, at the end of the process, there is a homogenization of musical styles as a function of its acceptance by a public used to certain musical styles.[11] Thus the attack on the national record market is converted into a reality of ideological consequences of great scope. But one cannot consider only the list of the most-sold records and their record companies; the data of public attendance and income collected at the main concerts during the summer are important too. In this sense Table 10.3 is very representative of the relation between income through record sales and artists contracted for live concerts.

Table 10.3. Main Summer Concerts in Spain, 1988

	Artists Contracted for Live Concerts			
Date/City	The Stage	Artists	Tickets sold	Sales ($)
MADRID				
22 May	Auditorium	Judas Priest	21,857	188,422
28 May	Auditorium	Sting	55,000	711,206
29 June	Bull ring	Whitney Houston	15,350	330,215
22 July	Stadium	Pink Floyd	45,497	1,176,646
7 August	Stadium	Michael Jackson	59,548	1,796,706
8 August	Stadium	B. Springsteen	59,980	1,680,474
6 September	Bull ring	Mecano	19,790	154,655
8 September	Bull ring	Miguel Bose	15,295	116,336
9 September	Bull ring	J. Sabina	18,000	155,172
18 September	Auditorium	Rock	19,111	329,500
15 September	Bull ring	A. Belen/V. Manuel	118,731	206,897
BARCELONA				
16 May	Auditorium	Joe Cocker	6,897	137,001
20 May	Auditorium	Judas Priest	7,962	137,275
25 May	Bull ring	Sting	18,500	398,706
28 June	Bull ring	Whitney Houston	10,634	241,048
20 July	Club Sports	Pink Floyd	42,728	1,105,034
3 August	Stadium	Julio Iglesias	70,649	1,141,982
10 September	Stadium	Amnesty International	88,500	1,905,172
PALMA DE MALLORCA				
15 August	Auditorium	Julio Iglesias	1,361	145,586
MARBELLA (MALAGA)				
5 August	Stadium	Michael Jackson	26,879	1,193,284
SEVILLA				
5 September	Bull ring	Julio Iglesias	8,513	291,909
BENIDORM (ALICANTE)				
12 August	Bull ring	Julio Iglesias	5,909	244,913

National singer and groups = 5; International singer & groups = 9

Source: Sociedad General de Autores.

The standard Anglo-American stars attain levels of ticket sales and of income at the box office that is very superior to that attained by the most representative artists of the Spanish music industry.

If we exclude the Amnesty International concert, against South African apartheid, in which were presented famous artists from Michael Jackson to Pink Floyd, passing through Sting (all products of the Anglo-American transnational industry), the comparison of the economic figures leaves out any doubt as to the popularity of transnational music in the country. The data pertaining to the summer of 1988 only confirm those of the previous years.

In conclusion, the contemporary Spanish music industry presents a group of characteristics, among which the most important are:

1. The absolute domination by the transnational producers and distributors, CBS, WEA and EMI being in a fundamental way the most strongly implanted.
2. Speaking of the national companies, Hispavox stands out as the most powerful in our context. But, if one observes the tables cited later on, one cannot speak strictly of national companies, given that Hispavox includes artists such as Dire Straits and Bananarama, which confirms the interconnection between transnational companies and national ones.
3. On the other hand, the existence of small record companies with national funding, which produce a type of music very restricted to small groups of consumers, cannot be forgotten. The marginal rock of the Basque Provinces would fall into this category. Such small recording and distribution studios very rarely reach with their products a Top 40 listing, and the diffusion of their music is through live concerts and a faithful public that relates to the nationalist fears and criticism in the content and themes of these artists and groups.
4. Finally, and as a summary, it can be said that the actual position of the relation between the national and transnational record companies in Spain is similar to that existing in the rest of the European countries of our orbit.[12]

MUSIC AND NATIONAL MUSIC: A PERSPECTIVE FOR THE NEAR FUTURE

Throughout this study we have described the most representative styles of the Spanish musical panorama, together with the implantation of those products created by the transnationals of this sector. From a prediction of the future, we could foresee the path that local music will follow, based on the one it has followed during the last decades. The musical creative styles which are stronger nowadays can be synthesized as follows:

*   The continuity of Spanish music--the type of flamenco-like song with themes reflecting the values of a traditional cosmos--will remain at the present levels of activity; that is, with high consumption in the middle-middle and lower-middle social classes.
*   The light song and pop music, as preeminent mass music, will remain at a level of the national market, which is transferred to Latin America thanks to their lyrics in Spanish and their musical forms of traditional format.

- Rock, and its multiple substyles developed upon exterior influence, will remain in its two most particular variables: as standard rock and as marginal rock of the peripheries, either from the nationalities or from the urban areas of the large cities, especially Madrid, Barcelona and Bilbao.
- The introduction of Caribbean and Latin American rhythms such as *salsa* will remain in a sector of the Spanish market dedicated to summer and vacation consumption. Each year there is a renovation of dances inspired by this musical style; therefore we can talk of a fixed market dedicated to an average public which attends concerts and discotheques.
- Autonomous music--Basque, Catalonian, Gallician, Mallorquin or Valencian-- remains within very narrow margins of distribution. At the end of the 1960s and beginning of the 1970s, this type of music had a great social acceptance influenced by the political and social conditions created by the transition from Franco's regime to a parliamentary democracy. Figures such as Raimon, Joan Manuel Serrat, Jose Antonio Labordeta and many others either have lost importance in the Spanish music industry or have retired due to the low demand their works create in a society in which conspicious consumption has been imposed as the mechanism on which the rest of the collective structures rest.
- Concerning cultural music, there is a complete dissociation between consumption industries and the social diffusion of classical works. Music authors such as Luis de Pablo, Cristobal Halffter, Tomas Marco, Carmelo Bernaola, Joan Guinjoan, Enric Rexach or Josep Soler are still listened to in limited circuits by a minority used to classical music and the avant garde, although this phenomenon is identical in France, Italy and Germany where authors like Karlheinz Stockhausen, Luigi Nono or Gyorgy Ligeti are known by a reduced public.*13*
- If in contemporary classical music Spain follows a process similar to that of other European countries, in the domain of sales and diffusion of classical music there will have been a significant increase. The most representative transnationals of serious music--Deutsche Grammophon, Decca, Harmonia Mundi, IMP and others--have at present an extraordinary acceptance by a sector of the population made up of professionals and university people who come from the middle class, representative of contemporary Spain. Nevertheless, the previously called "pseudocultural" music--that music which fragments classical music creations, reproducing them for the taste of a majority of consumers who see in them a sign of higher status--has been able to establish an extensive national market. Opera fragments are a preferred target of this consumption.
- Zarzuela and folk music, genuine popular music, maintain a stable consumption, but do not present any creative innovation. Thus, zarzuela which in the past century meant the development of a specific Spanish genre because of its themes and music, is barely cultivated in composition and it is not spread among the youth of the country.

Therefore, local music maintains the above-mentioned styles but the control of the market, without doubt, is in the hands of imported music. There is an anarchic development of Spanish pop and rock music, since we cannot speak of the creation of an authentic Spanish style. Some attempts in this sense have failed, and the same can be said about Latin American pop and rock music, which has not been able to break the barriers of language and of other cultures. Nevertheless, the levels of spending generated by the record industry in Spain reflect a society with a strong, growing musical consumption, as the figures in Table 10.4, referring to the years 1975 to 1989, reflect.

Table 10.4. Record Sales, 1975 to 1989

Year	Singles	Long Play	Cassettes	Compact Discs	Total	Millions of $
1975	7,380	8,850	11,850		28,020	63,921
1976	8,133	11,700	15,492		35,325	80,446
1977	7,211	12,005	22,806		42,022	92,637
1978	8,075	13,459	15,563		37,097	115,831
1979	9,607	15,531	19,467		44,605	145,903
1980	7,028	16,425	27,074		50,527	167,276
1981	6,939	15,019	20,979		42,937	182,799
1982	6,498	16,711	23,109		46,318	181,589
1983	5,900	13,815	14,389		34,104	157,669
1984	4,162	11,543	12,363		28,068	155,574
1985	2,365	11,712	13,429		29,114	165,164
1986	1,355	13,922	18,042	325	32,039	223,900
1987	837	14,902	20,830	1,125	39,075	303,674
1988	365	17,800	23,292	2,487	45,177	382,882
1989	252	20,563	27,240	4,920	54,596	496,278

Source: Asociacion Fonografica y Videografica Espanola (AFYVE).

The table shows that there is a growing level of economic activity and an evidently healthy industry. Despite this level of economic activity, when dealing specifically with local music and musicians, this optimism has to be attenuated, basically because the lion's share is enjoyed by transnational companies. As Agustin Girard points out in an article,

At the same time that the structure of supply becomes necessarily worldwide, in its technology and economics, the demand for programs, for cultural content, for fictional works and for music of a worldwide public also frequently includes international products. The hours of emission double every year, and this rhythm will accelerate when diffusion satellites start working: the demand for programs will double at that same rate, in the same way that consumption of recorded music grew 30% annually in the last decade.

The place that each country occupies in this market in expansion is proportional to the strength of its cultural industries and to the quality of its cultural productions. This can give each country, or region of the world, the opportunity to publicize the most universal features of its culture--which can be the most peculiar, most national, most deeply human aspects of this country--or on the contrary, impose on countries with a weaker production capacity a larger dependence on countries with a strong production.*14*

This text, despite having been written a long time ago, reflects the major problems of cultural industries: the disequilibrium between countries as the result of the evolution of a transnational sector which divides national cultures into receptors and controllers. Such a disequilibrium is perceived more clearly in the levels of activity of Spanish music. Authors and styles of great creativity do not cross national borders due to the economic monopoly and the style and values which the transnationals control.

Statistics about cultural habits in the Spanish state reveal a large group of citizens who listen music or who go to discotheques in their spare time.[15] (see Table 10.5).

Table 10.5. Habits of Cultural Behavior in the Spanish State, 1978 to 1985

	1978 Total %	1985 Total %	1978 Men %	1978 Women %	1985 Men %	1985 Women %
1. Reading books	36.2	46.0	48.4	51.5	50.9	49.0
2. Reading newspapers/magazines	42.5	58.0	47.4	37.7	54.1	45.9
3. Visiting the library	7.5	9.3	22.3	19.0	33.3	25.4
4. Going to discotheques	18.8	27.0	21.5	16.4	53.8	46.2
5. Attending musical shows	11.7	13.3	12.5	11.0	50.4	49.6
6. Attending the theatre	10.7	16.0	10.0	11.1	44.6	55.4
7. Visiting museums, monuments & others	15.5	20.0	15.8	15.2	48.1	51.9
8. Going to the cinema	46.3	37.0	49.9	43.1	50.7	49.3
9. Listening to the radio	55.8	35.0	50.7	60.5	44.1	55.9
10. Watching television	87.9	87.0	87.6	88.0	48.3	51.7
11. Watching sports	22.0	38.0	35.8	9.5	76.9	23.1
12. Playing sports	16.6	27.0	25.3	8.6	72.2	27.8

Source: Ministry of Culture, 1978 and 1985; and W.A.A. (1987). El consumo cultural. Ed. Fundamentos/Instituto National de Consumo; Madrid, p. 90.

If we look back, the cultural consumption of Spaniards in terms of music has experienced a positive evolution, and although TV is still the greatest national entertainment, it is true that listening to the radio--the main dissemination of imported music--going to discotheques and attending musical shows are among the preferred habits of cultural behavior. The use of mass communication by Spaniards is shown below (see Table 10.6).

Table 10.6. Use of Mass Media by Spaniards, 1973 to 1987

	1973 %	1975 %	1978 %	1981 %	1984 %	1987 %
1. Newspapers	25	26	27	26	32	30
2. Magazines	30	35	43	42	54	55
3. Radio	27	27	41	46	59	55
4. Cinema	40	39	45	45	51	37
5. Television	57	59	67	69	84	87
Base:	25,047	25,960	27,201	28,033	28,890	27,884

Base: Poblacion mayor de 15 anos. (1000) = 100%.

Source: General Study of Mass Media.

After analyzing all of the musical styles mentioned in this chapter (*cancion espanola*, pop, light, rock, classical, pseudocultural and so on), the levels of economic activity, and the relation between cultural consumption and the use of the mass media in relation to the music industry, it can be said that we are faced with a country in which the inequality between foreign cultural industries and the interior cultural industries is evident. In the case, for example, of audiovisual means--cinema and television--one can confirm the very unequal volume of imported products shown. And now in the subject that concerns us, the parallel with audiovisual means is similar. The conclusions that can be drawn, with respect to the data considered, cannot be other than these:

1. The different phases of production and commercialization of the international music market act against the development of local industries.
2. With such a condition of dependency the creative styles and tastes are homogenized in a way in which no innovative tendencies arise which are not controlled by the logic of the constituted market.
3. The inequality in the levels of activity, then, acts in favor of a supply and demand stabilized by the great transnationals, which renew styles and substyles as a function of their political and economic interests hidden beneath the apparent superficiality of fashion.
4. But, from a sociological perspective, the effects of the action of the importation of internationally homogenized styles and contents have the significance of bringing with them rules of conduct which are spread among the groups that are closest to these imported products. The values, codes and norms of conduct spread, creating a social mentality that assimilates an ideology centered upon a

very "Americanized" concept of life. An ideology which affects the processes of socialization and interiorization of collective attitudes which identify with the "modernity" of a society--a modernity that has to be understood as a pure strategy of market study and of transnational intervention in autochthonous cultures.

The future perspective, thus, of music and of local industries should not lead us into pessimism. Nevertheless, for now, the factors which determine the levels of economic and social activity--but at the same time ideological activity--of music in Spain demonstrate an orientation toward more and more dependence on foreign resources and on the market strategies which promote formulas of sophisticated intervention that contribute to the diffusion of collective ideological structures with strong elements of irrationality and "mythification." The future of Spanish music, it is to be hoped, will not convert itself, paraphrasing Sigmund Freud, into the future of an illusion; or even into a musical future conditioned and mortgaged by the impact and the lucrative ends of the control of the dominant monopolies.

BY WAY OF A CONCLUSION: A PROBLEM OF OUR TIME--NEW CULTURAL MODELS OR THE REPETITION OF OLD CONTENTS WITH INDUSTRIAL METHODS?

We arrive at a point where it is necessary to try to establish some conclusions about the contemporary music industry, especially in the Spanish case. A synthesis, then, of what we have expounded throughout this study could be structured on the following characteristics and consequences:

- The case of the Spanish music industry cannot be considered different from that of the other countries around us. The coexistence between a type of music adequate for internal consumption and an imported transnational music is similar to the rest of the ideologically and economically dependent countries.
- But such a coexistence is unequal in terms of the strength that the producer and distributor record companies have. This inequality destroys, little by little, the national companies, to the extreme that capital and finance originate, to a large extent, from foreign absorption and participation.
- In this economic perspective, nevertheless, musical consumption is increasing. Interior demand rose as a consequence of the consolidation of the mass media cultural standard in which the music industry and its diffusion is located. Juvenile groups, in this sense, appear as the preeminent consumers of these products.
- Thus, a prevision of the economic future that awaits our industry is certainly quite negative. The penetrating power that transnational industry possesses follows a path parallel to that which is followed by other sectors of the audiovisual means of communication and the mass media.
- Thus, one cannot observe indicators of strategies of recovery or a transformation of this state.

If, on an economic level, Spain finds itself in an obvious dependency, at the level of social effects, the characteristics to take into account are the following:

- The exposition of the political, social and economic conditions, expanded upon when dealing with the historic evolution of Spain, show that we have before us a country in which the fundamental processes of European modernity are arriving hurriedly. Thus, from the last day of the Franco regime up to the present, the governing groups have tried to join themselves narrowly to the group of structures of the Anglo-American model.

- The introduction, above all, of symbolic ideological processes has produced the effect of a country that is incorporating itself in "modernity." This is the specific effect of the action of mass media products. Music appears thus a paradigm of the transformation of Spanish society, with certain mechanisms of identification, functioning within the Anglo-American rules that affect in a direct way the social psychology of the population.

- One must not forget, in consequence, that the functioning of transnational music industries takes place within a consumer society. The structures of status formation, that such a society assigns, finds in idols and in the contents of imported music incentives and support which act in favor of the aculturalization of the nation. [16] The "American way of life" has taken hold in the sectors of the professional middle class and, logically, in the youth group that directly receives the impact of the phenomenon of consumption with a power that comes to that of religious devotion.

- There, and from the social point of view, Spain reproduces the typical rules of a consumer society with its implicit mass psychology, by which the products of the mass media compensate large social sectors. [17] Nor are we able to consider here the great diversities in relation to the international dependencies of transnationalized messages.

Another aspect to consider is the rethinking of a state policy in terms of helping Spanish creations. At this moment the music industry of the country is wrapped up in a continuous ideological and economic gamble. Nevertheless, one cannot speak of formulas of intervention plans of public politics that allow for the improvement of the conditions of the national music sector. Legal control of activities, the concession of subsidies, the priority at the time of promoting Spanish music abroad, embodying a strategy that would give autonomy to the music of the country, have not been sufficiently considered.

It can be said, then, that in both economic and social areas, and in the area of promotion of public policies, music continues to be the great unknown, and except for the usual labels by which Spanish music has been defined, the reality is that one can foresee a future in which there will be little change in the arguments concerning the country and its creations.

We do not want to complete these possible conclusions without establishing a wider analysis about the cultural effects of transnational products. Spain is a particular case, like the rest of the dependent countries, within a context that includes and extends more and more over the autochthonous cultures. Thus, the present study requires that we do not rely only on concrete and narrow data. Therefore, it is necessary to perceive the latent significance of the manifest aspects, from a global position, paraphrasing. Robert Merton. In this way we have left for the end the examination of the characteristics and effects that the new international cultural model is producing.

The progressive industrialization and technicalization of the productive means has created forms of culture completely distinguished from those of the creative and critical cultures of the past centuries. Creative culture held a place between the "common sense culture" of traditional form and the "culture of the dominant groups." This culture of the "third level" created forms, concepts and results from an amplification of styles which have constituted our European intellectual and musical history. Nevertheless, from the beginning of the twentieth century, the original creative processes have given ground to instrumentally elaborated products, defining this latter concept from the perspective of the "instrumental reason" of Horkheimer. Thus, instrumentalized creation slowly replaces that "third level culture" of a creative and critical character; and the industrial constructions continuously disseminated by the mass media, at the same time, take over the "culture of common sense," with its symbolic, almost preindustrial rules, and take over national intellectual traditions. Cultural internationalization, as a consequence of the power of new techniques of diffusion, is a phenomenon of multiple consequences.

We are not attempting a defense of a culture of nationalistic form, but rather of a creative humanist culture which broadens faculties, and to which we owe what we are.[18] It is very difficult, given the way in which the record market is articulated, that a Beethoven or a Falla would be able to create with the liberty that they had, if they had been inserted into the pressures of a consumer market. It has been repeatedly stressed that the most serious cultural problem existing at present is giving in to the iron laws of economic interchange. The economic process is that which determines the cultural models that dominate. Cultural production, then, created by the market, carries with it a radical change in the cultural organization of the past. Cultural institutions, creative forms and their diffusion through mechanical reproduction become part of the dimension of interchangeability of the cycles and circuits of the international markets. As Baudrillard affirms,

sociology is, in this sense, usually victim and accomplice: it takes the ideology of consumption as consumption itself. It pretends to believe that the objects and consumption (as in another time moral principles or religion) have the same meaning for the upper and lower sections of the social scale, it credits the universal myth of standing and, upon this base, sociologizes, weighing, stratifying, correlating, at the whim of statistics.[19]

In effect, for Baudrillard, the economic dimension of cultural consumption and its analysis on the part of a quantitative sociology forgets that there are underlying effects of a determinant symbolic and ideological character. In this way, music--as particular art--follows the same process that characterizes industrialized culture. The substitution of the individual creator for a team that studies markets and elaborates artists and styles in function of a prestudied average public consolidates the prototypical phenomenon of the new social and economic conditions of contemporary political culture. The cultural decentralization and democratization that postindustrial societies can make possible has not been realized due to the imperious commercialization of cultural products.

But, at the same time, the defense of auctochthonous cultural identity that each country develops is threatened by the tendency of the transnational concentration of the supply of artistic products. A text by Theodor W. Adorno synthesizes what is happening nowadays:

The relentless unity of cultural industries foreshadows what happens in politics. Established differences, such as those between A and B, or between articles published in magazines of different prices, do not depend so much on their themes as on their classification, organization and qualification of consumers. All of them receive something, so that none of them can escape. Distinctions are extensive and acute. The public is given an hierarchical structure of various qualities elaborated in a chain, which create the law of integral quantitative value. The public must react (as if it worked spontaneously) according to a preset end indicated in an index, and select the category of a serial product which is appropriate to the category to which it belongs.*20*

The words of Adorno--who considered the effects of industrial and musical cultures with a great foreshadowing capacity--can be summarized in the general law according to which the main criteria of industrial culture is to *unify economy and conscience.* For example, the styles and substyles that dominate in our time not only move large quantities of invested capital, they also, and above all, promote levels of classification of consumers. Rock, pop and *cancion espanola*, are in a global manner typologies to create tastes and necessities.

In consequence, one could say that we face a new cultural model in which music has a prominent role. This cultural model could be defined as a *pseudocultural dynamic* which appears as the general ideological nucleus of postindustrial capitalist societies.*21*

Pseudocultural culture--that is, deprived of its intellectual and aesthetic contents and reflecting at the thematic level the system of economic production--acts by simplifying its messages and directing the necessities considered by David Riesman as "the lonely crowd." *22* A number of effects summarize this action, among them:

- The fragmentation of contents which, repeated in a continuous way, acquire a great capacity of persuasion and conviction. In transnational music, the succession of substyles and fashionable music reproduce a critical and neutralized comprehension of the musical message.
- The uniformity of messages is a consequence that follows from the above. The apparent uniformity of cultural and musical industries moves, nevertheless, within a very limited set of variations of prototypes and styles. The appearance of creative propositions different from those of the dominant Anglo-American ones would mean the negation of such deeply rooted industries.
- But the fragmentation of contents and uniformity of messages flow into a homogenization of the publics and in the constitution of a collective social psychology in which the rational perception of the real is substituted for a group of artists and stars who function as symbols of primitive identification. Thus, a general

cosmos, clearly focused on the possession of things, reinforces or inhibits itself as a function of status and the capacity of consumption.

• But not only tastes are homogenized; there is a selection of values in the transnational industries that reveal a very partialized iconography. Musical aesthetics are repeated time and again in different combinations and with axiological schemes in which complex references to ethical, philosophical and other values are eliminated, and there remains only the exaltation of those values required for ideological adaptation to the transnational productive process. It can be said, then, that it is cheaper to adapt the consumer's psychology to the products than to change the prearranged schemes of standard products.

• The final consequence of this undermined pseudocultural model is a morality of success and of the winner that reminds one of the old social Darwinism. The anonymity of the consumer who utilizes the mass media or standard music as a release on weekends is compensated by the obsessive repetition that these products furnish a personality and make one a success with "others." The mechanism, thus, of giving incentives to conducts typical of individual success, used as productive ideology, represents the foundation of the principles of a market society, and of its mechanisms of production and international distribution.

All the presented characteristics, which define the products of cultural industries, function in a similar form within the industries of contemporary standard music. Thus, it is not a problem of describing the musical model of the Spanish state, but rather of inserting it into a dominant model, whose axes are finely defined values. The national music industry, then, reproduces an economic, political and social dialectic of great international scope. The domination of the Anglo-American model has to be understood as the result, and as the logical consequence, of the dominance of said society in the contemporary panorama.[23] But the specific study of the national music industries confirms, in the levels of creative and symbolic dimensions, the formation of a unifying ideological process in postindustrial societies. Symbols, codes, values, styles and systems are organized in a transnationally conditioned musical process. In conclusion, the hegemony of imported music assigns such a level of dependency to national industries, that the general title of this book becomes objective: the voice that stands out from among the national chorus is, logically, the voice of the "master" of the international market, the voice of its products and of its symbols.

NOTES

1.   See various authors. (1982). *Industrias culturales: El futuro de la cultura en juego.* Mexico City: Fondo de Cultura Economica/UNESCO.

2.   Terron, E. (1974). *Sociedad e ideologia en los origenes de la Espana contemporanea.* Barcelona : Peninsula.

3.   Tunor de Lara, M. (1974). *La Espana del siglo XX.* Barcelona: Laia.

4.   Miguel, A. De (1975). *Sociologia del Franquismo.* Barcelona: Euros.

5.   VV.AA. (1985). *La Guerra Civil Espanola, 50 anos despues.* Barcelona: Labor.

6.   Jackson, G. (1981). *Aproximacion a la Espana contemporanea. 1898-1975.*

Barcelona: Grijalbo.

7. (1983-1985). *Historia de la musica espanola*. Madrid: Alianza.

8. See Angles, H. (1965). *La musica en la Corte de los Reyes Catolicos*. Madrid: Consejo Superior de Investigaciones Cientificas. And from the same author, *La musica en la corte de Carlos V*. Madrid: C.S.I.C. Also, Querol Galvada, M. (1970). *Musica Barroca espanola*. Madrid: C.S.I.C.

9. Fernandez-Cid, A. (1973). *La musica espanola en el siglo XX*. Madrid: Fundacion Juan March.

10. Flecha, R. (1990). *La nueva desigualdad cultural*. Barcelona: El Roure: pp. 117-121.

11. Baudrillard, J. (1982). *Critica de la economia politica del signo*. Mexico City: Siglo XXI.

12. Manuel Valls (1974) in his book, *La musica en cifras* (Barcelona: Plaza y Janes) points out: "We are far from enjoying a defined music politic, egalitarian, coherent and efficient, in which music could be understood as a common good, integrated in the humanist education of future generations, and as something vital within our social context, and not as a kind of market which offers a luxury product" (p. 34).

13. Marco. T. (1970). *Musica espanola de vanguardia*. Madrid: Guadarrama.

14. Girard, A. Las industrias culturales: Obstaculo o nueva oportunidad para el desarrollo cultural?" En VV. AA. (1982). *Industrias culturales: El futuro de la cultura en juego*. UNESCO. Mexico City: Fondo de Cultura Economica.

15. AA. (1987). *El consumo cultural. Fundamentos*. Madrid: Instituto Nacional de Consumo, 90.

16. The work of Roland Barthes deals in detail with such mechanisms. See Barthes, R. (1980). *Mitologias*. Madrid: Siglo XXI.

17. Kristeva, J.; Rosolato, G.; et al. (1980). *Psicoanalisis y semiotica*: Barcelona: Gedisa. pp. 174 ff.

18. Moles, A. (1978). *Sociodinamica de la cultura*. Buenos Aires: Paidos. pp. 21-69.

19. Baudrillard, J. (1982). *La Critica de la economia politica del signo*. Mexico City: Siglio XXI, p. 51.

20. Adorno, Th. W. & Horkheimer, M. (1981). "La industria de la cultura." In Gurevitch, M. & Woolacot, J. *Sociedad y comunicacion de masas*. Mexico City: Fondo de Cultura Economica, p. 395.

21. This analysis is expanded by Munoz, B. (1989). *Cultura y comunicacion: Introduccion a las teorias contemporaneas*. Barcelona: Barcanova, pp. 128-139.

22. Reisman, D. (1950). "Listening to Popular Music." *American Quarterly*, 2 (4).

23. *McBride*, S. (Ed) (1981). *Un solo mundo, voces multiples*. Mexico City: Fondo de Cultura Economica. Also, Mattelard, A. (1974). *La cultura como empresa multinacional*. Buenos Aires: Galerna; Schiller, H. I. (1983). *El poder informatico. Imperios tecnologicos y relaciones de dependencia*. Barcelona: Gustavo Gill; and Sommerland, E. L. (1975). *Los sistemas nacionales de comunicacion. Questiones de politica y opciones*. Paris: UNESCO.

BIBLIOGRAPHY ON SPANISH MUSIC

Angles, H. & Subira, J. (1951). *Catalogo musica de la Biblioteca National.* Madrid: Consejo Superior de Investigaciones Cientificas. 3 volumes.

Arnau, J. & Gomez, M.C. (1982). *Genios de la Musica espanola.* Madrid: Zacosa. 2 volumes.

Fernandez-Cid, A. (1973). *La musica espanola en el siglo XX.* Madrid: Fundacion Huan March.

Le Bordays, A. (1978). *La musica espanola.* Madrid: Edaf.

Livermore, A. (1974). *Historia de la musica espanola* Barcelona: Barral.

Marco, T. (1970). *Musica espanola de vanguardia,.* Madrid: Guadarrama.

Salazar, A. (1982). *Musica contemporanea de Espana.* Oviedo: Universidad de Oviedo.

Sopena, F. (1976). *Historia de la musica espanola contemporanea,* Madrid: Rialp.

Subina, J. (1953). *Historia de la musica espanola e hispanoamericana.* Barcelona: Salvat.

Vaggiona, H. (1965). *La musica espanola contemporanea,* Cordoba: Universidad de Cordoba.

Valls, M. (1962). *La musica espanola despues de Manuel de Falla.* Madrid: Revista de Occidente.

VV. AA. (1983). *Historia de la musica espanola.* Madrid: Alianza Editorial.

Apart from these sources, the following general works can be consulted:

Pena, J. & Angles, H. (1954). *Diccionario de la musica.* Barcelona: Labor.

Scholes, P.A. (1964). *Diccionario Oxford de la musica.* Buenos Aires: Sudamericana.

VV. AA. (1986). *Historia de la musica.* Madrid: Turner. 12 volumes.

SPECIFIC BIBLIOGRAPHY ON CULTURE AND INDUSTRIALIZED CULTURES

Abella, R. (1975). *La industria cultural en Espana.* Barcelona: Peninsula.

Abella, R. (1985). *La vida cotidiana de Espana bajo el regimen de Franco.* Barcelona: Argos Vergara.

Abellan J. L. (1980). *Censura y creation literaria en Espana, 1939-1976.* Barcelona: Peninsula.

Adorno, Th. W. (1974). *Industria cultural y sociedad de masa.* Caracas: Monte Avila.

Bardavid, J. (1969). *La estructura del poder en Espana. Sociologia politica de un pais.* Madrid: Iberico Europea de Editiones.

Baudrillard, J. (1978). *Cultura y simulacro.* Barcelona: Kairos.

Bustamante, E. (1982). *Los amos de la informacion en Espana .* Madrid: Akal.

Castillo, J. (1987). *Sociedad de consumo a la espanola.* Madrid: Eudeba.

Debord, G. (1976). *La sociedad del espectaculo.* Madrid: Castellote.

Equipo Resena. (1977). *La cultura espanola bajo el Franquismo.* Bilbao: Mesajero.

Gonzalez, M.J. (1979). *La economia politica del Franquismo. Dirigismo, Mercado y Planificacion.* Madrid: Tecnos.

Hamelink, C.J. (1981). *La aldea transnacional. El papel de los trusts en la comunicacion mundial.* Barcelona: Gustavo Gill.

Jerez Mir, M. (1982). *Elites politicas y centros de extraccion en Espana.* Madrid: Centro de Investigaciones Sociologicas.

Lacy, D. (1968). *Problemas y perspectivas de la comunicacion de masas.* Buenos Aires: Troquei.

Marsal, J.F. (1979). *Pensar bajo el Franquismo. Intelectuales y politica en la generacion de los anos cincuenta.* Barcelona: Peninsula.

Mattelard, A. (1977). *Multinacionales y sistemas de communicacion. Los aparatos ideologicos del imperialismo.* Mexico City: Siglo XXI.

McDonald, D. (1969). *La industria de la cultura.* Madrid: Alberto Corazon.

Moles, A. (1974). *Teoria de los objetos.* Barcelona: Gustavo Gill.

Moles, A. (1978). *Sociodinamica de la cultura.* Buenos Aires: Paidos.

Morodo, R. (1984). *La transicion politica.* Madrid: Tecnos.

Munoz, B. (1989). *Cultura y comunicacion: Introduccion a las teorias contemporaneas.* Barcelona: Barcanova.

Pinuel, J.L. (1983). *Produccion, publicidad y consumo.* Madrid: Fundamentos. 2 volumes.

Ponzio, A. (1974). *Produccion linguistica e ideologia social.* Madrid: Alberto Corazon.

Pye, L.W. (1969). *Evolucion politica y comunicacion de masas.* Buenos Aires: Troquel.

Ramirez Jimenez, J. (1978). *Espana (1939-1975), Regimen politico e ideologia.* Barcelona: Labor.

Romano, V. (1977). *Los intermediarios de la cultura.* Madrid: Pablo del Rio.

Ros, J. (1978). *Capitalismo espanol: de la autarquia a la establizacion. 1939-1959.* Madrid: Edicusa.

Schiller, H.I. (1976). *Comunicacion de Masas e imperialismo yanqui.* Barcelona: Gustavo Gill.

Schiller, H.I. (1983). *El poder informatico. Imperios tecnologicos y relaciones de dependencia.* Barcelona: Gustavo Gill.

Serrano, M. (1977). *Los profesionales en la sociedad capitalista.* Madrid: Pablo del Rio.

Shaw, D. (1987). *Futbol y Franquismo.* Madrid: Alianza.

Sommerland, E.L. (1975). *Los sistemas nacionales de comunicacion. Questiones de politicas y opciones.* Paris: UNESCO.

Tamames, R. (1973). *La Republica. La era de Franco.* Madrid: Alianza-Alfaguara.

Tunon de Lara, M. (1977). *Ideologia y sociedad en la Espana contemporanea.* Madrid: Edicusa.

Turner, V. (1980). *La selva de los simbolos.* Madrid: Siglo XXI.

Vazquez Montalban, M. (1980). *Historia y comunicacion.* Barcelona: Bruguera.

Vazquez Montalban, M. (1987). *Los demonios familiares de Franco.* Barcelona: Bruguera.

Veron, E. (1971). *Lenguaje y comunicacion social.* Buenos Aires: Jorge Alvarez.

Vidal-Beneyto, J. (Ed) (1979). *Alternativas populares a las comunicaciones de masas.* Madrid: C.I.S.

Vidal-Beneyto, J. (Ed,) (1977). *Del Franquismo a una democracia de clases.* Madrid: Akal.

Vilar, P. (1983). *Crecimiento y desrollo.* Barcelona: Ariel.

Volpe, G. Della (1970). *Critica de la ideologia contemporanea.* Madrid: Alberto Corazon.

VV.AA (1983). *Historia de la transicion. Diez anos que cambiaron Espana, 1973-1983.* Madrid: Cambio 16.

INSTITUTIONAL BIBLIOGRAPHY ON THE SUBJECT

Centro Superior de Investigaciones Sociologicas (1982). *Tiempo libre de los espanoles en el fin de semana. Utilizaciones del tiempo libre.*

Informe Foessa (1984). *Cambio social en Espana.*

Instituto de la Juventud (1985). *Juventud y tiempo libre.*

Ministerio de Cultura (1987). *Demanda cultural de los espanoles.*

Ministerio de Cultura (1984). *Encuesta de habitos culturales. Cultura y ocio.*

CHAPTER 11

SEEKING THE BEST INTEGRATION: POPULAR MUSIC IN TAIWAN

Georgette Wang

To a former colony, cultural imperialism, or any form of imperialism, was just a way of life. This used to be true for Taiwan when it was placed under Japanese rule in the first half of the twentieth century. In regard to popular music, this was still true long after Taiwan was returned to China. But today the situation seems to be changing, a change that can be traced to both political and economic development of the society. Taiwan, a small island off the southeast coast of China, has never been considered as part of the mainstream culture in China's thousands of years of history. Since Chinese migrants began to cross the Taiwan Strait in the Sui Dynasty (A.D., 589-618), the island was exposed to deprivation and exploitation from bandits and foreign colonialists. In 1895 Taiwan was ceded to Japan when the ruling Chin Dynasty lost the First Sino-Japanese War, and independence was not recovered until the end of the Second Sino-Japanese War in 1945.

Peaceful days, however, did not last. Only four years after Taiwan was back on the map of China, the Nationalist government lost its power base to the Communists on the mainland, and was forced to move to Taiwan, bringing with it refugees, soldiers and technocrats. Today, except for some 33,800 Aborigines, a great majority of the island's 20 million population are Chinese. Of the Chinese community, largely three subgroups can be distinguished: South Fukienese, Hakka and mainlanders. Although all three share the same cultural roots,[1] the first two are considered as local Taiwanese because their families lived on the islands for generations, while the mainlanders only arrived after the fall of the Nationalist government on the mainland in 1949. For a resource-poor island the size of Maryland, in the 1950s Taiwan not only faced military threats from Communist China, its economy was in shambles. In 1949 the islands' per capita income was no more than US$50 (Minard, 1984). But after a successful land reform and vigorous planned transition from a primarily agricultural economy to a labor-intensive industrial one, economic growth began to pick up. The average growth rate in the 1950s (8.2%), 1960s (9.1%) and 1970s (10%) showed a steady increase over time. Although the growth rate seemed to have slowed down in the 1980s (8.2%) (*Questions and Answers*, 1991; and *Economic Yearbook*, 1990), per capita income reached US$7990 in 1989, approximately 160 times that of 1949, and the unemployment rate remained very low at 7.1% of the labor force.

By the 1990s Taiwan was considered one of the four newly industrialized economies (NIE) in Asia. The lifting of a 40-year Martial Law in 1988 brought further heterogeneity and diversity to an already rapidly developing society. For the first time in its history, Taiwan saw opposition parties advocating their ideas in the streets as well as in the legislative body. Economic development fosters political reform and together they brought other challenges to the society. In a matter of a few years, the people of Taiwan found themselves caught between the need for environmental protection and continual economic growth; the choice between an orderly society and the right to disturb such order while seeking minority welfare; and, ultimately, pursuit of unification with China, or the establishment of an independent state.

Culturally Taiwan also experienced an unprecedented openness; political taboos became targets of ridicule, and new communication technologies such as VCRs and direct broadcast satellites brought the audience into direct contact with foreign cultural products. Such developments not only rendered government policies of protecting media from imperialism meaningless,[2] it also put local producers into fierce competition with international giants for the domestic market. Already ratings have shown a decline in viewing of the three broadcast television networks; further decreases are expected when cable television is officially open for licensing.[3] Faced with such challenges, the popular music industry is perhaps the only one which would forecast an optimistic future; to those in the business, the battle has been fought, and the issues settled.

MUSIC TRADITIONS AND THE DEVELOPMENT OF POPULAR MUSIC IN TAIWAN

Ancient Chinese music, dating back to 1100 B.C., was mostly lost because a scientific system of keeping music score notations was never developed. In the Tang Dynasty (A.D. 618-907), music originating from nomad tribes on the Northwestern border of China was introduced into the country, gradually integrated with the culture and formed the backbone of what is known today as "Chinese music." Limited by the instruments, traditional Chinese music is seldom contrapuntal, nor does it emphasize tempo or summation tone. Melody and its flow therefore became the most important ingredients. Even today these characteristics are still visible in some musical works.

Popular music as it is understood today had its origins in Taiwan from Chinese movie theme songs in 1932 (Chang, 1991). Although quite a few songs were recorded and became well-known in the 1930s, suppression by the colonialist government soon put an end to this after the Sino-Japanese

War broke out in 1937. A fierce acculturalization campaign was launched by the colonial rulers in the late 1930s to mid-1940s and silenced all creative musical works, at the same time it left a lasting influence on the culture. When the Nationalists arrived in 1949, they brought along Mandarin songs from movies produced in Shanghai. In an effort to integrate the former colony effectively with mainstream Chinese culture, songs sung in South Fukienese dialect were discriminated against once again. Under the government policies of minimizing the use of dialects in the mass media, their appearances on the electronic media were limited, which contributed to an eventual decline in the mid-1960s. Ironically to adapt to local tastes, many Mandarin popular songs incorporated features of the South Fukienese songs, including their Japanese flavor, and thus developed a style which is no longer similar to their Shanghai forefathers (Tan, 1991).

But before the early 1970s, neither Mandarin nor South Fukienese popular songs really caught the hearts of the younger generation, especially the intellectuals. To them, locally produced songs were old-fashioned and sometimes of poor taste. Genuine "popular music," in their eyes, meant Elvis Presley, the Beatles and Tom Jones. Listening to the American Armed Forces Radio was fashionable, and singing Western pop music was modern. In 1975 an analysis of the local popular music preference patterns showed a striking similarity to that of the United States. In the late 1960s, a television program, *The Golden Song Award,* brought local popular music production to life. For the first time many youngsters had their attention drawn away from Western products. Unfortunately the novelty failed to last; in a few years the quality of the songs went down and the program disappeared from the air.

The real turning point came in the late 1970s when the United States, one of Taiwan's staunchest allies, broke diplomatic relations with it in order to establish ties with China. To many the news was shocking, but the severe setback also provided a stimulus for everyone to reexamine their society's dependence on the West--politically, economically and culturally. One day at a campus popular music concert, a student went on stage and surprised the audience by asking: "Where is OUR song?" No one could answer.

Not long afterward, a movement called "campus folk song" began to develop. At first it was the work of a few amateur students. But the mood caught on with the general public and soon the students' voices were heard outside the college campuses and they became new national idols. Their songs, in comparison with those available locally, were more refined and properly geared to the prevailing mood of their young audiences. Some especially sought to identify with the Chinese, rather than the Western, culture. The well-known "Heir of the Dragon" by Hou Teh-jien, for example, contains lyrics which emphasize the conviction that "for ever I am the heir of the Dragon (the Chinese tradition)." Others, such as "Chicken Farms," may be more lively and down-to-earth, and "The River of Lost Memory" more poetic than nationalistic--their attempt at cultivating a distinct style for contemporary Chinese popular music was unmistakable.

The success of the campus folk songs brought a tremendous profit to the music business. But when the movement became commercialized, its original idealistic flavor subsided, and gradually a new generation of popular music surfaced. As described in the *Publications Almanac* (1984, 781), this new generation of popular music featured a "combination of Western and Chinese popular music with sometimes a Japanese touch to it." By the free use of composition skills and instruments, these popular music writers managed to integrate what was considered "Chinese" with what was considered "Modern," and perhaps more important, to sell it on the market.

By the mid-1980s, Chinese popular music had firmly established itself in Taiwan. Not only had the industry undergone a complete restructuring, its major audiences changed from clerks and factory workers to students. While breaking diplomatic relations with the United States stimulated the birth of campus folk songs, the lifting of Martial Law in 1988 and the political reforms that ensued served to liberate creative minds.

By 1990 the government Office put an end to prior censorship. Greater autonomy was granted to radio and television program producers in deciding what to, and what not to, broadcast. Also gone were the requirements that singers be licensed before they gave public performances.[4] Although the ban on a sexually provoking song "Exposing Myself" proved censorship had not died out totally, political taboos were mostly in the past. This new-found liberty led to greater heterogeneity in popular music works, which helped to push the business to another climax. According to government statistics (*Publications Almanac*, 1990), in 1988 and 1989 for the first time the number of Chinese popular music records and tapes released (396) exceeded those of Western popular music (278).

The overnight success of several young singers indicated that some fundamental changes in the market structure were under way. With per capita income growing, the average age of the popular music consumers steadily came down. The fact that even elementary school students were buying records and audiocassettes stimulated the rise of teenage singers such as the Tiger Cub Team, City Girls, Chang Yu-sheng and Wang Jieh. To the younger generations, "growing up with Chinese popular music" has almost become a way of life, just as listening to Western popular music was a way of life to their parents' generation. Being Chinese, however, does not necessarily mean local. While Western popular music is on the decline, the Taiwan market is flooded with products from Hong Kong, and even from mainland China. In 1991, four of the ten best selling albums were imported from Hong Kong (*China Times Evening News*, December 15, 1991, 16). A majority of the Hong Kong singers who made it in the Taiwan market are well known movie or television stars. The only exception rose to fame for the role he played in a three minute television advertisement.

Compared with those from Hong Kong, the popularity of mainland Chinese singers was much more modest in Taiwan, a natural development perhaps, since the popular music industry was still on a limited scale in China. The lack of aggressive promotion strategies often put the Chinese at a disadvantage when market competition was fierce. Even though the success of Tsui Jien's "I Have Absolutely Nothing" was remarkable because after 40 years of embittered hatred and mutual distrust, this was the first time a song across the Taiwan Strait attracted buyers in Taiwan.

The rise of teenage and Hong Kong singers was part of a trend toward greater variety in the market. In fact by the early 1990s, the market was an exemplar of the sales cliche: "Whatever you need, we've got it." With appropriate promotion strategies, even the least likely could come true. Chao Chuang, for example, achieved a dazzling success by taking his not-so-handsome appearance to the heart of his audience with this song: "I Am Ugly, But I Am Tender." Using attractive sales pitches, some old songs found a new life: Tong An-ger's "In Fact You Do Not Know My Heart," reached another high point in sales after the singer's new interpretation. In terms of melodies and style, there are the songs which are distinctly traditional or folk in nature. Kao Lin-Feng's "The Yellow Plateau," for example, is a rendition of a Northwestern Chinese folk song. The works by Yoker and Leeling, on the other hand, reminded their audiences of the campus folk songs back in the late 1970s. Some others, including many of Yu Chen-ching's songs, sounded like clones of American raps, only the lyrics were Chinese. Of the great variety we witnessed in the market, two other trends of development are of special interest here; the birth of "new music," and the newfound popularity of South Fukienese popular songs.

"New music," is a term generally used to denote nonmainstream music which began in the late 1980s with the Taipei New Music Festival. Sponsored by the Crystal Record Company, the festival was designed as a forum for musical works with little chance of acceptance by the major producers. Some of these songs, such as "Chen Ming-chang's On-stage Collection," later became popular, but many others remained favorites of only a small segment of the audiences (Yee, 1991).

In comparison to the mainstream popular music, new music is characterized by its ambition of integrating local musical tradition with popular music, a desire demonstrated by its radical attempt to meld traditional music, folk songs and even Taiwanese opera with rock, blues, rap and computer music. "Love in a Foreign Land's Season," for example, is the dialogue between folk song, computer music and blues, while "Opera Ants" is the rock version of Taiwanese opera. To underline its local flavor, many of the new music songs were sung in the South Fukienese dialect, not in Mandarin.

Also highly visible is the attempt by the new music to convey ideologies that are clearly not mainstream. Chao Yee-hau's "Exposing Myself," for example, touched on suicide, greed, nihilism and sex. Others, including "Crazy Song" and "Democracy Ah-Tsao" have become indispensable in street demonstrations and social movements. Their popularity among selected groups of young intellectuals and the middle class is hard to ignore. In connection with the birth of new music is the rise of South Fukienese popular songs in recent years. As mentioned earlier, South Fukienese popular songs began to lose audiences in the mid-1960s despite a history going back to precolonial days. It was not until some 20 years later when young intellectuals and established musicians such as Jien Shang-jen and Chiu Chen began to venture into this deserted land. Stimulated by a mounting interest in Taiwan's roots and history after Martial Law was lifted, a new generation of South Fukienese popular songs began to emerge with remarkable success in the late 1980s.

In comparison with what used to be typical of the South Fukienese songs, the updated genre generally features more refined music, often turning to poems for lyrics. The distinct styles of individual singers has also brought life to their traditionally sad and pessimistic orientation, a characteristic said to have been developed under ages of political repression

(Hsian, 1991). Lin Chiang's "Marching Ahead," for example, is a lively song describing the determination of a young man to make it in a strange big city, while songs by new music singers are inevitably critical. With a fresh new image, the South Fukienese songs are on their way to a bright future, although their market is still developing.

The variety apparent in Taiwan's popular music is an indicator of the society's greater heterogeneity. However in the critic's eyes, today's popular music conveys nothing but the same old love stories, the loneliness of city dwellers and the rebellion of younger generations (Luo and Yu, 1991, 34). This lack of a sympathetic view of popular music, and its market successes, can be attributed to the island's philosophy of the music industry.

THE MUSIC INDUSTRY

Just as one cannot discuss new music without mentioning Crystal Records, we cannot ignore the changes that have taken place in Taiwan's music industry while discussing its popular music. As one important part of the popular culture in Taiwan, popular music has made its way to the audiences through several channels:[5]

1. Radio: music is heard over radio for at least 75 broadcast hours a week.
2. Television: at least one weekly TV program, *Golden Songs--the Tiger Dragon List* was entirely devoted to it; sometimes even spot advertisements have unexpected promotion effects: Lee Ming-yee's "As Long As I Like It" achieved an overnight popularity with a soft drink advertisement.
3. Magazines: altogether five monthly magazines are devoted to popular music.
4. Karaoke bars and KTV centers: places which allow customers to sing-along in public or in private rooms.
5. Direct sales of records and tapes.

According to the most recent statistics (*Publications Almanac*, 1984, 780), total sales of audio products increased over five times in the 12 years from 1971 to 1983. It is interesting to note that during the 12-year period, the number of records and tapes sold reached a high of 4.2 million in 1978 and 1979, at the peak of the campus folk songs, then began a drastic fall to an all-time low of 2.1 million when the movement come to an end. Although statistics were not available after sales picked up in 1983, we can almost be assured of a steady growth as the sales of any single Top 10 album is estimated to be around 400,000 (*China Times Evening News*, December 15, 1991, 16).

Another indicator of the industry's development is the number of record companies. According to government statistics, in 1962 there were a total of 38 record companies islandwide. In 1989 this number reached 710 (*Publications Almanac*, 1990, p. 991), with about 76% concentrated in metropolitan Taipei.

For a population of 20 million, 710 record companies seems to be a staggering figure, even when not all are in the popular music business. Hidden behind this number, however, is a different picture. Owing to the increasing production and advertising costs, the business is becoming more capital-intensive than ever. Most of the companies which dominated the market during the pre-campus folk song era (e.g., Four Seas) had their golden years before the mid-1980s. Fierce competition among new players in the market led to buyouts and mergers, which led to a complete restructuring of the industry.

Although no official figures on record companies are available, very few could deny that by the early 1990s, Rolling Stones and Flying Saucers were the two leading companies in the popular music business in Taiwan. On average, about two-thirds of the albums that make it to the best seller lists come from these two giant companies. In addition to their solid financial background, top-notch talents in music and promotion and extensive distribution networks, the two companies have other characteristics in common. They both started business when campus folk songs became popular; they are owned by young entrepreneurs who were singers or songwriters themselves; and they are growing into conglomerates with ventures into areas other than music production such as popular music magazines and music instrument sales. In addition, both are in the process of entering partnerships with multinationals. Flying Saucers, for example, would have been bought by Sony-CBS if there had not been management changes at Sony's Asian office. Rolling Stones, on the other hand, formed Taiwan Pony Canyon with Japan's Pony Canyon and Hong Kong's Jia Ho.

As the changing nature of the business makes it increasingly difficult for smaller companies to compete in the market, a few dozen have managed to survive by exploring market niches and developing their areas of speciality. Ji Ma, for example, has devoted its entire manpower to producing popular music in South Fukienese dialect, while Crystal Records is best known for its support of the nonmainstream music.

One important recent development in Taiwan's popular music industry which contributed to the formation of a large number of companies was the rise of the so-called independent studios. These studios, often organized by singers and songwriters, took music production as their primary job and relied on larger companies for promotion and distribution. Chen Mingchang and Lin Wei-chen's "Democracy Ah-Tsao," for example, was produced by the Black List Studio but marketed and promoted by Rolling Stones. This complementary rather than competing relationship with the giants was made possible by the growing popularity of MIDI (Music Instrument Digital Interface), a computerized music synthesizer. With it individuals can try their talents at music production, and if accepted by the major companies, will have a chance to test their works on the market. Although not many studios are set up to last, their appearance undoubtedly contributed to the heterogeneity we have witnessed in Taiwan's popular music production and also to the further specialization of the industry.

THE FOREIGN INFLUENCE: IMPORTED POPULAR MUSIC AND TRANSNATIONALS

While imported popular music suffered from a serious setback in Taiwan a decade ago, its audiences have not disappeared. In fact through years of hard work, imported popular music has finally become a profitable business. When popular music was introduced to Taiwan in the 1950s, the market was entirely dominated by pirated records. The situation remained more or less the same until 1967 when Shan Yang, a company doing business in sound systems, began importing records from abroad. The move was unsuccessful, the price of US $7.50 per record scared away most customers. In 1981 Shan Yang made another attempt to bring order to the market: licenses were obtained from a dozen companies in West Germany, the United States and Great Britain to reproduce locally and sell their products. Companies which granted Shan Yang such rights included RCA, Telefunken, Virgin and Kitel.

While Shan Yang was fighting against piracy through authorized reproduction, the copyright law was revised to put the problem under control effectively. In 1985 the new copyright law was implemented and stiffer sentences, including fines and up to five years in prison, were introduced against violators.

Since Shan Yang produced much better quality records than the pirated versions, they soon became favorites of consumers interested in fine music, even though the pirated copies cost half as much as the legitimate records. Encouraged by market reaction and the implementation of the copyright law, other companies soon followed in Shan Yang's footsteps. The list includes Himalayas (Sony-CBS, Japan), Flying Saucers (WEA, United States) and Fu Mao (Companies in Great Britain, France and West Germany). In exchange for the right of sales and reproduction, these companies usually have to pay an average of 20% royalties for each record sold, they have to keep the sales of imported albums above a certain level, and pay a deposit in case the minimum requirements are not met. As observed by Tao Hsio-ching, a well-known disc jockey, owners of these companies are typically young with a determination to promote copyrighted music products.

It is difficult to give a list of the singers and groups and the major hits these licensed companies have introduced. As pointed out by Gon Whai-chung, owner of Himalayas (Wen, 1986, 26), every month his company selects about 20 albums from among the 50 released by CBS to market locally.[6] The 20 may range from classical to popular music, almost whatever the group of judges considers having a market potential. Very often, listings of *Billboard* and *Cashbox* are the best indicators of sales.

Although Western popular music has dominated the popular music world in Taiwan for a long time, multinationals have not yet played a major role in it. Subsidiaries of multinationals in Taiwan include but a few, such as PolyGram, BMG, and EMI (*China Times*, December 29, 1991, 22). In competition with local companies, they have the clear advantage of having an established reputation, solid financial background, extensive international network and effective management. The major interest of these multinationals, however, is not necessarily directed at local production. Sony-CBS, for example, has managed to introduce many of its Japanese singers to Taiwan through cooperation with Himalayas, a local company. For the very few who do have contracts with local singers, the purpose is to produce popular music for overseas, rather than for just the local market.

In the past, the works of several local singers (Fei Yu-ching, Huang Ying-ying and Fei Hsiang) were promoted in South East Asia through multinationals, especially in Singapore where the majority of the population is Chinese. But singers including Su Rey and Tsai Ching have also made a name in the overseas markets through local companies such as Flying Saucers. In the eyes of local producers, the "internationalization" of singers has a long way to go yet, as multinationals, the ones who are best qualified for the task, are not so keen on promoting them; and on the other hand, not many singers have the potential of achieving success across the national boundary (Lan, 1990, p. 115). Although multinationals have not yet dominated the Taiwan market, it is difficult to predict how long the situation will remain unchanged, especially when rumors about mergers and buyouts are thick in the air (*China Times*, December 29, 1991, 22).

MUSICIANS

Since the rise of the campus folk songs, popular music in Taiwan has turned from Western to Chinese; at least it appears so. The issue, however, will become more complicated when we try to trace its entangled family lineage, as is demonstrated in the result of a musicians' survey conducted by the author in Taipei in 1985. These musicians, 34 in all, were mostly in their twenties. Growing up in Taiwan at a time when industrialization had barely taken off, their cultural roots were either rural or urban, and were unmistakably local. When it came to religious belief, over one quarter identified themselves to be Buddhists or Taoists. How much this cultural heritage contributed to their music, however, is open to question. When asked if their music reflected the culture they used to identify with or identified with at the time of the interview, over half gave a negative answer. Western music, on the contrary, seemed to be a more powerful source of influence.

Regarding the musician(s) who had the greatest influence on them, 18 of the 29 who answered the question named someone they did not know or who had a different nationality--for example, the Bee Gees, Bach, Barbra Streisand, Men at Work, Bob Dylan or Judy Collins. Of all the names mentioned, American musicians were the largest group, followed by Chinese and British. A similar pattern of response emerged when the respondents were asked if their work had been influenced by internationally distributed music; this time an overwhelming majority (30 of the 34) said yes. The expression of tempo, composition, instruments and equipment used, performing style, costume and even spirit were said to be under foreign influence.

From the musicians' point of view, foreign influences may be more pronounced in their music than those of their own cultural tradition. Not everyone, however, felt that this was something to be worried about. Yu kwan, a well known disc jockey, once said that talking about the socializing effect of foreign popular music is "exaggerating the issue" (Wang, 1983, 17). To Hsu Chang-huey, an established composer himself, even if foreign influence does exist, only the tunes and melodies are affected; the spirit can still be Chinese.

Hsu's view point is well in accordance with that of Lee Tai-hsian's, also a well known composer. In his observation, no one can avoid being influenced by foreign culture today, but to be entirely cut off from tradition is equally difficult. Therefore it is not necessary to be defensive about one's culture: a point of balance will eventually be achieved. The development of Chinese popular music in Taiwan seems to have testified to Lee's predictions. From the earliest campus folk song singers to the advocates of new music in the 1990s, seeking cultural roots has always been the preoccupation of not just a few, but of a much larger segment of the musical community.

All too often, the success or failure in embodying the cultural essence in their music became the criteria for measuring achievement. The decline of the campus folk song movement, according to many of those who participated in it, could be attributed to the inability to grasp the indigenous music language despite their earnest efforts (*Independent Morning Newspaper*, January 30, 1991, 19). According to a campus folk song singer, even Lee Shuang-tse, the key person who started the movement,[7] had to struggle with himself because the real Chinese music was nowhere to be found when his mind was occupied by Bob Dylan's songs.

To these first generation Chinese popular musicians, their heavy exposure to Western music and limited personal experiences impoverished their potential for greater development. Lee's plight was exhibited in other popular music singers of the same generation. Hou Teh-jien, after his song "Heir of the Dragon" became famous, defied government regulations and left Taiwan for China seeking his "cultural roots." His sojourn in China, however, was cut short when he was expelled by the Chinese authorities for joining the student's democratic movement in Tienanmen Square in 1989. Now he claims that there is nothing wrong with pure rock music. In his words, "one has to be a human being first, then a Chinese" (*China Times*, January 30, 1991, 21).

While Hou may have liberated himself from the burden of producing something Chinese, Lo Tah-yo, another popular singer from the early 1980s, took a path of growth different from Hou. A self-appointed social critic, Lo's music was essentially Western, although the humanitarian concern was distinctly local. After his departure for Hong Kong, however, his songs seemed to become more commercially oriented. "Comrade Lover," for example, was a movie theme song. By the 1990s, Lo again produced works targeted at the Taiwan audience. For the first time his songs were sung in South Fukienese, and also for the first time, traditional melodies and instruments were used.

Compared with the first generation of local popular music singers, those who rose to fame more recently seemed to have been less burdened by the "mission" of creating something uniquely "ours (Chinese)," as in contrast to "theirs (Western)." As Chinese popular music has more or less established itself, the newcomers were allowed more freedom in defining popular music in their own terms. Chen Ming-chang, one key figure in the new music family, is a self-taught musician who committed himself to the future of Taiwan music. Coming from the grass roots, a background totally different from the campus folk song singers, Chen did not have to struggle with what he knows (Western popular music) and what he intends to produce (local music). To him, the lavish use of melodies, singing and composing styles of local folk music was as natural as the vitality of those in the lower social stratum he portrays in the lyrics.

Chen Ming-chang is but one of the many who continued to experiment with blending the old with the new, and the indigenous with the imported. Whether the effort is made out of personal interest, market demand or a sense of mission, Lee Tai-hsian is probably correct in saying that a point of balance will eventually be reached. By then cultural imperialism or the loss of cultural identity will no longer be an issue.

NOTES

1. The South Fukienese and the Hakka speak dialects that are different from Mandarin, the Pekin dialect that the government enforces in schools and public institutions as the official dialect. But all three groups use the same written language, celebrate the same festivals and many worship the same indigenous gods and goddesses.

2. As Taiwan was a former colony of Japan, Japanese programs were not allowed on the electronic media. On television, imported programs must be kept under 30%. This protection, however, became meaningless when signals could be received directly from Japanese broadcasting satellites, and imported movies and television shows were available on videotapes anywhere.

3. Officially cable television has not been open for licensing, but underground cable systems have been around for over ten years, and have reached a considerable degree of penetration.

4. Like many other regulations, this one has never been strictly enforced.

5. The information presented here is based on media programs as of December 1991.

6. Himalayas became the agent for Sony when CBS was bought by Sony in 1991.

7. Lee Shuang-tse died young when trying to save someone from drowning.

BIBLIOGRAPHY

Chang, Chao-wei (1991, August). "Major Events of Popular Music and Musicians. *United Literature, 7 (10),* 130-151.

Economic Daily News (1990). *Economic Yearbook of Republic of China.* Taipei: Economic Daily News.

Hsian, Yang (1991, August). Notes on Youth and Worries. *United Literature, 7 (10),* 90-94.

Lan, Shu-jen (1990). "Crossnational Cooperation in the Recording Industry." In *The Past, Present and Future of Taiwan's Recording Industry* (pp. 111-115). Taipei: Chuang Hsing Magazine.

Luo, Shei-hsien and Yu Jien-kuo (1991). "Contemporary Poetic Music." *Tam-kan Youth,* 30-31.

Minard, Lawrence (1984, 7 May). "The China Reagan Cannot Visit." *Forbes,* 36-42.

Publications Almanac (Various years). Taipei: China Publishing House.

Questions and Answers about the Republic of China (Various years). Taipei: Kwong Hwa Publishing Company.

Tan, She (1991, August). "The history of Taiwan Popular Music--A Preliminary Observation." *United Literature, 7 (10),* 72-80.

Wang, Georgette (1983, August 17-19). "Popular Music and Youths in Taiwan--A Look into the Socio-Cultural Factors." Paper presented at the Wingspread Conference on Youth and the International Music Industry. Racine, Wisconsin.

Wen, Rei-yo (1986, January 15). "Spokesmen for Foreign Tunes." *Chuan Hsin Magazine,* 16, 24-28.

Yee, Hsieng (1991, August). "The Subversion and Paradox of Taiwan New Music." *United Literature, 7 (10),* 95-98.

CHAPTER 12

VISCERAL VIBES AND A PLACE IN THE SUN : U.S. POPULAR MUSIC

Deanna Campbell Robinson,
Jack Banks
& Nancy Breaux

INTRODUCTION

Recently, we had a good time listening to Junior Walker and the All Stars at Blues Alley in Washington, D.C. While foot-thumping and hand-clapping, we thought about how that performance epitomized what we want to say here. Like much of American popular music, the All Stars' stuff is visceral. It's loud. It's energetic. The vibes go right through you. And its African roots poke through its European surface. The music of these five middle-aged black men is quintessential American, representative of the many conflicts that characterize United States popular music: black and white, acoustic and electronic, big business and local production. As anyone could tell at Blues Alley that night, popular music is more than just the sum of its musical elements. It is an experience among musicians and audience members in an onion-like context. Musicians, listeners, music and performance conditions are layered within local circumstances, national characteristics and international competitive strategies. Robinson et al. (1991) believe that popular music "is defined by the relationships in which the music works, gets and realizes its meanings and functions, and has effects."[1]

Within this comprehensive perspective, Junior Walker and the All Stars' performance "said a lot" about music in America. The band was 100 percent black. The audience, people able to pony up the $20 cover charge, 95 percent white. Walker played the local-yokel, older black man to his largely 30-40 years-old yuppie listeners, a performance strategy that seemed to appeal to them, reinforcing the bigotry of still-segregated United States society. The cover charge was greater than usual for a small club, but the scene was typical with musicians crowded onto a small stage at the end of a jam-packed smallish room with columns cutting into some people's line of sight and cocktail waitresses squeezing drinks through impassable spaces. Because Blues Alley is a jazz bar, it has no dance floor, unlike many United States popular music venues where zealous dancers provide even more heat and motion to already sweaty, chaotic scenes.

Blues Alley is a prestige club that showcases top jazz artists. Areas like Adams-Morgan, an ethnically and economically mixed neighborhood in the District of Columbia, feature smaller venues for lesser known musicians. There are many, many thousands of such bars across the United States that offer an incredibly varied range of popular music that includes residual, current and emergent genres and subgenres, an array further complicated by constant importation of foreign music and musicians.[2] Adams-Morgan, a community with many immigrants, even has a special performance place for Ethiopian popular musicians, although the number of residents from that country is relatively small. Popular music is like food in the United States. It comes from all over the world and freely combines musical elements from ethnic traditions and high tech innovations. It is big business, producing homogenized music that everyone downs like McDonald's burgers, but also idiosyncratic, like very localized street food. It produces creative hybrids but also preserves traditional genres, jamming together new "Chinese-Mexican stews" with "French cooking," electronic microwave-zaps and acoustic classic preparations.

The food-music analogy falls down in one respect. Supposedly, Native Americans contributed foods like corn and turkey to the U.S. diet but they have had no comparable influence on American popular music. All American popular music elements and combinations have been imported. It is the unique merging of African and European traditions that characterizes most U.S. popular music and that has made it so acceptable to fans worldwide. The international spread of European classical music readied global ears for European-derived popular music.

The African diaspora prepared international sensibilities for the explosive combination of the two traditions. Strangely, even though Asians also have had a strong presence globally, especially Chinese and Indian immigrants, their cultures have not spread music in the same way as those of Africans. In the United States Asians have had a particularly strong presence in the West, but only in the last few decades have American jazz, New Age and world beat musicians begun to add Asian elements to their composition repertoires. In rock the Beatles may be the only internationally well-known group to have incorporated Asian traditions, most notably the sitar, perhaps partially because of England's postcolonial ties with India.

TWENTIETH CENTURY UNITED STATES POPULAR MUSIC DEVELOPMENT

Good popular music can be found literally everywhere; United States musicians have no exclusive hold on creativity and skill. Their music has dominated twentieth-century internationalized popular music not only because of visceral vibes and familiar elements, but also because of the socioeconomic environment in which United States music thrives. American popular music has been so influential worldwide for at least four major reasons: (1) the United States had an advantageous capitalistic economy for quick commercial exploitation of music technology and markets; (2) United States recording companies enjoyed favorable circumstances after World War II; (3) the United States has a relatively stable and generally noninterfering political structure; and (4) the United States is a primary site for musical struggle and merging between two of the world's dominant musical traditions.

United States Capitalism

Early in the twentieth century, the United States enjoyed an ideal climate for commercial development of recording, film and broadcasting technologies. The country believed strongly in laissez-faire capitalism, a philosophy that permitted largely unfettered industry development of technology and, except for some antitrust laws, unregulated corporate division of exploitable markets.3

Most countries instituted national telephone and broadcasting systems, but the United States permitted free enterprise to determine the shape of all its communication systems except for the postal service. AT&T, General Electric and Westinghouse were the major creators of RCA, and those four entities spawned the first broadcasting network, NBC. RCA also launched a recording company, as did the second broadcasting network, CBS. With the exception of CBS, these companies, along with Western Union, divided communications systems and services among them before the United States government drew up the country's first comprehensive broadcasting plan.

The companies benefited from the sheer size of the American market. Before the development of broadcast radio in the early 1920s, Americans spent more of their leisure dollars on phonograph records than any other leisure product. The large American consumer base allowed recording companies to use domestic profits to build efficient international marketing and distribution mechanisms.

Although record sales dropped drastically during the Great Depression, United States popular music thrived on radio sets around the world. The 1930s sales falloff meant the demise of small companies, but the larger ones, affiliated with radio networks, used the opportunity to expand their interests.

The United States After World War II

The United States emerged physically unscathed by both World Wars. Although World War I was followed by the Great Depression, World War II ushered in the period of America's greatest economic strength. While war-devastated countries were trying to reestablish economic and political structures and their citizens were struggling to feed and clothe themselves, Americans were enjoying more money to spend on leisure products than ever before.

During the post-World War II decades, United States majors, always internationally oriented, continued a process of vertical as well as horizontal integration, easily maintaining their positions within the world's top five recording companies.[4] Many of the independent companies, who had taken the financial risks necessary to develop rock 'n' roll in the 1950s, were acquired by the majors in the 1960s, along with the independents' greatest rock stars like Elvis Presley.

The British rock that grew out of black-generated United States popular music forms also proved lucrative for United States companies.[5] Before the 1960s, American and European recording companies set up partnerships to repackage each other's materials for local sales, but U.S. companies rarely exercised their options. In the early 1960s the Beatles and other British groups established fans in the United States; the American majors took up their options at that point and sold to a ready-made audience.

The entrance of the big companies into rock 'n' roll marked the final stage of the internationalization of Anglo-American popular music. Satellites and transistorized radios made it possible for young people in the farthest corners of the world to listen to the same music. Despite its great influence, the inundation of Anglo-American rock abroad did not kill other countries' indigenous music production. Although many of their musicians initially played covers of the internationalized tunes, they moved from there to indigenous creations that sounded like Anglo-American rock and, eventually, to original compositions that wove together their own musical traditions and rock elements.[6]

The international companies continued to favor Anglo-American music, however, because a single master could garner a very large international audience. A non-Anglo-American group might be popular in their own country, but a master of their music could not guarantee sales outside of that country.

World War II helped United States recording companies in one additional way. Postwar babies began to reach their teenage years in the 1950s and became the dominant age group in the 1960s. Popular music became they cry of rebellion as they protested United States involvement in Vietnam, called for social change and challenged their parents' values and lifestyles. Although rejecting consumerism in other areas, these young people, especially the well-heeled Americans, enthusiastically spent their money on recordings.

At the end of the 1970s, the strength of the United States recording industry began to wane as the country fought a recession, rock diffused into many fragments, the baby boomers became parents, and musicians in other countries recaptured their own creativity and fans. Between 1978 and 1982, the recording industry suffered a deep recession.

But American commercial ingenuity once more offered a respite to record companies and renewed consumer interest in popular music. MTV was launched in August 1981 as a 24-hour cable program service presenting an endless stream of music videos--short visual productions featuring current pop and rock songs.[7]

Music video has since become an indispensable means of promotion for recording artists, who are expected to have accompanying videos for their songs in order to become commercially successful. By 1989, 97 of the top 100 pop hits on the *Billboard Hot 100* chart had accompanying videos.

Foreign musicians were especially eager to be on MTV as it could insure their success in the huge American market. Groups like the Australian Men At Work and the Icelandic Sugar Cubes became international stars through MTV exposure.

The United States Government and Popular Music

During the early years of radio, the Federal Radio Commission[8] established a policy of encouraging stations to air live rather than recorded music. They argued that people could hear recordings elsewhere so did not need to hear them on the air. Because the airwaves are regarded as public property, radio stations were expected to serve the "public interest," and it was not in the public interest to play records on the air. The fact that two of the three national broadcasting networks owned recording companies tested the credibility of this policy.

The Cold War prompted fear of Communist influence during the 1950s in the United States. Anyone who worked in a culture industry was subject to congressional scrutiny for politically "incorrect" thinking. Although film and theatre people may have suffered more from McCarthyism,[9] popular musicians endured police closings of performances and other indignities during this time.

The 1950s congressional investigations came as close to widespread censorship as ever experienced in the United States. Unlike other countries, however, the United States has never instituted *routine* prescreening review and political censorship of cultural products. In the 1980s a group of powerful people did persuade Congress to hold hearings on popular music lyrics, with the result that recording companies agreed to warn parents about potentially offensive lyrics and to print those lyrics on recording covers.

Obscenity laws are sometimes evoked to suppress what some people regard as politically or aesthetically valuable works. In the early 1990s some record store owners were fined for selling rap recordings found by a court to be obscene. Scattered instances of outright government censorship occur occasionally (for example, the temporary banning of a Canadian film about the United States contribution to North American acid rain problems), but none of these have involved music.

Outside obscenity, which is not protected by the First Amendment, outright bans on recorded material are not likely in the United States. The socio-political upheaval of the 1960s prompted the Federal Communications Commission to order radio station executives to monitor all popular music lyrics for drug promotion in the early 1970s. The order evoked such strong First Amendment protests that the Commission was forced to rescind the order only three months after its issuance.

Black and White Conflict

One impetus for shutting down rock 'n' roll concerts during the latter half of the 1950s and early 1960s came from racial bigots scared by the mixing of black and white youth in musical audiences. Whites had attended black music performances during the entire twentieth century, but until the 1950s these performances were limited mainly to drinking-age adults. Blacks and whites rarely mixed socially on these occasions. Despite the lack of person-to-person rapport, the interaction between black and white musical traditions may be the single most important factor for the global appeal of American popular music.

United States music evolved from the Atlantic Ocean "musical revolving door," whereby musical elements and various ways of combining them have been shuttled back and forth across the ocean via seamen, merchants, soldiers, missionaries, settlers, slaves (including those who returned to Africa when freed), and, eventually, the recording and broadcasting industries. Now new transportation and communication technologies--plus the economic and social internationalization they engender--propel musicians, their music and their audiences ever more frequently and quickly through that revolving door.

Until the rise of the broadcasting and recording industries, musical exchange relied on live performances and sales of sheet music. Black and white remained relatively separate even after the births of radio and recording at the beginning of the century. During the 1920s, some independents' and majors' secondary labels specialized in "race" music, but most of them fell victim to the Great Depression in the 1930s.

Music publishers in the early part of the century looked to vaudeville and music halls for new material and located their offices next to these venues on what came to be called "Tin Pan Alley" in New York City. Theatre and films also furnished material for large recording companies who distributed the tunes around the world. In the 1940s, however, the importance of show tunes decreased in the face of new black swing played by big white bands.

Mergers of the two strands of black and white popular music genres were hastened by the movement of rural blacks and whites to metropolitan areas during World War II, their growing intimacy with each other, and their new familiarity with each other's music via radio broadcasts and live performances. After the war, consumption of music jumped dramatically as returning servicemen courted their sweethearts and began to produce the baby boom generation. The first wave of teenage baby boomers became a ready market for the mid-1950s sensuous, visceral, politically and aesthetically powerful combination of black and white musical strands--rock 'n' roll. From that point on, American popular music (and to a lesser extent British) flooded the world market.

Although United States music still dominates the international market, indigenous production has accelerated around the world and, at least to some extent, the international market has opened up.[10] The same phenomenon applies to local U.S. music production, where many musicians have begun to self-produce, market and distribute their own recordings.[11]

CURRENT UNITED STATES PRODUCTION

Because the working conditions of United States musicians have been explored in depth in an earlier ICYC book[12] we will concentrate on some recent trends in United States music production here.

Production Outside the Recording Companies

All popular music begins on the local level; each musician comes from somewhere and usually is a narrowly known performer until picked up by a fairly large recording company and promoted heavily. Although a constant tension exists between local musicians striving to survive in spite of pressures from the central recording industry, both sides traditionally have needed each other.

Recording companies need local creation in order to reap innovative ideas and fresh music. Otherwise they will be unable to meet each generation's demands for its "own music" and will be reduced to formulaic reproductions of past successes. Independent, smaller companies often play the role of intermediary between local musicians and large recording companies. Independents are more flexible and more willing to take financial risks.

We have used the phrase "traditionally needed each other" because the total dependence of local musicians on recording companies has eased recently. Very good quality recording equipment has become economically and physically accessible to a wide range of studios and musicians, thus facilitating small-scale studio and musician self-production. Musicians almost anywhere can rent studio time, arrange for production of artistic album covers, have recordings reproduced (including in CD form), and market the products directly to their fans via live performances or indirectly through local stores.

Nevertheless, the distribution part of self-production still remains limited. A group would have difficulty making itself well-known nationally, let alone internationally. One West Coast group managed to sell 45,000 copies of its first two albums but even such modest success is not the norm. Distribution remains a problem. Local musicians still need big record contracts if they want to market their music widely.

Genre Trends

The rock stars of the 1960s are the heroes of today's parents and not necessarily today's youth. Consequently, a curious phenomenon has occurred where rock's big names are moving into children's literature. Michael Jackson, Carly Simon and Jimmy Buffett, among others, all have written children's books, an interesting example of cross-product exploitation.[13]

Another sign of the greying of rock is the emphasis the music industry is putting on CD boxed sets of older material. In fall 1991, Led Zeppelin's $70 set (some sets cost over $100) had sold 750,000 copies for Atlantic Records.[14] Such sets cost little to produce and have a big payoff, particularly at a time when consumers are replacing their old vinyl discs with CDs. CD sales virtually replaced those of record albums at the end of the 1980s. Reissues of material on CDs includes many genres, not just rock. For example, Atlantic also released a huge compilation of classic rhythm and blues songs in 1991. Bret Easton Ellis, the 26 year old author of several novels, writes that young Americans have grown increasingly frustrated by the lack of salience, by the sheer bigness of aural texture, in American rock. We have turned instead toward college-radio bands like REM, and the newly revamped B-52's, whose enigmatic cool and harmless view of contemporary culture seem appealing and suggestive toward the viciousness and monotony of heavy-metal, which speaks to a huge section of this audience in crude, basic ways, and toward the pounding, chilly ominous dance-pop of a Janet Jackson.*15*

In the United States the 1960s role of rock may be being filled by rap, currently the music for the politically rebellious. The growing general support, white as well as black, for rap is ironic because, since their role in the foundation of rock 'n' roll, blacks have become increasingly alienated from rock. This is due at least partly to the way music marketers split the audience into mainstream (white) and black compounded by "album-oriented-rock" (AOR) stations and MTV's reluctance to play black musicians' music.

If rock has been predominantly associated with white males, many of whom are now ageing, rap, which emerged in New York City in the mid-1970s, is the music of black males, mostly young street blacks. It also follows African oral tradition, especially as refined in the Caribbean by "sound-system" musicians, and largely defies white intrusion.

White big-name rappers often are, from a radical fan's point of view, watered down to gain greater popularity--for example, M.C. Hammer, more radical rappers like Public Enemy and Laquan pump out comments on real problems in the United States, especially between races, but also drugs, crime and education (all of which are intertwined with race in the United States context). Some rap is quite ugly. Ice Cube's "Death Certificate," number 2 on *Billboard*'s album chart in late 1991, contains rap that bluntly insults and threatens violence against "homosexuals, women, whites who exploit blacks, whites who covet black women, blacks who date white women, Korean shopkeepers, rappers who cross over to pop, the Los Angeles chief of police, self-destructive ghetto blacks and more."*16* Album lyrics advocate shooting Jews and burning down Korean stores.

Rappers speak primarily to their "brothers," other young street blacks and frequently Black Muslims, but their albums sell to whites also; otherwise, Ice Cube could not have made it to the number 2 position and N.W.A. to number 1. Rappers epitomize the penchant for record companies to record whomever will make money, no matter if that "whomever" is trying to remake the economic and political structure of the society upon which the record company depends. Because rebellion and struggle are popular themes for many young people, especially street blacks, they also provide lucrative lyrics for would-be stars and perpetuate questions about sincerity as opposed to market exploitation.

Rap also has been successful internationally, although the reasons why are not clear. Keith Cahoon, Far East manager for Tower Records, told *Fortune* magazine that "a lot of people thought rap wouldn't sell [in Japan] because they don't understand the lyrics. Well, they don't, but they buy it anyway."*17* Foreign musicians creating rap within their own cultural contexts adopt the musical style and general rebellion of United States rap but adapt the messages to their own environments and values. French *rappeurs* are ardent supporters of a single world and find American rap artists' message to be divisive and angry. These foreign rap artists, however, are little known to American fans. United States rap musicians scathingly call foreign artists' efforts "bandwagon" rap.*18*

Heavy metal continues to be popular in the United States, the most extreme subgenres with rebellious white males, a sort of white counterpart to rap. Guns 'n' Roses, Metallica and Skid Row--all angry, crude groups--have all made it to the top of the *Billboard* chart.

One form of experimentation in the 1980s and 1990s is rock-classical crossover, wherein classically trained artists like David Byrne, Peter Gordon and John Zorn launch into manic rock. A more recent addition to that list is Great Kat, who plays heavy-metal Beethoven takeoff on the guitar, an interesting twist for a female classical artist.

Women's popular music, although not as widely publicized as rap and not a single genre, also is acquiring new notice in the United States music scene. In 1988, Tracy Chapman, K.D. Lang, Michelle Shocked, the Indigo Girls, Melissa Etheridge and Phranc burst upon the American music scene, and music critics pronounced the arrival of a "new breed of women" in popular music. Neither their songs nor the images they project cater to stereotypical male fantasies of female pop singers, the critics declared.

What has remained undetected by media critics, or what has been taboo to be openly addressed, is that these artists have studiously avoided male pronouns in romantic ballads and, as with Lang, have carefully constructed their personas to assert a strong, sexually ambiguous female presence.

This "new breed" of women artists is significant for at least two reasons. First they have each achieved commercial success in what is probably the most patriarchal and masculine institution within the culture industry. And, in doing so, they have infiltrated the dominant culture with a subtle but evocative feminist ethnic. At the very least, they have projected female centrality, even lesbianism, on the level of the text. And more visibly, as with the example of K.D. Lang, they have presented themselves as objects of female desire.

A second and perhaps even more important reason to note for this group of women is that they represent the progeny of the first wave of artists in what can be called the "women's music industry." The women's music industry is distinguished from the dominant, mainstream industry as that music which is produced and performed by and for women.

Each of the aforementioned artists began their careers through the nationwide network of coffeehouses, bars and music festivals associated with the women's music industry. Although they chose to enter the more commercial popular music domain, they represent an evolution that has been expedited by the first wave of artists in the women's music tradition.

Olivia Records and Redwood Records, both located in the San Francisco Bay area, have been the seminal producers of women's music since the early 1970s. They both continue to exist on the periphery of the music industry, choosing an alternative "political/spiritual" discourse addressing feminism, a commitment to protect human rights and to promote world peace through the celebration of diverse music and culture.

It is important to place Redwood and Olivia in a financial perspective.

They both continue to operate as barely more than grassroots organizations. For each project they must begin by raising the funds to produce and promote the work. Both companies manage to produce technically competitive products for a quarter of what the major record label would spend. An average budget for Redwood Records, for example, would be $20,000.

These studios began by addressing an audience that was struggling to assimilate its own spiritual and political place in the world. As Anise Jacoby, the promotional coordinator at Olivia Records, describes, the younger generation of listeners have their spiritual understanding already in place.[19] The politics of the younger generation are louder, more direct and often assaultive. Both Olivia and Redwood are attempting to address this more militant level of cultural resistance in their music. As Jacoby stresses, they are trying to incorporate the Sinead O'Connors as well as the Chris Williamsons of the musical spectrum.

In popular culture, women have long had to contend with both a scarcity of images and images that are either negative or unidimensional. While they have always found ways to interpret culture despite this lack of models--in fact, much of the most important recent cultural criticism has arisen from a feminist critique of culture--there is no substitute for the visibility of positive, powerful images of women in cultural representation. In this respect women's music is similar to rap and its promotion of strong black male images.

A fourth type of popular music important in the 1990s is country music, which is enjoying a renaissance of sorts. Jon Pareles writes that it has "reclaimed the sound of its glory days, the honky-tonk of the 1950s and early 60s."[20] Country's revival brings back emphasis on acoustic instruments but, according to Pareles, can only temporarily evoke nostalgia for a past time, a life on the open range as opposed to hunkered down in the suburbs. Country artists such as K.T. Oslin might reply to Pareles that country not only has adapted to modern times but is writing some of the most poignant lyrics about very personal contemporary problems.

Sight Versus Sound

One problem with country music is its lack of visual excitement. Record company consideration of visual appeal preceded MTV. Philip Harper describes how Motown decided not to feature some black artists' pictures on record covers so that more record stores would carry the recordings. He tells how Motown operated a "charm school" to groom its black musicians for the crossover market (i.e., both black and white).[21] Apparently Motown also emphasized use of the still relatively new television medium to sell musicians like the Supremes to the early 1960s white audience.

But music videos raise visual considerations to a new level of importance. MTV emphasizes good performance as opposed to good music. The channel initially featured new music by several visually oriented artists who had been excluded from commercial radio stations with playlists limited to classic rock albums. It successfully developed several new recording artists such as Madonna, Boy George and Cyndi Lauper, who adeptly showcased their mildly outrageous visual images in this new media form.

Now, major record labels increasingly tend to sign artists with attractive, provocative visual images such as Cyndi Lauper, Madonna and Grace Jones. Conversely, artists with musical talent who lack a visually appealing image are less likely to receive record label contracts. Larry Mazer, a manager for popular heavy metal groups, says he has bands that labels will not sign because executives fear "they won't get on MTV."[22]

With the advent of music videos, lack of musical abilities is no longer a barrier to success in the music industry. The pop group Milli Vanilli achieved commercial success largely on the basis of their stylish looks and dancing abilities that were elaborately displayed in the group's popular videos. The group was exposed as a fraud because the performers did not sing nor play any of their own material.

Milli Vanilli's popularity suggests that the new importance of visual appeal combined with enhanced audio engineering capabilities is encouraging development of a new division of labor in the music industry. Studio musicians can record songs to be lip-synched by camera-ready performers who appear in videos or onstage, a process reminiscent of the 1930s practice of substituting more appealing voices for silent actors/actresses who sounded rotten. Only one step below this is the widespread practice of musicians who prerecord their material and lip-synch while on stage, or instrumentalists who preprogram electronic equipment and simply turn it on while performing. Emphasis on slick, highly technical performance, as opposed to live music making, interacts with the split between what is possible on the stage as opposed to what can be done in the studio. Beginning with the Beatles' recorded-effects experiments in the 1960s, recordings have evolved into an entirely different art form from live performance. Studio manipulation enables a single artist to sing all the parts of a choir or the play all the instruments in the group.

Voices and instruments are freed from flaws and liberated from reality. Such effects and the sheer perfection of recorded music are impossible to reproduce on stage, but the fans are used to them. Big stars whose recordings made them into technoheroes become much less exciting, sometimes downright boring, in real life if they cannot reproduce that slickness on stage. So a merger has begun to occur between recording technology and the high tech concert, producing an increasingly murky distinction between what is real and what is not. Equally muddy is the question of what fans want--real music or even more extreme technical effects and beautiful bodies. Grammy Award officials may care if Milli Vanilli sings--fans may not. Peter Watrous points out:

Advanced technology, and the aesthetic that comes with it, has created a generation gap between the anti-tape brigade and the younger audiences for whom the new technology is standard practice. Today's music is constructed in a studio, as opposed to being honed in garages or juke joints. It is polished and precise, often structurally complicated, nonlinear in its narrative and filled with snippets of music from older recordings.[23]

Audiences used to listening to high tech music on CDs may relate to lip-synching performances more positively than to "authentic" ones--they may even challenge the traditional notion of what authentic means today. Watrous concludes that "what critics and legislators are overlooking is that, along with the change in technology, the nature of a musical performance has changed as well. Musicianship isn't the point anymore, if it ever was."*24*

THE UNITED STATES INDUSTRY TODAY

In the late 1980s and early 1990s, the fortunes of United States recording companies began reversing. New technologies like CDs, digital audio tape (DAT) and recordable CDs are now developed abroad with no possible United States exploitation. No single American genre like rock exists any more. Record companies mine talent wherever they can find it--Jamaica, Nigeria, Ireland, wherever. Recording company costs have skyrocketed. A significant part of the profits due recording companies is being eaten up by pirates. But the most important blow of all is that foreign interests are buying up the United States recording industry.

Copyright

Copyright has been a big issue in the United States, for whom cultural production has been a huge export industry. The potential sale of digital audiotape recorders in the country was the subject of the controversial Digital Audio Tape Recorder bill in the 1990 congressional session. The recording industry favored the bill's solution to the problem of DAT ability to make nearly perfect reproductions of albums, a Serial Copy Management System that permits people to make unlimited copies of works but then prevents copies being made of the copies. This solution was opposed by the National Music Publishers Association, which wanted to impose royalty charges on DAT and blank tape purchases. Sony went ahead and began selling copy prevention recorders, but by the time they did this Philips had developed a rival system of recordable CDs which seemed more likely to become the next big change in recording equipment.

Recording companies have used development of new technologies to try to curb the tide of piracy and home copying with only periods of temporary success. Most technologies eventually become accessible to pirates who use them to make ever-more perfect copies. This has been especially true in Asia. The United States has applied harsh trade pressure to countries reluctant to pass and enforce copyright legislation, threatening to remove their General System of Preference status if they do not comply.

United States companies may have lost as much as $61 million in 1989 in Thailand alone according to 1990 government estimates. Pirated tapes in Thailand sell for about 80 cents and are the same quality as legitimate copies costing six times as much. Indeed, the pirated versions may be made at the same factories as the legitimate ones. According to the *New York Times*, 95.5% of tapes sold in Thailand, 27 million cassettes per year valued at $32.6 million, are pirated.*25* While most Asian countries have bowed to United States trade threats and International Federation of Phonogram and Videogram Producers pressure, many Thai legislators walked out of the Parliament during a recent discussion about possible enactment of copyright legislation.

In those countries that have passed copyright laws, enforcement remains a problem and South Korean, Chinese, Taiwanese, Indian, Philippine and Indonesian general copyright losses exceed those within Thailand. Even if countries do comply, the companies may be waging a losing battle to technology.

Previously home copying has not been thought of as a great problem. And certainly it cannot be controlled as even the digital audiotape decks permitted in the United States can be used to make one copy of a work. Now a newly issued radio patent promises radio receivers that could deliver written identification of music to be played at some future time so that fans could easily get their tape decks set up in advance.26 This system plus the future digitization of FM radio signals will enable people to produce very high quality recordings of broadcast material. A new system developed in Europe to prevent "ghosting" of FM signals (Coded Orthogonal Frequency Division Multiplexing) combined with advanced recording technology may enable consumers to make virtually flawless copies "off the air." Given such developments, it is hard to see how massive copying can be prevented so a tax on blank tape purchase may be the only equitable solution.

Escalating Costs

Record companies can spend $300,000-500,000 producing a popular group's album and will have to sell many thousands of copies to recover those costs, plus those associated with marketing and distribution. These costs account in part for the current repackaging of old material in CD sets. Sets of old materials cost so little to produce that companies need to sell only a thousand copies in order to recover costs. Furthermore, because the recorded artists already have established audiences, little has to be spent on promotion of "reruns." If the artists are still recording, then older material reissued on CDs can help promote new albums.

Promotion is a big expense, and bigger now than ever before. Steve Pond tells us:

Once Michael Jackson had performed magical illusions on stage, and Janet Jackson had appeared with a live leopard, once Prince had been wheeled on stage in a Corvette and Madonna had vamped and vogued through a tour with theatrical conceits so overwhelming that the music seemed nearly irrelevant, the stakes were raised.27

Promotional tours can cost millions, physically wipe out the artists and are increasingly difficult to mount. And recording companies are footing less and less of the bill. Paula Abdul invested over $1 million in her 1991-1992 tour. Fans are used to the technical sounds possible in the studio and the visual feats possible on-screen, neither of which are easily produced on-stage. Yet, according to Virgin Records' Jeff Ayeroff, "in the MTV era . . . the [artists] who can pull off a tour are the ones who are here for the long run."28

Whether or not tours promote staying power more than television appearances is questionable, but whether MTV exposure gets more attention for groups than tours is fairly self-evident. Millions of people see a group on TV, whereas only several hundred thousand will see that group on a six-month tour.

Videos and Centralized Control

Video music became an established part of the music industry as record labels increasingly relied on music clips rather than live tours as the primary element of a promotional strategy for their artists. Now, the major record companies spend more than $50 million a year on music videos and generally maintain control over all aspects of the production of video clips for their artists.

The general acceptance of music video as a form of promotion has had uneven consequences for musicians seeking commercial success. New artists will often produce their own music videos on a limited budget in an attempt to gain broader exposures. Some video clip makers claim that low-cost videos can assist an artist in obtaining a record label contract by bringing an act to the attention of record company executives. However, music videos typically presented on major program services are much more costly productions, with an average budget of $60,000 that must be financed by a musician's record label. Michael Jackson's late 1991 video "Black and White" reportedly cost over $1 million because of its extensive use of special effects. But that investment will be well worth it if the video even comes close to the success of his 1982 "Thriller" video which sold 21 million United States and 48 million international copies.

The United States for Sale

Rock music was the big money-maker for United States recording companies in their heyday. Many music critics now speak of a "loss of center" in rock music. Rock has now become so diffused that it no longer has the same political and aesthetic clout that the genre once enjoyed and maybe not the same economic power either.

The music scene has become very fragmented, partially because of the reverse influence of foreign-originated music on American musicians, many of who experiment widely with foreign musical styles and new aesthetic possibilities afforded by change in music technology. A decade ago, other countries feared the cultural effects of a one-way flow of American music. Now musicians from all over are engendering a multidirectional stream of music; experimental United States musicians are helping to make that possible. Foreign business executives now are looking to cash in on that flow, no matter what its direction.

American music is a $20 billion-per-year international business. Some 70% of its revenue comes from international sales. Only aerospace topped entertainment software, responsible for an $8 billion dollar United States trade surplus in 1990, as the country's most lucrative export sector. But the recording industry's economic success may prove to be its downfall.

The largest problem of the United States record industry is that it is not American anymore. All but one of the majors have been bought by foreigners. Warner remains United States controlled, CBS is Japanese, RCA now is German and renamed BMG.

One reason for these acquisitions is that developers of new audio technologies need sufficient software to play on their equipment so that consumers will buy it. For this reason Sony, burned by lack of software for its

Betamax video recorder, bought CBS Records and Matsushita bought MCA. But this is not the only reason why Japanese companies are scooping up American entertainment producers nor the reason the German Bertelsmann bought RCA records earlier and the Dutch/German PolyGram acquired other American labels.

Other counties have awakened to the economic importance, as opposed to the cultural value, of entertainment software. Before the last few years, governments worried about United States cultural imperialism. Now the same governments are busy puzzling over how they and their companies can obtain an economic piece of the internationalized cultural pie. If this means buying United States talent and profiting by it, then so be it.

Even though musicians in other countries may care that their music is recorded by the big international companies, the people in charge of those companies do not care whose music they record as long as it sells. The take-over of the United States recording industry has created a bizarre situation. American talent is still valuable but it is owned elsewhere. In the early 1990s two pictures appeared in the *New York Times Magazine* that well represented the current United States popular music scene: Michael Jackson sitting among a sea of Japanese children and Akio Morita, head of Sony, hugging one of his company's new musical acquisitions, Cyndi Lauper.

CONCLUSION

Junior Walker and the All Stars' recent Blues Alley performance echoes performances occurring around the United States every night. All the old tensions still exist: black and white, acoustic and electronic, local and international. But in other ways, Junior's group is an example of residual culture. The All Stars do not care at all about visual appeal or technical slickness. They have no angry messages. They do not have high promotional or production costs. In a way they are like the United States recording industry itself--old warhorses with a lot of talent and energy but not necessarily the international street smartness to compete or even survive much longer.

The United States no longer is in a position of economic ascendancy. Countries that suffered widespread damage in World War II, like Japan and Germany, and newly industrialized countries, like Taiwan and Korea, now offer intense competition in hardware and are beginning to do the same in software. Foreign musicians have recovered from their adoration of Anglo-American music and are looking to their own musical traditions for creative inspiration. The international majors, only one of which is now American controlled, grab potentially profitable material anywhere.

Perhaps, when all is said and done, no country will ever dominate the international popular music scene again. People all over now have access to music from everywhere. Cheap audiotapes cross borders easily along with radio and TV signals. In terms of what is available to consumers, it does not matter who owns the recording industry. It is in the interest of international companies to encourage international consumerism. Peter Sealey, a senior vice-president at Coca-Cola, notes that "the time is right; the world has changed," meaning that an international consumership has been built for many, many products.[29] There are global media now, like MTV. And there are global teenagers. The same kid you see at the Ginza in Tokyo is in Piccadilly Circus in London, in Pushkin Square in Moscow, at Notre Dame in Paris. MTV's major advertisers are athletic shoe, movie, blue jeans and soft drink companies, all catering to a rapidly increasing youth market worldwide. Nor do we have to fear world cultural homogenization. Globalization is offset by an equally strong trend toward indigenization, the realization that one's own local traditions are worth keeping, related to a growing need to establish a self-identity based on the immediate environment.*30* Every community will continue to have local musicians, some of whom will make it into the international big time and add their idiosyncratic styles to what is a grand mix already.

What matters most to the United States, country as well as a recording location, is that it is losing its economic dominance, a position that partly depended upon strong cultural influence abroad. Americans are now learning to share their place in the sun.

NOTES

1. Robinson, Deanna Campbell; Buck, Elizabeth B.; Cuthbert, Marlene et al.; and the International Communication and Youth Culture Consortium. *Music at the Margins: Popular Music and Global Cultural Diversity.* Newbury Park, CA: Sage, 1991. See also Wicke, Peter and Ziegenrucher, Wieland, *Handbuch der popularen Musik.* Leipzig: Deutscher Verlag fuer Musik, 1985.

2. Williams, Raymond. *The Sociology of Culture.* New York: Schocken, 1982.

3. See Head, Sydney and Sterling, Christopher. *Broadcasting in America: A Survey of Electronic Media.* Boston: Houghton Mifflin, 1990, and earlier editions of the same title.

4. Recording "majors" are defined as the largest companies who do their own production, marketing and distribution. While some "independent" companies are quite large, they usually rely on either the majors or other companies for marketing and/or distribution. PolyGram (Dutch-German) and EMI (British) are the other two members of the top five international companies.

5. See Gillett, Charlie. *The Sound of the City: The Rise of Rock and Roll.* New York: Outerbridge & Dienstfrey, 1970.

6. See the last chapter of Robinson et al. *Music at the Margins.*

7. See Banks, Jack. "The Historical Development of the Video Music Industry: A Political Economic Analysis." dissertation, University of Oregon, 1991, for more information about video music than can be presented here.

8. The Federal Radio Commission was established as a temporary agency by the 1927 Radio Act. Its successor, the Federal Communications Commission, was created in the 1934 Communications Act which is still applicable in the United States.

9. A ruthless United States Senator from Wisconsin, Joseph R. McCarthy, chaired the congressional Un-American Activities Committee during the 1950s.

10. See Robinson, et al. *Music at the Margins.*

11. Ibid.

12. Ibid.

13. Fein, Esther B. "Rock and Pop Stars Reach a New Audience in Children's

Books," *New York Times*, October 21, 1991, B1.

14. Lev, Michael. "Music Industry Bets on CD Sets." *New York Times*, September 4, 1991.

15. Ellis, Bret Easton. "The Twentysomethings: Adrift in a Pop Landscape." *New York Times*, December 2, 1990.

16. Pareles, Jon. "Should Ice Cube's Voice be Chilled?" *New York Times*, December 9, 1991, 30.

17. Huey, John. "America's Hottest Export: Pop Culture." *Fortune*, December 31, November 18, 1991, B1.

18. Grimes, William. "Rapper and Rappeur Meet, in Bafflement," *New York Times*, November 18, 1991, B1.

19. Personal interview by Nancy Breaux. 1992.

20. Pareles, Jon. "When Country Music Moves to the Suburbs." *New York Times*, November 25, 1990, Section 2, 1.

21. Banks. "Video Music Industry". 1991.

22. Goldberg, Michael. "MTV's Sharper Picture." *Rolling Stone*, February 8, 1990, 62.

23. Watrous, Peter. "Lip-synching Can Make Music Sweeter." *New York Times*, July 22, 1990, 23.

24. Ibid.

25. Erlanger, Steven. "Thailand, Where Pirated Tapes Are Everywhere and Profitable." *New York Times*, November 27, 1990.

26. Andrews, Edmund L. "Patents." *New York Times*, November 16, 1991, 18.

27. Pond, Steve. "10 Months, $1 Million and 100 Headaches." *New York Times*, November 17, 1991.

28. Ibid.

29. Lev, Michael. "Advertisers Seek Global Messages," *New York Times*, November 18, 1991.

30. See Bright, Charles and Geyer, Michael. "For a Unified History of the World in the Twentieth Century." *Radical History Review,* 39, 1987, pp. 69-91.

BIBLIOGRAPHY

Andrews, Edmund L. (1991). "Patents." *New York Times,* November 16, 18.

Banks, Jack (1991). "The Historical Development of the Video Music Industry: A Political Economic Analysis." Dissertation, University of Oregon.

Bright, Charles and Geyer, Michael (1987). "For a Unified History of the World in the Twentieth Century." *Radical History Review*, 39, 69-91.

Ellis, Bret Easton (1990). "The Twentysomethings: Adrift in a Pop Landscape." *New York Times,* December 2.

Erlanger, Steven (1990). "Thailand, Where Pirated Tapes Are Everywhere and Profitable." *New York Times,* November 27.

Fein, Esther B. (1991). "Rock and Pop Stars Reach a New Audience in Children's Books." *New York Times.* October 21, B1.

Gillett, Charlie, (1970). *The Sound of the City: The Rise of Rock and Roll.* New York: Outerbridge & Dienstfrey.

Goldberg, Michael (1990). "MTV's Sharper Picture." *Rolling Stone.* February 8, 62.

Grimes, William (1991). "Rapper and Rappeur Meet, in Bafflement." *New York Times.* November 18, B1.

Head, Sydney and Sterling, Christopher (1990). *Broadcasting in America: A Survey of Electronic Media.* Boston: Houghton Mifflin Company.

Huey, John (1991). "America's Hottest Export: Pop Culture." *Fortune,* December 31, 30.

Lev, Michael (1991). "Advertisers Seek Global Messages." *New York Times.* November 18.

Lev, Michael (1991). "Music Industry Bets on CD Sets." *New York Times.* September 4.

Pareles, Jon (1990). "When Country Music Moves to the Suburbs." *New York Times.* November 25, Section 2, 1.

Pareles, Jon (1991). "Should Ice Cube's Voice be Chilled?" *New York Times.* December 9, 30.

Pond, Steve (1991). "10 Months, $1 million and 100 Headaches." *New York Times.* November 17.

Robinson, Deanna Campbell; Buck, Elizabeth B.; Cuthbert, Marlene. et al.; and the International Communication and Youth Culture Consortium (1991). *Music at the Margins: Popular Music and Global Cultural Diversity.* Newbury Park, CA: Sage.

Rohten, Larry (1991). "Pop-Music Fashion Becomes a Sales Hit." *New York Times.* January 8, C1.

Watrous, Peter (1990). "Lip-synching Can Make Music Sweeter." *New York Times.* July 22, 23.

Wicke, Peter and Ziegenrucher, Wieland (1985). *Handbuch der Popularen Músik.* Leipzig: Deutscher Verlag fuer Musik.

Williams, Raymond (1982). *The Sociology of Culture.* New York: Schocken.

CHAPTER 13

URUGUAYAN POPULAR MUSIC: NOTES ON RECENT HISTORY

Carlos Alberto Martins
& Carlos Dumpiérrez

To speak of Uruguayan popular music in most places outside South America almost automatically means to think of Daniel Viglietti. It is his name that has reached farthest, thanks first to his qualities as an artist, and second to his important international discography. The latter is the main difference between Viglieti and his other colleagues who had to choose to go into exile after the coup d'etat of 1973. But, although he is also one of the most popular and influential folk singers in Uruguay, he is not the only one, and he was not the first to create, sing and play within what has been called *Nueva Canción* in Latin America. This chapter will try to seek some antecedents and will specifically stop to consider the popular music phenomena which developed after the military upheaval.

Uruguay is the smallest country in South America: just 187,000 square kilometres in size, with less than 3 million inhabitants, it is embedded between Argentina and Brazil. Almost 80 out of every 100 Uruguayans live in cities, and nearly half of the total population resides in the capital, Montevideo, and its surroundings. The country had enjoyed a quite peaceful democratic political history with few interruptions since its first constitution, in 1830. Its population had been formed mainly from European immigrants, especially from Spain and Italy, but also from other parts of the world.

Disastrous conditions for others (e.g., wars) were favorable for the sale of Uruguayan meat and wool, the country's major exports. An early development toward international commerce, and its corresponding structures in services, helped the urbanization process and the creation of an important middle class. The "welfare state" established since the late nineteenth century helped these developments in social structure and consequent cultural changes by means of free education, equitable conditions for women, universal franchise, health services and retirement pensions. This kind of paradise began cracking in the mid-1950s, when international conditions started changing. No previous government had undertaken any measures for developing self-reliance. The distribution of the country's wealth--capital and land--went from bad to worse during the 1960s, a period which was not golden for everybody. The card played by the government after 1968 was repression. The unity of the workers into one central trade union had happened four years earlier; the amalgamation of all left-wing parties under one single banner became a reality for the 1971 national elections; in the meantime, urban guerrilla groups had developed considerably. On June 27, 1973, the military engineered a coup d'état: Parliament was dissolved and judiciary power was transformed into a Department of the Executive. A crude and long repression followed, and thousands were forced into exile, while those who stayed were reduced to impotence and silence.

Renormalization began with a constitutional plebiscite promoted by the armed forces and held on November 30, 1980. The official proposal, which would have institutionalized the dictatorship, was rejected by 57% of the voters: some say that it was the first time that a dictatorship lost an election. Two years later, a law was promulgated that led to public elections for officials within each party. In both large political parties, the opposition sectors largely won. The national election of November 1984 marked the return of the country to its traditional democratic culture.

These are just some of the facts describing the context within which Uruguayan popular music has developed, with almost two beginnings, up to the current state of its being a part of the national musical establishment. This is the story we intend to synthesize here, starting from the roots.

ANTECEDENTS

Roots

Uruguay does not have indigenous inhabitants, and the cultures of those people who lived in its territory before the Spanish colonization have been lost. Uruguayan music has then only two primary external influences: European and African. In Uruguay four great folkloric areas can be seen, which, without infringing upon each other, live together in its territory: (1) an area of dances and rural songs on the River Plate side, forming a unity with the Argentinian provinces of Buenos Aires and Entre Rios, where we find such music as the estilo, the cifra, the milonga, the vidalita, the pericón; (2) a northern area which participates, together with the Brazilian state of Rio Grande do Sul, in some dances and songs of the so-called fandango Riograndense: the chimarrita, the carangueijo, the tirana; (3) the old European songbook--as called by the eminent Argentinian researcher Carlos Vega--which survives intact in Uruguayan territory through children's repertory: with more than a hundred songs, many of them very old, but common to nationals of Western culture; (4) the dramatic dances of the African slaves which derived from candombe in the nineteenth century, and survive today in the Carnival masquerades and in the very rich llamada, or drum ensemble, which walks through the streets of Montevideo in the summer months. (Ayestarán, 1967, 8).*1*

The introduction of slaves in what is today Uruguay began at the end of the seventeenth century. During colonial times the percentage of the population which was of African origin has been calculated as being 20% to 30% of the total (Ayestarán, 1953, 61). It greatly increased in the following century. However, estimates of current figures range between 3% (Ayestarán, 1953, 55) and 6% (Instituto de Estudios Sociales, 1979, 7). Candombe, the Afro-Montevidean folk music, is a rhythm pattern played by a family of four drums of different registers; the original choreography has seemingly passed through important changes, but is still very popular during Carnival festivities. The European popular musical heritage has the guitar as its basic instrument, and also, sometimes especially for rural dance music, the accordion.

Uruguayan Popular Music before 1950

Toward the end of the nineteenth century, new urban musical sounds were being created simultaneously in the suburbs of both national capitals on the shores of the River Plate. Tango, the music the Argentinians promoted throughout the world as their "typical" music, is really binational. More precisely, it is the music of two cities. "Son" or "younger brother" (Ayestarán, 1953) of the Milonga and the Habanera, tango has had a complex development process from these distant origins up to today's *tangueces*.

Another popular urban phenomenon is the murga, inherited from Andalusia, Spain. Up to the late 1960s murgas was limited to the Carnival month. It consists of a group of some 20 men who perform a structured show. The music is made up of melodies from the previous year's hits, and the lyrics are usually written by a group member and are generally critical of social and political events. The voices are accompanied by three percussion instruments: bass and snare drums and cymbals.

The musical panorama of this first half of the century was completed by several products from abroad, especially from the rest of the American continent: from jazz to samba, including Afro-Cuban music and boleros. But the country was unable to export its own music. It had to watch Buenos Aires promoting tango everywhere as its own, and including in their musical embassies many more Uruguayans than they imagined or acknowledged.*2*

Another important phenomenon in Uruguayan popular culture, but pertaining to the whole Latin American continent, is that of the improvisers, the *Payadores,* who continue a thousand-year-old artistic practice.

The 1950s: Birth

The lack of research about Uruguayan popular music is especially felt when we have to consider the antecedents of recent years. There is the historical case of Bartolomé Hidalgo, poet and singer, who participated in the rebellion against Spain in the second decade of the nineteenth century. And there are some isolated names from the first decades of the twentieth century, who have stayed in the popular memory, but often it is just the names that are remembered, not the music. Anyway, no comprehensive studies have been done which enable us to formulate a continuous and coherent historical development. Questions are far more numerous than answers.

Nevertheless, the first influential phenomenon to appear at the beginning of the second half of this century was foreign: the great Argentinian folk music explosion. Some groups appeared who were to conquer their country with their northern folk music: Los Chalchaleros and Los Fronterizos, the first and most popular ones; but Buenos Aires was just the launching pad from which they seduced their neighboring countries. Many of their songs may be considered as mass products, but it is a fact that before their arrival the music from distant Argentinian provinces was unknown in the cultural centre of the country. This was in spite of the previous efforts and great talent of such singers/writers as Atahualpa Yupanqui and Eduardo Falú.

There were important sociopolitical conditions that enabled this "musical boom" to happen. The lead role played by the lower class was the basis for the first government of General Juan Perón (1946-1955). These lower classes, mainly a neoproletariat of rural origin living in the bigger cities, became the nucleus from which this folk music phenomenon could draw its principal--at least its first--audience. For its development, a wider basic cultural infrastructure[3] was fundamental, in order to produce attitudes which promoted the defense of the national artistic patrimory and production. A concrete example of a political input to such attitudes was the measure which obliged radio stations to air a minimum amount of Argentinian music.

It is very difficult to evaluate the impact of this process in Uruguay, especially for the 1950s. It is unlikely that the leading Uruguayan folk musicians from that time had begun creating and performing as they did just because they were *following* the paths of their neighbors. In fact, Amalia De la Vega began her career backed by Ayestarán and his collection of folklore songs. And Osiris Rodríguez Castillos created, from the outset, his poems and songs based on Uruguayan rural folklore, inspired by the people, places, history and culture of the Uruguayan countryside.

But the influence was very apparent among the younger generation, those who appeared in the early 1960s; many of the new singers began playing a guitar in order to play the songs from the Argentinian north and littoral provinces that radio had helped to popularize. Many recordings from the early Uruguayan groups and soloists of the 1960s included Argentinian rhythms, namely zambas. This happened not only with ephemeral artists, but even with almost all of those who were to develop a long and solid career.

The 1960s: Developments and Protest

So, at the beginning of the 1960s an unforeseen number of new singers, players, composers and lyricists began to break onto the Uruguayan public scene. A list could be made of the groups and soloists who left their recorded traces from those years, but we will limit ourselves to mentioning just those whose activity has continued for a long time. Trying to keep some chronological order, the first meriting mention are Aníbal Sampayo (living in the northern city of Paysandú), Anselmo Grau and Santiago Chalar (both from Montevideo). Immediately after them come the three that were to have the most popular success: duo Los Olimareños (formed by José Luis Guerra and Braulio López), and singer-lyristic-composers Daniel Viglietti and Alfredo Zitarrosa. It is in fact very difficult to differentiate between generations in those years, and it would be unfair not to add some of the other popular singers whose activity helped to enlarge the audience found and created by their immediate predecessors: Marcos Velásquez, Tabaré Etcheverry, José Carbajal, Washington Carrasco, Eustaquio Sosa, Yamandu Palacios and a bit later, Roberto Darvin, Héctor Numa Moraes and Manuel Capella. By the end of the decade they were a coherent and relatively homogeneous group of artists sharing some characteristics and especially a series of cultural and political values. Almost all of them were singers accompanying themselves with a guitar; they composed most of their repertory themselves; their rythmic patterns were influenced to a great degree by Uruguayan folklore. Their cultural values were closely linked to their aesthetic options, because these were opposed to mass media offerings on two levels: geocultural origin and quality. Quality was greatly valued by most of the singers, especially where lyrics were concerned. They frequently set their music to lyrics written for them by poets, or used published poetry for the words of their songs.

The most important lyricist/composers were Ruben Lena and Víctor Lima; among the poets/lyricists we must mention Wáshington Benavides, Juan Capagorry, Circe Maia, Líber Falco, Humberto Megett, Idea Vilariño, Enrique Estrázulas and Mario Benedetti. In many cases also, singers/composers set poems written by non-Uruguayan poets to music, choosing from the best that were written in Spanish: León Felipe, César Vallejo, Federico García Lorca, Rafael Alberti, Nicolás Guillén, Ernesto Gardenal, and others.

This care for the quality of the lyrics appears also in the singers' own texts; some of them displayed great talent in this aspect of their work. We can see here, among other elements, the influence of the French popular song tradition (*chanson française*), permeated via Spain. This influence was accepted by an intellectual milieu able to value the lyrics more than the music in a song. Concern about the musical training of popular music performers came principally from Viglietti, who was looking forward to a promising career as a concert guitarist when he decided, for political reasons, to become a popular singer.

It seems evident that what we separate out for analyzing as an "aesthetic option" is in reality a part of a complex system in which the main motivator is political: the effort to propose active alternatives to what existed and was approved. This political sensibility found different personal ways of expression. It is also important to underline that these artists were not against everything that was foreign; their attitude was antiimperialist but not chauvinist. Many of them admired and even took ideas from colleagues from other countries, in whom they recognized undoubted values.[4]

The movement came to be known as *Canto Popular* (Popular Song), a label which put the accent on just one of the elements, the text. Capagorry has explained: "From Hidalgo until today, popular singing has defined its style: it is to sing 'on firm foundations' (*con fundamento*, with solid arguments) about problems common to all" (Capagorry & Rodríguez Barilari, 1980, 13).

The name *Canto Popular* was first used as the title of one of the records by singer José Carbajal. He explained why: "we wanted to differentiate Uruguayan 'folklore' from the Argentinian one. If we said we made folklore, people wanted us to sound like Los Fronterizos." (cited by Jaime Roos, in Magnone, 1984).

Until 1973 there was a neat separation between *Canto Popular* and the rest of the Uruguayan musical production. Uruguay, like most other countries in the world, suffered the British musical invasion led by the Beatles. It was a true urban explosion helped by the previous penetration of North American rock 'n' roll. In the middle 1960s Uruguay was (re)producing local copies of Anglo-Saxon rock performers. Some of these artists did go two or three important steps toward a transformation of what they were doing (in their roles of reproducers of a much too foreign culture) in a different, cosmopolitan contribution to the popular music of their country.

A first step consisted of composing songs for their own repertoire: this meant finding a new personal identity through self-expression. The second, which was more difficult because it meant assuming the local collective identity, which was originally less prestigious, was to sing in Spanish, and not in English. A third step took some of them to the incorporation of regional rhythmic elements: first of all candombe but also malambo, carnavalito, chacarera, etc. Some groups achieved only the first step: they were quite ephemeral and dedicated themselves to playing at dances; others reached only the second, and have formed the small but solid--albeit also ephemeral--world of (excellent) Uruguayan rock music, whose best examples were the groups Psiglo and Días de Blues. In the third category we find the names of singers/composers Eduardo Mateo, Ruben Rada and Dino and the groups El Kinto, Totem and El Syndikato.

THE 1970s AND 1980s: FROM RESISTANCE TO INSTITUTION

1972-1973: Abyss

Serious works written about the generation of popular musicians which came after the coup d'état coincide in underlining the continuity between the previous stage and the second. Talking about 1977, which they consider as the "year of reappearance," Capagorry and Rodríguez Barilari (1980, 125) say: "[It was] not the zero year, because both the most remote and the most recent antecedents indicated that the national song was not dead." Castillo (1983) cites several examples of artists who began in the first period and followed more or less without interruptions in the second.

Nevertheless, at the beginning of 1974 we wrote in a Montevidean weekly:

Approximately until 1971 there was a progressive growth of the "pop" musical movement in our country. Each time more records from our artists were released, several concerts were organized each month, our TV channels dedicated four to five hours per week to national music shows; in short, the situation was encouraging. There has been no development in music since 1972. And the famous lack of PVC for making records was the "coup de grace" toward the end of the year. At the level of *Canto Popular* there have been no great revelations, and in the area of national rock music there were two names at the top of popularity: Totem in 1972 and Psiglo in 1973 (Martins, 1974).

Exile, political and/or economic, was one of the most important consequences of the events of those early 1970s. Most of the lead players from the first generation of *Canto Popular* followed the path of forced emigration, sooner or later. At certain levels their absence was partly compensated by clandestine circulation of cassettes with copies of their European or Mexican recorded albums. Besides, a conscious effort was later made by some members of the newer generation, in order to help to keep their memory alive.

The Uruguayan Popular Music Movement During Dictatorship

What happened thereafter would have been considered impossible at the moment of the military coup d'etat, in 1973. Nobody could have imagined the steady development, from an almost zero level, of a new and strong movement of Uruguayan popular music. But it not only did happen: it was also a composite, heterogeneous system, where all previous, separate elements came together.

The main vehicle for the melting of musical differences into something unique was the musicians themselves. It was never said, but widely understood, that Uruguayan popular music was the symbol of an alternative, the voice that could not speak, the people who could not move. So, musicians--and even some peripherals: poets, radio DJs, journalists, actors--joined their different styles, backgrounds, tastes and also political views in a common pot. In it, everybody was putting forward the same message of cultural resistance. This also meant that music itself was becoming more united, when in the previous years there was quite a neat separation, as we mentioned, between *Canto Popular* and the rock/pop-influenced sounds.

But this did not produce a new blend, something hybrid. It just happened that the younger generation, the musicians who began playing during those years, introduced personal new approaches to popular music. Here were, for example, Fernardo Cabrera, Roberto Masliah, Los que iban cantando. Most of them worked toward an evolution of musical sounds, and usually also of the lyrics. The influences upon them were universal, but selected: the Latin American folk roots, the best British pop music and contemporary classical music.

The latter, a very rare source of influence on popular music in the world, came as part of an important element in Uruguayan popular musical culture since the 1960s: training. It was considered that popular music was as serious and important as the other two big categories of music (folk song and so-called classical). This led over half of the musicians to study not only their instrument (more often, the acoustic guitar) but also harmony, orchestration, composition and so on. Some of the teachers, the people who became the true opinion leaders in the field during the dictatorship, were contemporary classical music composers. Their influence is most evident on Masliah, and on some members of the group Los que iban cantando, like Jorge Lazaroff and Luis Trochón.

All these musicians, in any case, lived and worked together with others who were more attached to the folk traditions. Carlos Benavides and duos Los Eduardos, Larbanois-Carrero, Tacuruses, were mostly linked to folk song roots, but they also showed that they had good instrumental training.

The movement as such developed slowly, from small shows in theatres, up to big gatherings in stadiums. This process took about ten years. In the first five years progress was very slow. The path to the big one-act shows was built through dozens of medium-sized events which billed several artists. This was the first way to attract thousands of people, giving them the only possible opportunity to get together and express their support for cultural-political alternatives.

As well, the sale of records was affected by a general stagnation in the record market, in line with the global economic situation. Nevertheless, there were big hits in those years, mainly albums (Los que iban cantando, Canciones para no dormir la siesta, Omar Romano, Benavides) and some songs ("Como un jazmín del país" by Benavides).

Music for Democracy

It was after the end of the dictatorial years, from 1984 onward that this movement began losing strength. It seemed clear that once the civil society recuperated institutional ways of participation, the resistance character of popular music lost its main reason for being.

Additionally, now Anglo pop music influences were apparent in the performances of the most popular musicians, Eduardo Darnauchans and Jaime Roos, as well as Cabrera and others. Moreover, the newer generation consisted mainly of rock groups, who mostly followed British models. The most important positive result of the activity of the 1970s concerned the institutionalization of murga music, a process that had in fact already begun in the 1960s.

As mentioned previously, murga is one of the typical Carnival musics in Uruguay. During the early years of *Canto Popular*, some of the most popular singers adapted murga rhythm to their songs, using it as a normal resource. Duo Los Olimareños and singer-composer José Carbajal have had many hits with songs with murga accompaniment. Ten years later murga was a twofold phenomenon. On one side, it had become a new dance rhythm, with people repeating the choreographies of murga singers as seen in the Carnival *tablados* (stages). This meant that murga became an all-year-round sound. On the other side, musicians from the newer generations continued the trend: Jaime Roos, the group Rumbo, Omar Romano. Later on, murga was already there to stay as a permanent reference, and some murga groups even began playing in theatres, outside the classical Carnival dates.

Also with democracy reborn, Uruguay experienced a new and quick improvement in its rock music. Since that moment, a few events happened that started an adolescent rock movement with particular characteristics and without much connection with the predictatorial Uruguayan rock:

- A certain degree of saturation occurred in the market for the *Canto Popular* repertoire: the return of the great stars of the genre (Alfredo Zitarossa, Los Olimareños and Daniel Viglietti), back from exile, monopolized public attention to the detriment of the new artists who came to prominence during the dictatorship.
- The new generation did not seem to find *Canto Popular* very attractive, since the need for opposition arguments had passed. Young people were looking for a new sound that they could identify with.
- The introduction of programs from the various new FM radio stations helped to promote the new bands.
- Some musicians of the *Canto Popular* genre shed their mass rock connotations, distancing themselves from the rest of their colleagues.
- The appearance of a group who would inspire others to follow the same stylistic line: Los Estómagos.

The first LP from Los Estómagos, a group from the city of Pando situated 35 kilometers from Montevideo, was produced at the end of 1984. However, their first best seller came from a very particular punk version of the *Cambalache* tango, a classic written by the celebrated composer Enrique Sántos Discépolo, which they adapted to match perfectly their philosophy.

Cambalache appeared in the middle of 1985 in a compilation album called "Graffitti," the name of the hall where they had started to play at that time. The hall presented, for the first time, some of the groups which, together with Los Estómagos, were to become the nucleus of the new movement. Of all these groups the most noticeable were Los Tontos and Los Traidores, and also Neoh 23, Adn and Zero. A common characteristic of all of them was the influence of British punk. They produced basic fast rock 'n' roll, sinister melodies, if any, and disillusioned, nihilistic lyrics.

Los Tontos, starting from the same base, but using sense of humor as a weapon, became the second great success. Their song lyrics about nuclear wars, violence in the streets, discrimination against the elderly, slimming diets, police brutality were given an absurd and sadistic treatment. Their first great hit was the "Hymn of the Dangerous Drivers," with lyrics by their drummer Leo Baroncini and music by Alberto Wolf. The group had their own television program, which was very unusual for Uruguay.

Los Traidores were perhaps the most radical group in the movement. Once, during a performance at the Summer Theatre in Montevideo, they started insulting the president Julio Ma. Sanguinetti, and the police arrested them. Their success led both Los Estómagos and Los Tontos to produce their records in Argentina. Los Tontos won a gold disc in Chile and a certain stardom in Peru. However, it did not last. About 1989 Los Estómagos split up and some of their members started a new band called Los Buitres. The same fate happened to the rest of the groups as a consequence of factors such as desertions, the narrowness of the market and manipulation by record companies and managers. With the exception of Los Estómagos, from a strictly musical point of view the quality of the songs left much to be desired, and, once the novelty wore off, the public seemed to notice this.

Around 1990, the Uruguayan music scene displayed a certain synthesis between the influence of rock and the local sounds. The adolescent bands ceded more and more territory and started to share the limelight with some of the previous generation of creators who, having participated in the *Canto Popular* movement, had maintained less local stylistic references, or were more open to influences. This group of artists included Jaime Roos, Eduardo Darnauchans, Fernando Cabrera and the brothers Hugo and Osvaldo Fattoruso, probably the most important Uruguayan musicians of the last 30 years and founders of the Shakers (a pioneer group of Uruguayan and Argentinian rock in the 1960s), who lived permanently outside the country, recording in the United States and in Brazil together with artists like Airto Moreira, Chico Buarque, Hermeto Pascoal or with their own group Opa.

On the strictly rock side of the coin, the reborn group Níquel brought a new era of maturity into this style, with a much clearer connection with the predictatorship rock scene. The members of this group also play in the band of Jaime Roos. They are one of the best live bands performing national rock. Other important groups performing in the early 1990s are Zafhfaroni (jazz-rock), José Luis Pérez y La Fuerza del Destino (fusion), Repique, also ex-members of Jaime Roos' band (candombe), and Alvacast (heavy metal).

Additionally, we must mention the stardom of one of the most important singers of Uruguayan music, Laura Canoura (ex-solo voice from Rumbo), who, after recording the melody for one very-well-known soft drink advertisement, had her first LP, produced by Jaime Roos, earning a gold disc--something which was very unusual for a female artist to achieve.

Among all of the musicians of this period, the most important is undoubtedly Jaime Roos. A musical son of the Beatles, and the direct heir of the best musical traditions of the country, he led the trend toward the inclusion of more Uruguayan musical forms: the murga, the milonga and the candombe. In this process he achieved the most impact, popularity and record sales ever obtained by any musician in Uruguay since Viglietti's great successes, and those of Zitarossa and Los Olimareños in the 1960s. Roos managed to create a new sophisticated music which was simple and danceable at the same time. His repertoire is full of great hits, and some of his recordings are among the most successful in the history of the Uruguayan record industry (his LP "Brindis por Pierrot" won two platinum discs and two gold ones). At the same time he worked as an artistic producer of records with similar success: in addition to the above-mentioned record of Laura Canoura, we must mention the albums of Canario Luna, the main murga singer. Roos also produced Repique, the Travesia Group and Jorge Nasser, the singer of the Níquel band. However, Roos has not become an international star yet, although he played to a capacity audience in the Luna Park Stadium in Buenos Aires.

THE URUGUAYAN RECORD INDUSTRY

In the close relationship to the economic evolution of the country, the Uruguayan record industry sales have dropped to minimal levels from which it is very difficult to recover. Numbers talk: in 1972 the annual sales of records was around 1,500,000 units. In 1987, 15 years later, the figure was 300,000 units. This situation spelled disaster for most of the companies started during the previous 20 years. Companies like Clave, Macondo, Apsa, Prodisa, Fonomúsica, De La Planta, Discovery, Ed. Amanecer and Eco Mallarini have disappeared forever.

The CUD (Record Producers Association) has established that a gold disc (the only award officially recognized by record sellers) is given after 300,000 units are sold, an amount which is achieved only two or three times a year. Through lack of support, only the cassette, which takes 90% of the market, has survived the crisis. The vinyl record, with rare exceptions, is not made any more because of its very low profitability. The compact disc is only beginning to enter the market and few local artists have seen their work produced in this way: Jaime Roos, Fernando Cabrera, Mariana Ingold, Osvaldo Fattoruso, Eduardo Darnauchans, Laura Canoura among others.

At the beginning of the 1990s the only existing production company was Palacio de la Música which monopolized the market, mainly thanks to its chain of record shops, and when its competitors started to disappear, it became licensee for all the multinationals (EMI, PolyGram, WEA, BMG, Sony) in addition to collecting the most important national signings as well. The other two companies still in existence are Sondor, the pioneer company of the Uruguayan music industry, famous in the past for its support of local artists; and Tacuabé, a cooperative of Uruguayan musicians which produce their own records. The fact that the big multinationals have never had a place in the market has allowed Uruguay to be relatively isolated from the big marketing campaigns and the strong pressures these have on the communications field. However, the characteristics of the market are not different from those of big markets, and follow the lines dictated by the United States and Great Britain in Anglicized music, and by Spain and Argentina in Spanish-language music. As an example, some of the international names which reached the best seller lists and were played on the radio during the last few years were: Sting, Bruce Springsteen, Dire Straits, Phil Collins, U2, Prince, Michael Jackson, Madonna, Mecano, Joan Manuel Serrat and Julio Iglesias. We must also mention the circumstantial hits from groups such as Kaoma and the Gypsy Kings, and the soundtracks of Latin American soap operas.

As to sales according to musical style and country of origin, obviously music with lyrics written in the Spanish language lead the market, taking a 53% share in the late 1980s. This 53% included all the national music (rock, *Canto Popular*, murga, local salsa, etc.) and Spanish and Argentinian pop music. Immediately challenging this situation comes the English-language music with 42%, with artists as strong as those mentioned above. In this market segment, also for consideration are the compilation records made up of the hits of the moment, which are normally more successful than the individual records. Making up the last 5% of the market are the other styles: tango and traditional folk song, jazz and classical music. Record promotion comes basically through radio. Just in Montevideo there are 22 AM stations and 10 FM ones. Their programs are entirely dedicated to English-language music, or international pop music in Spanish, with very little airtime left for national music.

CONCLUSIONS

Any small country, especially if it is surrounded by big countries, finds itself in a dependent situation. In this context, its relations with its environment and neighbors become vital. To have a strong local culture will enrich it, in the sense that the local culture will be added to the external elements that it will have to adopt in order to survive. Uruguayan musical culture has been linked historically to its neighbors, especially to Argentina. It was able to develop strong indigenous elements mainly in its capital city, and these were linked to the very popular Carnival festivities. The fact that the country was a part of the Occidental and capitalist economic system helped the penetration and influence of the hegemonic musical cultures, in particular the Anglo-Saxon ones.

The nationalistic popular music movements which developed since the 1960s were brought about within particularly constricting political and economic circumstances. But, on the other hand, they could not have developed as a collective phenomena of important popular success had there not been a cultural historical context of an old middle class, with a wide general education and deeply rooted democratic mores. Twenty years later this sociocultural context was totally impoverished and decadent. These conditions forced a contraction in Uruguayan popular music, in the same way that the record market in general contracted. This situation depleted the impetus that Uruguayan music could have had in the previous years of making itself known in other countries. This was not a problem confined to music, but encompassed the country as a whole. It was evident, for example, to Uruguayans, that in 1983 in Europe, the ten years of the coup d'état in Chile were commemorated. Uruguay did not exist for Europeans at that moment, even though the country was suffering exactly the same anniversary.

This chapter has tried to make a complex reality more widely known--a very rich reality in its moment, but barely known by the outside world. The chapter has also served to consider the cross influences between musics in the world. It shows, among other elements, that the so-called world interdependency is nothing more than a theoretical-ideal concept, which hides what normally are relations of dependency. Of cource, when analyzed these relations appear to be non-deterministic. In other words, the Uruguayan case confirms that any dependent system has *always* some degree of autonomy. Uruguayan popular musicians managed to make the most of the available possibilities. The progressive openness which came later and made communications easier created an apparently paradoxical loss of that capacity to use rarely available degrees of liberty.

The musicians of those earlier years, from those producing original work of the highest quality up to the more simple imitators of foreign sounds, have shown another example of what the world is losing in richness as it ignores them.

NOTES

1. All references to musical roots are based on the work of the first Uruguayan musicologist, Lauro Ayestarán, cited in the Bibliography. The death of Aye-

starán in 1966 left uncompleted a formidable research, teaching and diffusion work, begun in the 1930s.

2. Maybe even Carlos Cardel, tango's most famous singer of all time, was born in Uruguay, but some Argentinians prefer to believe he was French. Some of the most important names in the history of tango have been Uruguayan: Francisco Canaro, Enrique Saborido, Gerardo Mattos Rodríguez (and his composition "La Cumparsita," the tango that has earned the most money from world rights), Julio Sosa, Horacio Ferrer, to name but a few emigrants.

3. We beg pardon of the eventual orthodox readers.

4. The example of Viglietti's opinion on the Beatles is cited by Benedetti (1974, 46-47). We have not found a single declaration by the Beatles--not even from Lennon--expressing their admiration for Viglietti. Didn't they like him?

BIBLIOGRAPHY

Ayestarán, L. (1953). *La música en el Uruguay.* Montevideo: Servicio Oficial de Difusión Radio-eléctrica.

Ayestarán, L. (1967). *El folklore musical Uruguayo.* Montevideo: Arca.

Benedetti, M. (1974). *Daniel Viglietti.* Madrid: Ediciones Júcar, Colección Los Juglares, No. 13.

Capagorry, J. & Rodríguez Barilari, E. (1980). *Aquí se canta. Canto Popular 1977-1980.* Montevideo: Arca.

Castillo, R. (1983). "Génesis de la Música Popular Uruguaya." In Muñoz, C. & Castillo, R. (Eds.), *Las artes del espectáculo.* (pp. 203-210). Montevideo: Centro Latinoamericano de Economía Humana, Serie El Uruguay de Nuestro Tiempo, 1958-1983, No. 9.

Instituto de Estudios Sociales (1979). *Population Statistics.* Montevideo: Department of State and Public Institutions.

Magnone, C. (1984). "Soy un músico que está con el pueblo." (Interview with Jaime Roos). *Aquí,* 47 (24), March 3, 1984, Montevideo.

Martins, C.A. (1974). "Uruguay Pop '74: Balance de otoño. *Ahora,* April 25, 1974.

Martins, C.A. (1980). "Discografía." In Capagorry J. & Rodríguez Barilari, E. *Aquí se canta: Canto Popular 1977-1980,* 134-140.

Martins, C.A. (1986). *Música Popular Uruguaya 1973-1982. Un fenómeno de comunicación alternativa.* Montevideo: Ediciones de la Banda Oriental and Centro Latinoamericano de Economía Humana, Colección Argumentos, No. 6.

Martins, C.A. (1987a). "Music in Cultural and Communications Policies in Uruguay." *ISME Yearbook,* Vol. 14, 136-151, London.

Martins, C.A. (1987b). "Popular music as Alternative Communication." *Popular Music,* 7 (1), 77-94. Cambridge: Cambridge University Press.

Martins, C.A. (1988a). *Communication, morphogenèse et identité culturelle.* Louvain-La-Neuve, Belgium: CIACO Editeur.

Martins, C.A. (1988b). "L'oeuvre expressive et son rapport au contexte. Chanson populaire et identité culturelle." *Recherches Sociologiques.* 19 (2-3), 313-326. Louvain-La-Neuve (Belgium).

INDEX

ABOUT THE CONTRIBUTORS

HANNA ADONI is a Senior Lecturer in the Department of Communication and Journalism at the Hebrew University of Jerusalem. Her major research interests are mass culture and mass communication, in particular print media, in the processes of political socialization and social construction of reality. She published, in collaboration with A.A. Cohen, C. Bantz and an interaction team of researchers, *Social Conflicts and Television News*. She is also a coauthor of *Music at the Margins*.

SUSANNA AGARDY is the Head of Research at the Australian Broadcasting Tribunal. She has conducted a large number of studies of public opinion in relation to television and the reaction of children to television.

JACK BANKS is the ICYC General Secretary and a Ph.D. candidate in telecommunications, Department of Speech, University of Oregon. He is researching political-economic aspects of music television. He is also a coauthor of *Music at the Margins*.

NANCY BREAUX is a Ph.D. candidate at the Department of Speech, University of Oregon. She is researching aspects of the feminist rock schene.

AVONIE BROWN is a Master's degree candidate, Department of Communication Studies, University of Windsor, Canada. She emigrated to Canada from Jamaica and her research interests include feminist theories, alternative media and the Canadian Caribbean community.

ELIZABETH B. BUCK is a political scientist and Research Associate, Institute of Culture and Communication, East-West Center, Honolulu, Hawaii. She is author of *Paradise Remade: The Politics of Culture and History in Hawaii* and is a coauthor of *Music at the Margins*.

NELLY DE CAMARGO, a sociopsychologist, is Head of the Multimedia Department at the Institute of Arts, University Campus, Sao Paulo, Brazil. A researcher on Media, she is President of CETCO (Transdisciplinary Center for Mass Communications Studies), has been Vice-President of IAMCR (International Association for Mass Communications Research) for ten years and still serves as a member of its International Council. In the 1980s she was UNESCO Regional Advisor for Communications in Latin America. Among her publications is *Communication Policies in Brazil.*

MARLENE CUTHBERT is Professor and Chair, Graduate Studies, University of Windsor, Canada. She lived and worked in the Caribbean for 22 years and her research focuses on communication and cultural policy, technology, dependency and development and the recording industry. She is a coauthor of *Music at the Margins.*

CARLOS DUMPIÉRREZ has extensive experience in promoting music on radio, TV and in the press. Now he lives in Madrid, working for the Spanish television and radio and studying audio-visual techniques at the Institute for Latin-American Co-operation.

ALISON J. EWBANK is a freelance writer after spending many years at the Institute for Mass Communication Studies at Leeds University, researching political aspects of the mass media. She is coauthor of *Social Conflict and Television News* and of *Music at the Margins.*

CARLOS ALBERTO MARTINS worked for 20 years in the popular music scene in Uruguay, as a DJ, producing records and shows, being on the jury at festivals, critic, journalist, and foreign correspondent for *Billboard* and other publications. He is now working as a consultant in policy matters for the film and television industry for the European Community and for the government of the region of Madrid.

TORU MITSUI, Professor of English and Music at Kanazawa University in Japan, has written numerous articles (sometimes in English) and a dozen books on folk and popular music in the United States and United Kingdom, including *The Story of "You are my Sunshine": The Music and Politics of the American South.* Recently he has taken an interest in the historical development of domestic music in Japan.

BLANCA MUNOZ is a Professor at the University Carlos III of Madrid in the Department of Political Science and Sociology. She has written: *Ideological Problems of a Model with Scientific-Experimental Typologie; Utopia and Aesthetics: Historic Realization as Aesthetic Realization in the "First Generation" of the Frankfurt School.*

FOULI T. PAPAGEORGIOU is Director of the Center for Development Studies Planning and Research in Athens, Greece. She has extensive research experience on issues related to policymaking in the fields of leisure and recreation. She has worked as a lecturer in the Athens National Technical University and a research fellow in the universities of Aston, Leeds and Edinburgh between 1976 and 1985. She is a coauthor of *Music at the Margins.*

USHA VYASULU REDDY is Professor of Mass Communications and Director, Audio-Visual Research Center, Osmania University, Hyderabad, India. Dr. Reddy has published widely, in newspapers, magazines and scholarly journals in India and elsewhere. Her current research activities include work in popular music and its impact upon youth, and work on technology applications in different parts of the world. She is a coauthor of *Music at the Margins.*

DEANNA CAMPBELL ROBINSON is Director of ICYC, Director of PacCom (Pacific Communications Research Group) and Professor and Graduate Coordinator, Telecommunication and Film, University of Oregon. She specializes in communication law and systems, especially American and South Korean. She is coauthor of *Social Conflict and Television News* and of *Music at the Margins.*

GEORGETTE WANG is Professor in the Graduate School of Journalism, National Chengchi University, Taiwan. She is coeditor of *Continuity and Change in Communication Systems,* editor of the *Treading on Different Paths: Informatization in Asian Nations,* and coauthor of the *Looking for the Information Society.* She is a coauthor of *Music at the Margins.*

LAWRENCE ZION is writing a Ph.D. dissertation at Monash University entitled "The Pop Music Scene in Australia: 1963-1969." He has tutored in politics at Monash University. He is also working as a broadcaster on a public radio station in Melbourne, and as a scriptwriter, songwriter and musician. He has published a number of articles on aspects of the Australian rock scene.